D0889854

THE STRATEGY OF MULTINATIONAL ENTERPRISE
Organisation and finance

The strategy of multinational enterprise
Organisation and finance

Michael Z. Brooke, M.A., Ph.D.
Lecturer in Management Sciences,
University of Manchester Institute of Science and Technology

and

H. Lee Remmers, B.S., Ph.D.
Associate Professor
Institut européen d'Administration des Affaires, Fontainebleau

American Elsevier Publishing Company, Inc.
New York

Published in the United States by
American Elsevier Publishing Company, Inc.
52 Vanderbilt Avenue
New York, New York 10017

© Longman Group Limited 1970

First published 1970
New impression 1972

International Standard Book Number: 0-444-19647-1
Library of Congress Catalog Card Number: 70-122440

Printed in Great Britain

Contents

Figures

B

Tables

Preface

Some years ago a French newspaper described an encounter which conjures up a striking picture.[1] On one side stand a group of Provençal peasants, on the other an American businessman. Between them is an interpreter, struggling 'to explain, in his high-school English, men who are rather complicated for a son of the Middle West'. Two civilisations face one another. The president of the American firm 'knows what he wants and wants it badly—to provide the Libaron factory this year with the materials to produce 15,000 tons of preserves and tomato-juice of Libby quality'. That was then just six times the total output of tomatoes in all the existing French canneries added together. The men who grow the vegetables are told to forget their hard-won experience and their traditional methods. In future they will be thinking in acres and not in kilogrammes; they will prosper so long as they do exactly as they are told by their new masters. These latter have conducted three years of intensive research before choosing this particular patch of Europe—research which has investigated every aspect of growing, processing and selling. A team of meteorologists has been brought over from Wisconsin University; soil experts have been consulted; three hundred varieties of tomato, a hundred and fifty types of bean and many other fruits and vegetables have been tested. Economists have amassed mountains of figures. Nothing has been left to chance.

That picture is a suitable frontispiece for this book. We describe and analyse policy formation, control systems, centralisation, decentralisation, finance, ownership, organisation, a hundred ways of saying: 'You will prosper so long as you do as we tell you', and a hundred ways of reacting to this statement.

The years of research which lie behind this work have involved travel over countless thousands of miles. We acknowledge a grant of £1000 from the Organisation for Economic Cooperation and Development towards this. The other 'resources' of the project were the generosity of the Institutes which employ us in encouraging the work, and of the firms which cooperated in granting us facilities.

The material for this book has been collected by interviews with senior executives from over eighty companies. They patiently, and often enthusiastically, endured conversations that have sometimes lasted many hours. Since we undertook not to reveal which companies cooperated in the research, we are unable to thank those who helped us by name. Every word that follows should be taken as an acknowledgement of our indebtedness to them. Their zeal, enthusiasm, ability and helpfulness may not come out in the necessarily analytical discussion which follows. The reader may regard them as he will—apostles of free enterprise or lackeys of the capitalist system, according to his taste. He may think of them as organisation men, or as creators of the affluent society. In human terms they are hard working and constantly involved in unfamiliar and disturbing situations. They live in a harsh, aseptic world as different from the world of some of the professions as the modern operating theatre is from the drug-store. They are producing some fascinating organisations, and if they are over-fascinated by them one can think of worse vices.

The project was originally conceived by Peter L. Smith, who combines a professorship of finance at the Institut européen d'Administration des Affaires at Fontainebleau with a senior lectureship in the subject at the University of Manchester Institute of Science and Technology. Both authors owe an enormous debt to Peter Smith.

The authors would also like to thank their wives, who have been for long periods 'grass widows' to the multinational firms, and their families; Jacqueline and Robert Brooke spent much time sorting and indexing the material. They would also like to acknowledge the help of many colleagues and friends who have discussed the problems with them, and especially Dr Hans van der Haas whose own book (*The Enterprise in Transition*) came out in 1967, as well as the staffs of numerous libraries, especially the librarian of the *Financial Times*.

M. Z. Brooke
H. L. Remmers

March 1970

Acknowledgements

We are grateful to the following for permission to reproduce copyright material.

British Institute of Management for extracts from Paper 7 by J. Simon and Paper 4 by W. J. Kenyon-Jones of *International Operations Conference Papers*; The Proprietors of the *Financial Times* for extracts from various issues of *The Financial Times*; The Macmillan Co. Inc. for a table from page 12 of *A Comparative Analysis of Complex Organisations* by A. Etzioni, Copyright © by The Free Press of Glencoe Inc., 1961; McGraw–Hill Book Co. Inc., for extracts from *The World-Wide Industrial Enterprise* by F. G. Donner (1967).

The multinational company

1.1 General considerations

THE WIDER IMPLICATIONS

'He has only to take care that they do not get hold of too much power and too much authority, and then with his own forces, and with their goodwill, he can easily keep down the more powerful of them, so as to remain entirely master in the country. And he who does not properly manage this business will soon lose what he has acquired, and whilst he does hold it he will have endless difficulties and troubles.'[1] This quotation from the most famous textbook for the Organisation Man discusses the relations of The Prince and the Barons. It might equally well apply to the relations of King Henry VIII and the Abbots, or of the President of the United States and the large business corporations. The power within a power has always been a major preoccupation of government, and a preoccupation that is accompanied by a dilemma—that the rival contestants albeit regarded as usurpers are also seen as forces for civilisation, progress, and other changes considered desirable by governments. Hence a love–hate relationship is apt to develop, influencing the policies of both sides. The President of the United States does not, like Machiavelli's hero, invite executives of large companies to the White House in order to have them strangled after dinner; but his attorney-general does prosecute them for such a 'crime' as 'price-fixing', while other governments threaten nationalisation.

External pressures on a company, then, may suggest an age-old problem of government; the internal situation seems to point to an analysis in terms of philosophy or even theology. Ask an executive of a company with global operations how the whole apparatus works, and he is liable to reply in words reminiscent of an early creed—there is unity in diversity, free will (local autonomy) is combined with an omnipotence (central control) which is then seen to be limited by its own creation. In explanations of this incomprehensible state of affairs, the ancient use of analogy has been replaced by the organisation chart covered in dotted lines.

A multinational company is for present purposes one which has activities, other than marketing, in more than one country. This type of concern is not new. Indeed one of the firms approached during this study had been multinational for over 200 years. Many European companies which own mines or plantations overseas have always been in this position. Parts of North America, as well as large areas of Africa and Asia, were originally governed as well as developed by companies with boards of directors in Europe. Three hundred years ago the East India Company, a pioneer joint stock venture, was having difficulty in raising capital for new operations in the East, although it was offering a minimum 100 per cent interest. A hundred years after that, Adam Smith was deprecating the diversion of capital from needed projects at home to plantations overseas even though the return was higher there.[2]

Naturally the company's environment contains more factors than the governmental one just mentioned; it contains a variety of different populations, cultures, languages, market conditions, competitors, financial systems, climates, and many other influences through which a course has to be steered. Each of these can contain its own range of problems; but in spite of the difficulties this type of company has increased rapidly, and three notable changes have marked the increase in this century, and especially in the 1950s and the 1960s.

One such change is that it has become usual instead of abnormal for an industrial firm to manufacture in more than one country. Detailed figures are given elsewhere in this book, but, as an example, the foreign assets of British firms more than doubled in the decade ending in 1966; meanwhile in twenty years American foreign investment increased over eight times.[3] Large increases could also be quoted for other European countries, as well as for countries outside Europe like Japan and Canada. These facts also illustrate the second of the three changes, namely that foreign investment has ceased to be solely, or even principally, European in origin. American investment overseas considerably exceeds that of all the rest of the world put together, whereas there was once a time when most Transatlantic investment was European in origin. Even so European investment in the United States has been increasing, a fact which Europeans tend to overlook when they argue for limiting investment the other way. The third change affecting the character of the multinational company is that of acquiring a cosmopolitan appearance. Both the extent and the limitations of this are discussed below, but at least the expatriate firm today usually attempts to minimise rather than to assert its foreign ownership. These changes are accompanied and largely caused by identifiable economic, political and social developments.

Great international companies give rise to many fascinating paradoxes. Highly profitable and often accused of being examples of organised greed, they yet provide many examples of the weakness of the profit motive. Many of the firms which cooperated in this study gave evidence of the problems of making managers profit-conscious.[4] Much was said about short-term incentives to stimulate profitable decisions. Otherwise the desire for a quiet life, the processes of growth, and other factors would produce large increases in the size of the organisation without corresponding increases in profitability. The force of this point is in no way altered by the fact that evidence is also produced to show how successful these incentives have been. Another paradox is that companies, which would obviously disclaim any non-material motives, evoke a high level of commitment from their executives. As high, one is tempted to assert, as any of the traditional professions. This is particularly noticeable among expatriate managers building an organisation in a foreign country, and living through all the tensions to which this gives rise. Eschewing idealism, and indeed the whipping boy of the idealist, the international company is in fact showing considerable skill in breaking through international barriers and animosities.[5] Business has proved a reconciling force in more than one explosive part of the world. On the one hand, the large international companies raise living standards where they operate and endow civilisation richly with new possessions; but it does not follow from this that they are the most efficient or the most discriminating instruments for raising these living standards. On the other hand, these companies also represent large aggregations of power; but it does not follow that they use this power less scrupulously or less humanely than other powerful organisations. These wider implications of international business are not the subject of this study, although we would hope that some relevant evidence is collected here. For we recognise that 'the very process of policy formulation presupposes political and ethical values that are independent of economic theory'.[6]

We wish to suggest that later chapters show the considerable creativity that takes place in the building and financing of organisations which meet the huge demands put upon them. The organisations themselves, and their role in society, will obviously be judged in terms of wider social and political criteria which do not concern this study. This is not to say that such considerations are irrelevant. For instance, many multinational companies instruct their subsidiaries to adopt the 'best local employment practices' in any given country. This fact is incorporated in this study together with the corollary, usually insisted on but seldom put into writing, which says 'not too good' for fear of unpopularity with other local employers. These facts, we repeat, are mentioned, but not the numerous interpretations by which different schools of thought would explain them. Such policies can be described as 'enlightened' or they can be explained as 'sinister'. This is the type of comment, we are trying to say, that has usually been excluded from this book. Naturally the evidence assembled here is relevant to ethical and political discussion, but we are content to leave such interpretation to the reader.

What we have attempted to do is to identify the management processes of a number of companies. We have done this by examining the organisational and financial issues involved. The scope to which this has committed us and the methods used to study the problems are described in the appendices at the end of the book. The other sections of this chapter explain the presuppositions and the plan of this work. We have attempted to describe the policies and practices observed, to analyse the pressures and trends underlying them, and to make some predictions about future developments. This represents, we hope, a modest contribution to a vast and absorbing subject.

The study itself has been set up on interdisciplinary lines. We use that overworked phrase because one of us teaches finance and the other sociology. In the study of the business organisation, we would claim, this combination is particularly appropriate. The student of finance is concerned with such sociological concerns as motivation and attitude, in the case of the present study especially attitude to risk, while the sociologist is much interested in the consequences of the application of different financial and control systems, including planning and appraisal. We hope that, despite our own inadequacies, the two disciplines will be seen to have made each its own distinctive contribution to an integrated study.[7]

We originally drafted a report which described the procedure in particular companies in the form of 'Company A reported that they organised this particular matter in this way . . .'. Diagrams of individual companies were included. In accordance with agreements made when access to the companies was first sought, all these descriptions were referred back to the firms described. In checking the evidence this reference back was probably better than a questionnaire; it produced an unexpected bonus in that much was learned from comments made and further discussions held. In this book the descriptions of particular companies have been omitted; it was decided that a generalised account and analysis was more satisfactory. This does entail a certain vagueness in some passages. For instance, there are phrases like 'a few companies' use a 'certain procedure'; this statement means that at least three or four undoubted cases of the practice were discovered, and one or two more doubtful ones. It has been found impossible for security reasons to include profiles of the companies. Some of the firms are so large and so individual that any detail would identify them. Indeed, some relevant facts have had to be omitted from the text for security reasons; but every effort has been made to identify the significant processes as precisely as possible.

Both of us have worked on all the chapters, and agreed the contents sentence by sentence. This agreement has been preceded by interminable conversations scripted something like this:

REMMERS: Can't you cut out more of this sociological jargon? We shall lose any readers we have managed to attract when they come to phrases like 'calculative involvement'.
BROOKE: What! You say that and defend mumbo-jumbo like 'intracompany transfers'?

As a result of such exchanges we have used the technical terms of our respective crafts only where we are convinced that they are widely understood or that any translation would be too inexact. Specialists will be able to translate back. Terms used occasionally are explained in the text, the following are used frequently:

DEFINITIONS

Our definition of a *multinational company* is broader than that of some authors who would restrict the phrase to firms without any geographical bias.[8] In such a company, according to this limited definition, there would be no domestic or overseas divisions, only various parts of equivalent standing in different areas of the world. Decisions with respect to markets, sources of finance, promotion of management personnel, uses of funds, and plant and head office location would be made on the basis of socio-economic analysis without reference to national pride or local loyalties. In the real world, there are few companies that at present remotely approach such a narrow definition. Our definition of a *multinational company* is any firm which performs its main operations, either manufacture or the provision of service, in at least two countries. Other terms are:

Host country. Any country which receives foreign direct investment, especially a country in which a particular subsidiary is operating.
Home country. Any country whose residents make foreign direct investment, especially the country of origin of the company described.
Parent company. A company which owns and controls foreign direct investment.
Head office. The central organisation of the firm as opposed to the foreign subsidiaries. The words *head office*, *parent company*, *headquarters*, or sometimes just *company*, are used normally to refer to the *home country* organisation of the company, whatever that may be. It can include production facilities and research centres in the home country as well as just the administrative centre of the company. But in some cases, including some of the regional centres described later, there are references to parts of *head office* outside the home country.
Foreign subsidiary. The corporate form which represents the foreign direct investment, also referred to simply as *subsidiary*, and sometimes as *affiliate* or *local company*.
International division. The part of the head office with a foreign geographical responsibility. The companies themselves use numerous names for this; in Britain it may be an *overseas holding company*.
Intracompany. Used to describe events which take place within a single multinational firm such as intracompany transfers of goods and services, or intracompany loans. Other authors sometimes use the term *intercompany* with the same meaning.

International management. Used of executives from any country operating away from their own country. The phrase *international grade* is used where firms have specific policies of global promotion for nationals from more than one country.

Foreign management. Managers in the company (usually the foreign subsidiary) not from the home country, also referred to as *local management.*

Expatriate management. Managers from the home country working abroad.

Directors. Used normally in the British sense whatever the nationality of the firm.

1.2 Finance

The discussion of financial management in multinational companies will focus, in particular, on the policies and practices which firms have developed for the finance and control of their foreign subsidiaries and affiliates in Europe. Much of the area to which we will devote our attention is relatively new, and only recently has become the subject of extensive research efforts. As far as we know some of our material has never been available before, at least in the form and detail in which it is presented here. Our aim has been to cast further light on this rapidly growing and increasingly important, but relatively unexplored, area of business activity. In so doing, we would hope to stimulate further study by pointing out some of the special problems which face a company operating in a foreign environment.

At first glance, the financial management of a foreign subsidiary is very similar to that of a private company—which it usually is. There are relatively few foreign subsidiaries which are quoted on any stock exchange. The great majority are either wholly owned or jointly owned with a small number of shareholders, usually companies. As such, generally speaking they rarely publish their financial accounts, and detailed knowledge of their operations is lacking. In addition, they have no large local shareholding public who might be concerned with profitability and dividends.[9] Although they often may be very large in relation to most other firms in any particular country and important to the local economy, they avoid close scrutiny by the financial press, and can conduct their affairs with somewhat more flexibility than a public company. For example, their dividend policy can be shaped by more widely based views than if they had to be concerned about local shareholders. Their financial structure can deviate far from what is generally held to be appropriate for a particular industry or national environment. Indeed, many of the usual considerations of financial management, which are appropriate to publicly owned domestic companies and which appear in the literature, are not necessarily valid in the case of the foreign subsidiary. From the standpoint of management, there are usually good reasons for these divergences, and we will look into them later in the study.

Another characteristic of many foreign subsidiaries makes them difficult to measure according to the usual yardsticks of performance. Many of them are part of a more or less integrated organisation, with activities closely interrelated within a region such as Europe, or perhaps an even broader sphere of operations. As a consequence, one subsidiary may specialise in a limited range of products for supply to other subsidiaries within, say, the Common Market countries. This is a trend which has been developing rapidly in certain businesses, notably in the chemical, automobile, electrical engineering, and electronics industries. In such companies, the profits reported by a particular subsidiary may not at all reflect its true performance. For a number of reasons, profits may be either lower or higher than they would otherwise be if the company were completely independent. The pricing of intracompany transfers of goods and services presents difficult problems in the best of conditions, and where managements may have an incentive to increase or decrease revenues in a particular subsidiary, transfer prices or allocations of head office expenses sometimes offer an attractive opportunity to shift profits. While management does not have an unlimited discretion to do this, there is still enough scope to distort profits to such a degree that in some cases a meaningful measurement of performance is rendered difficult.

Besides making performance difficult to measure, these and various other policies can lead to conflict of interest both between the subsidiary and the host country, and also sometimes between the management groups in the subsidiary and in the parent company. A policy of exporting at a price other than what might be normally arrived at through arm's-length negotiations will generally have the effect of increasing the tax revenues of one country at the expense of the other. The transfer of funds by foreign subsidiaries during an exchange crisis is clearly in opposition to the short-term advantage of the host country. Antagonism between the subsidiary management and the parent company can sometimes arise over these matters, particularly where the local management identify themselves with the national interests of the host country. In general, whenever a policy is imposed which benefits the group as a whole at the expense of a subsidiary—where, for example, the subsidiary's profits are kept artificially low—there is nearly always a possibility of disputes developing, the morale of local management being weakened, and their effectiveness impaired.

The possibility of such conflict is inherent in international operations. In virtually all multinational companies in our experience, there was little doubt in the eyes of the parent company where ultimate loyalty was to be directed, whose goals were to be maximised, or whose risks were to be minimised: *the parent company*. The following views of two British managing directors of United States owned subsidiaries make the point:

The manager of a British subsidiary of an American company has in a sense to be an internationalist. For him, patriotism is a parochialism which he cannot afford. . . . It is clear, therefore, that [he] must—(a) set aside all restrictive nationalistic attitudes; (b) accept the managerial restrictions and limitations which the subordinate status of a 'foreign-owned' subsidiary generally implies; (c) and, finally, [he] must regard [himself] as the means whereby the parent company's requirements and national interests can be successfully married.[10]

The Manager of a subsidiary must accept that he enjoys a subordinate status, that a subsidiary company is an organ of the parent company, and that policy is basically formulated and handed down by the parent company . . . if an executive finds it difficult to accept his essentially subordinate role then the best thing he can do is to resign and go elsewhere. He must, too, set aside any nationalistic attitudes and appreciate that in the last resort his loyalty must be to the shareholders of the parent company, and he must protect their interests even if it might appear that it is not perhaps in the national interests of the country in which he is operating. Apparent conflicts may occur on such matters as the transfer of funds at a period of national currency crisis, a transfer of production from one subsidiary to another, or a transfer of export business. A decision of this sort may be very difficult to take, but it must be accepted if a proper relationship is to be established.[11]

This does not necessarily mean that the goals of the subsidiary need always to be subordinated to those of the parent, nor that so doing would inevitably damage either the subsidiary or the host country. In most cases, the long view is taken, and policies are formulated accordingly. Nevertheless, it is these characteristics that provide another reason why usual standards or considerations regarding company behaviour must be used with especial care when one is dealing with foreign subsidiaries.

In contrast to the local companies against which it must compete in the host country, the subsidiary of a multinational group is often held to have a number of advantages. Usually multinational companies are large, and possess extensive technological, managerial, and financial resources.[12] Their availability to the subsidiary, often at little or no cost, can make it a formidable competitor. This probably goes a long way towards explaining the success that many have achieved. Other benefits spring from the nature of multinational operations. There is, first, the strength which lies in mutual support that members of the group are often able to give each other. Secondly, in terms of operational efficiency, there is often the possibility of economies of scale which come from integration along regional lines. Thirdly, in the area of finance, there is the opportunity for companies to raise funds where they are most readily available and cheapest, to lessen the impact of taxation through various practices that we mentioned earlier, and to shift funds and earnings about the group to its best advantage. In the multinational company these and other openings do exist and are certainly important.

However, these advantages can be more than offset by the greater degree of risk and complexity in managing such geographically dispersed operations. Instead of a single business environment influencing most of its activities, a multinational company can have as many different environments as it has foreign subsidiaries. The economy of each country is still affected by more or less local conditions and this gives rise to an assortment of national policies designed to deal with whatever current problems each may have. Tax systems vary a great deal between countries, with a host of different rates and methods of assessment. Local inflationary pressures may bring about credit restrictions with the double-edged effect of making it less easy to obtain local finance and at the same time, since demand is cut and with it profits, making internal finance more difficult. At its worst, inflation may eventually cause devaluation. Balance-of-payments deficits may also lead to devaluation, or compel a country to place restrictions on capital movements, or limit the access of foreign subsidiaries to local capital markets. Exchange controls may limit the amount of earnings which may be remitted, or the exchange rates at which foreign currency may be purchased for this purpose. Administrative measures to stimulate regional economic development or certain local industries may impose severe restrictions on new investments, or on the expansion of existing ones.

The picture then is a complex one, for the multinational company typically finds itself subject to multiple political and economic systems, each with its attendant controls and risks, advantages and disadvantages, opportunities and dangers. These grow with the number of countries in which it operates, and place a heavy burden on management which must assess the additional economic and political variables that result from each expanded field of activity. Not only are the variables more numerous, but relevant information about them is more difficult to obtain, and usually less accurate and timely than the businessman is accustomed to find in the familiar domestic environment. It is understandable, therefore, that management frequently appears to respond to this new challenge cautiously, and pursues what have been called risk-minimising policies.[13] This sensitiveness applies whether the risks are perceived as a potential monetary loss, a smaller market or lower profits than expected, or even unfavourable publicity.[14] Thus we shall see that many companies are reluctant to commit equity funds to their foreign subsidiaries; they prefer to finance them with local debt, reinvested earnings, and with intra-company loans which are generally more easily repatriated than equity funds. Risk-minimising policies will also be evident when we look at practices concerning remittance of earnings, control of operations, and ownership of foreign subsidiaries. There are other major determinants of financial policy, but the avoidance of risk is an important

C

factor influencing management decisions in this area, and will appear as a recurrent theme throughout the discussion.

1.3 Organisation

Company policies have, of course, to do with economic objectives—the creation and maintenance of markets, the manufacture and supply of goods and services, the provision of finance, the ensuring of a suitable return on investment, the organisation of labour. Above all, policies are framed with the intention of ensuring the profitable operation of the company. The exercise of power within the company is designed to subserve this intention. Power is wielded by economic means for economic aims. That this is the appearance but does not adequately explain the facts is now commonplace. In fact two trends, normally emphasised by different schools of thought about organisation, are of interest here. The one school demonstrates how constraints on rational decision-making are shrinking, because the areas of uncertainty and doubt are growing less as a result of the development of modern management techniques. But, at the same time, behavioural scientists have been unearthing more and more evidence about the irrational elements in the formation of policies and practices. For instance, the study of social systems brings out the network of conflicting objectives and group relationships as well as all the other factors which lie behind the decision-making of the organisation. Policies are framed through the working of these social systems, whose patterns change when a company sets up offshoots in a foreign country. New groupings arise. These are discussed in this study under labels like *international, foreign, expatriate* and so on; and it will be seen that this stress on the completeness of the change is by no means incompatible with the suggestion that the so-called cultural differences between one country and another are apt to be exaggerated.

Over sixty years ago the need to investigate the social and personal issues involved in commercial decisions was being stressed.[15] Among many writers who have taken up this point R. A. Gordon, in a chapter already quoted, has emphasised the need to look at the power relations involved: 'Power . . . increases with the size of the firm. Here lies an important explanation of the tendency of many large firms to become larger, even if sometimes the profitability of such expansion is open to serious question.'[16]

It has also been pointed out that the maximisation of profits is limited by a tendency commonly known as empire building, where the organisation has grown partly due to individual managers increasing their own departments. This is the kind of insight which helps to explain the complicated and devious decision-making involved in the move abroad. Meanwhile it is in the nature of an organisation to impose a conflict of loyalties on its participants, and this must limit the single-minded pursuit of any particular objective. Certainly policy discussions are mostly concerned with profits, and decisions are justified on the grounds of results at least in the long term. But this 'long term' can stretch out of this world when applied to such contemporary preoccupations as the company image or labour policies in a foreign country.

POWER

The concept of power is used to interpret evidence that has been collected about the relationship between the parent company and the subsidiary. In interviewing executives at a head office, there would at first seem to be two different concepts of this relationship. According to one view the subsidiaries were regarded as semi-independent companies, in which case some of our questions were regarded as meaningless. But the majority took for granted some degree of central control. That the actual situation is different again soon became evident, and is reflected in the dialectical processes outlined in this book. Relationships are seen to develop and change according to patterns that arise out of problems rather than concepts. These patterns are then analysed in terms of power. Some might argue that the relationships should be analysed in terms of cooperation, and there was impressive evidence both of cooperation and of its problems; but power seems to fit the facts more closely. Power is exercised in an organisation in order to ensure that the members conform to its purposes and objectives, or at least to those of the dominant group.[17] A business typically uses money for this purpose—the payment, the increase of payment, or the withholding of payment. Some form of calculation is involved, so the member of the firm can be said to be influenced by *calculative* pressure in his involvement in the organisation. The inmate of the prison, on the other hand, is kept there by force—represented by the locks, the handcuffs, the truncheons. His involvement can be said to be *coercive*. At the other extreme is the zealous adherent of a movement who plays his part because of a strong desire to do so. His involvement may be called *voluntary*. Thus a line could be drawn from the most *coercive* organisations to those where *voluntary* commitment produces the required results. Naturally many organisations will have a mixture of types of involvement, the 'trusty' will not need the locks to keep him in prison.

While all business organisations are primarily of the *calculative* type, the exact balance between the *calculative* and the *voluntary* varies and is itself a fascinating subject of study. Attitudinal studies on the shop floor have sometimes shown that there is a higher proportion of *voluntary* stimulus than is expected.[18] Naturally the *voluntary* element is greater among those in more senior positions. If a man's income is very large and his chances of dismissal very small, then further *calculative* incentives are likely to be unconvincing.

So the relationships between head office and subsidiary can be considered by examining the methods the organisation uses to attain conformity to its objectives. These relationships can also be considered in terms of where operating decisions are taken—the issue usually described as centralisation or decentralisation. In this book the words *open* and *close* are preferred in the hope that this verbal change allows the subject to be approached from a new perspective. This change also avoids the problems caused by the misuse of the word decentralisation. A trend to tighter and more sophisticated control which, in any ordinary sense of the word, must mean the opposite can be described by an enthusiastic executive as 'part of our decentralisation plans'. In fact, the evidence collected on this point well illustrates the reciprocal action that can be involved in the formulation of procedures and policies. It was said by companies that the degree of centralisation varied from function to function; but it can be observed that the development of new techniques in all the functions, at least up to a certain point, constitutes a pressure towards a more *close* arrangement, whereas the desire to increase independence and reduce wasteful communications is a contrary pressure. The arguments for allowing this greater independence are strengthened by a well-entrenched ideology which condemns interference with the 'man on the spot'. This ideology is as powerful in inducing people to say 'we are decentralising here' as the profit ideology is in forcing preoccupation with a single *calculative* motive, however unconvincing this may be. In both cases a mixture of technology and professionalism helps to produce this contradiction.

The characteristics of both the *open* and the *close* relationships between head office and the subsidiary are discussed below and we note that they are subject to constant change as a result of an identifiable series of problems and conflicts.[19] So much is this true that it might well be possible to classify the organisational changes in terms of the problems that set them off. The problems are also outlined in the following pages. Missed opportunities, slow communications, cultural differences and duplication of effort are the main issues which touch off the search for fresh solutions, and thus produce changes in the relationships. The analysis of these changes is an important feature of this study, and is most suitably related to what may be called problem-centred decision-making. The result shows a centrifugal tendency. In theory the relationships could be as *open* as that of an investment link where the holding company will withdraw its money if an adequate return is not forthcoming, but otherwise will not interfere; or they could be so *close* that every significant decision has to be submitted to head office. In practice the most *open* and the most *close* relationships prove the least stable, and the trend is towards some average relationship in which frequent reporting and visiting the home and the host-country organisations is accompanied by efforts to maximise the independence of the local management. Here, as elsewhere, different statements can apply to the same reality. Take, for instance, such statements as: 'We are not interested in just being a holding company, we control our operations strictly'; and 'We are a completely decentralised concern, but we have to ensure that our money is properly used'. These two can describe arrangements which turn out to be remarkably similar when the actual decision-making is examined.

STRUCTURE

Power, then, is one of our behavioural themes, structure is another. Studies of organisation structure have often examined the change from personal rule to bureaucracy.[20] Consider, for instance, a position in an organisation, say that of managing director. In a bureaucracy his appointment is made in the light of required qualifications and experience, and his activities are circumscribed by rules and regulations. On the other hand in the personal organisation the holder of a post is far less limited in the way he does his job. Naturally the two types of organisation merge into one another, but in the most extreme form of personal rule everything depends on the ruler. His decisions are self-willed and autocratic. Typically he is the strongminded character, the maker of history, the man who rules his country or his church or his firm arbitrarily but by his own forcefulness, promoting and demoting according to his will. All other officeholders depend entirely on him, and his departure is a major crisis. At the other extreme, each member of the organisation has a fixed and clear set of duties and privileges, authority to give instructions is distributed throughout the organisation in accordance with abstract and consistent regulations, and authority is vested in the position rather than the person. Thus the departure of any particular manager or subordinate makes little difference. He is easily replaced. Most organisations can trace some process of development from the personal to the bureaucratic type of structure, but an outstanding personality can reverse or distort this process.

As firms encounter the complexities of large-scale international business, they may react by an increasing formality or in the opposite way. Throughout this study there is evidence that both are happening. Sometimes, even, both occur at once, when greater formality in the business methods is accompanied by less formality in the organisation. One example of the latter is a conscious effort to fit the job to the person as well as the person to the job, to modify the specialisation and formalisation of the bureaucratic process. This modification is assisted by the great intricacy of the large company with its variety of functions and products and countries. It is also helped by the use of techniques like 'management by objective', which tend to place the significance of the individual over against the demands of the job.[21] This reinstatement of the person *vis-à-vis* the post is further enforced by the widely held view that a manager has to 'earn the right to be heard'. Naturally most organisations are inclined to move backwards and forwards along the spectrum of personal and bureaucratic structures; but some multinational firms, which are subject to special pressures and employ men who understand these processes, have made conscious efforts towards what may be called *repersonalisation*. Indeed, one of the pressures is the simple fact that the foreign manager may understand the role of the individual, whereas the significance of the position escapes him.

In this book the convention is followed of analysing organisations in terms of standard types supplemented by examples of actual organisations. These types are not descriptions of, for instance, an actual bureaucracy but rather of its typical characteristics. Similarly a general account of the symptoms of a disease will not necessarily fit any particular patient. The standard type makes the identification of a bureaucracy, as well as the route of structural change, possible.

A characteristic problem of the multinational company is the conflict between the geographical and the product-group projections of the organisa- tion.[22] This is discussed at length in terms of models which are 'standard types' and not actual companies, but which have been carefully constructed from the companies studied. In these models can be seen the influence of the overseas operations on the structure of the head office as well as on the handling of the subsidiaries. This influence is plain in every company studied once the foreign operations have become a substantial part of the company's business, and is a continuing influence not to be understood in terms of one major reorganisation. This structural process can also be analysed in terms of a 'quasi-resolution' of conflict.[23]

This curious phrase stems from the view of an organisation as a coalition of groupings each with their different and sometimes conflicting goals. In this situation any complete resolution of the conflict is an illusion. But each problem area is dealt with in turn as it becomes obvious, and to this end ever more complicated structures evolve. The goals of the organisation itself, as of its constituent parts, are liable to conflict with one another; and this conflict is prevented from becoming too open by dealing with each goal in turn. An example of this is the antithesis between the company's desire for good relations with governments both in the home and host countries, important if only to avoid damaging restrictions being imposed, and its desire for unrestricted movement of capital to get the best return. Such external factors should not be underestimated in studies of organisation, but it remains true that the most obvious influences on company structure are conflicts between the different projections.

Once again it can be said that the sophisticated firm understands the conflict of goals amongst its employees and tries to use this. 'Constructive conflict'[24] is a phrase used in some companies to describe the complications that have arisen. But there may well be a suspicion that this phrase can mask an unwillingness to clear up a difficult situation. The conflict may be creative, but it may also be unnecessarily wasteful of human effort. An ill- defined situation which may be handled satisfactorily at head office can produce a much less satisfactory situation when mirrored in the overseas subsidiary. For it has also become plain during the study that the foreign company reflects head office arrangements to a greater extent than is realised. This tendency may well be accentuated by improved communications. The executive at head office in some newly devised function may, perhaps unconsciously, bring pressure to bear on the local company to ensure that he has an opposite number with whom he can communicate. Among the issues noted in various places in this study are the problems that improved communications can bring. So often such an improvement has been canvassed as the cure for all ills, but this may be too facile. For instance, a conflict that is hidden while communications are poor may become acute when an improvement takes place.

Another instance of communications problems of special relevance to this study has been called *organisational shock*.[25] This refers to a situation where a firm has been reorganised without any knowledge or comprehension among those affected. Hence such preparation as there has been comes by rumours, probably ill-informed. In an organisation where this can happen at all, any change is likely to come as a deeply felt crisis which may well produce resistance or non-cooperation. So the results of the reorganisation may be quite different from those expected; and the organisation enters what has been called the *vicious circle*. This means that attempts to correct the problems that arise produce further unexpected results, which then lead to further efforts at correction and so on.

If the problem has been a change which was totally unanticipated and unprepared, then further alterations will only increase the resistance to change as such. This chain of events, noted in many types of organisation, can obviously be expected to occur in the multinational company with its great opportunities for just such problems. The phrase *vicious circle* is relevant to much of our account of intra-company relationships. The effect is likely to be increased by the way in which a reorganisation at head office, possibly welcome there but in any case not thought to be very significant, can have much greater repercussions overseas. The cutting of a link regarded by the subsidiary as vital, as well as the setting up of a link considered a nuisance, may impose great difficulties on the local company. This may weaken a subsidiary's performance, and in turn set off other measures to impose tighter controls designed to bring that performance back to standard. A circular motion is produced with the correction of problems unrelated to the causes of those problems, and indeed making them worse. It is characteristic of attempts to cure the effects of *organisational shock* that they tend to produce fresh shocks. For two systems—communications and control—have got, as it were, out of phase.

In addition to discussions of structure and power, this study looks at the role of the manager with decisions to make across frontiers.

ROLE

The concept of role, the collection of activities attached to a particular appointment, is an analogy from the theatre, and is sometimes criticised as such. In the theatre it can be assumed that any activity of the player while on stage is part of his role, and that he ceases to be in this role as soon as he leaves the stage. So precise a boundary cannot be placed round the exercise of any particular role in the social sciences. For one thing a man is always playing several roles at once—family roles, work roles, leisure roles and so on—and these interact with one another. Trouble in one role may affect his performance in another. While at work he is likely to be simultaneously a superior, a subordinate and a colleague to different groups of people. One man can be a manager, an employee, a company representative on a negotiating panel, and much else besides. One aspect of this which is illuminating for the present study has been called the *role-set*.[26] This phrase refers to the bundle of relationships which are necessarily involved in any one particular role; and these include the different parts that a man must play in relation to his superiors and subordinates within the same appointment. The large multinational corporation has developed for many of its executives, especially those abroad, a role-set of the greatest complexity—a veritable spider's web.

Another theme under the heading of role is the effect of appraisal systems on behaviour. Much is already known on this subject, and how an inept appraisal system can distort the aims of an organisation. One case-study has shown how the collection of statistics of placement in an employment bureau worked against the development of the counselling service which was a main objective of that particular agency.[27] A parallel situation can be seen in international firms. The particular factors thought by the subsidiary to count most in their appraisal determined their priorities. It was noticeable that many companies concentrated attention on certain special issues. The result might be called hidden centralisation, producing a *close* relationship where an *open* one had been intended.

Among other issues that can be grouped around the concept of role is that of leader. Some leaders of large companies appear consciously to try to build a legend around themselves, and use many devices to construct the mystique. In the few examples of such characters noted in this study, they were clearly seen as agents of cohesion in the company. They created a unity of purpose which penetrated to the foreign operations. In other companies the foreign executives only mentioned the men with whom they actually communicated as representing headquarters. They used words like my director, or my functional chief, and judged the company by these characters.

With leadership goes the question of succession. The exceptional character may be hard to succeed, but always succession has its problems. The successor as chief executive frequently finds it necessary to establish his authority by an immediate statement of policy. How much such policies affect the actual operation of the company may well be doubted. The struggles that are built into the structure go on in spite of the stances of the chief executive. His influence is more to be seen in motivation and cohesion than in organisation, however expert he may think himself to be at this. To say that is not to belittle the influence of the exceptional individual at any point in the hierarchy. The importance of such has been pointed out in several studies of innovation,[28] and innovation is often crucial to the large international firm; but so is a unity built on individual attitudes rather than on structural changes. The machine has got to work—hence the significance of the person who can wander freely between different cultures. In the end, personal as well as social roles are meaningful in the study of the multi-national firm. The personal role enables the company to be a unity rather than a reluctant assortment of different operations held together by a common shareholding.

These categories—power, structure and role—are selected for convenience of arrangement; the division is necessarily artificial. The real interest of the study is the connection between the three and how this determines policy. Questions arise like: How do policies emerge within the structure established through the power conflict? Where do significant ideas come from? What forms of organisation encourage them, and which suppress them? How does the existence of some of the role problems condition the financial arrangements? Material for answering such questions appears in the evidence assembled on these pages; meanwhile the principal hypotheses to which this evidence points are assembled below.

1.4 The arrangement of this book and the principal issues covered

The material thus briefly introduced has been rearranged in the following chapters into three major divisions. These are not necessarily watertight since the decision-making processes that we are studying cannot be neatly separated out. With this qualification part I deals with the organisation, part II discusses finance, and part III is concerned with a number of miscellaneous but significant issues.

The field-work for this study has mainly been carried out in Europe. Most of the statistical material available on the subject is from American or British sources. Hence the phrase 'principal issues' refers to operations in industrialised countries for the most part. We have formulated these into a series of propositions developed in the course of this study and intended to weld the different parts into a coherent whole and provide a rationale for the ensuing discussion.

Part I analyses the processes and pressures which influence the organisation

C*

of the multinational firm. Chapter 2 looks at various aspects of the structure of the companies, while the two following chapters examine the relationships that develop between head office and the foreign subsidiary. Chapter 5 takes another look at the organisation with a view to examining the role of the executive who finds himself caught up in the processes of decision-making and communicating across frontiers.

PROPOSITIONS

—that the trend towards increasing emphasis on the product group projections of a company raises problems when that company goes abroad. Communication blocks arise from overemphasis of either geographical or product group aspects of the organisation. Hence some companies are developing elaborate organisations with multiple reporting systems. These are producing what may called a repersonalised bureaucracy.

—that a decentralising ideology masks a centralising reality. The factors which create this situation include an increasing speed of technological change and the rapid development of global techniques, strategies and information collection. These influence the units of a multinational firm quite differently from those of a domestic one.

—that considerable personal pressures are involved in the management of multinational companies, and especially difficult is the position of national management in a product group organised firm. Global promotion is another issue with significant implications for the future.

Part II analyses the sources and methods of financing foreign investments used by multinational companies. This section has been divided into two parts. Chapter 6 is concerned with the reinvestment of earnings and remittance practices. Chapter 7 deals with external finance—both that which is raised in the host country, and that which is brought in from foreign sources—with the focus on the foreign subsidiary.

PROPOSITIONS

—that general policies and particularly financial policies in multinational companies are specifically designed to further the goals of the parent company, and only incidentally those of subsidiaries or host countries. Such a built-in bias is bound to create conflicts between the different parts of the organisation, between the whole organisation and its home and host countries, and between the home and host countries themselves. Typical of such policies are the various schemes which are used to shift earnings from one country to another in order to avoid taxes, minimise risks, or achieve other objectives.

—that the additional economic and political variables which come from operating in several environments produce financial policies different from and generally more complex than those typically found in domestic companies. The implications of this are that (1) normal standards of company behaviour with respect to disposition of earnings, sources of finance, structure of capital, pricing of intracompany transfers, liquidity, and so forth are not necessarily relevant to a foreign subsidiary; and (2) the performance of subsidiaries becomes difficult, if not impossible, to measure.

Part III deals with issues which, together with organisation and finance, complete our picture of multinational strategy. First are examined the opportunities and pressures that lead to developments abroad. Chapter 8 describes the size, rate of growth, and profitability of foreign investments in selected countries. Their success alone might be considered sufficient reason for other companies to consider foreign operations seriously. Chapter 9 analyses the reasons that companies give for the initiation or extension of these operations. This chapter also names situations in which withdrawal has occurred. Chapter 10 takes a brief look at the problems involved in relationships between companies and countries. The implications of this on ownership policies for foreign subsidiaries are examined in chapter 11. In these chapters we have selected a few examples of the problems in a particular aspect of the subject where the situation is constantly changing.

PROPOSITIONS
—that under some circumstances foreign operations are more profitable than domestic. This provides one motive for such operations; the search for raw materials and other scarce resources provides another. Apart from these, the main motives stated by companies are defensive—the protection of markets. There are personal pressures involved, with identifiable groups working both for and against the move abroad.
—that national differences as such are becoming less significant; it is the fact of international operations that is important rather than the particular local differences. Nevertheless there are likely to be problems in the future as the growing internationalism of the company executive becomes out of step with local national opinion.
—that while the desire to enforce company-biased objectives and policies helps to explain the strong and compelling preference of most multinational companies for wholly-owned subsidiaries in the industrialised countries, this will sooner or later need to be reconciled with the rapidly growing demand for greater local participation in their ownership, and greater autonomy in their operations.

A final chapter looks at multinational strategy as a whole, restates our hypotheses in the light of this discussion and draws some conclusions.
There are also two appendices, the first of which describes the method

and scope of the studies which underlie this book. This description has been put into an appendix since it will not interest all of our readers, but it does give some idea of the type of enquiry undertaken, and some of the characteristics of the companies investigated. Appendix 2 contains an analysis of the financial data of British subsidiaries of foreign firms operating in the United Kingdom. Most of this has been collected from unpublished sources and shows their profitability, rate of growth, capital structure, and sources of funds over an eight-year period. A limited and selective bibliography of books and articles that the authors themselves have found useful is provided at the end.

PART I

Structure and relationships

This part identifies some of the main problems and pressures that influence the structure of the multinational company. Chapter 2 looks specifically at the various types of organisation that are produced in the firm because it operates in different countries. Chapter 3 looks in a broad sense at the power relationships that develop between head office and subsidiary, while the following chapter discusses in some detail the control and planning procedures which companies develop across frontiers. Finally chapter 5 is concerned with personal issues, the role of the executive who is influenced by the international character of the company.

The organisation

2

2.1 The limited options

The organisation of a company is compounded by many factors—historical accidents, personal foibles, technical inventions, commercial disasters, perhaps also a theory of organisation. Conscious of the many chances and coincidences which have produced the existing arrangements, each company will describe itself as unique or odd by some imagined standard of normality. Phrases like, 'Well, I'm afraid we cannot be of much use to you, because we have a very unusual set-up in this firm' were heard in company after company. One of the reasons for this sense of uniqueness was the influence of an outstanding character. The processes of change from personal rule to a bureaucracy have been discussed in chapter 1. It should be said here that these processes follow standard routes, the options are limited. Among the influences here are the defining of responsibilities, the planning of promotion schemes, the drawing up of education and training programmes and so on. Frequently to the outside observer, with a collection of examples of different firms in front of him, the standardisation is as plain as are the individual idiosyncrasies which seem so important to the insiders.

The purpose of this chapter is to identify the organisational changes that are taking place in terms of the pressures that are producing them. In our introduction this change process was looked at in the light of existing accounts of the bureaucratic process. It was there suggested that some long-accepted trends are being reversed in the organisations here studied. Take, for instance, the process of development into clearcut lines of command, fixed areas of authority, and specialisation: 'Its specific nature . . . develops the more perfectly the more the bureaucracy is "dehumanised", the more completely it succeeds in eliminating from official business, love, hatred, and all personal irrational and emotional elements which escape calculation.'[1] The multinational company which reverses this process does not just work by rules, but demands much greater initiative from its key executives. Hence the efforts described in this study to establish more independent and responsible positions. Subsequent studies of bureaucracy have been more concerned with showing exactly how particular organisations work in practice, and with examining the informal aspects of their procedures. The leaders of some of the large companies, or their advisers, have themselves studied organisation theory and set out consciously to change the trends, and so to establish more personal responsibility and initiative.

This statement is not, as it might appear, inconsistent with the evidence assembled in the next chapter showing greater centralisation. For increased independence can accompany a reduction in the area of decision-making; indeed there have always been jobs which by their nature combined great independence with limited discretion. The locomotive driver, for instance, is necessarily independent but his powers are limited. A closer analogy would be that of the proprietor of a small business who works on sub-contracts for a larger firm. His decision-making is severely limited to the terms of his contract, but within that he has considerable independence. He is not subject to constricting rules, nor to close oversight, and he can control how he performs his task and arrange his own conditions of work. Some firms, especially those of the D type described below, are developing what might on this analogy be called *contractual management*. It might be added, although this is true also of domestic companies, that some firms are pressing experiments in this direction right down to the shop floor. Within a tendency to greater concentration of ownership, greater centralisation of decision-making, there is yet a discernible trend to greater individual independence within the organisation.

The development of contractual management relieves some of the problems of the multinational firm, but reinforces others. Both processes are demonstrated in the action and reaction described below. Diagrams show some arrangements to which these processes lead. The diagrams are standardised as a rule except for one or two which show actual companies. The charts are meant to be regarded as something like stills from a film. They show isolated, but typical, moments in a process of organisational change, and are chosen because they illustrate the working of significant forces producing organisations of increasing complexity. They show that changes in company organisation work along a number of identifiable lines. For the main outlines the options are more limited than is sometimes suggested by companies which claim to be different from everyone else.

2.2 Head office

One reason why companies can so easily claim to be unique is that there are so many possible combinations and permutations of managerial functions. Thus many companies have specialised departments, perhaps with a director at the head, which are not found among other companies. Some of these situations arise for historical reasons, some as a result of the type of business. Thus a consumer products business may have advertising as a major function with a director in charge at head office and in each subsidiary. Indeed such a practice will be used in the next chapter as evidence of centralisation. However, the development of integrated functions—marketing, finance, research, distribution and so on—has had the effect of reducing the differences at policy-forming level. Hence, commonsense classifications based on the nature of the business are irrelevant. There are many other suggested classifications for international business which are unrelated to the operation of any significant forces, and are incapable of clear definition. However, one major and inescapable pressure for change in the multinational company may be described as the conflict between the three principal projections of the firm.[2] These three projections are given various names, but for present purposes they are called: 'central services', 'product group' and 'geographical'. The central services include functional departments such as finance, marketing, research, personnel and engineering. The domestic company may possess all three projections, but it is unlikely that the geographical will be important. There may be a distinction between home sales and export, there may also be regional management within the country; only in very few firms does this extend to manufacture as well as sales. Once a company does go abroad, the geographical organisation obviously becomes very important indeed, and the conflict between the three projections is, as we have said, inescapable. The resolution of this conflict has become much more difficult as a result of the trend towards product group organisation at home,[3] and the particular problems that arise between this and the geographical projections. In some companies the central services are minimal, having been moved for the most part into the product groups. But even without the current emphasis on product group organisation, the multinational firm would be involved in this conflict—a conflict which, in any case, many executives describe as beneficial because it increases the sensitivity of the firm to its environment and its opportunities. But the significance of the conflict enables an analytical classification to be set up based on actual pressures in the organisation.

This leads us to consider the four types discussed in the rest of this chapter. Type A has no separate geographical or product group organisation, and most of the firms in this category are single-product. Type B comprises companies where the geographical organisation is the main link with the foreign operations. Type C, on the other hand, is product group organised worldwide. Type D is a complicated mixture of the different projections. Table 2.1 sets out some detail of a small sample of thirty-nine firms which can be placed confidently in one or other of the categories. The transition from one type to another can be sudden, the abolition of an international division moves a firm from type B to type C on the day that division closes down. But usually the change is slower than this, and hence some companies are in transition and not readily classifiable.

The table attempts to relate size and growth to organisation. Naturally

Chief executive,
colleagues and advisers

Central services
manager

HOME   Finance   Production   Marketing

ABROAD

Chief Executive

Finance   Production   Marketing

  Other lines of communication   Hiring and firing line the sample is too small to be dogmatic, but the trends shown have been confirmed by spot checks on other firms. Thus type A companies tend to be small but growing fast. Type C companies grow more slowly than type B. Type D companies are very large, but with a wide range of different growth rates, especially with regard to profits. Industry groups are given in the table, but a distinction has not been made between those principally selling to consumer or to industrial markets. Both are spread through each of the four types and many of the larger firms are in more than one. No oil companies are included since these would distort the figures.

THE TYPE A COMPANY

The single-product companies are mostly small. With growth, pressures towards diversification build up. There are one or two exceptions, notably the oil companies; but even they are sometimes product group organised, with petroleum and chemicals as the principal divisions. There is the problem of distinguishing the multiproduct and the single-product firm. For a large company can have some minor sidelines without in any sense changing the organisation. Hence the criterion for type A is the central services organisation at head office (fig. 2.1). If the major units at head office are functional with perhaps one department dealing with miscellaneous products, this is classified as a type A organisation. As soon as there are significant product group departments, this becomes type B or C.

In the smallest companies, the links are likely to be of the simplest—a straightforward contact between chief executives. But they can become very elaborate, especially in a larger single-product company with a high proportion of its business abroad. In this case there will be a number of functional executives at home who have constant communication with their opposite numbers abroad. The type A company is the least stable—a merger or a reorganisation along product group lines can change it into type B—but nevertheless a few large companies still operate this way. An actual example of the decision-making process in a type A company is shown in fig. 2.2. Here is demonstrated the discussion process as between home and overseas executives in the evolution of two decisions. One was a move into a new market which had first been suggested by the foreign subsidiary concerned. The other decision was the establishment of new production facilities and was proposed by head office.

THE TYPE B COMPANY

One common arrangement for both European and American companies at present is some variation of type B—a product group organisation at home

Fig. 2.1 The organisation of the type A company: usually a single-product company with links through central services

Table 2.1 The organisation of the multinational firm. Showing comparative sizes and growth

Type[1] and no. of firms	Main link in head office with foreign subsids.	Industry[2] groups	Assets 1968[3] £ million			Growth since 1963		Profits 1968[4] £ million			Increase since 1963		Route of change	No. having regional centres
			Range	Median	Mean	Range £m	Mean %	Range	Median	Mean	Range £m	Mean %		
A 9	Chief exec. or deputy and central services	Engineering Food Textiles	4, 449	48	150	1, 211	33	1, 103	16	27	0, 33	30	to B or C	3
B 10	International Division	Engineering Chemicals Paper Misc.	23, 1372	143	327	9, 529	46	4, 122	27	38	2, 50	40	to C or D	4
C 13	Product Group	Engineering Chemicals Building Paper Textiles Mining Holding	32, 815	115	209	6, 199	24	4, 135	17	28	–1, 42	38	to B or D	2[5]
D 7	Product Group and International	Engineering Chemicals	628, 1137	997	923	165, 535	41	79, 267	122	154	–30, 65	23	—	5

Notes. 1. The first column shows the type as used in this chapter, and the number of firms in each type.
2. The industry groups follow the classification in *Who Owns Whom*.
3. Assets: net current assets + fixed assets less depreciation. The next column shows the growth in assets.
4. Profits: net income before interest or tax. The next column shows the growth in profits.
5. In both cases the regional centres are managed by one product group, which sometimes acts as agent for others.

and a geographical organisation overseas. This is a logical development from a usual method of growth overseas through starting first assembly and later manufacture in the principal export areas. This means that the first overseas operations are likely to remain the responsibility of the export department at home. As the overseas operations grow, they outgrow the resources of this department, and new arrangements are made. In an English company the new arrangement will often be called an 'overseas holding company'; in an American firm it is more likely to be called an 'international division'. Whatever the name, the result will produce an organisation much like that in fig. 2.3 below. The international division or company at home will be headed by a divisional manager of similar status to the product group managers. The distinctive problem that arises from this type of organisation is a block in communications within the headquarters. Into the international division are crowded all those with knowledge and skills relevant to the overseas operations. They are appraised according to the success or failure of those operations. Conversely, the product groups are staffed by people with little interest in what happens abroad.

The establishment of foreign manufacture will reduce their programmes or at least cause them to search hard for alternative markets. Since overseas manufacture is likely to start in an area where the product sells well, the reduction in programme may jeopardise a whole product line. Hence the product management will have a strong interest in opposing the efforts of the international division. Companies sometimes make elaborate efforts to overcome this problem. The product group management are allowed a 'book credit' for the overseas manufacture of their product. This point is further discussed in chapter 4. Executive bonuses, where these exist, may be adjusted to allow for the loss of business, and so on. There is still, however, a built-in prejudice against the foreign companies, a lack of interest, an unwillingness to help. So the block in communications arises; between the international division and the product management there is a clash of interest. This is exacerbated in companies where there is also little interchange of personnel—where an entire career can be in the international side of the business. The difficulties of the type B firm will be especially serious when a lot of technical support is needed overseas, or when there is a wide range and diversity of products to look after.

THE TYPE C COMPANY

A few of the companies studied overcame this problem by scrapping their international division, or at least reducing it to a small liaison organisation mainly for export. Thus these companies reorganised into type C—the product group organisation at home and abroad. The more usual route to type C was the more direct one, that as products went overseas they remained the responsibility of the product group. There was also the effect of

30

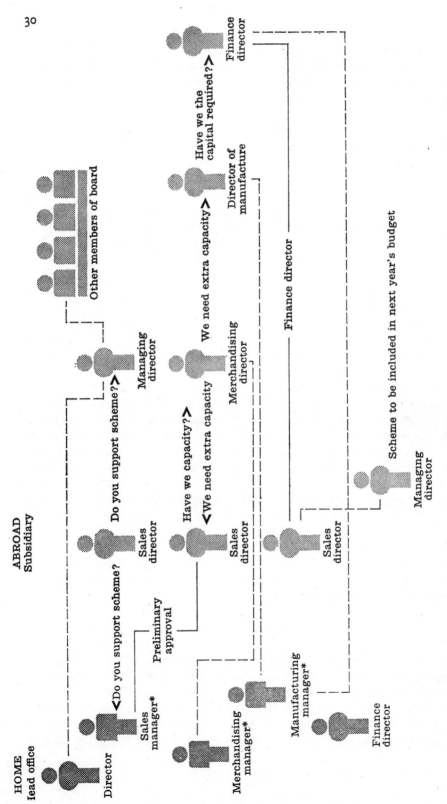

HOME
Head office

ABROAD
Subsidiary

Director

Sales manager*

<Do you support scheme?

Merchandising manager*

Manufacturing manager*

Finance director

Sales director

Do you support scheme? >

Preliminary approval

Managing director

Other members of board

Sales director

Have we capacity? >
<We need extra capacity

Merchandising director

We need extra capacity >

Director of manufacture

Have we capacity? >

Finance director

Have we the capital required? >

Finance director

Sales director

Scheme to be included in next year's budget

Managing director

* The appropriate member of the Board or department dealing with the part of the world in which the subsidiary is situated.

HOME
Head office

ABROAD
Subsidiary

Your productivity figures suggest
need for new equipment

Manufacturing
manager

Do our labour costs justify this?

Investigation by head office staff shows
that new equipment would not be justified
on labour costs, but: these costs are
rising, quality is an increasing problem,
there is scope for expansion

Manufacturing
director

We agree with these
proposals. Do you?

Yes, detailed scheme is
to be provided by the
manufacturing manager
and sent to the board
of the subsidiary

Board of subsidiary

Board of company

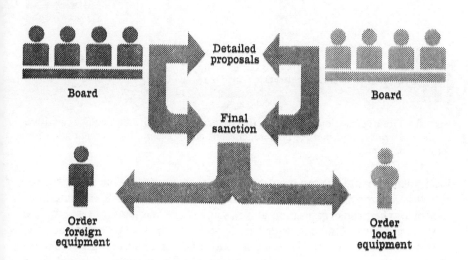

Board

Detailed
proposals

Board

Final
sanction

Order
foreign
equipment

Order
local
equipment

Fig. 2.2 (i) (*Page 30*) The decision-making process in a type A company: entering a
new market
Fig. 2.2 (ii) The decision-making process in a type A company: re-equipping a factory
overseas

mergers already described. The type C company (fig. 2.4) often has a more complex organisation than the type B. There may, for instance, be sub-product divisions which may also have foreign operations under their own direct control. Hence this type of company is apt to develop considerable 'organisational distance'; that is, there may be several stages between the

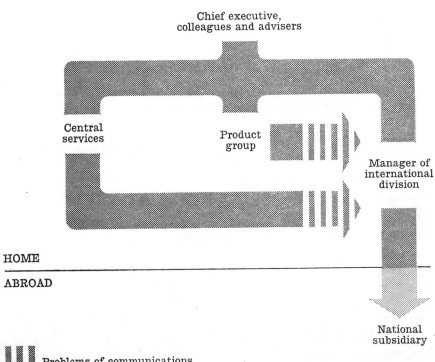

Fig. 2.3 The organisation of the type B company: a multiproduct company with a product group organisation for home operations and a geographical organisation for foreign operations

local operation and the top management of the company. This will make for the close relationship described in the last chapter, although this is sometimes modified when the organisation at any stage is one man and not a complete functional set-up. One characteristic difficulty of the C type organisation is a block in communications between head office and the foreign company. As Robinson says in describing a product group organised firm: 'This absence of attention to foreign markets was primarily a matter of organi-sation.'[4] With the B type company the trouble is one of communications within head office; but communications with the foreign companies should be good, the international division exists just to promote them. Abolish the international division and no one is specifically and solely responsible for the subsidiaries. The product group management still has a built-in interest in concentrating manufacture at home, and the establishment of local manufacture is regarded as a concession due to unfortunate circumstances. Besides, what expertise there may be at headquarters in the foreign concerns

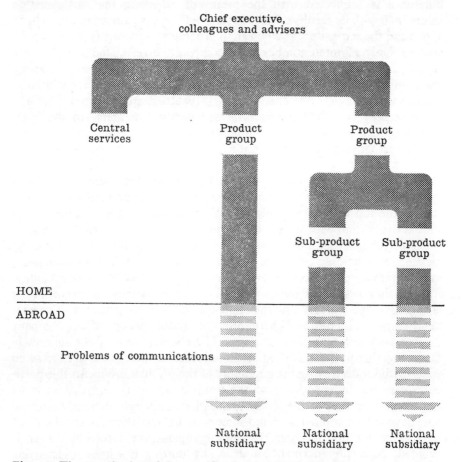

Fig. 2.4 The organisation of the type C company: the multiproduct company with a product group organisation for both home and foreign operations

about local conditions will be diffused, and may well be very thinly spread indeed. Hence the block in communications is liable to occur between headquarters and subsidiaries, and where the link is one man with numerous subsidiaries reporting to him the link may become very tenuous. In these circumstances the foreign company may feel that it has all the disadvantages of an international company, such as slowness of decision, and no advantages. It has nowhere to turn. The other characteristic difficulty of this type of company is the possible waste of resources involved in setting up more than one organisation in any particular foreign country. Some companies become C type by intention—they start abroad by product group or re-organise into this pattern. Others become C type as a result of adding over-seas operations in extra product groups after a merger or take over (the difference is connected with the means of achieving the amalgamation rather than with its results). Both routes to a C type organisation can happen at one and the same time, as when an international company is taken over by another. Only a limited number of the companies investigated in depth were type C, and few of these had developed from a merger as well. Nevertheless, this number was supplemented by others from more superficial acquaintance, and this was enough to demonstrate clearly that there are two types of merger.

These may be called *bureaucratic* and *personal* mergers. In the latter (which applied in a very few examples) the two organisations were brought together either immediately or, if at a later date, suddenly and dramatically. This has been called a personal merger because it relied on some special driving force generated by one man or within the organisation. The much more common *bureaucratic* merger is a very slow process indeed. It can start at the top with some experimental group services; more often it will start at the bottom with some tentative joint ventures.[5] The whole operation is characterised by an unwillingness to disturb the traditions of either orga-nisation. It is holding on to the fastness of the rock, with an unwillingness to swim into deeper waters. It is a good example of safety before profitability. And all this in spite of the fact that both organisations are prepared for change. No one expects a merger to leave the two companies with perma-nently separate identities. Where different product groups of one company go overseas a different problem arises. There is not the need for delicacy in fitting together well-established organisations; but there is the need to avoid waste without destroying the autonomy of the product group. In this parti-cular case the independence of the product set-up is regarded as more important than that of the local organisation; although obviously national laws have to be complied with and some form of 'arm's-length' relationship[6] is required for tax purposes. In some companies wasteful duplication is avoided, especially in small countries, by putting the local organisation into the hands of the product group which has the largest stake in that market. This will then act as agent for the other products represented.

THE TYPE D COMPANY

None of these arrangements overcome the basic problem that the product-oriented firm has a lack of interest in foreign manufacture. Hence has developed type D (figs 5 and 6). This represents an elaborate combination of product group and geographical management. The relative strength of the two branches of management may vary. In one company the geographical organisation would provide the administrative framework within which the product groups operated. When plans were laid to operate in a new area, the international division would set up a local company, recruit personnel and look for sites. But this would be done in consultation with the product management who would have done the market research required. Once the organisation was set up the product management would run it; they would become tenants, as it were, of the international division with the latter providing many of the services. The international division would also be friend and advocate at headquarters for the foreign companies. Pressure would be kept on the product management at home to ensure that the overseas operations were not neglected, and the latter would feel that there was someone to take up their problems. This organisation is designed to overcome the blocks in communication which can arise in types B or C.

The very complexity of this organisation can be challenging and stimulating. It has its characteristic problems but managers feel that they are given status and independence. Recruitment to executive posts is crucial, and all companies with this type of organisation pay great attention to management development schemes. There is emphasis on the importance of 'getting to know your way round' such a complex structure. In one particular example executives in the subsidiaries had to report at least two ways—to the appropriate product group and to the regional management for their part of the world (some C type companies did not report along the geographical lines at all). The chief executive of a local company had these two lines. His production manager would be answerable to him and to the product group which would add to his reporting lines. But some of the marketing managers would find themselves reporting in many directions at once, and in varying proportions for different sections of their business. This company was described as having 'a spectrum of reporting proportions'.

A new product group would be most likely to set up abroad through the international division; it would move some of its staff into the area concerned to study the situation and recruit salesmen and other local people. Once the company was established, the expatriate management would teach local nationals the intricacies of the reporting and communications system before handing over to them. With this 'spectrum' of reporting the D type company departs as far as can be imagined from the old type of organisation with its military model of clear and simple lines of communication and spans of command. The company just mentioned went up to nineteen reporting routes for one man. In another D type company the marketing director in one host country reports to his national chief for personal and disciplinary matters; but to his product group manager in the home country for matters concerning his handling of the products. He may also have other products for which he is acting as agent, and for these he will be answerable to their managements. There will be a link, probably not a reporting one, to the

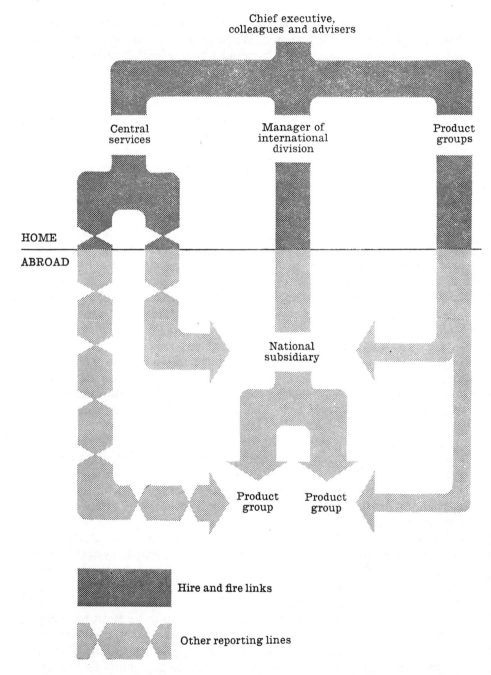

Fig. 2.5 The organisation of the type D company where the geographical organisation has priority

central marketing function, and his future may well depend on the central management development function.

The product group marketing manager in the host country, who is working for a different product, will report to his own product group manager, his local marketing director, and his product group marketing

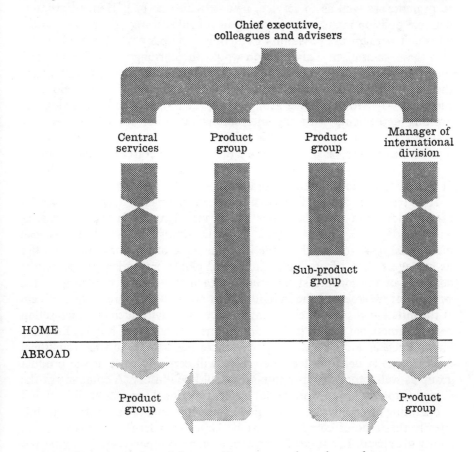

Fig. 2.6 The organisation of the type D company where the product group organisation has priority

director in the home country. Modifications of this scheme are possible. For instance, one firm separated the marketing function completely from production, so that there were two separate reporting lines within the product group. Another firm made a separate reporting system for finance, and in this case the local finance managers reported direct through their functional chief to the head office finance director, as well as along the product and geographical lines. This was a rare case of direct reporting to one of the central functional divisions. These would normally provide an advisory service, although top management would often be recruited from them. There would not usually be a strong official link.

The official process of policy formulation in the D type company is by negotiation between the different units—a 'meeting of minds' one company called it, 'creative conflict' another. The geographical organisation has to promote, as well as to service, new activities abroad. Hence the international division may see a marketing or manufacturing opportunity somewhere, or perhaps the possibility of buying a company which would fit well into the organisation. This division would then arrange a conference with the product group concerned and any other interested parties to investigate the possibilities and to make recommendations. Or the process could work the other way with a product group taking the initiative and discussing and drafting agreements with the international division for operations in a certain area. Such agreements might involve more than one product group. The whole emphasis is on contractual rather than hierarchical management. This contractual management allows a planned variation as to the degree of centralisation in different subsidiaries.

It is true that only a limited number of companies have this type D organisation; and these have not had it very long. It is also evident, as has already been suggested, that type D arrangements call for special managerial qualities. At the same time this type of firm has much to offer its managers. Apart from high salaries and global promotion prospects, the demands of the job are substantial. At each step in the organisation the strength or weakness of the individual can be crucial. There is the problem of the inflation of personnel. It may well be asked why such an organisation needs a functional set-up in its host countries at all. Or if it does, for some reason such as local conditions, why there need to be further functional departments at headquarters. For these will certainly exist in the product group as well, otherwise its autonomy would be illusory. A company of the C type (product group worldwide) has its functional services at the top and at operating level only; but the type D company usually has more than this. Clearly this type of company must be large, with large resources and an ability to expand. In a time of contraction such a company could be expected to find itself with a considerable problem of how to reduce the organisation without breaking essential links.

While this type, at the moment, does seem to provide a final stage of development for companies that are large enough, it cannot be said that there is any set method of development from one type to another. A multi-product company may start with a C type organisation, find problems of communication with the overseas operation, and reorganise into a B type company with a strong international division. One British company that had recently done this had found that the product group organisation overseas had been too wasteful. The change to a B type geographical organisation had been accompanied by a *closer* relationship throughout to develop

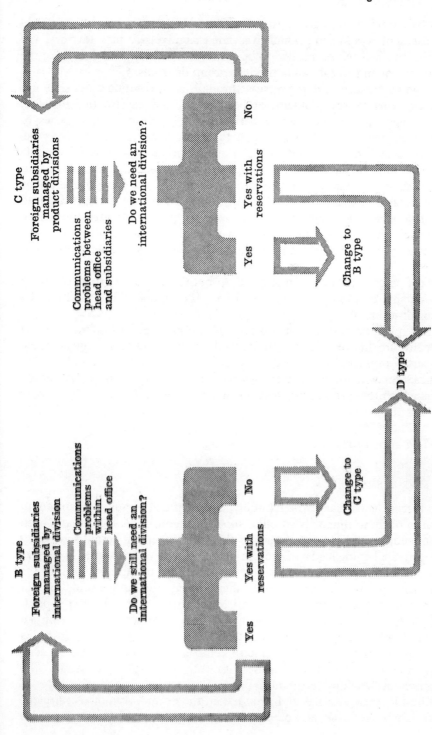

Fig. 2.7 Pressures towards organisational change—the limited options

a global strategy. As part of the reorganisation, also, a central functional management was set up, which was not executive nor just advisory. On certain specified subjects it had to be consulted. This applied equally to the international and to the home product group divisions.

A company can develop overseas through its international division and find that this causes problems at head office, and abolish this division. Either type of company can embark on a reorganisation or a series of reorganisations which effectively leads them into the more complex D type. Hence words like 'evolution' are quite inappropriate to what is a reversible process under the control of the company's management. What can be said is that these reorganisations show the influence of the foreign operations on the total organisation of the company. Once a company commits itself to a considerable proportion of its assets overseas, it commits itself to internal upheavals which do not affect a purely national company.

There is some difficulty in deciding what is the 'considerable proportion' of the assets of the firm which starts the process of reorganisation. The figure of 20 per cent has been suggested,[7] but this must vary from company to company, according to the overall size, the nature of the product, the personalities involved and so on.

Thus it can be said that the number of options open to the international company are limited. If it is multiproduct, it cannot for long continue to operate overseas as if it were a purely national company, and the reorganisation will follow one of these three main types: B, C, D. Some forms which this process can take are shown in fig. 2.7.

2.3 The subsidiary

THE MIRROR EFFECT

The foreign subsidiary will naturally have a much simpler organisation, but it is likely to mirror head office to some extent. This has already been mentioned; several clear examples of this 'mirror' effect were discovered.[8] The principal evidence is where the parent company has some distinctive grouping of functions, or calls certain offices by unusual names. If the subsidiary adopts the same style, then clearly the organisation or reorganisation of the subsidiary is mirroring head office. In the type B (geographical) company the subsidiary can be expected to develop an organisation along its own lines, in accordance with local customs. And this often proved to be the case. The local company less clearly mirrored head office in type B firms than in those with other forms of organisation. The reflection of headquarters could be seen in various ways—the type of relationship between sales and production, the normal area of recruitment for the chief executive, and others. Of the companies where this particular point was investigated, in about one half of the cases the subsidiary clearly mirrored head office, and only rarely did it fail to bear any resemblance whatsoever.

This mirror effect may not be produced by instructions from head office, but by an almost unconscious development along the lines of communication. For the subsidiary will need managers of sufficient status to communicate with and visit head office in functions where such communication is demanded, and will not be able to afford other officials even if local conditions suggest their employment. Even in some companies where much was said about encouraging local autonomy, the set-up in the subsidiary was found faithfully to mirror some unusual arrangements at headquarters. One consequence of this was confusion in the lower levels of subsidiary management. 'We understand the system because we have had a spell in head office,' said one subsidiary manager, 'but our subordinates do not. They get impatient of arrangements that seem irrelevant to our local conditions.' Some companies make conscious efforts to assist contacts between lower levels of management. But this can be complicated when a subsidiary manager is operating in more than one product group. One company had actually placed all specialists in the subsidiaries directly under head office, but this had not worked.

The foreign operations are bound to have some legal framework to comply with the fiscal laws of the home country. Although there still exists a number of examples of foreign branches, the complications of different national taxation systems usually lead to the setting up of a subsidiary company. In any given country there may be several of these. In a geographically organised company the legal entity is likely to be also the operating unit; but in a product group organised firm this may not be so at all. However, a set of accounts for all operations within the country that satisfy the tax authorities will be needed. If a company has a very *close* relationship with its subsidiary, some form of arm's-length[9] dealing is needed to satisfy the tax authorities, and this is another pressure preventing the treatment of foreign operations in exactly the same way as home ones. Apart from the legal problems of producing satisfactory accounts from a number of separate organisations, some minor administrative difficulties were reported by companies with a product group organisation overseas. These included sharing office space and equipment between different product divisions; there were also problems of salary differences between officers who worked together, but worked for different divisions with different scales. The companies concerned tended to make light of the problems, but clearly special skills are required to coordinate activities for which one has legal but not operational responsibility.

These organisational pressures on the subsidiary demonstrate the trend to a *closer* relationship indicated below in chapter 3. That these pressures come from within the subsidiary as well as from head office

D

will be shown in a later section (3.5). There are also the counterpressures of nationalism, and these are discussed in chapter 10. But these do not appear to have great effect in practice; normally home country patterns reappear in the local operations. It has been suggested[10] that the geographical features of the organisation will disappear in the future. We suspect the contrary. The abolition of the international division may be appropriate at a time when growth is relatively easy, but as growth becomes more difficult, and particularly if this is accompanied by increasing hostility in the host countries, a reinstatement of the geographical organisation can be expected. No doubt firms will also attempt to reduce any waste involved in conflicts between the two projections.

THE TWO HEADQUARTERS

One difficulty found in many different situations is here called the problem of *the two headquarters*, represented by the national head office and the international one. This problem arises, ironically, from a company's sensi-tivitity to local national policy, and thus the placing of considerable authority with the subsidiary management. But in the eyes of some of the operating executives in the subsidiary, especially the technical experts, the actual effect of this can be to produce two headquarters with which they have to deal, three if there is a regional centre. Where most of the relevant knowledge, skill or resources are at the international head office, there may be a strong urge to bypass the local arrangements. Operating managers say, and some-times say forcefully, that they want direct contact with the source of knowledge and that the national headquarters is an irrelevance, 'just a tax office' one of them said. Thus the problem of *the two headquarters* can be expressed in terms of the development of informal communications systems which follow skill rather than nationality. Studies of staff-line relationships and of professionalism sometimes show evidence of similar situations.[11] However, the attempt to short-circuit head office, although most frequently noted among the staff, was also found among line managers.

Nationalism attracts so much attention that the existence of other more powerful links often passes unsuspected. But it would seem that professional links across frontiers, already fostered by international conferences, are going to become more significant in the future. Indeed, in one company these links are already being institutionalised by methods such as those suggested in fig. 2.8. This diagram shows relationships between the staffs of a specialist department in headquarters and a similar department in a foreign subsidiary. One aim is to assist in the transmission of new ideas from one country to another. Whether it makes the difficulties of *the two headquarters* more or less is open to question; intracompany politics is also an issue here, but so is the relationship with the host country. This whole question is connected with issues of national policy, as against the inter-

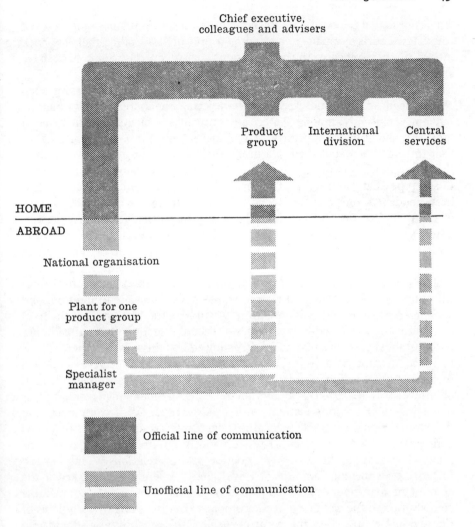

Chief executive,
colleagues and advisers

Product group

International division

Central services

HOME

ABROAD

National organisation

Plant for one product group

Specialist manager

Official line of communication

Unofficial line of communication

Fig. 2.8 The problem of the two headquarters
One specialist manager estimated that 90 per cent of all his communications were with someone in head office: this was a type D organisation

national organisation, which are looked at again in chapter 10. Meanwhile the organisational issues are troublesome for those in charge of the national subsidiary.

2.4 The regional centre

An important piece of geographical organisation that some companies have developed between head office and the subsidiary is the regional centre.

This is designed to coordinate the activities of local companies in a group of countries, and is normally regarded as a unit of head office that has been moved physically nearer to the operations that it controls. Some firms have abandoned their regional centres, and expressed the view that they were irrelevant in the air age. However, the number of firms actually having such centres seems to have increased in recent years. The increase shows mainly, but not exclusively, among American companies. Fourteen of the firms in table 2.1 above had some form of regional organisation, while in another four this had been abolished. Naturally those companies which emphasised the geographical organisation were most likely to operate this way, that is to say type B and some type D firms; of the four in which the centre had been abolished, one was type A and the other three are now type C. Two of the type C firms had regional machinery in particular product groups. These sometimes acted as agents for selling other products. The principal regions were Europe, the Americas and the Far East. The organisation of the regional centre usually closely followed that of head office.

The establishment of the regional centre could be expected to reduce the autonomy of the national operation, whatever the stated intention, and add an expensive and possibly time-wasting extra link in the chain of communications. Several examples of reactions among local subsidiaries to the establishment of a regional centre showed that this was their view. These included attempts to bypass the centre, belittling of the executives stationed there, and even resignation from the company. For the presumed addition of a level was regarded as demotion by some national managers, and as damaging their communications with headquarters. With companies that did have regional centres the local management was apt to react this way, and considerable personal effort was obviously required on the part of the regional executives to establish good working relations. This 'effort' included an enormous amount of travel, and it might well be asked if the amount of man-hours spent on journeys in this way made a comparable contribution to the wellbeing of the company. In discussing the problems of the regional centre from the point of view of the subsidiary it should also be said, however, that companies which did not have such centres often recorded a demand for them. Local management often demanded some office nearer their operation, only to react when this was put into practice, and especially when a charge for it appeared on their budget. One company which had experienced many problems with subsidiaries after setting up a regional centre had had much heart-searching on the subject. But in the end the argument for having such an office in close touch with the foreign markets, and matching up to similar centres established by competitors, proved decisive; and in fact this company developed regional centres in more than one part of the world. The other disadvantage of the regional centre was that its establishment was inconsistent with the policy of making the subsidiaries stand on their own feet.

Among the advantages of the regional centre was this point of bringing some part of head office into closer contact with the local operations. This particularly applied to marketing, and hence some companies had regional marketing centres only. To a more limited extent it applied to finance. Indeed, among United States companies tax considerations had been a pressure towards regional centres in countries which constituted 'tax havens'. When changes in the law removed their usefulness in this connection, some of the centres remained. It would seem, however, that there could still be fiscal advantages in a regional financing policy. In any case bringing functional management nearer to the operation was one justification for the regional centre; and it was pointed out that an extra level was not necessarily involved if the management posts moved to the regional centre already existed at head office. The difficulty about this argument is that regional management at head office has the function of being the friend in court, the representative there of the local subsidiaries. The physical move of regional management from the centre to the region can also move it, in the eyes of the subsidiary, from the nurturing to the disciplinary function. This concept, discussed below in chapter 3, can be crucial in the interpretation of apparently minor reorganisations. If the elements of nurture and discipline are not recognised, then unskilful re-arrangements can abolish the nurture and multiply the discipline. This is one cause of the phenomenon of an alleged decentralisation which appears in the opposite sense to the man in the field. It also explains why the company encounters strong opposition when setting up a piece of organisation which the subsidiaries had previously been suggesting.

Some substantial advantages are claimed for the regional centre. The most important is that a strong and experienced team is established for development in the area. It can provide the expertise for setting up new national organisations. For the regional executives are near enough to the situation to establish the new company, and yet withdraw gradually when suitable. The centre can avoid the danger of premature withdrawal and the danger of holding on too long. That is the theory. Naturally this function of the regional centre can be exercised by any well-established national subsidiary in the area. But the next purpose of the regional centre cannot so easily be left to another local company. This is to underpin a subsidiary where there are problems. One regional centre has an advisory relationship only with companies in its region that are operating satisfactorily. Where, however, a subsidiary is in difficulties the regional officers take over direct line management. This underpinning allows greater risks to be taken with the national companies. This particular firm has a D type organisation, and uses the geographical projections as support for the product groups in this way.

Management development is another activity of some regional head-quarters. The identifying and training of future managers on a regional basis is something the centre can do; and this is extremely difficult for the local company, unless it is a very large one. Personal problems may well be reduced by regional, rather than global, development of the future executives. Indeed, the advantages of bringing a man up through a regional centre may be enormous, but if these are the only advantages it becomes an expensive management school. Problem-solving on the spot is another purpose of the centre. If this is part of the underpinning mentioned above, it is obviously valuable. But there must be involved here a fine calculation between the quick solution of problems and the expense of the centre. If this assistance takes away the initiative of the local company, this method of problem-solving may become very expensive indeed. Rationalisation of production within an area was another possible purpose for the regional organisation. Rationalisation across frontiers is discussed elsewhere. This is obviously a special opportunity for the international company, but much delicacy is needed to make use of it. It is argued that the regional centre can develop sufficient local knowledge and a wide enough view to handle the rationalisation more competently than head office. This may be so, but it needs saying that the firm in this research which seemed to have the most advanced methods of rationalisation across frontiers, together with great sensitivity to local opinion, was one which had a type D organisation but without any regional centres. The ability to operate long-term planning techniques was another advantage mentioned for the regional centre. In this connection it could provide a general service for the area, whose cost would be beyond the resources of any of the local companies. It could also conduct studies to decide questions like the optimum size of the local companies in the area.

The exact amount of authority vested in the regional centre could vary considerably. It could be just a post office for messages in transit, or it could be an important decision-making unit. If the latter, then complex operations in the area could be coordinated, and important deals settled quickly. Indeed, it was the possibility of major strategic advantages over competitors in the region that gave the centre a significant place in some organisations. The regional controller of one company said that they had lived through many of the snags of the regional centre but it remained 'open to question whether or not we could have doubled our income in the region if we had not had a regional headquarters'. He took the view that an unnecessary multiplication of staff was the great danger, and that this was overcome by a frequent reappraisal of each office. A substantial regional centre might have a staff of about 150 with about half on tour at any one time.

Two companies said that all the major controls were exercised at the regional centre, which was answerable to head office as a subsidiary in its own right. In these cases the centre had a significant authority and a role in developing regional policies. It is significant that in both cases the expenses of the centre were paid by head office and not charged directly to the subsidiaries. Budgets were drawn up between the regional centre and the subsidiary. Head office was only brought in when major problems appeared. Limiting the amount of discussion which involved head office was frequently mentioned. Regional centre executives described themselves as a 'filter', and no doubt this was just the aspect which the subsidiaries most disliked. Some of the reasons for setting up foreign companies at all also applied to the regional centre. For instance it could be a 'listening post' acquiring knowledge of new developments in the area. It could also be useful in matching up to both competitors and customers, if they were organised regionally. It could be on the other hand that fashion rather than economic considerations produced the regional organisation.

Figures 2.9 (i)–(iv) on pages 48 to 52 show some of the ways in which the regional centre may fit into the organisation.

Thus the regional centre is a development of the geographical organisation which meets certain immediate problems, but may well produce long-term difficulties. The advantages of the centre can be summed up in saying that it meets the lack of local knowledge at headquarters and the lack of expertise in the subsidiary. There would seem to be a cast-iron case for building up a trouble-shooting team to underpin local operations. But such a team hardly needs the apparatus of a regional centre. The disadvantages of the centre lie in its role in the organisation—the known disadvantages of lengthening the lines of communication and the expected effect on the operations of the subsidiaries in its area, together with a change in function as seen by the foreign company.

2.5 Communications and policies

EXTENDED COMMUNICATIONS

The multinational company represents an extended system of communications. Within this there are a number of processes by means of which information and instructions are passed. These range from formal correspondence to the 'grape vine'. Some of these processes are intentional and formal, others are less formal, and others are unplanned. In some cases one item of communication can be used to stimulate others. The circulation of productivity comparisons is an example of one of these. Among the many purposes that this can serve is the dissemination of technical knowledge. For a technical advance in one subsidiary is thereby notified to others. In this section some of the problems of communication are considered together with the processes actually used. These latter include the issuing of written instructions and operating manuals, the reporting and control systems, the circulation and discussion of plans,

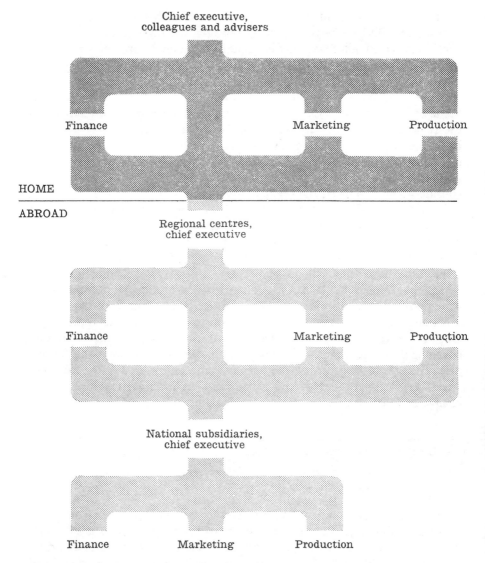

Fig. 2.9 (i) The place of the regional centre in the company: the single product centre (a type A or C company)
The number of functions located in the regional centre may be limited

minutes of meetings, intrafirm comparisons, visiting by executives and the holding of company conferences. The effectiveness of these methods is related to the actual organisation of the company. Thus we have already seen how certain organisation structures have their characteristic communications problems. We will also look at the way in which the communications system influences the formation of policies. In subsequent chapters

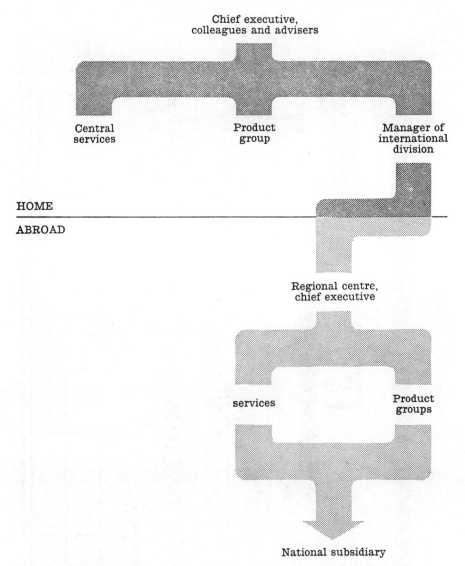

Fig. 2.9 (ii) The place of the regional centre in the company: the multiproduct centre (a type B company)
The reporting lines may by-pass the centre for long-established subsidiaries

these processes, briefly set out here, will be examined again in the context of the power systems, the control systems, and the personal relationships of which they also form part.

The general assumption that a slowdown of communications is to be expected in a large organisation was certainly shared by executives in the larger companies investigated, but, perhaps because this problem had

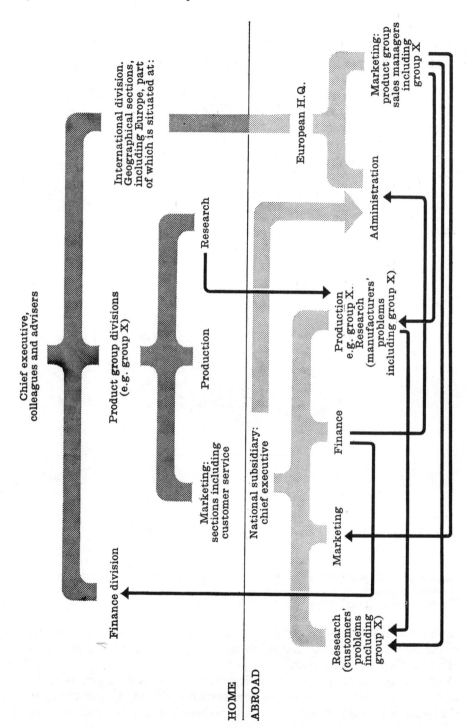

Chief executive, colleagues and advisers

Finance division

Product group divisions (e.g. group X)

Marketing: sections including customer service

Production

Research

International division. Geographical sections, including Europe, part of which is situated at:

European H.Q.

Administration

Marketing: product group sales managers including group X

Production e.g. group X. Research (manufacturers' problems including group X)

National subsidiary: chief executive

Finance

Marketing

Research (customers' problems including group X)

HOME

ABROAD

been anticipated, little convincing evidence could be found. Some people in subsidiary management complained about disadvantages in competitive situations, but the problems mentioned did not seem to be related to the communications systems. Where these were formalised, information and feedback seemed remarkably rapid—as fast as could be expected in a much smaller organisation. One specific issue did appear, however, and that was the significance of the number of levels. Many years ago empirical evidence was produced to suggest that both speed and reliability of communications were related to the number of levels in a hierarchy.[12] This would lead one to expect that an increase in the number of levels by, for instance, the introduction of a regional centre might be damaging to the communications system. In some of the evidence collected about regional centres it would appear that this expectation was justified.

Two comments, however, need to be made. One was that the establishment of a regional centre was not always regarded by the company as the addition of a level at all, but rather as the movement of an already existing part of head office nearer to the scene of the operations with which it was concerned. This was sometimes the case, although even then it might not appear in this light to the subsidiary. The other comment is about the significance of the authority and status of the regional centre. If most problems could be settled here then it would speed up communications. But this was only certainly the case in one such centre, and even then only for the weaker subsidiaries. In this case the rapid expansion of the foreign operations was credited to the policy of developing regional centres which had at least the power to ensure the rapid settlement of contracts.

The actual number of levels between the foreign subsidiary and the top of the firm is called the *organisational distance*. Companies evidently find difficulties about appropriate methods of determining this, since most of the larger companies reported frequent changes. On the whole more levels with less officials at each was the pattern that seemed to be emerging in both the product organised (type C) and the geographical (type B) companies.

Fig. 2.9 (iii) The place of the regional centre in the company: the multiproduct centre (a type D company)
This is an actual company which has developed an organisation on whose complication the chief executive of one subsidiary commented: 'This works because everyone is determined it should work.' It has been developed to meet certain requirements:
1. Maximum initiative for each executive and minimum red tape to be combined with global efficiency and the ability to take full advantage of the international position
2. Lines of communication appropriate to each function with the least possible bottlenecks
3. Need to combine a group-mind with individual responsibility on problems
This figure is not an exact chart of the organisation of the company but an attempt to show how the objectives are realised in practice

The two main positions where staffs easily became inflated and the length of the communications lines extended were subproduct group establishments in the C type company, and in the specialised departments of the type B firms.

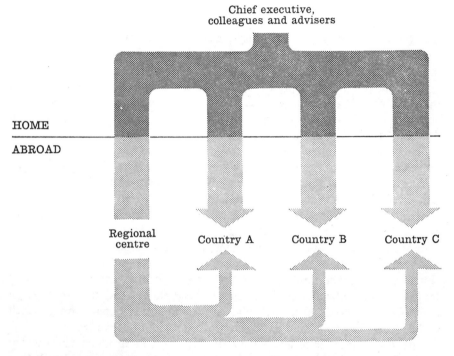

Fig. 2.9 (iv) The place of the regional centre in the company: the regional centre with advisory functions only
The regional centre may come into direct line management for a subsidiary which is especially weak

It should also be said that the extended communications of the multi-national company give scope for the reformulation of policies along the line. Changes can in their turn be reflected back to the parent company. Several examples of this were encountered. One company, for instance, had a worldwide ruling against leasing any of the large and expensive pieces of equipment it manufactured. A manager of one of the sales branches of a national subsidiary in this group found that this put him in an awkward position. Since late deliveries seemed likely to lose him an important customer, he decided to lease some equipment. Before doing this he consulted some of his fellow-managers, but only those who were in charge of other branches like himself. He felt it was pointless to consult his superiors, who were bound to quote the regulations. In the end, his decision to lease the equipment came to light when his national head office asked for the machine involved. There were some troubles at the time, but later the regulations were amended to give more discretion to branch managers. Such a conflict between global policies (in this case pressures to increase market share) and global regulations (not to lease) is typical of the type of conflict likely to arise in the multinational firm.

Another example of reformulation of a different, but also typical, nature was in a company that manufactured two qualities of the same product. The policy was that the better-quality article, which was also the more profitable, was the one which was heavily advertised and sold. The poorer-quality product was used in support where needed. One subsidiary, however, found that the cheaper product sold more easily and gradually shifted their sales emphasis to this. The overall result was a greater bulk, but a lower profit. The global rules of the company were subsequently reframed to enforce the sales of the higher-quality article.

CIRCULATING REPORTS AND INFORMATION

The system by which head office collects reports from its subsidiaries constitutes a major formal channel of communication. The main problems here are to make reports meaningful and to avoid disrupting the activities of the local company. A reporting system that is significant in a large headquarters can be both irrelevant and burdensome in the subsidiary. A striking example of this was the complaint of a subsidiary marketing manager that his report on the competition was a terrifying task, whereas in that particular country the competition itself was negligible. In his view, inflexible regulations which did not apply to his particular circumstances kept him deskbound for substantial periods producing lengthy reports; the problem was exacerbated by a lack of multilingual secretaries in his particular area. This complaint was typical of many where subsidiaries were asked to produce information which they did not require for their own use. This collection of irrelevant material did present itself as a major problem of being part of an international group, but there was the further complaint that reports so laboriously compiled were not read at headquarters. 'They show no sign of using the information at all,' said one foreign manager, 'indeed we get visitors from head office who have apparently studied none of the material about our operation.'

At least one-third of the subsidiaries visited mentioned this matter in some form or other, sometimes saying that their reports elicited no comment or response whatever. Apart from the lack of response and the demand for information that the subsidiary did not itself require, the other main source of complaint was to be instructed to report on matters that had been specifically delegated to the subsidiary. This occasionally produced strong reactions, and we found evidence in some subsidiaries of efforts to avoid supplying information where it was felt that to ask for it at all was an infringement of autonomy. A sample of the complaints voiced by subsidiary management included the following:

A British controller in a US-owned subsidiary in the United Kingdom complaining about the standard reports which were used throughout the group: 'They are forced down our throats. They use them in America, and by the great god conformity, we have them here.'

A French executive speaking scornfully of reports demanded by the parent company in Sweden: 'Il y a un service statistique en Suède qui s'amuse à faire des comparaisons entre les différentes compagnies du groupe. Ça ne sert strictement à rien.'

A British executive writing to headquarters in the United Kingdom: '. . . that much of the work in question is marginal to our proper duties and repetitive in character . . . the competition report alone comprises 180 pages of details to the point where the sales manager has been worried not what to do about competition, but how to pass on the news of it to [headquarters] by due date. We are compiling statistics for [headquarters] far in excess of those needed here for practical operations and we thus question the overall need for them elsewhere. . . . There is [also] the needling feeling . . . that if a man quietly doing his best must, at each turn, prove to an anonymous reader that he has done it, then there might be an implication of lack of trust in his ability.'

A Canadian manager in a US-owned subsidiary in Britain: 'It is a damned nuisance keeping up with the reports. But after all, I suppose they are entitled to know what is happening, they are the owners.'

Another British manager complained of too much reporting: 'The whole thing has gotten out of hand. They keep us from doing our job by making us send home half a ton of paper to prove that we are doing it.'

One response of head office executives to these complaints is to say that the subsidiary managers are not necessarily the best judges of what information they do in fact require for their own use. Reporting, we were told, has an educational purpose—to teach subsidiary managers how to appraise continuously all aspects of their business. Further, if reports are relaxed, then some important matters may be neglected. Thus one firm cited delinquent accounts. These had been removed from the list of required reports, but were later restored when it was discovered that one subsidiary had ceased to watch them carefully. So in this way reporting systems can be used as a stimulus as well as a control. To the complaint about lack of response, the reply was that it was only thought necessary to make comments when the reports showed that some matters required attention. It should be added that some companies were making efforts to meet the complaints of the subsidiary. These efforts included reappraisal of their reporting system to see where pruning was possible; they also included regular feedback of information and comment to the local companies.

Nevertheless, the usual view at head office is that large investments overseas need careful monitoring, and that this requires a great deal of information. An opinion which well sums up this attitude is the remark attributed to the president of one large corporation: 'A fellow once said to me, "Listen, leave me alone to do my job. And if I don't do it, well you can fire me." I said that that was impossible. By the time we'd found out he hadn't done the job right, we might be on our way to losing $5 million.'[13]

However, there are other less burdensome ways of collecting and circulating information. One is the circulation of the minutes of meetings. This practice is operated both ways between head office and the overseas companies. It does, of course, enable the subsidiary managers to be selective about the information given. They can doctor their minutes, but they can also do this to their reports. On the other hand, they are more likely to receive information this way—for instance, the minutes of research committees at home will keep subsidiary managers abreast of new technical developments, a matter which is otherwise easily neglected. One C type British company had two committees—a management and a research committee—charged with maintaining the flow of information. Another company kept formal reports to a minimum; but considerable attention was given to the flow of opinion and information. Frequent newsletters on any subject of concern to the company's business were circulated, and the chief executive regularly exchanged tape recordings with the men in charge of the foreign companies. These tape recordings were completely private and no decisions taken through them became effective until reported in writing. Such ingenious methods of keeping the local company in the picture evidently raised the morale. In this company, great enthusiasm was shown for the system, whereas in many companies it came out that subsidiaries were often starved of information, and that this was one of the ways that international companies failed to make the best use of their advantages.

Few companies had a systematic check that all relevant information was getting round. Indeed, although the main complaints were about excessive communications, there were also many about the lack of it. In some companies, regular monthly or quarterly meetings, often lasting two or three days, are held at which corporate top management and subsidiary management review the operating results of the past periods, revise plans as needed, and discuss various matters of common interest. Although the meetings are effective devices to keep pressure on subsidiary management, one of their main objectives is to air problems as soon as they arise. 'Woe become the man who keeps a problem to himself and lets it get worse,' said an official in a company which held such meetings. Subsidiary management may find this approach irksome, and in any case it is time-consuming. One managing director told us his guess was that he spent more than a third of his time engaged in either preparing for or attending such meetings. There is something to be said for active response. It avoids the feeling in the subsidiary that little is known about it at headquarters in spite of all the laborious reporting, and thus does give subsidiary management the satisfaction that head office is in touch, and that a good performance will quickly be recognised.[14]

The element of speed in reporting was also mentioned. Some companies made a fetish of speed in their upward communications. Monthly reports had to be telexed to headquarters at ever earlier days in the month. But the same sense of urgency was not so often shown in downward communications. It did not help in winning a contract where quick decisions had to be taken if a discussion had to to take place between three parts of a company which were in three different countries. The domestic company might well have an advantage here, an advantage that would not be decreased if the international company's 'expertise' at headquarters was not entirely relevant to the local situation. This might not just arise in selling; it might also happen when buying was involved.

In one company it was possible to observe an actual contrast in procedures between a domestic and a foreign subsidiary. In both cases a decision on capital expenditure outside the discretion limits of subsidiary management was involved. In the domestic instance, the manager was able to phone one of the directors, who told him to go ahead. This director was thoroughly familiar with the situation and willing to be answerable to his colleagues. In the foreign company, the decision took several days. This was a company which was multinational and multiproduct, and had recently slimmed down its head office staff. Hence it took some time to contact those with whom consultation was required. With a larger head office staff, despite other disadvantages, the consultation might have been quicker. But undoubtedly speed of decision-making was not mentioned as often as it might have been. This would seem to be just because it was so thoroughly anticipated by head offices. Procedures had been built in to speed up communications, even at the expense of inflating the organisation. But the standardisation of these measures in turn inflated the communications, and this is where most of the complaints come.

The speed of communications may well become a problem once more with the spread of new managerial techniques. For instance, a decision time for a new capital investment, within limits which had been acceptable in the past, could be quite unacceptable when critical path analysis was to be applied to the project. The communications problem could be even worse when the analysis was made in one country and the vital decisions had to be taken in another. In this matter the international company is likely to have an advantage over many national ones. Speed of communications has more to do with efficient organisation than with physical speed.

Aware that an excessive flow of communications is a burden on the subsidiaries, some companies are using sampling techniques. By this means information can be collected in depth on some product lines and not others; one company spoke in terms of 25 out of 300 lines. This may be a convincing way of balancing the cost of ignorance against the cost of information; it certainly does not help the morale of the subsidiary if it comes to believe that its unproductive work becomes greater every time head office buys a new piece of data-processing equipment. But not every company accepted the proposition that the communications flow should be kept to a minimum. Three advantages were claimed for increasing this. One was that the passing up of new ideas was related to the volume of general communication. The present sample of firms was not large enough to confirm this, but the evidence available seems to show that this is at least also related to the sophistication of the product and the industrial condition of the host country.

Another claim for an increased flow of information was that it was necessary to monitor the responses of the local management to new methods and techniques. This indirect monitoring was less inhibiting than the less frequent but more direct questioning. And the third claim was similar to this—that the more independence was left to the local managers, the more it was necessary to watch for the first sign that they were not running their businesses properly. This point may be the answer to the one made earlier that the difference between the view at head office and that at subsidiary level as to whether the latter was autonomous or not far exceeded expectation. For at subsidiary level demands for information are usually equated with control. From head office standpoint they may appear in just the opposite light—as a check that makes control unnecessary. It may well be that companies are insensitive to this contradiction, that it is not realised how much the communications system determines the organisation at subsidiary level.

One item of 'communications' is the international comparison. Some companies concentrate on one measure of performance which is constantly circulated, and is the main subject of discussion at all appraisal sessions. Other companies circulate a great many different sets of comparisons. Yet over half the companies studied used no such comparisons. This was one of the subjects where opinions were equally strong in different directions. Some companies regarded the circulation of these comparisons as crucial to their growth; others regarded them as an expensive waste of time. There is evidence to support both these views, and it is clear that considerable care is needed to use comparisons effectively. Two examples were encountered where the circulation of such figures merely led some highly paid executive in the subsidiary to spend a great deal of time collecting evidence to rebut the comparison.

POLICIES AND REGULATIONS

Another aspect of the communication system is to ensure that the subsidiary is familiar with the policies and rules of the company, and retains this familiarity through changing circumstances. Policies can be written into formal documents or they can exist in unwritten traditions or understandings. As has been pointed out before, the organisation with elaborate written rules is not necessarily less flexible than that without. Those which have unwritten rules may change very little over the years; whereas organisations with written constitutions can be considerably changed. It is easier to make changes to rules which are framed precisely than to unwritten but powerful conventions. Hence it must not be assumed that companies with no written rules are necessarily more adaptable. They may be even more rigid; but at the same time there may be considerable differences of opinion as to the role of any particular officer. One executive said that written rules and organisation charts were only irritants; in his organisation everyone knew where they stood. As a matter of fact conflicting accounts of the role of one of his fellow-directors had already been given. On the whole foreign managers do not know exactly who to deal with on any given matter by instinct.

There does seem to be a relationship between the use of written rules and the employment of local managers. It is the expatriate who operates a rigid system without written regulations. If a company has elaborate written manuals, it may well also have local management wherever possible.

Multinational companies are likely to have a mixture of written and unwritten regulations. For written rules to cover every eventuality would be unlikely, if only because there might be legal problems. European firms operating in North America, for instance, are unlikely to issue written instructions about arrangements with competitors—such instructions might bring the local company into trouble with the law. On the other hand, companies with the greatest dislike for written rules are likely to have such rules for financial reporting, otherwise consolidation of accounts becomes a problem. One aspect of this subject which came out clearly during the investigation was that head office and the subsidiary can have quite different views as to what constitutes a written rule. In one company head office explicitly stated that there were no written regulations, apart from a short list of items on which consultation was required which was given to each chief executive of a foreign subsidiary on his appointment. Yet in the same company functional executives abroad produced carefully bound folders of rules and requirements giving in much detail how their departments were to be administered. They had bound these themselves, hence head office were correct in affirming that they had not sent out books of rules; but they had bound them from instructions they had received, not ones they had deduced. The fact that his 'rule book' had come in so many instalments that no one could remember having sent it did not make it any less real to the foreign manager. Indeed by prescribing in great detail how he must report to head office, it effectively determined how he would administer his own department.

While some companies had manuals for each function, which set out standards and methods in great detail, the more common practice among companies which had written rules at all was a policy document which set out the point in the organisation at which specific decisions could be taken. The force of a manual could vary from subsidiary to subsidiary. For instance, one company had a worldwide manual of sales depot procedure. This was obligatory for the smaller companies but advisory for the larger ones. Some of the more comprehensive manuals, more favoured by American than European companies, purport to discuss 'company philosophy'. Phrases like 'promoting a sense of belonging among employees' tend to occur. These manuals seemed to have two main uses. They were used as a basis for management development courses, and they were referred to by officials who found themselves often on the move.[15]

The following were the main headings in the policy manual of one large company:

1. Safety: most careful check on new equipment.
2. Quality: worldwide procedures to ensure that product meets specification.
3. Promotion from within.
4. Training: personnel development programme.
5. Individual recognition: right of appeal against decisions at any level.
6. Social responsibility towards host country.
7. Growth.
8. Belief in competition, including willingness to supply potential competitors.
9. Service through products (e.g. to supply better products at lower prices to help raise standards of living).
10. Efficiency of management.
11. Advanced personnel policies.

In another firm, written rules took the form of a letter to the managing director:

As managing director you are the Executive head of the business in [country X]. You are responsible for the proper functioning of all branches of that business, for all decisions and action taken in [country X], and for carrying out policy as formulated.

The nature of the Company's business requires that certain decisions, for policy or other reasons, should only be made after consultation with Head Office, and a note of these is given at Appendix A.

In addition, sufficient knowledge of the Company's affairs in [country X] can only be acquired with head office if a reasonable volume of information is sent there from time to time. A note of the reports and returns required is given at Appendix B.

Apart from the particular requirements stated in these two appendices, you should feel free to consult with head office on any matter at any time, in order that the volume of experience there may be used to the best advantage in furthering the interests of the business.

Appendix 'A' referred to above was entitled 'Matters on which head office should be consulted before action is taken', and encompassed most significant decisions that would be normally taken in each functional area. However, these instructions were tailored to each subsidiary—generally, the larger and more important were given substantially more autonomy.

A much smaller company had set up management committees with the basic policies of the company set out in instruction to these committees, which tried to preserve the autonomy of the operating units, and included the following passages:

> . . . to facilitate and expedite the work of the Board of Directors in
> 1. consideration, formulation, definition and modification of policy
> 2. effectuation of such policies . . .
> 3. methodical review of the effectiveness of any such policy . . .

A later clause described these committees as 'strictly non-executive'. The committee which dealt with subsidiary companies was charged with having due regard to:

1. the recognition of the autonomous character of such companies.
2. the maintenance of the legal authority and responsibility of the Directors thereof.
3. the differences in constitution, control and management arising from differences in the law of their domicile governing overseas subsidiaries.
4. the essential fact that the position of the parent company in relation to its subsidiary companies and the extent of its effective control thereof is that of sole or majority shareholder; and that accordingly in theory such control can only be made effective at and by means of General Meetings of such companies.

This last was a statement of an extremely *open* relationship, and demonstrates that such relationships are sometimes defined in writing.[16] Hence all four possibilities do in fact occur—written policies and close or open relationships, unwritten policies with either close or open relationships. But there is a natural correspondence between the written manual and the close relationship. Indeed, the very loss of opportunities—for example, failing to make the most of technical advantages—which will be noted as a factor for impelling a close relationship, also impels a written manual.

Thus the policy manual is connected both to the structure and the relationships within it. In the case of the structure, the problem of piecing together an organisation in which the component parts may have very different traditions should not be overlooked. For tradition is a powerful type of unwritten policy. This problem has certainly produced a trend towards more written statements. A writer for the American Management Association has reported that in the companies in her sample there was a clear trend towards written agreements with subsidiaries, but even so about one-third did not have them.[17] In the present study, the number without such agreements was nearer a half, presumably showing that European firms are less likely to have them.

FORMAL AND INFORMAL

The principal types of official organisation in the multinational company have now been identified. A distinction is often made between the *formal* and the *informal* aspects of organisational behaviour. There have been reservations expressed about making this distinction, but for some purposes it does seem useful to contrast the official links in the firm, those prescribed by the regulations and organisation charts, and the unofficial procedures that develop. However, there are undoubted drawbacks in that companies that have developed a sophisticated organisation, such as the D type, are led or advised by men who may themselves have studied organisations in theory and are aware of the need for informal links. Discussing behavioural studies in relation to production processes the chairman of one large international group has said: 'Experience has shown that employees' interest in their work is stimulated in this way and their performance improved.'[18] Obviously informal links across frontiers are different altogether from those in small groups in the workshop or office. But they have some characteristics in common, and appear to match similar needs in enabling the people concerned to meet the strains and stresses inherent in the formal organisation. Companies that are led by people who recognise this are likely to make provision for informal contacts and to facilitate their formation. The difference between these firms and the more rigid ones can be seen by different reactions to questions about their lines of communication. Some companies actively discourage any links across frontiers and insist that all communications go through the official channels. Others reply that the short-circuiting of the official system is encouraged; they are trying to use the natural development of informal links to improve executive performance.

These circumstances mean that there is a greater difficulty than usual in distinguishing between the formal and the informal aspects of the organisation. There are, in other words, some procedures which fit neither category and yet are a significant element in the behaviour of some of the firms observed. We have chosen to call these activities *recognised informal.* Official facilities encourage recognised informal links, and no action is taken against them, but they remain unofficial. Hence they differ from both the formal and the informal, but *recognised* is not exactly the right word. We would rather refer to them as manipulated informal, if the word manipulated could be used in a neutral sense; for they are an attempt to handle the more subtle links in the organisation in such a way as to improve the efficiency of the whole.

Take, for instance, a regional grouping. The formal regional organisation has been described earlier in this chapter. But informal regional arrangements also exist. In some cases they exist with the active encouragement of the head office, which does everything possible to encourage subsidiaries in a given area to get together. So a recognised informal grouping develops within a region with managers discussing common problems and formulating common strategies. Other firms actively discourage such arrangements, and indeed issue instructions that all communications are to pass through head office. Evidence was discovered, however, to show that in these companies, too, regional groupings do develop. Subsidiaries get in touch with one another and develop a common policy with regard to the demands of head office. It could be argued that since in certain parts of the world some regional grouping is going to arise anyway, it is beneficial to formalise this and so bring it under control. But unless the regional grouping is sabotaging long-term plans, it may be cheaper to have an informal than a formal one. At any rate this example of three different types of regional grouping well illustrates the formal, the informal and the recognised informal processes.

Informal procedures often develop in multinational companies by the bypassing of units of the organisation, such as the efforts of operating managers to establish direct links with headquarters mentioned earlier in this chapter. There the point was made that head office was regarded as the source of knowledge; it may also be regarded as the source of promotion. Where there is a recognised informal link with functional or product management, there may also be additional informal connections with the central services. For instance, in a D type firm there may be a management development officer at the centre who plays a crucial role in promotion, and with whom an informal link is important. This importance may account for some journeys to head office for which the stated reason is to consult with some other official. Indeed, the promotion arrangements of the D type company can appear calculated to produce informal structures. For the manager in a national subsidiary may have a direct reporting link with his local managing director, but this latter can be in a different product group from himself or perhaps part of the international division. Hence he will have little chance to observe the work of some of his own subordinates, including the one just mentioned, although nominally he hires and fires them. The next move of this particular subordinate may be to a different part of the world, perhaps as chief executive in another national subsidiary. He may not owe his promotion either to his present chief or to the product group managers who also see some part of his work. Each one of them may have only a limited knowledge of him, and the crucial figure is the official who is collating their appraisals. It is with him that informal contact has to be established.

In general it can be said that the number of informal links increases with the formal, and helps to make the latter more supportable.[19] It is this supplementary nature of informal links that seems to be important, and that often cuts across national differences. Naturally there are links that follow national lines, especially among expatriates.[20] Perhaps less noticed are the links that follow functional lines, the groupings that followed knowledge, skill and specialisation and resisted national considerations. These were often, in fact, recognised informal links, with the strictly informal groupings growing up behind them again.

Some of the processes described in this chapter can be regarded as a *repersonalisation* of the structure, with a trend to less regulation and more individual responsibility, especially shown in the development towards *contractual management*, the blurring of the lines of command, and the emergence of the *recognised informal* facet.

3

Relationships between head office and the foreign subsidiary: power systems

Power in an organisation can be discussed in terms of two closely related questions. The first is *how* does the organisation attempt to ensure that all its parts conform to the objectives and rules fixed for the whole? And the second question is *where* are the decisions taken that 'the organisation' is attempting to enforce? Both these questions assume a developed and size-able bureaucracy in which the decision-making could be widely spread. In attempting an answer this chapter looks at the power systems involved in two pairs of concepts. The first of these is whether power is exercised by *calculative* or *voluntary* pressure.[1] The second pair is what we have called *open* and *close*, that is referring to where the decisions are actually taken. This latter pair is discussed in the second part of the chapter. The state of the relationships between head office and subsidiary is compounded of facts understood in the light of both these pairs and the paradoxical situations produced between them.

3.1 Calculative and voluntary

Force is used to keep the inmate in prison, money to motivate the employee in the firm, and persuasion to keep the adherent in support of his 'cause'. These are the primary means of producing conformity to their respective objectives among the members of different types of organisation[2]—'primary' because the organisation normally depends on the use of its particular means. No amount of persuasion or conviction will induce a person to work for a firm that is unable to pay him. Similarly monetary inducements will not usually get a person to change deeply held convictions. Thus the business organisation must always use its particular means of controlling its members; we have called these *calculative*. But *voluntary* inducements, those that do not involve a straight financial calculation for the individual, can be used as well. Indeed, for many of its members the firm is a 'cause' as well as an employer. The exact relationship between the two means can be an interesting study at the lower levels; it becomes more complicated higher up. For here there is confusion as to the nature as well as the appropriateness of different ways of exercising power, and this can be seen most notably in the kind of authority the companies try to exercise over their foreign managements. This confusion is here described as a calculative theory masking a voluntary practice, and this constitutes one of the two paradoxes around which this chapter is written. Calculative phrases are used, but few calculative sanctions. This view is reinforced by the fact that the use of these calculative phrases is more often concerned with efforts to promote competitive rivalry between one part of an organisation and another than it is with the straightforward consideration of individual reward and penalty.

The publication of *The Organisation Man*[3] has made it unfashionable to admit a sense of dedication to the business organisation, even if this was not already the case. But in fact the relationship between the calculative and the voluntary exercise of power, which is not simple among the lower ranks, becomes far more complicated among those in executive positions. It can be said that on some occasions when firms appear to use the calculative appeal most strongly, they are in fact using the voluntary method most effectively. An example of this is the *profit centre*; this phrase is increasingly used in companies to describe a unit of the organisation where the man in charge will be judged by the profitability of that unit. An increase in the calculative element in the control system is suggested; but this can be an illusion. The attaching of profit responsibility to a post does not of itself make the post more or less secure than it was before. Indeed, there is evidence that firms which use concepts like the profit centre are also firms which maintain stability of employment among their managers. If, on the other hand, there is a salary bonus tied to the profitability of the unit, then the calculative element is increased; but the significance of this can be exaggerated. What the profit centre arrangement does do for the manager is to increase his independence. The theory behind this is usually expressed in phrases like 'making the man feel that his unit of the firm is his own business'. The implication is that a man will work much harder and for much longer hours at his own business than he will for someone else. But it is the independence which produces this at least as much as the income.

The independent business man is regarded as one who prefers to work for himself at a lower salary than he could command by working for someone else. So the aim is to produce the attitudes associated with self-employment in the large corporation. Thus such a calculative phrase as profit centre can express a different reality. Other phrases like 'owner-manager concept' similarly mask what is effectively a voluntary commitment. There are some possible circumstances where the reverse can be true. A statement that appears to have voluntary undertones can have a price tag. For instance the improvement of the company image can also 'improve' expense accounts. There are, however, two considerations which place limits on this diagnosis of voluntary involvement among senior executives in a business organisation. One is that their careers, and perhaps their investments, are likely to be more heavily committed to the firm than those of more junior employees. So the wellbeing and indeed the very existence of the company involves for them some calculative involvement. The other consideration is the extent of the demands made by the firm; if these are limited, then voluntary involvement is limited. If most of the executive's waking hours are absorbed by the company, then voluntary considerations can be assumed to be of greater importance.

In general, calculative power involves an appeal to a person's self-interest, as opposed to voluntary power which appeals to his interest, his values. One of the characteristics of the foreign executive is that calculative considerations are likely to be even less convincing than to the home executive. For his salary and his promotion chances[4] are both determined mainly by considerations that have little to-do with his performance; so are the limited possibilities of dismissal or demotion. There remains the executive bonus, either in cash or stock option. This practice is distinctively American although increasing in Europe. But if a man's position is high enough to qualify for this executive bonus, in most firms this means that his salary is already very large. So it is hard to believe that he will perform much more effectively for a little more highly taxed income.

If it is hard to find credible evidence that calculative influences are strong with men who have reached the top positions in overseas companies, this is not to underestimate the concern some companies have that a man's performance may decline once he has achieved his ambition. It is to say that multinational companies can command a great deal of enthusiasm and vision, more (one suspects) than many of them realise, certainly more than they give themselves credit for when questioned. The multinational company has much to offer in terms of strategy and scope to engage the whole attention of the most able men. It seems as if the very complexity of the organisation is a factor here, in that it gives the manager something to pit his wits against. One keeps hearing about the fascination of driving a great organisational machine, and the struggle to meet targets in a competitive and often unpredictable environment. One should, however, repeat that the personal involvement of the senior executive in his organisation includes the calculative element that, if the company does go under, his career and fortune are more completely at stake than those of his subordinates. This, of course, is hardly likely to happen in most of the firms we are discussing. Some national governments are less stable. So the principal influences are voluntary and include the creation of profit centres, already mentioned, the setting of objectives to be discussed in chapter 5, and the promotion of competition between the companies in the group.

The fostering of competition within a country between operating units is comparatively simple. However, competitive comparisons between companies operating in different countries can be very complicated, and indeed self-defeating if not handled skilfully. An example of where this can go wrong was in a firm which used cost comparisons to measure the relative performance of the operating units. The way these were framed seemed totally unfair to one subsidiary in a group we investigated; and the most obvious result of the exercise was that all too much highly paid executive time was spent proving that the figures were misleading. Recognising the dangers, some firms displayed considerable ingenuity in promoting competition between their subsidiaries. One example was provided by a company which used a productivity index to measure performance. This was based on an elaborate calculation designed to make genuine international comparisons possible. The number of man-hours taken to produce a standard number of products was calculated for each country; this measure will be called an MH. For each company in the group, there were four calculations: the present MH, an attainable target, a theoretically possible target without any capital expenditure, and a theoretically possible target with new equipment. This measure allowed fully for local differences, and decisions about capital expenditure would obviously be related to labour costs in the country concerned. Further, the MH would be broken down in order to measure the key operations within the company. This was intended to allow international comparisons to be made in the working of each function. Such a system provided an elaborate and plausible method of comparison so long as labour costs were a significant part of the expense of the product. The company concerned regarded this as a principal reason for a considerably improved return on investment, especially when the scope for an increase in market share was limited. Connected with this was the bringing to head office in turn of the chief executive of each subsidiary to discuss the MH situation in his company. During his time at head office he was put through a period of intensive questioning by different officers of the company. He was expected to stand up to this questioning without having any colleague present to test his familiarity with every aspect of his business. No doubt his job ultimately depended on the way he coped with this inquisition, and to that extent calculative considerations were involved. But, like the MH concept of which it was part, the main aim was to stimulate each subsidiary by competition with the others and with themselves by examining the possibilities of improvement in their own business. Towards this end, reports on all the MH factors in the group are regularly circulated. This is a voluntary control. It is on a par with the systems used by religious and political bodies for the better achievement of their objectives. By forcing the local executive publicly to defend his performance at head office, a greater compliance with central policies is ensured without using calculative methods.

One of the reasons why the distinction between calculative and voluntary involvement becomes blurred is that the multinational company has an acute problem of conflict of interest between the whole and the parts. This conflict makes it difficult to calculate the contribution of the individual manager, as we shall see in a later chapter. Meanwhile the problems of such appraisal make the calculative element even less convincing, and the voluntary element more important. What seems to be developing is some sort of contractual arrangement. The actual supervision of the contract may be *open* or *close*; but some real or implied agreement arises which determines the involvement of the foreign management. This was usually implicit only, but in one company where it was explicit there were procedures for discussion between the subsidiaries. An additional force for voluntary commitment is that of the outstanding character, as has been shown by other studies.[5] His drive and character build up a loyalty which keeps the company together, and blurs problems which might otherwise become pressing.

There is clearly much scope for detailed study on the exact part played in any system by the voluntary and the calculative elements respectively. But the study of the multinational firm provides interesting examples of the use of the one where the other is intended.

3.2 Open and close

DEFINITION

The relationships between head office and the foreign subsidiary have been discussed in terms of the means of ensuring conformity. We will now look at *where* the decision-making powers lie. If the significant decisions regarding the subsidiary are taken at head office, this is called a *close* arrangement; the reverse is described as *open*. These words have been preferred to centralisation and decentralisation, which are used in a similar sense. A typical statement on this subject is:

> There has been a tendency towards decentralisation of management which to a large extent overcomes the undesirable features of central control. Comparatively independent operating divisions have been set up which are practically equivalent to separate companies, except in certain financial obligations to the parent company. While not an entirely new practice, it has found increasing favour in recent years.[6]

Most of the companies interviewed expressed a policy with regard to both their product groups *and* their overseas operations in terms much like this statement. We have seen that the facts are often different from the avowal, and one reason for this is presumably that unlimited autonomy for the product group must mean some limitation on the autonomy of the foreign operations, and vice versa.

Another reason that has been mentioned is that decentralisation by functional specialisation is also occurring.[7] You cannot 'decentralise' everyone; less centralisation at head office may mean more abroad. These and other reasons lie behind the contrast between the ideology of decentralisation and the reality of centralisation. A similar insight has been expressed differently by another writer in a summary of the centralisation-decentralisation controversy, distinguishing between 'preference' and 'conditions' in considering style of management. The preference is for decentralisation because of the expected advantages. But the conditions limit the realisation of this preference. This author further distinguishes between the limitations imposed by those matters that are within the control of the organisation—structure, rules and so on—and those that are not. He clearly regards the controllable factors as most significant. In contrast this study of multinational companies has found that a number of uncontrollable limitations are very important, notably technology, available staff and necessary responsibilities. For it is in these areas that occur the 'missed opportunities' which touch off many of the changes described below as 'a dialectical process'. The importance of technology here is twofold. On the one hand research concentrated in the home country can produce rapid developments both in products and in methods, and the dissemination of these will limit the local autonomy. On the other hand the development of new data-processing equipment will produce demands on the communications system which effectively determine many practices in the subsidiary. Hence the sense that opportunities provided by new inventions were being missed if local autonomy was allowed to block the application of these inventions. But, as explained above, a thorough swing to centralisation was also prevented by a sense of missed opportunities. For this would lead to a loss of personnel and a low standard of performance by those who remained. Hence the concept of the *normal line* (see fig. 3.1) has been devised to illustrate how the influences on the relationships cancel one another out, with this sense of missed opportunities working both ways. It still remains that the practice in most firms is more centralising than the theory.

It might be anticipated that the relationship with the foreign subsidiary would be connected with the maturity of the latter and probably the cultural development of the host country as well.[8] This proved to be not quite the case. For one thing, the subsidiaries in which a more open relationship might be expected, the sophisticated ones, are often part of a company that is much influenced by technological development, and hence impelled to a closer relationship whatever might be the intention. Then again the environmental constraints (local laws) might be more important in forcing an open relationship than cultural differences were in promoting a close one. And finally there were the controllable factors. One of these was *organisational distance*. This occurs in companies where there are powerful units of the organisation between the overseas subsidiary and the top management.

This was described in chapter 2, it will be recalled, in connection with product group and subproduct group divisions (see fig. 2.4). This could also occur in geographical organisations, particularly where there were regional centres. The proliferation of functional staffs which create *organisational distance* is clearly a controllable factor, but one that is apt to produce a relationship that is more close than intended. It was anticipated that the relationship would vary with the function, and therefore with the orientation of the company. This was not borne out by the evidence: what was discovered was a far greater difference than anticipated between the intention of the head office and the result at subsidiary level. This has led to the theory that different groups of managers were involved. The top managers of the parent company were sometimes more concerned to force a subsidiary to stand on its own feet than to limit its autonomy. But at the next level of management, the procedures which operated for collecting information and for planning were a much greater influence on the subsidiary than was realised at head office. This conclusion, that levels of management influence relationships rather than specific functions, was unexpected but clearly demonstrated by our evidence. This came out in the majority of subsidiaries investigated, but there were exceptions, and in some firms procedures were specifically established to avoid undue limitations on the autonomy of the foreign affiliates.

Another of the controllable factors influencing relationships is the confidence that head office executives have in the subsidiary managers.[9] The latter will be kept in a close relationship until their performance improves, but this relationship may block the improvement. When they are given more initiative, this may lead to the making of mistakes which will give ample justification for those at head office who argue against decentralisation anyway—the corporate hawks, as they might be called. Further, these mistakes, if they do not lead to new procedures removing discretion from the local managers, may well lead to the development of further central services which will effectively reduce the autonomy of the subsidiary.

An increasing pressure towards a closer relationship is the opportunity for rationalising production across frontiers. This may well become a necessity with modern methods of production, and some subsidiaries specialise in the manufacture of a limited range of products for sale in both their home market and to other members of the group. This naturally results in extensive intracompany trading marked by cross-shipments of finished goods, subassemblies, industrial intermediates, and components. This development has gone furthest in Europe, receiving an impetus from the trading opportunities presented by the establishment of the Common Market and European Free Trade Association. The chemical industry, in particular, has led the way in this process, but it is also becoming a feature of the automobile, farm machinery, electrical equipment, and other industries. The economies of scale in an ever-increasing number of industries are too large to be obtained from a single national market, and plants are being designed to produce for an entire region. Such decisions are taken on the basis of considerations such as low production costs, proximity to markets, or specialised manufacturing knowhow. The logic behind this development is evident, but so is the fact that the problems of planning and coordinating such operations are enormously complex. A measure of this can be obtained from the following example given by the former chairman of General Motors:

> If the South African assembly operation and its recently added manufacturing facilities are to function smoothly and efficiently, they must today receive a carefully controlled and coordinated flow of vehicle parts and components from West Germany, England, Canada, the United States, and even Australia. These must reach General Motors South Africa in the right volume and at the right time to allow an orderly scheduling of assembly without accumulation of excessive inventories. This is a challenging assignment which must be made to work if the investment is to be a profitable one.[10]

To make this work, authority over a wide range of operational matters must be transferred from the subsidiary to a higher level in the organisation which has a broader view of the overall business. Of course, not all foreign operations are suitable for integration. In particular many consumer goods must be especially adapted to a national market, and it may often not be feasible to produce for export. Local production may also be required if sales are to the government, or if the product has a high weight-to-cost factor. But where there is scope for integration, close control over the subsidiaries seem to be an inevitable development. This stimulates further development abroad, for it opens up the possibility of a regional strategy.

Within the company, then, the relationships may be open or close—reinforced by an exercise of power by both calculative and voluntary methods. These relationships may be identified by examining a range of issues between head office and subsidiary. Where are important decisions taken? How do subsidiary managers know the limit of their discretion? How much surveillance is exercised and by whom? If answers to these and similar questions show considerable autonomy in the eyes of both head office and subsidiary management, this is called an open relationship; the opposite is called a close relationship. For reasons discussed below it is not possible just to say 'This is an open firm', or 'That is a close firm'. It is only possible to classify them by their present stage of development. While all firms claimed a more open relationship, 60 per cent of those investigated showed evidence of a more close one. And this represents, in fact, a higher proportion of the larger firms because most of the smaller firms showed an open relationship.[11] Since the relationship could best be understood as a trend in each individual company, it was thought convenient to look at firms in terms of the origins of their foreign operations. This involved looking beyond the evidence that was immediately available, and considering the backgrounds of the companies, and therefore seemed a convenient starting-point for analysing what was happening.

THE EXPANSION STRATEGIES

The origins of the move abroad can be understood in terms of four broad strategies,[12] two of which involve close relationships and two open. The first of these strategies is the exploitation of *natural resources* abroad. This category includes companies which own plantations for tropical agriculture—cotton, coffee, cocoa, tobacco, sugar and so on—as well as mining and quarrying. In Europe this particular strategy has a long history, going back into colonial times. The next strategy is called here the *manufacturing*, and includes companies which go abroad to make a wider use of their technical lead. The third strategy is called *commercial*. As we shall see in chapter 9, this is the most common route to multinational operations at the present time. It is essentially defensive in character, the development of manufacture abroad to counter threats to the market, and starts with an open relationship. The fourth strategy arises where some geographical diversification is a main motive and where the parent company regards itself as a holding company. This is called an *investment* strategy, and the contact between head office and the subsidiary may be really that of consultant to client.[13] This particular situation arises when a company wishes to acquire foreign assets without committing managerial resources, or when the particular foreign subsidiary is an insignificant part of the company's effort.

The oldest among the companies investigated started as part of the colonial system—they were descended from the traders who prospected for minerals or chemicals, or organised plantations for tropical products like tea, cotton, sugar, tobacco, fruit. The firms were managed almost exclusively by men from the home country. On principle the exercise of power was personal; it was also usually close. The essence of the close relationship is one where all important decisions are taken at the centre, and those delegated to the local operation are only such as cannot be settled centrally. Even with these, very clear guidelines may be laid down. These may be found in writing or may be informal and arise from the manager's knowledge of the company. An ironical fact is that while the invention of the telephone and the increase of air travel make centralised control more practicable, and possibly less burdensome, these developments were at first accompanied by less close relationships. It seems that companies exercised considerable ingenuity to make central control work in the days of less rapid communications. The telegraph was, of course, available long ago; and such arrangements as a senior executive from headquarters arriving on each alternate P and O liner to Far Eastern ports are still remembered in some companies.

Perhaps the typical position in a colonial company is where a young man goes out with a thorough personal knowledge of the company he serves. He may spend his life overseas, but promotion is from country to country and for the lucky ones eventually back to head office. Almost all the senior executives at home have followed this route. The new executive develops an intuitive knowledge of what he is supposed to do in any situation and who he is supposed to consult, and he knows that his promotion depends on following this line. He knows that he must consult with his superiors to the maximum which the available means of communication make possible. The expatriate manager is thus the link in the organisation. His own discretion is limited; no one else has any. This is a close relationship although the overseas firm may not be hedged in by written policy manuals.

No company today uses the word 'colonial'. Even the innocent question, 'Your origins were colonial?' is apt to bring a sharp retort. So we have used the phrase *natural resources* for this type of strategy, but many of the firms involved still have arrangements which stem directly from their colonial origins. They have attempted to retain something of the close relationship, informally exercised, when this can no longer be done by the transfer of managers from the home country. Thus one British firm has set up a staff college in the United Kingdom. To this are brought managers from overseas companies; each course may include men from fifteen to twenty different countries. These courses are designed so that the participants may get to know the company more intimately. They meet personally members of the board, and in general the aim is to keep the intimate and personal relationships of the old system. The whole process of executives growing up together in the company, and passing through the same process of conditioning, becomes so difficult once the promotion of local nationals becomes normal that there is tendency to change the system altogether. The staff college just described fulfils several functions, but its most significant is to retain the old system under the new conditions. It aims to give the local national something of the intuitive, informal understanding of the ways of the company that the expatriate always had.

The colonial type company had a close relationship, it can almost be said, because of the environment in which it grew up. In the environment of today there are personal and ideological pressures towards a more open relationship. The impact of these pressures will be discussed later; meanwhile, the technically orientated company which is manufacturing new inventions overseas or is concerned with maintaining a high level of quality is likely to wish to retain a close relationship. The main headaches of the company will be related to such matters as the protection of patents and trade marks, the maintenance of specifications and standards, and the constant improvement of the products. These concerns are not easily

E

decentralised, and whatever form of organisation the company devises, within it the relationship tends to be close. The risks of local autonomy are too high to do otherwise. For other types of companies, those described as *commercial* and *investment*, these considerations are often less relevant. Those which market relatively simple products and are commercially orientated tend to emphasise local control. So do firms where the relationship is largely one of investment.

THE NORMAL LINE

The types of companies we have classified as *natural resources* and *manufacturing* tend to produce *close* relationships of the sort described. The *commercial* and the *investment* types start from a more *open* relationship. In these, the short-term financial returns tend to be the main method of appraisal. So long as the subsidiary produces an adequate return on investment the contact from head office is minimal, and considerable discretion is left to the local management. The situation can be represented diagrammatically (see p. 75).

Figure 3.1 also illustrates that there is a trend away from the original situation that is centrifugal rather than the reverse. There is, in theory, some *normal line* to which companies appear to move whatever their origin. This line is very hard to identify in terms of actual operating procedures, but the trend towards it can be clearly seen in almost all the companies investigated. Special circumstances or strong personalities may distort the trend, but constantly the close companies report 'we used to be more decentralised', and the open companies say 'we have had to tighten up our organisation'. One company said 'we are not interested in being just a holding company, but we like to leave the initiative to the man on the spot'; and another, 'we are not an operating company, but of course we have to make sure that our money is used to the best advantage'. It was far from obvious that there was much difference between the two in practice. As the two quotations suggest, the main pressure towards both more open and more close relationships is a sense of wasted opportunity. The open company finds that the expertise at the centre is being wasted; the close company finds that talents in the operating units are being frittered away and often lost. The actual pressures which make up this centrifugal force are listed in table 3.1.

This list is not exhaustive, but it contains some of the principal pressures frequently mentioned by companies. Those which appeared occasionally, sometimes only in one company, are mentioned in the text but not listed in table 3.1. This list gives only the common pressures and shows clearly the nature of the dialectical process that is being described. The balance of argument is clearly a fine one. The experience of companies is in both directions—loss of managers on the one hand, and poor results on the other. But some of the categories also suggest powerful pressure groups. For

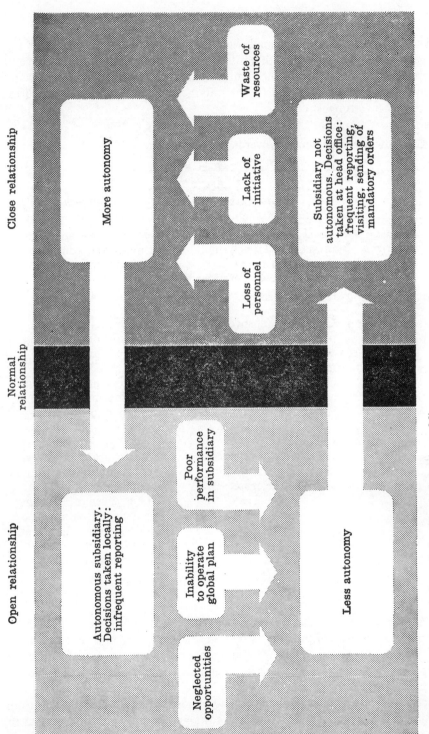

Fig. 3.1 The *open* and *close* relationship and the *normal line*

instance, head office will normally work towards a closer relationship, but in a geographical organisation there is in almost every case a pressure group for decentralisation in the international division.[14] All other things being equal, however, (1), (2), and (6) were found to be the strongest pressures, with (6) the strongest of all.

Table 3.1 Some pressures towards the *normal line*

	Pressures to an open *relationship*	*Pressures to a* close *relationship*
In host country	Local feeling and political pressure, relatively high standard of living, personnel considerations. (1)	Relatively low standard of living and education expatriate management. (4)
In subsidiary	Good results, successful planning, relatively high sophistication, loss of managers, containment of problems. (2)	Poor results and unsatisfactory planning, failure to grasp profit opportunities, local management developing goals contrary to those of the rest of the firm. (5)
In head office	Geographical organisation, marketing orientation, ability to delegate. (3)	Product group organisation, technical orientation, emphasis on global strategy, use of operating manuals, development of modern techniques in all functions, international rationalisation. (6)

In general it can also be said that these pressures operate differently according to the originating situation of the company. For instance, technical orientation refers to the company which is manufacturing a sophisticated product or providing a complex service. Unless the colonial considerations apply, this company is likely to be overseas reluctantly and recently. For it is likely to have a good export record and a product group organisation at home. Low labour costs, high transport charges, tariff barriers and the actions of competitors draw it into overseas operations.

Since the company is overseas to manufacture complicated products where quality is important, a close relationship is natural. This will be modified by several likely developments. One that will most immediately stimulate a change towards a more open relationship is the actual or supposed loss of managerial talent, another example of missed opportunities. Managerial talent is widely assumed to be very scarce, and actual resignations are quickly investigated. Although not many examples of this were mentioned, some companies were concerned about the potential loss of talent through recruitment problems and inadequate motivation of managers. A solution of both these problems was considered to be more independence for the local management. 'The best men are snapped up by our competitors, because they don't think there's enough scope in a foreign firm.' This was also given as one of the advantages of global promotion.

Another pressure towards a more open exercise of power is the growth of personnel at head office. In recent years, partly no doubt under the influence of Parkinson, the pruning of head office staff has been a fashionable activity. One newly appointed chairman was described by the *Financial Times* as 'huffing and puffing' his way around his organisation.[15] Where there is a genuine reduction in the numbers of functional staff at headquarters, this can appear to the subsidiary as producing a more open relationship. For several levels of management between the subsidiary and the main board make for close supervision, especially if there is a group of specialists at each level. This is most likely to happen where there is a product group type of organisation. Briefly, where a subsidiary manager in a large company says that he reports direct to the chief executive of the parent company, this probably indicates an open relationship, and the reporting will be limited both in extent and frequency. If he reports to another executive at the top of the firm, this will also appear open; it is reporting to intermediaries that begins to make for a more close relationship. It may be worth recording that when asked to state a preference, the overwhelming majority of subsidiary managers preferred to deal with a specific senior executive— a member of the main board in a European company, or a vice-president in an American firm. To have a personal relationship at that level gave them a friend in court without unduly limiting their independence. There were a few who preferred the link with a less senior executive more specifically concerned with their side of the business. But there are problems involved in fitting a subsidiary into its allegedly logical place in an organisational chain, which combines a close power relationship to headquarters with a personal remoteness from the top.

The general rule that the technical firm will set up a close relationship with its overseas companies finds exceptions in some of those most recently established for two reasons. One is that a management ideology is involved in the setting up of a new company. This ideology combines a belief in 'participation' together with 'individual responsibility'. A man, it is assumed, must be held clearly responsible for his part of the business, and must be involved as far as possible in the decision-making process. The latter half of the proposition becomes more difficult in an international company, but the former becomes easier. The manager's area of responsibility can be more clearly delineated. Many managements are deeply imbued with this ideology, as are the consultants employed to advise them. This is reinforced by the second reason which is the concern for nationalism, and the nightmare of falling foul of the host country government. Hence more independence may be given to the local operation than it has technical sophistication to cope with. One dramatic instance of this was witnessed during this study, and the expatriate managers who had to be rushed in to meet the problems that arose spoke of the personal problems involved. There were considerable difficulties in reverting to a close relationship after an open one had produced a breakdown.

The firm with the less elaborate product is likely to start with a strong commercial bias, and to manufacture overseas in order to protect an existing export market. The protection of a market where tariff barriers and transport costs made export no longer possible was the typical reason given for this type of company to be overseas. The open relationship is the normal condition for a company using the commercial strategy. The tendency in these companies is to stress the importance of local knowledge and 'leaving things to the man on the spot'. There will be the minimum of reporting although a careful watch will be kept on the finances of the local company. Characteristically, the investment situation will be more open still, with the parent company only intervening over the raising of capital and the allocation of profits. Even these may be handled informally, with the parent company holding in reserve its ultimate sanction of changing the management.

Powerful forces are changing these open type arrangements and making them more close. These forces are in general more powerful than those operating in the opposite direction on the close arrangement. The most open of all are the holding companies of various types which have collected most or all of their subsidiaries on the grounds that they would be good investments. If a company is just a holding company it is likely to have some financial control, some personal links hopefully intended to stimulate the subsidiary, but otherwise no central services. The problems of this type of relationship have had some publicity of late. For instance: 'Little or no direction from the top may have been all right in the inflationary 'fifties, but it can be a grave source of weakness in today's competitive conditions—the date of the autonomous subsidiary is past.'[16] This is another 'sense of wasted opportunity'. The subsidiary may have seemed a good investment, it may have given the company the security of a geographical spread, and it may have been selected because of inspired management. But the security of the group may also take away a spur from the manager of this subsidiary without providing an alternative impetus. This ironical fact has been mentioned in several case studies. When a phrase like 'buying management' is used, it is used of buying a company led by a man who has proved his ability to perform well on his own. As part of a larger organisation, however nominally independent his position may be, he does not always come off. Hence it is common for the holding company to find situations about which some remedial action is needed. One thing that can be done is the establishment of central services and some sort of product group organisation. Either of these is likely to constitute pressure groups for a close relationship.

The firm with the commercial strategy will start with some central services, and the pressures to centralisation are likely to come from within these. Once again neglected opportunities, either real or potential, are likely to suggest that more power should be exercised at the centre, and this suggestion will receive a special impetus from the development of modern techniques. For instance, marketing is a function which seems most congruent with the open relationship. The emphasis is on local customs, local outlooks, the independence of the market suggesting the independence of the subsidiary. But modern marketing concepts are not local in their application at all. Adapting them to local conditions is a comparatively minor task beside the evolution of the methods themselves. Then again local differences are themselves growing less. For example, tastes in so many consumer goods are becoming international. Companies manufacturing such goods report a switch in many markets to international brands rather than local ones. One company especially mentioned that in the 'forties and early 'fifties in the newer countries national brand names were important. But as the date of independence recedes there is a noticeable swing to brands with international names. The local 'culture' is everywhere becoming less important except as a tourist attraction. It can be said indeed that the growing use of international brand names is a pressure away from local autonomy. What is more, this type of business is likely to grow even faster and to realise more fully the advantages of the multinational firm. To make full use of such advantages will involve standard specifications and the close controls that these involve.

The possibilities of international advertising were vividly illustrated in one company which used television for promoting some of its products. Sales of an international brand increased in part of a country that was just across the frontier from that in which the advertisements were being screened. The increase was much the same on both sides of the frontier, while sales of a local brand only increased in the one country. Another point about advertising was made by a company which had suffered from inconsistent images of its product caused through independent promotion in different countries. This is an experience which might well lend itself to centralising tendencies.

THE INFLUENCE OF DIFFERENT FUNCTIONS

It was sometimes suggested that the degree of centralisation within the firm varied from function to function. This variation may be becoming less, as has just been suggested in marketing. Moreover, in all the functions the development of modern data-processing systems at head office is increasing the closeness of the relationship. Such equipment does this by its very nature; but, when operated by men who are deeply imbued with the principle that your 'decisions are only as good as your information', this can be a very centralising force indeed. It is often not realised at head office just how burdensome the information collection can be to the overseas company. Innocent-looking requests for information can place great strains on the smaller set-up, even forcing changes in the organisation which were not at all intended. The problem of language becomes acute at this point. To be allowed to report in your own language produces a more open relationship than such a minor concession would appear to suggest. The further step of being allowed to report by methods most suitable to your own country makes for even greater openness. This concession was, however, rarely made, and in its complete form only met with in one company of our sample, in spite of all that was said about decentralisation.

The personnel function is one that might be expected to be decentralised and traditionally has been. Labour legislation and trade union negotiations make central control impossible. Vague directions are frequently mentioned, in the form of: 'We are instructed by head office to ensure that our employment practices are at least as good as the best in the country.' They are usually instructed, although they do not produce the information so readily, that they must not be 'better' than the local employers either. But a closer relationship in the personnel function is now appearing. Some companies are beginning to use aptitude tests worldwide, others are producing standard attitudinal surveys.[17] Techniques are more and more imposed internationally, such as those used in the study of organisation. As a portent of the future, global promotion has been made easier in at least two of the companies surveyed by putting all senior personnel records on a central computer, and other firms are planning a similar development. In general, a fresh impetus to centralisation has come with international management development programmes. This increasingly close relationship applies to management development, and it may also apply to selection and training techniques on the shop floor. But it remains that the laws and customs of labour relations stand as strong obstacles to centralisation. Thus one firm reported that consent to the deduction of trade union dues in a subsidiary in a country where this was normal was considered as a major deviation of principle by head office. Nevertheless the 'deviation' had to be accepted.

Production, on the other hand, is expected to be a centralising function. Clearly a common trade mark requires a worldwide quality and standards control. But this has not always been as close as might be expected; the attempt to standardise products, and especially components and spares, around the world has proved a landmark in the history of some organisations. The production manager in a national subsidiary which had experienced the changeover to global standards asserted that the savings could be more apparent than real. He cited two main problems. The first was the lengthy transitional period during which double stocks had to be held. This might be still further prolonged if customers could not be persuaded to accept the new standards. The other problem was that standard products required standard raw materials, and this might be very difficult indeed. The setting and policing of the global standards and of the purchasing policies were undertaken by the appropriate product group of this firm at head office, and any variations had to be registered there. The situation thus produced could seem very onerous to the subsidiary—'one hell of a problem', one production manager called it—and yet at the same time, not too authoritative to head office who would claim to apply the rules 'in a commonsense way'.

In some of the larger firms the centralising trends were recognised, and efforts made to protect subsidiary management from undue interference—'taking the nonsense out of centralisation', one chief executive said of such efforts. To keep up the pretence that decentralisation is taking place when the truth is the reverse may prevent such a recognition. One method of 'taking the nonsense out' is to put a limit on matters with which head office is allowed to concern itself. Such a device also serves the opposite purpose of ensuring that the subsidiary stands on its own feet where this is a problem. The limit can be, for example, expressed in terms of the capital expenditure allowed to local management without reference to head office. This would have overcome a difficulty mentioned by one local company which otherwise had wide discretion. The problem was the acquisition of a small piece of land adjoining the plant which they needed for the future, and which was available at the time. They wanted to buy it at once because development plans for the area were clearly going to boost land values. The price was trivial, but the parent company refused permission on the grounds that their policy was against 'entering property' at that time. Later, when the expected development was taking place, the land had to be bought at a much inflated price.

The last paragraph suggests a point already mentioned, that centralising and decentralising pressures may not vary so much according to the function as to the level of management. The directors of many of the companies studied showed as much concern with making the subsidiaries stand on their own feet as with getting them to accept the global policies. Regular reviews of operating procedures with encouragement to the subsidiary to make criticisms was one of the ways this was done. The enforcement of global rules (like the one mentioned at the end of the last paragraph)

E*

and new techniques was the duty of the next level of management at the centre. Hence the contradiction between enforced autonomy and enforced centralisation can be explained by the fact that two different managerial groups are involved. This latter group would be constantly concerned with gaps in the knowledge or effectiveness of head office which would lead to the formulation of new regulations to fill those gaps. The subsidiaries would react to these and there might be a reformulation as a result. The actual quantity of regulations and orders might seem small at the centre, small enough to remain within a general policy of maintaining an open relationship; they might not seem small at all to the subsidiary. The resentment would be most likely to collect around specific issues where there was considerable local expertise. An example of this was purchasing. Head office might be able to obtain long-term contracts of advantage to the group as a whole, or might enforce purchasing within the group itself. Subsidiaries would go to great lengths to avoid this type of interference, which would often appear to benefit the group but not their own part of it.

Research is normally a centralising function, and there was general agreement that decentralised research could be very expensive. Hence most research was done in the home country. Some of the companies involved in this study attached great importance to innovation. This upgraded the work of their research organisation which thereby became an even stronger pressure to a close relationship. However, some subsidiaries did have strong research departments, and thus became more independent. The detailed study of this is a subject in itself. In considering decentralised research it is important to consider the type of research being undertaken. While there is a problem of definition between the threefold classification of research usually adopted, it can be said that no clear example of basic research in a foreign subsidiary was discovered. As a matter of fact the amount undertaken by parent companies is not very great. The second category, applied research, can cover a number of different activities, from the search for new inventions or new formulae to short-term product support. If done abroad these were likely to be done in regional centres, but the latter was found in the subsidiaries as well. So also, to a much larger extent, was the third category, development work.

There were some circumstances in which research had to be done abroad, and these could produce a more open relationship. A common reason was the search for government, and especially defence, contracts in the host country. This might involve not only research in the subsidiary, but the possession of secrets which could not be passed to head office. Another condition was that the problems to be solved by the research might be different in different countries. For instance, the head office of a multinational company is normally in a high labour cost country. Some of the subsidiaries may be in lower cost countries where different techniques of manufacture are appropriate. One or two multiproduct companies did research in different countries for this reason. But this did not necessarily mean greater autonomy; indeed, central surveillance could be more thorough where research expenditures were heavy in the affiliate.

One disadvantage of too great a concentration of research at headquarters was the possible rejection of projects that might have been viable abroad. One company had noticed this problem and employed an executive especially to watch out for such projects. The peculiar difficulty of his brief, however, led to the lapse of the post on his retirement; but the tendency for a research department too completely concentrated at head office to overlook the needs of the overseas operation remains a problem. A third condition pressing for foreign research is the 'listening post' function of the foreign company. If one of the purposes of buying a company in another country is to gain access to that country's knowledge and techniques, then local research will be important. This will particularly apply to firms based in a technically less sophisticated country, such as European companies with subsidiaries in the United States.[18]

OTHER FACTORS

The problem of the *two headquarters*, explained in chapter 2,[19] is an example of pressure from within the subsidiary for what amounts to a more close relationship. What happens in this situation is that the subsidiary has been given a considerable autonomy, but is not large enough to carry all the expertise that the scope of its operations demands. Hence there are many managers who will manoeuvre all ways to short-circuit the lines of communication the company has so conscientiously established. This is, naturally, a rare situation. Normally a close relationship is not the aim of the foreign subsidiary, on the contrary it is a source of complaint.

Indeed the managers abroad predictably exaggerate the degree of centralisation to which they are subject. The head office executive will speak glowingly about local autonomy, and the subsidiary manager will protest about interference from the centre. But in some of the companies studied the difference of viewpoint exceeded anything that common sense would suggest. The reason for this seems to be the multiplication of functional staff at headquarters, already mentioned as a centralising development. The process seems to be that the top management at head office decides that a certain subsidiary is now large, well established and profitable enough to justify greater autonomy. The usual decentralising pressures are operating—loss of talent in the subsidiary, expensive waste in the communications system, complaints about slow decision-making. As a result many decisions are moved down. At the same time head office is increasing its functional staff. This means increased information collection, especially as the headquarters' specialists need the information to consider innovations whose possibilities they have been appointed to develop. Mandatory orders may be needed to ensure that usable information is available when required. All this effort influences the organisation of the subsidiary which must have officers capable of meeting the demands of head office. It further influences the systems used abroad, and leads to a greater independence. On the actual use of innovation the head office will probably not dictate, but considerable pressure can be brought on the foreign company to accept the methods and techniques which have been found to work in the home country. Indeed, the use by head office of the word *advice* can be ambiguous. To managers there the advice can be genuinely intended as such; to the subsidiary there can be strong pressure implied. In the eyes of the local management there can be rich rewards for accepting the advice and corresponding penalties for rejecting it.

An illustration of the effects of advice is given by Cyert and March in a case study concerning the selection of a consultancy firm.[20] The appropriate department recommended a suitable consultant. However, a suggestion was made that before a final decision was taken other consultants should be investigated. From the others named, the controller suggested one as a possibility. This one was selected. The authors of the case study point out that the suggestion to look for another, and only one other, gave the men who had to make the recommendation the impression that this was the consultant favoured by top management. But the controller remained convinced that he had in no way influenced the decision. If this can happen within a single office building it might be expected to happen even more in an international company. In fact, the significance of advice in the development of policies in multinational firms was found to be considerable. As one foreign executive asked: 'What does this English word *advice* mean?' It should be said that some companies showed great awareness of this problem, and their executives accept considerable personal pressures in trying to avoid it. They do this by constantly visiting the subsidiaries and talking issues through with them thoroughly.

In general it may be said that if information is asked on subjects which have been left to the discretion of the subsidiary this will appear as a removal of the discretion. The affiliate manager will ask himself why information is required on matters which are only relevant to decisions he is supposed to take himself. 'We are very careful to avoid giving this information,' said one such manager. He may react that way; but, on the other hand, he may take the request for information as an instruction in the way he should run his business, and the whole exercise as involving a close supervision of his activities. It was found that this could occur in the more developed subsidiary; whereas the less sophisticated ones, where greater control was intended, might ignore the request or the advice. It would seem that a clear definition of the limits of autonomy constantly reiterated and strictly adhered to, combined with regular meetings with head office executives, gives the subsidiary the greatest sense of independence.

In another study, the point has been made that one of the consequences of concentrating decision-making at the top is to make adjustment to change difficult throughout the organisation.[21] This insight could well be useful to the international company as a reason for modifying the present trend wherever possible. The companies involved in this study which reported problems of innovation appeared to be meeting these problems by greater centralisation. Hence, in terms of the hypothesis stated above, the firms might well be reinforcing the problems. This is where a process of action and reaction develops which it may need some skilful diagnosis to break. For if subsidiary and head office view the relationships differently, and if the former resists innovation as a result, the resultant action on the part of head office will confirm the subsidiary's fears.

Much has now been said to show that there are forces impelling firms away from existing positions whether open or close. In theory the more powerful forces are those making for the open relationship; but in practice the opposite proves to be true.[22] Nevertheless the action and interaction is such as to cause constant fluctuation around what we have called the *normal line*. The process envisaged is shown in table 3.2.

In this table the pressures towards the normal line are clearly shown. Companies starting with totally different philosophies are drawn together by the influence of the characteristic problems which each encounter. An examination of this is complicated by the fact that there can be different relationships with different subsidiaries; there can be changes of system *vis-à-vis* the company as a whole; there can be different relationships in different functions. All will show some, but varying, effects of the 'lure' to the normal line. The formulation of genuinely objective criteria for assessing the normal line is a problem.[23]

Let us suppose, for instance, that a detailed operating manual is a symptom of a close relationship. Then a company which supplies every executive with a suitable manual is obviously operating such a relationship. The manual may cover instructions for every detail of his work, and in fact may be an assertion of all-embracing power on the part of head office. It may leave little to his imagination. But if enquiries in the company show that an executive can say that he has never read the manual and does not know where his copy is, and yet has kept his job for many years, this suggests that the relationships within the company are not so close after all. Hence the supposedly objective criteria need some investigation. The foreign subsidiary may take to itself more autonomy than appears by simply ignoring the advice or instructions that come from head office. A few examples of this were found—where the facts showed a more open relationship than the organisational arrangements would suggest. Naturally, subsidiaries which can get away with this are successful—or at least good at producing results which appear successful (another problem for the parent company) —and presumably they have strong-minded leadership as well. With

Table 3.2 Conditions which identify the normal line towards which relationships between head office and foreign subsidiary are drawn

	1 Close *relationships*	2 Normal *relationships*	3 Open *relationships*
Organisational considerations	Organisation of subsidiaries mirrors that of home country.	Registered company in host country shows some correspondence to that in home country.	Subsidiary organised on lines normal in host country.
	Head office appoints board of subsidiary.	Head office appoints board of subsidiary, but with consultation, latter may nominate candidates.	Board of subsidiary self-appointing with consultation over chief executive.
	Long lines of communication.		Short lines of communication.
Reporting and visiting	Monthly, fortnightly or weekly reports in great detail in all functions.	Quarterly or monthly financial reports in some detail. More general reports in other functions.	Budget, balance sheet, profit and loss account, quarterly or less. Informal reporting, if any, in other functions.
	Head office forms and language for all reports.	Head office forms for financial reports.	Reporting by methods and in language of host country.
	Frequent and regular visits both ways. Regular meetings in all functions, including global conferences.	Visits from head office regularly, and to head office frequently. Visits in all functions and several ranks. Occasional global meetings, likely to be regular for chief executives.	*Ad hoc* visits only, mainly by chief executives.

Table 3.2 (*cont.*)

	1 Close *relationships*	2 Normal *relationships*	3 Open *relationships*
Decisions normally reserved to head office or regional centre	*All those in col. 2 plus:* All capital expenditure. Use of subsidiary profits. Major pricing decisions. Short-term borrowing. Depreciation policy. Credit terms.	*All those in col. 3 plus:* Medium-scale capital expenditure. Raising funds within country. Entering new product range. Entering new markets. Appointment of senior executives.	Major capital expenditure. Raising funds internationally. Final sanctioning of future plans. Final sanctioning of budgets. Dividend payments sanctioned. In addition there will be one or two special decisions which vary from company to company, e.g. appointment of chief executive, development of new products, licensing of patents, trading outside subsidiary's own country.

reservations, the normal line may be said to constitute a collection of arrangements around which most companies fluctuate.

The situations outlined in figure 3.1 can obviously be distorted by a strong personality in the subsidiary management. A number of cases were identified where one subsidiary had a special position in a group simply because it was thought risky to interfere. Phrases like 'he's a law to himself' could be used at headquarters, and 'we try to make it too dangerous for them to intervene' would be heard in the subsidiary. But the distortion by personality in the subsidiary seldom seems to be a permanent one. The strong character is tolerated because he makes the local company profitable, but he is a nuisance to the system and pressures are likely to build up against him at the centre. And these pressures are likely to be strong when it comes to the appointment of a successor.

Whatever other factors may be involved, the closeness of the relationship appears to be related to the size of the company. The small firm may be close at home, but when it goes abroad it tends to adopt a very open type of relationship. Of companies included in this study with a net investment below £10 million, all described an *open* relationship. One of these companies had had to remove the managing director of a subsidiary, and spoke of this as a 'traumatic experience'. In another firm, an Australian affiliate had only local management and was visited once a year by someone from head office. Annual or half-yearly reporting was common among these small companies. Sometimes personal factors were involved. For instance, one small company with an open relationship yet had to consult head office on capital expenditure, methods of distribution of its products, composition of the higher management. This last was included because it was a subject on which the chief executive at home had strong views. Another firm which needed a closer relationship because of the technical nature of its products, had an expatriate managing director in each overseas company, but relied on the personal relationship to ensure adequate control.

The apparent connection between size and the relationship surely shows that expense as well as attitude comes into the decision. For a close connection across frontiers is clearly expensive, and the small company does not have the resources. In the company which does have the resources, on the other hand, this very fact may be an extra pressure to a close relationship. Some of these 'resources', in the form of functional staff at head office, will be an active pressure group advocating a closer arrangement. The big company, to whom the profit of any individual subsidiary is less important than it is to the small firm, establishes a closer relationship because it can afford to.

Thus the lure towards the normal line can be distorted by personalities and can be influenced by the size of the firm. The arrangement will become less stable the further it is from the normal line. If one can envisage a continuum of relationships from the most close to the most open, the pressures to change will be strongest at either end. The concept of the normal line has been introduced to explain this observation.

Before leaving the subject of relationships between head office and foreign subsidiary, it needs to be said that on any definition this relationship contains the two elements of discipline and nurture.[24] Naturally, the overseas people will tend to see the connection in terms of discipline, while those at home talk about the nurture. But it seems that it is possible to separate the two. Occasionally an example was encountered where a subsidiary regarded one person at head office as a 'friend in court', and another as always finding fault with them. This may arise naturally, but it could be built into the organisation. Indeed, complex relationships between the geographical and the product group projections of the organisation may well have this effect. It is even possible that a clearcut distinction between the nurture and the disciplinary functions may reverse the usual problems of centralisation and decentralisation. Certainly whether or not a close relationship is a problem to the subsidiary will be partly determined by the nature of this connection. An open relationship, as was found, can be a problem if there is a lack of 'nurture', if the subsidiary does not get the benefits of belonging to an international group. The distinction may also produce a greater sense of autonomy in the subsidiary while retaining all necessary head office control. It may, although no certain example of this was actually found, produce a situation where the local company finds the relationship more open than the parent.

3.3 Summary

The clearest point that emerges from this account of the relationship between the home and host country organisation is of their dialectical nature. The main force involved is that of frustration—for the close relationship is thought to produce expense and loss of initiative, and the open one waste of resources and loss of opportunities. Some of the factors that at any given time help to resolve this dialectical problem have been identified. Traditionally technical orientation has meant a closer relationship, while marketing emphasis has meant a more open one. However, it has been seen that modern techniques press for a closer relationship in all the functions. Why then is there not a clearcut trend to a closer relationship? And why does almost every company talk in terms of decentralisation? The answer seems to be in the current ideology of management which speaks in terms of personal responsibility and participation. These concepts are hard to realise in a multinational company. Further, the ideology of the host country may be different from that of the home country. But, whatever other factors are operating, there are strong checks to further centralising pressures. These are reinforced by the other current fashion which speaks in terms of giving a manager total responsibility for his area of the company. Much thought is currently being given to this in an increasing number of companies, and hence organisational efforts are made to block the increasing trend to a closer relationship. The interconnection between the exercise of power and the actual mechanics of organisation in a large firm is a difficult one to disentangle; but to assess the formulation of policy, the distinction is a necessary one. For the more open the power relationship, the more diffuse the formulation of policy. Characteristically, the centralised company reports that 'for all our efforts' little contribution is made to important policy-thinking or new ideas. The company with an open relationship acknowledges the reverse more readily.

We have tried to analyse the various lures, as they might be called, in the relationships between the centre and the foreign affiliates. The short-term pressures are towards our hypothetical normal line. But the long-term trends seem to be towards a closer relationship. Indeed it seems inconceivable that this trend will change unless the world is so unfortunate as to have another major war. For surely decentralisation is part of the outlook of a postwar world—a world in which conditions are uncompetitive and senior business appointments go to ex-service officers, a world in which the emphasis is on reconstruction rather than innovation. All three elements in this combination have been reversed and look like staying that way. The new leaders of industry have not been brought up in the military tradition of leaving the man on the spot to muddle his way through, and they have been brought up in an environment where giants compete hard. They are not greatly impressed with the difference of running a plant whether it is 300 or 3000 miles away, nor with the 'cultural differences' their products are rapidly reducing. But the increasing closeness of the relationship does not mean that the overseas manager will suffer from constant supervision. He will not, as the saying is, 'have someone breathing down his neck all the time'. The new close relationship is like that described in the oldest companies of colonial times, where the man on the spot was left alone for long periods, but his area of discretion was limited. No doubt this represents the trend throughout business, domestic as well as foreign, a trend towards greater personal independence within narrowing limits of decision-making. This is the form that the close relationship can be expected to take in the future.

Relationships between head office and the foreign subsidiary: control systems

In the two preceding chapters, we have considered some of the general relationships which develop between the parent company and its foreign subsidiaries in a multinational company. We have attempted to describe and analyse these in terms of the organisational and power structures that are evolving in these firms. Within the overall framework that these structures provide, there is an apparatus of formal rules, plans, forecasts, budgets, and reports—mainly of a financial nature—which help to give direction to and assure coordination and control of the organisation's activities. This is what we mean by *control systems*. But it has already been seen, and will become further evident in the discussion which follows, that such formal methods of control are but one aspect of the process of control in an organisation. No amount of plans, reports, or correspondence can replace competent and committed management in the various parts of the company, and the personal contacts, consultations, and exchange of views which underlie a control system and breathe life into it.

We shall focus on the more technical aspects of control systems, and will set out to identify and analyse some of their principal characteristics. In many ways, it will be noted, these features are not unique to the multinational company, but are found in most large organisations. For this reason, we shall try to bring out how and where control systems in a multinational company differ from those in a purely domestic firm. Also, our primary concern will be the control of subsidiaries, not the process which takes place within subsidiaries, interesting though the problems of internal control may be. The chapter has been divided into the following main headings: (1) general considerations; (2) planning activities; (3) capital budgeting; (4) control activities; and (5) measurement of performance.

4.1 General considerations

Most companies we interviewed considered it essential that planning and control information be prepared and submitted on a uniform basis by all subsidiaries and divisions so that meaningful comparisons might be made between them, and also to facilitate the task of preparing consolidated accounts by the parent company. It is also thought to be extremely important that the information be timely. To help meet these requirements, a detailed set of instructions was often provided by head office in an accounting manual which sets out the necessary procedures, timetables, a standard chart of accounts and definitions, and standard forms to be used by the subsidiaries in submitting their plans and reports. These were generally slightly modified versions of the procedures and forms used in the company's domestic operations. Often included in these instructions is a 'statement of corporate policy' which is intended to provide an overall framework to guide the subsidiary management in the preparation and use of plans and reports. Examples of such statements include the following:

> In the area of financial control over operations, the preparation and constant use of the operating budget is the most important tool a manager has.

> The operating budget is established within the framework of the goals (growth, product diversification, etc.) set by the board of directors and top management of the company. These goals, which are of a long-range nature, will be the 'targets' for overall performance and will be made known to local managers.

> One of the essential features of the operating budget is that it is built from the ground up rather from the top down. In other words, budget preparation and utilisation starts with individual department heads and individual salesmen, for it is these people who can best control expenses and achieve satisfactory sales growth. The basic principles involved are that budget responsibilities should start at the lowest management level and that if a manager has responsibility for the control of expenses or the achieving of sales goals, he should actively participate and ultimately agree on expense or sales budgets for his area of responsibility.

> The board of directors and corporate top management hold company managers directly responsible for the careful and timely preparation of the operating budget for their companies and for explanations of significant differences between actual and budgeted operating results.

> The operating budget is much more than a formal forecast of the future results of operations. It is primarily a plan for future operations. It embodies the principle of charting in advance the plan of operations and expressing the financial consequences of the plan in money terms. It puts the primary emphasis on the question 'what are we going to do next year and how will we accomplish it?' rather than on the question 'what did we do last year and how did we accomplish it?'

> The budget is a realistic target. Managers will be judged on their ability to make reasonably accurate budget estimates of their operations.

The operating budget is designed to supplement, not to supplant judgment. The budget is a valuable tool to help management make decisions based on a greater amount of factual knowledge. It is not a substitute for intelligent management.

Such policy statements, written rules, and operating guidelines extend to other areas as well, as will be recalled from the examples shown in chapter 2, and appear to be standard procedure for a great many companies operating abroad. In many ways, the need is probably greater for foreign than for domestic operations whose management usually share a common educational background. As we have already suggested, accounting standards and practices vary a lot between countries, and to avoid misunderstandings, detailed explanations and examples are necessary. One company's manual went to considerable lengths to cover all aspects of its planning and control system, explaining in detail what was wanted, and often why it was wanted. For example, strict guidelines governed the disposition of the subsidiaries' cash balances. A temporary build-up of cash excess to normal working balances was expected to be fully invested in interest-bearing bank deposits or in marketable securities. What constitutes normal working balances was, according to the company manual:

... heavily dependent on local conditions having to do with the availability and net cost (i.e. the interest rate differential between invested and borrowed funds) of short-term borrowing. That is, in any given situation the better the availability and the lower the net cost of short-term borrowing, the greater the risk which can be taken in keeping cash working funds to a minimum. . . . In the normal situation (i.e. where short-term borrowing is available at an annual interest cost of not more than two percentage points above the percentage return on invested funds and/or where short-term investments can be freely converted back to cash for annualised losses of less than six per cent) minimum cash balances should represent approximately two weeks' average disbursements, excluding large unusual type disbursements such as tax or dividend payments or fixed assets additions, which should be separately and specifically planned for. To the extent that the situation is less than normal in your country, minimum cash balances should be correspondingly higher. . . . Since money market conditions in most countries are constantly changing, the calculation of minimum cash balances should be on a continuous basis.

Regarding the investment of excess cash, the company operating manual had this to say:

The general rules to be followed in making investment decisions are first to minimize risk of loss and secondly to maximize income from the investments. Since investment of funds is far outside the course of [our] regular business, no attempt should ever be made to maximise income at the expense of risk of loss of funds invested. In other words, while no investment is ever risk free, only those investments where the risk of loss is truly insignificant should be considered. Beyond this, the attempt should be to maximize the income, with due regard to the necessity of having cash funds available at specified future dates. Further, no investments should be made having a fixed maturity of more than six months unless specific permission is received from the corporate treasurer.

If these guidelines appeared to leave local management with little question as to what they were expected to do, any last traces of doubt would be removed by the provisions that disposition of temporary cash funds is 'subject to the advice and guidance' of regional management. In reference to another very detailed set of instructions, concerning preparation and reconciliation of intracompany accounts, the manual cautioned: 'It is very important that [the procedures] be strictly adhered to, since they are a vital part of the quarterly consolidations of the group's financial statements.'

The currency used in the control system and related communications is another matter for consideration, and occasional difficulty. Although in some of the firms we studied, budgets, forecasts, and reports were expressed in the local currency, in most the parent company's currency was used— another reflection of the standardised procedures employed by many (and particularly the American) firms. Nevertheless, some managements believe there is an argument for permitting the subsidiaries to report in their local currencies—partly to make them less conscious that they are foreign-owned, partly to lessen their administrative burden. Even in companies where the parent's currency was generally used for the control system, special arrangements are sometimes made to accommodate particular subsidiaries.

Certainly one of the most compelling reasons for centralising authority over the finance function is the attempt to make the maximum use of funds. The policies and practices discussed in chapters 6 and 7 only become operative when coordinated from a position in the organisation that has an overall view of its activities. Needless to say, this seems to be invariably at head office. The following quotation is typical of the arguments used by companies in centralising these decisions.

The chief accounting officer is fully responsible for local financial matters subject to the financial policy of the company, but problems affecting corporate finances must be referred to the financial officer (at head office) for approval. For instance, very few overseas employees understand or appreciate the influence US taxation has on local problems. It is perfectly reasonable to expect the overseas manager to propose the revaluation of fixed assets or the creation of special reserves to diminish local taxes. But what is the overall goal? Are dividends to come forward with regularity to the domestic company? If so, each dividend becomes subject to

US income tax. The effective rate of reduced taxation on earnings out of which the dividend is paid, when taken as a tax credit by the parent company, may result in the parent company's paying more tax in the United States than would have resulted otherwise; therefore, the efforts of the overseas manager are fruitless. This is a good illustration of the type of responsibility and authority which cannot be delegated to people in the field under a decentralised organisation for financial activities.[1]

Secondly, centralisation of these matters is adopted for the sake of uniformity. Consolidation of the group financial statements requires uniform preparation and reporting of accounting data. Although head office staff can translate and reconcile subsidiary accounts which have been prepared according to local standards and practice, it was found that most companies consider it more expedient to push a part of this burden down to the subsidiary. They are provided with standard forms on which to submit financial data based on a standard chart of accounts, and prepared according to a precise and detailed set of procedures. Overall, this may well be the most efficient way to produce this information, but it adds to the subsidiary's work load when another set of accounts must be prepared to satisfy local legal or fiscal requirements. Standardisation is also important if management is to be able to identify and make valid comparisons between alternative courses of action. For example, if accounting data were not uniformly prepared throughout the group, comparisons of production costs or of profitability between different subsidiaries would have little meaning. However rational this justification may be, it was far from clear that firms actually were making much use of financial information for purposes of comparison.

4.2 Planning activities

The line between planning and control activities in the overall process is difficult to draw and arbitrary. In many respects they are interdependent and occur simultaneously.[2] If this were not enough, we run into a problem in semantics in distinguishing between what is often called—using military terminology—strategic planning and tactical planning.[3] Here we shall be essentially concerned with tactical planning activities,[4] the planning which is done at the level of the subsidiary within the guidelines, objectives, policies, and other directives of the parent company. This type of planning is detailed, routine, generally short-term, not exceeding two or three years ahead—though the more distant part resembles strategic planning, and covers the whole of the subsidiary's operations.

Planning serves many purposes. It is important, in the words of the company's manual quoted above, for 'charting in advance the plan of operations and expressing the financial consequences of the plan in money terms'.

In another company, management considered that: 'Le plan est une occasion pour faire réflexion sur toute l'opération.' But planning also serves as an initial control over operations; for, in its final form, it makes a choice among alternative courses of action and uses of resources. In a similar way it is a device of commitment, for in agreeing to the plan subordinate managers are held responsible for its realisation, or for explaining what went wrong. Again it can act as a means of pressure, for they know that their performance will be partially judged by how well they meet the plan. The follow-up process consists mostly of control activities, and is based on a feedback of information through a series of reports that are designed to measure how well plans are being carried out. Variations from planned performance can then lead to a corrective action (a control activity), and to replanning, or to both, in order to adjust to new operating conditions.

The core of a planning and control system is the annual budgets which will often be accompanied by rather less detailed plans covering the following one to three years. These comprise two main elements: the operating budget covering sales, expenses, and cash flow, and the capital budget.

OPERATING BUDGETS

During our interviews with company executives, we were often told that planning works from the lower levels of the organisation upwards. Plans built up by individual departments in the subsidiary are consolidated to produce regional and overall corporate plans. This is based on the principle quoted above, 'that if a manager has responsibility for the control of expenses or the achieving of sales goals, he should actively participate and ultimately agree on expense or sales budgets for his area of responsibility'. Perhaps the key words here are 'ultimately agree', for we found in most companies that corporate management would not be satisfied to accept the plans of subsidiaries without modifications.

The influence of head office in the subsidiary's planning is manifested in several ways. The president of the parent corporation may have publicly announced some overall growth target such as '$1 billion a year in net sales by 1973', or 'double our sales and profits in the next five years'. Corporate expectations are also made known to subsidiary management on an informal basis through personal contacts with other executives at meetings or during visits long before any formal planning begins. In some companies the corporation's long-term objectives are set down with more or less precision in an intermediate-range plan covering the three to five years ahead. Thus, in one way or another, subsidiary management generally know before the annual planning process begins the order of magnitude of their targets.

Especially where the relationships are *close* between head office and the subsidiary, there is a fairly intensive period of give and take during which time local management go over their various plans and proposals with their superiors. In one company this normally took place during the planning period, the summer prior to the budget year, through repeated but informal meetings with a regional management group. In fact, all through the year the managing directors of each subsidiary met at least once each month with them, often more frequently. Thus the regional management was kept closely informed about the subsidiary's strengths and weaknesses, and was able to make a fairly shrewd judgment of the realism with which plans were made. This was thought to be a crucial part of the entire process for the sales targets that were agreed upon became the cornerstone for all of the rest of the subsidiary's plans. Although the plans were built up by the subsidiary management, the meetings and reviews with regional management usually served to modify their targets in line with head office views. Firm, though subtle, pressure was put on the local management to conform to the parent company's expectations of overall performance. This phase of planning was also important because it provided the company with its best opportunity to coordinate the activities of the various European subsidiaries. For example, it was at this point that the product-mix was agreed upon. This was considered especially critical because this company was attempting to integrate production and specialise subsidiaries in the manufacture of certain products. In addition, the transfer prices on intracompany transactions were reviewed at this stage, an operation that preceded the setting of profit goals.

In one large multiproduct company, the planning process was a continuous year-long activity involving executives from all levels. The company used a five-year revolving plan which was updated each year. The planning cycle began during January and February of each year at subsidiary level. Sales and profit targets were set down for the subsidiary by product group on the basis of the previous year's results, and the forecast figures for the following two years, from the previous five-year plan. Although there was no hard-and-fast rule subsidiary management believed that head office expected to see a 10 per cent sales and profits increase over the previous year. These preliminary targets were then reviewed at regional headquarters, in particular by the product group managers, to assure proper coordination between the various subsidiaries whose production and sales were integrated. From there they were forwarded to head office for further study, possible modification, and approval in principle. Following this, the final preparation of the plan got under way in early summer. Based on the approved sales and profits targets, detailed plans covering sales, operating expenses, finance, personnel, and a host of other elements were built up for the following five-year period. These were again, in the jargon of one executive, 'massaged, pushed, pulled, discussed, and rationalised' by regional and corporate management. Face-to-face contacts were an essential part of the process, and these took place frequently on both an informal and formal basis between subsidiary management and their superiors.

The parent company's role in subsidiary planning is also well brought out by the following account of the Dunlop Rubber Company's system:

Up until this stage [the preparation of the plan at subsidiary level] Headquarters has not come into the planning at all, although, of course, there would already be a broad basis of agreement between the local Managing Director and the Overseas Director and General Manager derived from previous Plans and discussions, visits, etc.

From the beginning of October, and to a carefully prepared timetable, overseas companies send their Plans to Headquarters for examination by the Executive Director and his staff supported by specialists from certain central functions.

The Plans are received at one central point by the official responsible for coordinating all procedures connected with management planning.

He distributes copies or relevant extracts to specialists in various fields for study—specialists, or specialist department, such as Group Marketing Controller, Overseas Production Executive, Overseas Technical Department, Overseas Buying Department, Group Comptroller, Group Training and Personnel Department, etc. They in turn comment back to him. Thus, in the light of wider Group experience, the strengths and weaknesses of the Plan are exposed.

At this stage, again to a predetermined timetable, the Managing Director of each overseas company comes to England to present his Plan. After preliminary talks in London, his itinerary includes visits to various Group establishments in the UK where he can discuss any aspect of his Plan with the appropriate specialist and, if necessary, be given a demonstration or shown records of the practical working of any project similar to those included in his Plan.

It does not necessarily follow that targets are always revised upwards. They may well be lowered. In some cases the local Managing Director might be asked to reconsider a particular project—if, for example, there appeared to be any misconceptions as to its viability. It could be that where new products or major changes in operating conditions are concerned the specialists find that some targets are over-ambitious and not really capable of achievement.

The visit ends with a Final Review Meeting chaired by the Executive Director. It is at this stage that all suggestions for amendment or variation from the Plan resulting from specialist comment or changed circumstances or outlook are brought together and the Plan in its final form endorsed with Headquarters' support. The visiting Managing Director discusses any modification that he may consider necessary for his Plan as a result of his work over the past ten days; and the capital expenditure proposals are once more reviewed together with their financial consequences in terms of return on capital employed.

After that the local Managing Director returns to his territory ready to implement his Plan in the knowledge that it has been exposed to the most searching review by the best available skills in the Group.[5]

In another company, most of the contact between head office and subsidiary management during the planning process was conducted by correspondence. Planning began in the subsidiary during the late summer with the submission of its sales and profit targets, ceilings for salaried personnel, and capital expenditure proposals for the coming year. Meanwhile, the parent company's policy-making group had decided on an overall company profit goal. This was allocated among the major operating groups which in turn reallocated the respective profit goals to the various subordinate operating units—domestic divisions and overseas subsidiaries. These goals were not arbitrarily determined, but the result of head office's own assessment of local facilities and operating conditions expected for the following year. Besides, the company produced revised twelve-month forecasts each quarter which provided a continuing view of future prospects. Within these parameters, the preliminary targets submitted by each subsidiary were reviewed, altered if necessary, and returned. Based on these approved targets, the subsidiaries prepared their detailed operating plans.

Of course, by no means all multinational companies conduct their planning activities in such a closely integrated manner; even within a group, procedures may often be modified to accommodate certain subsidiaries that cannot, or will not, fit into the general pattern. Frequently, where it enjoyed a relatively *open* relationship with its parent, the plans drawn up by the subsidiary were based on its evaluation of expected local conditions, and accepted without change by the parent company. Basically, parent company participation in the subsidiary's planning depends on the same factors which are determinants of the division of authority between them. The nature and demands of the business are no doubt important. Where change —either favourable or unfavourable—is slow and only likely to occur within rather narrow limits, or where a subsidiary's operations are independent of the group and confined to its own market, the parent would be less likely to intervene in its planning. The opposite is usually true in industries where change is rapid, such as in electronics or perhaps chemicals, or where operations are integrated within a region and must be coordinated at higher level. The trend, as we have pointed out in the preceding chapter, is probably moving towards *closer* head office participation. Planning has become a fashionable, if not an essential, tool for management, and its usefulness has been clearly demonstrated as one of the keys to improved performance. Ensuring that this improvement takes place at all levels of the organisation will inevitably draw head office closer into the subsidiary's planning activities.

In the type of planning we have been discussing here, the focus is on the year immediately ahead. But, in addition, many of the companies we studied prepared operating plans which covered a period up to five years ahead. In some these were extremely detailed, being essentially a projection of the annual plan. In others the figures beyond the first year were intended to be, as it was outlined in one manual, 'as accurate as possible, but it is not necessary to go into the same detail in building them up as for the first-year budget figures'. At Philips', the giant Dutch electrical manufacturer, 'details are not required' for the third and fourth years of its four-year operating plan, 'but reliable estimates are'.[6] In yet other companies, while plans were not prepared beyond the first year, they were revised each quarter so that management could always have before it a detailed forecast of operations for the following twelve months. Finally, a number of companies produced an annual operational plan to cover only the year immediately ahead and no further. In these firms, the vagaries of the market were considered too great to make planning beyond one year of any relevance. This is not to say that no thought was given to the more distant future. But rather than make detailed forecasts which were put down formally on paper, they were often rather more in the form of a general indication of the future direction of the company.

In companies where detailed formal planning covered several years ahead, the justification was on various grounds. One frequently heard was that such a procedure forced managers to think out thoroughly all aspects of their business and thereby avoid many future difficulties by anticipating problems and taking corrective measures in advance. By plunging into great detail, it was thought, all concerned would inevitably know more about their business, and be able to perform better as a result. Related to this reasoning, some companies believed that the elaboration of a detailed plan extending over several years helped avoid what is sometimes called budget manipulation. Since current profits are generally one of the principal measures of performance, there is often considerable incentive to improve current profits by postponing certain expenditures to a later date or by various other means. Such practices tend to be discouraged where operational details are continuously projected several years ahead. Another major justification of continuous long-term planning was the better integration of operating plans with those covering investment, manpower, and finance, all of which have long lead-times. As one example, at Philips, the time dimension of planning was

> . . . determined by the length of time necessary to carry the policy or decision involved into effect. Philips chose a four-year plan as the backbone of its planning system because major changes in capacity require several years to effect (for example, land must be bought and factories built) and long-term financial adjustments also require several years from preparation to realisation.[7]

We suggested above that plans served as a commitment device in that they would be used as a measure of the performance of subsidiary management. Possibly with this end in mind, most companies we studied made a distinction between the final annual plan—or budget as it was frequently referred to—and forecasts. The budget provided the yardstick for performance, and as such was usually not altered during the year. It is often argued that such a yardstick is too rigid a standard by which to judge performance because the failure of plans is often due to events external to the firm over which the management has no control. A solution commonly suggested is to abandon the original budget when it has been invalidated by external changes which affect operating performance and substitute a revised one. However, few companies appeared to do this. It was thought that if the original annual budgeted figures were not altered, the local management would be better reminded of how well they were keeping to their original goals—in other words, pressure would be put upon them. In particular, by measuring past plans against past performance, a better estimate of the reliability of future plans might be obtained.

Although allowance is undoubtedly made for externally caused variations from planned results, it appears that managers are nevertheless judged in part on their ability to make reasonably accurate forecasts of their operations. But for short-term control purposes, that is for the plan to be of use to operating management in taking appropriate action to correct an unfavourable situation due to internal factors, a flexible budget for perhaps three months was generally adopted. This can be revised to reflect changes in external conditions. A revised plan is of equal—if not more—importance to management as a means of adjusting the other activities of the firm to the new operating conditions. It is a way of providing head office with the subsidiary's latest view of how future operations will go, in particular, their effect on the cash flow.

The frequency with which plans are revised is, generally speaking, dependent on the nature of the industry. The more volatile or rapidly changing the business, the more frequently plans need updating if they are to be of use to management. Of the companies we studied, those in electronics appeared to spend the most effort in constantly revising their plans. Their need for this is not difficult to understand. There are probably few industries with a faster changing technology, and loss from obsolescent inventories is an ever-present danger. In addition, it is a labour-intensive industry, and costs get quickly out of line. In order to keep abreast of the situation one firm, for example, revised its plans each month for the following six months. The detail was considerable, and included a complete income statement, inventory levels, receivables outstanding, capital expenditure, employees, order backlog, and other information. Needless to say, management spent a great deal of time and energy at the task. In other industries, the pace was less frenetic. Most of the chemical companies we studied tended to revise plans less often, usually quarterly. In some, the revised plan covered the following twelve-month period; in others, a revised year-end forecast was prepared quarterly.

Our discussion has been mainly devoted to planning for sales and expenses, but most of the same points can also be made with respect to cash flow forecasting, or cash budgeting as it is often termed. One of the main differences was that cash forecasts were made—or revised—more frequently than other types of plans. The minimum in the companies we studied appeared to be each quarter, and most prepared a revised forecast monthly. The need for forecasting cash balances on a frequent and continuing basis can be appreciated when considered in the light of fund transfer policies which we will discuss in chapters 6 and 7. And besides being continually updated, it is essential that these forecasts be timely if the maximum use of corporate funds is to be made. In a typical case, monthly revised cash forecasts were due to be sent to corporate headquarters by the fifth working day of the following month. This was to enable the corporate treasurer to know by the sixth or seventh of, say, June, the subsidiaries' expected cash balances for 30 June as well as the actual cash balances on 31 May. In general, the details required were fairly extensive, covering cash on hand and in bank, cash in time deposits, marketable securities, a breakdown of foreign currencies on hand, expected receipts and payments due within the period, and other relevant information.

CAPITAL BUDGETS

The subject of capital budgeting has received a good deal of attention during the past few years from academics, applied economists, and businessmen. Most of this, however, has tended to focus on providing an analytical approach to investment decisions, especially on methods of appraisal such as discounted cash flow. Although logical and with strong intellectual appeal, companies, in practice, find it is often difficult, even sometimes impossible, to apply these methods in capital budgeting.[8] Moreover, for the appraisal of investment projects in foreign operations, their difficulties are compounded by the generally poorer quality of information that is obtainable, the added risks, and the different costs of capital which arise from operating in multiple business environments. In the discussion which follows, we will explore some of the special features of capital budgeting in multinational companies. Although we will consider both, and indeed in many ways the problems encountered are similar, our attention will tend to focus more on the process in established foreign operations than on the appraisal of entirely new ventures.[9]

It is difficult to generalise on the organisational framework and on the criteria used by companies to evaluate and approve foreign investment projects. Proposals can range in size from a multimillion-dollar purchase of new plant and equipment to small outlays for hand tools and office furniture. Some require years to come to fruition, and others are completed in a matter of days. Some involve the entire organisation, and others only one individual. Chances of failure or success can vary greatly between projects.

Some of them are obligatory with no expected return, and others are undertaken only for prestige. Companies find a need, therefore, to use some rational and systematic method for coming to grips with such a wide range of investment opportunities. Their approach to this task is almost as diverse as the types of project put forward; there are, nevertheless, some specific comments which can be made.

Generally, a distinction is made between the type of review required for a major, non-recurring investment, and that for investments which are of a more routine nature, such as are needed for the normal development of the subsidiary. Usually, the very large projects are handled in an *ad hoc* manner, subject to a special feasibility study which is often extremely detailed and thorough, and generally requiring a relatively long gestation period. Such projects include creating a completely new subsidiary or a major expansion of an existing one, entering a new market or launching a new product, or the acquisition of a foreign-owned concern. The other more routine and generally smaller requests for capital funds are submitted periodically in the subsidiary's capital budget. However, the kinds of information required, and the methods of analysis are often similar for both types of investment. The differences are more those of degree than approach. The larger investments require more information, in greater detail and depth, and the analysis is more painstaking than for the smaller proposals.

As with decisions over many other types of activity in the subsidiary, one of the major issues in capital budgeting is the division of authority between local and head office management. From at least one standpoint, the subsidiaries could be justified in demanding considerable autonomy over investment decisions. It will be recalled that most of the investment by subsidiaries in fixed assets is self-financed (around 90 per cent in the aggregate for the sample of subsidiaries used in this study, and over 80 per cent for all United States investment in Europe). Further, we pointed out earlier that the policy of many companies was to limit investment in their foreign subsidiaries to internally generated funds plus local borrowing. Nevertheless, in spite of such practice and regardless of the merit of the subsidiaries' argument to have more say in the spending of capital funds, this is one area of decision-making where they are seldom delegated broad discretionary powers. Control over investment represents the ultimate control over the operations of a subsidiary and, as such, is almost always closely held at head office.[10]

In the companies studied, the primary means of control was by limiting the amount of expenditure that could be made without reference to higher authority. In some companies, all expenditure required such approval. In most, however, each level of management was given an upper limit for expenditure that could be made on its own authority. This amount varied between subsidiaries, even within a group, usually in relation to their size (which normally meant in relation to their importance to the group and the competence of their management). Generally, the expenditure limits placed on United States-owned subsidiaries were lower than those for British-owned, a manifestation of the relatively more *open* relationships often found in the latter. In a typical American-owned subsidiary, for example, the local managing director could authorise on his own responsibility expenditure up to $10,000; projects between $10,000 and $100,000 had to be approved by the vice-president for international operations at head office; projects over $100,000 had to have the sanction of the parent company's board of directors. It would not be uncommon for these limits to be two to three times larger in a British company of similar size.

For the routine type of investment analysis some companies prepared both short-term and long-term capital budgets; all companies we studied budgeted at least on an annual basis. The long-term capital budget, where it was used, normally formed an integral part of the long-term (three- to five-year) plan of operations, and provided an overall, coordinated projection of the company's future activities. Although the larger projects were some-times listed by name in these long-term plans, and provided the order of magnitude of the estimated funds that would be required, they were gener-ally not elaborated in detail. This step in the process represented only a preliminary screening; approval as part of the plan did not normally sanction the projects, and they were again submitted in the annual capital budget for a more rigorous appraisal. At this stage of the review, the marginal projects were discarded or postponed, and only those which had received an indication of reasonable support from senior management got included in the annual capital budgets of the subsidiaries.

Not all companies followed such a procedure. In a number of companies interviewed there appeared to be relatively little coordination between capital budgeting and operational planning beyond a one-year period. Even some capital-intensive companies whose major investments took five or six years to get on stream did no systematic formal planning of sales or expenses for more than one year ahead. These tended to be companies run by engi-neers, and in which investment decisions were based much more on tech-nical than on marketing grounds. An assessment of the market was made, but often only in general terms. Management appeared to feel instinctively that markets would grow sufficiently to meet the enlarged future capacity that they were authorising. Theirs was more of a production-oriented than a marketing-oriented approach to planning capital investments.

The annual capital budget is as much a control device as a planning tool, and is much more precise and explicit than the long-term budgets which some of the firms prepare. Rather than providing merely a rough indi-cation of the amount of financial resources required, the annual capital budget is normally drawn up on the assumption that these are known and more or less fixed. It thus helps to serve as the mechanism for allocating or rationing funds among the various investment proposals that are submitted. In the subsidiary, no less than at other levels of the company, preparation of the capital budget is a continuous process. As projects are put up and elaborated during the year, they are discussed and reviewed by various members of management in the subsidiary. The larger ones are normally taken up with someone in the parent company or, in some cases, in a regional headquarters—generally a member of a budget or investment committee. The process is one which in most companies involves many levels of management from the time of the initial proposal to the final approval.

The capital budget itself is a list of investment projects that are expected to begin during the coming year, and generally includes the amounts likely to be spent on projects approved in preceding budgets which have not been completed. It is drawn up and submitted usually during the autumn of the year preceding the expenditure in most companies according to a standardised set of procedures. Standard forms are used to describe each project and typically include such information as the following:

1. Project title, code number, date of request, submitting organisation, department, and individual.
2. Type of project: capacity increase, product improvement, new process or product, replacement, cost reduction, amenity, safety or working conditions and so on.
3. Description of project, its purposes, alternatives.
4. List of equipment: estimate of the amount and timing of expenditure, installation and other associated costs.
5. Market projections (if relevant).
6. Cash flow from investment: estimated amount and timing of earnings and depreciation flows, salvage value, increases in working capital needs.
7. Justification of project: estimated rate of return, payback, technical and other types of evaluation (such as local management's urgency rating).
8. Other relevant information including reference to reports and correspondence, approvals.

Usually, order of approval at the subsidiary level goes from the initiator— a functional executive in marketing or production in most cases—to a financial executive, and finally to the managing director. Depending on the limits of expenditure permitted, the proposal is either authorised or passed to the next level of management, regional or international. As already noted the largest projects go to the top management of the company for final review and approval. Once the capital budget is passed, a further approval is usually needed to spend the money. Often known as an appropriations request, this generally contains much the same information as appeared on the budget, but is more precise and reflects the latest expectations of the amount and timing of the costs and revenues for each project. For some companies this is little more than a formality, and the subsidiary's managing

F

director is delegated authority to approve all requests except those which exceed a certain sum, or are otherwise special. In other companies, the capital budget represents much more an approval in principle to proceed with a more detailed study of the projects, and here the appropriations request takes on more importance.

Most companies also make progress reports at periodic intervals during the budget year on projects under way or authorised by the capital budget. These generally show such information as the state of the project on the reporting date, the amount budgeted, the amount appropriated, the amount already committed (such as orders placed with manufacturers), the amount already spent, the completion date or the estimated completion date as appropriate. These reports serve two purposes. They show what has already taken place; and, more important, they provide an estimate of the timing and amount of future expenditure for use in the company's financial planning.

Overall, there appeared to be relatively little difference between the routine capital budgeting procedures used by multinational companies for their foreign subsidiaries and their domestic operations. This part of the process was normally standardised throughout the corporation, especially where the relationships tended to be *close*.

What were the criteria used by companies to evaluate foreign investment proposals? While there were a variety of financial, technical and subjective considerations, the majority of companies we investigated used some sort of financial measurement as one of their criteria. These were some variant on a rate of return calculation: an 'accounting' return on investment (net earnings on the new investment divided by the total outlay), return on sales, a time-adjusted return (discounted cash flow: internal rate of return or net present value, and, or as an alternative, payback period), return on the parent company's stake. Obviously this sort of appraisal would only be relevant for investments which had a direct and measurable effect on costs or revenues—a new process, cost improvement, an increase in capacity or replacement of existing facilities. A number of companies put considerable emphasis on the technical merits of a project, leaving the financial criteria other than amount and timing of expenditure as optional. These tended to be engineering firms where it was considered essential that the machinery conform closely to certain prescribed standards of performance. The subsidiaries of two of these firms nevertheless prepared time-adjusted returns for their internal use. Subjective appraisals made by subsidiary management were used by a few companies as the primary basis for selection. In all companies non-technical considerations were taken into account.

There are some special problems in the use of financial criteria in the multinational firm. For instance the criteria can be different at head office from at subsidiary level because of the effect of taxation, the method of financing the investment or the element of risk.

Tax differentials between the host and home countries can cause a given rate of return from an investment project in the subsidiary to be acceptable to its management but unacceptable to the parent company management. Take, for example, an American or British-owned subsidiary in a country which grants lower rates of taxation for certain types of investment. In such circumstances, the subsidiary might enjoy a tax rate as low as 25 per cent on its earnings. However, when this income was received by the parent company, an additional tax would have to be paid; as will be shown in chapter 6, this would normally be an amount which would bring the total taxation on the earnings up to the parent company's rate. Thus, if the parent were to evaluate foreign investments in terms of remitted dollar earnings or those of any other currency, the given rate of return in the subsidiary would be reduced on account of the additional taxation.

This leads to the question, then, whether the parent company should evaluate earnings from foreign investments as net of local taxes only, or as if they had been remitted with all additional taxes paid.[11] One answer to this is that companies should ignore the effect of any additional taxes that would be incurred upon repatriation of the profits, on the grounds that subsidiaries have tended to reinvest close to half their profits, and two-thirds of their cash flow.[12] Since a major part of the return from investment is not remitted, it seems illogical to argue for evaluating a subsidiary's earnings as if they were remitted and the additional taxes paid. The flaw in this argument is that it ignores the problem of how the additional reinvested earnings expected from the investment should be treated. They can reasonably be thought of as increasing future earnings of the subsidiary and thus lead to an increase in its value. They can also be partially (or wholly, if the subsidiary should be sold) repatriated at some future date. There is some evidence that companies do take reinvested earnings into account when appraising a foreign investment opportunity. In a survey made of 110 multinational companies, it was found that over half the firms included as part of the income from an overseas' investment the earnings reinvested in the subsidiary *adjusted for taxes*, that is as if they had been remitted.[13] From this it might be argued that the firms were implicitly recognising a subsequent repatriation of the reinvested earnings, and therefore were taking this eventuality into consideration in their analysis. Nevertheless, as we shall try to bring out below, the margin of error in the earnings estimates is such that variations due to tax differentials cannot usually be a deciding factor in the investment appraisal.

In addition to the effect of taxation, the subsidiary's financial structure will also cause variations in the rate of return, depending on whose point of view is taken. The subsidiary may calculate its return as, for instance, net earnings (after interest and royalties, and either before or after local taxes) on total investment. The parent company, on the other hand, may regard as its investment only the funds which it has itself put into the subsidiary—equity and intracompany loans. Then it may take as its return the sum (either before or after taxes) of expected dividends, interest, royalties, fees, repayment of loans, earnings from additional exports, and perhaps also some figure for reinvested earnings. Given these measures of income and investment, from the parent company's point of view, the greater the amount of local finance used, the less *its own* stake, and therefore the greater its potential return. However, companies still will look at the rate of return based on total investment in order to test the viability of the subsidiary (or its project) as such.

Similarly, the evaluation of investment risk is seen much differently from head office than from the subsidiary. Whereas an investment may yield a high return and be highly attractive to the subsidiary's management, currency depreciation or exchange controls may so reduce the amount which could be remitted to the parent as to make the same investment unacceptable. Worse still, political instability may result in the complete loss of the investment. There are various schools of thought as to how to handle this type of risk. One is to modify the cash flows by, say, demanding a rapid payback from the investment. For example, countries could be classified into groups according to the degree of risk felt to be attached to the eventual recovery of an investment, repatriation of earnings and so forth. The greater the risk, the faster the payback that would be required. Using this approach, the parent company could apply its usual investment criteria, for example, a given cut-off rate of return, but discount the future flow of earnings over the payback period required by each group.[14] Another somewhat similar approach that attempts to quantify these risks would require additional 'compensatory' financial goals from overseas investments over and above the normal goals used by the parent company to appraise similar domestic projects.[15] This could also include varying the company's usual required rate of return.[16]

In practice, many companies seem to approach the problem differently, and rather than attempt to quantify potential risks, try to avoid them as much as possible by limiting the commitment of their own funds. Parent company management appear to take the view that it is impractical or impossible to reduce such risks to figures or percentage points; and therefore they rely more on subjective evaluation criteria and the recommendations of those in the field, hedged around by risking a minimum of their own capital. The problem of risk does not seem to be so much an issue affecting routine capital budgeting, but more a problem that is faced by head office at the time of the initial investment or when considering a major expansion of existing facilities. Policies for a particular country are established at that time which set the pattern for subsequent investment appraisals and give rise to rules of thumb such as reinvesting only depreciation allowances, financing with locally obtained debt, and so forth. Finally, many companies with extensive overseas interests—including for example some of the international oil companies—have fairly explicit policies for investing in high-risk areas. They usually try to limit risk by not investing more than a given percentage of total overseas capital in countries which are felt to pose unusual hazards, and look at high-risk projects in terms of their effect on the company's overall investment position.

It was not at all clear which of the various criteria were given the most weight by companies in making an assessment of a project, indeed if any were weighted more heavily than others. Company officials generally seemed unable to explain in explicit terms the reason for using a particular appraisal method, and usually ended by saying decisions were 'based on a combination of things'. It was our impression that financial criteria were seldom the dominant factor, and in even those companies that used the most sophisticated methods of planning and reporting, it appeared that more weight was often given to strategic, technical, or subjective considerations than to financial data. There are probably two main reasons for this.

The first is that most companies tend to place the need to maintain or improve their market position above all other considerations. This attitude is particularly strong in the consumer goods industries, and finds its expression in words such as, 'It's no good being satisfied with second place in our business. The key to success is to get prominent display in the shops. If you're second, you may as well be in last place.' Or, from an office equipment manufacturer: 'All we worry about are sales. If we can increase them, the profits are there.' And: 'In our capital budgeting, what we do is to look at the sales forecast and ask, "what new equipment will we need?"'

The dominance of marketing strategy in investment decisions was a major conclusion of an American study of US companies' overseas operations in which the authors wrote:

> They [considerations of market position] determine the need, the urgency, and the desirability of an investment, while financial evaluations are used mainly to test the validity of marketing assumptions and to determine both the financial requirements and the financial means for attaining marketing goals. Thus, for the most part, financial considerations are pertinent to the *how to* rather than the *whether to* finance a foreign investment.[17]

The other principal reason that financial criteria do not dominate these decisions in most cases might be called the 'traditionalist view'—the variables are so many and the possibility for error so great that it is thought to be a waste of time to put too much faith in the projected figures. In particular, refined techniques such as discounted cash flow analysis were considered by many companies of little use under such circumstances. In spite of this, we were sometimes told by headquarters' management that a detailed financial analysis was still useful because it provided a way to oblige the subsidiary management 'to think the project through'. By so doing, it was believed that they would be less inclined to submit marginal projects. The companies' lack of confidence in the quality of the information appeared also to be one of the reasons that they generally did not make detailed comparisons among the investment proposals which arose in different subsidiaries in the group. In this regard, we did not encounter any company that attempted to rank projects for the entire group worldwide, or even regionally, in, say, order of descending profitability. In one company this was explained as 'We don't consider the world as one, but take each individual country by itself.' However, they generally did review the major projects of the different subsidiaries to prevent waste such as duplication of production facilities where one would suffice.

Because of these various factors, investment decisions seemed to be judged much more on broad strategic or on subjective grounds than on the basis of rates of return or other financial criteria. In particular, internal politics of the firm play an important role, and most decisions of any consequence have involved management at various levels over a period of time. Projects are put up long in advance, and are reviewed and discussed by management in the subsidiary, in regional offices or at international division, with technical personnel in domestic divisions, and in the case of large projects with corporate top management. They are incorporated into long-term plans which are vetted by various members of the organisation. By the time they reach the stage for final approval, most projects have already survived a series of preliminary screenings, and where a rate of return was prepared for head office, it seemed to us that this was more to limit the area of judgment, or to reinforce an argument, than to provide the major criteria for the decision. Major projects will generally be familiar to, and find supporters among, at least some individuals among the senior management of the parent company.

In most companies approval of the smaller, more routine, projects is delegated to the subsidiary management; the parent company does not vet them individually. One company, as an example, had a rule of thumb that the subsidiaries could normally count on being allowed to reinvest their depreciation allowances plus one-third of earnings after tax. Within this framework the subsidiaries determined their own priorities. This did not mean that they spent this sum without reference to the budget committee in the parent company, for all projects had to be included in the capital budget. However, it seemed to be implicitly understood that investments up to this amount would generally get approval; and for routine-type expenditure, which this usually comprised, the company apparently felt that the subsidiary management was the best judge of the local situation. Expenditure which exceeded this amount usually had only arisen when a new plant was constructed, or a major expansion of an existing one was undertaken. These projects had generally been planned long in advance, having appeared as an adjunct to the long-range operating plan. Thus when they appeared on the annual capital budget, justification had already been made, and it became then a question of whether to cut back on other investment, temporarily reduce the level of remittances, or raise additional finance. While this had seldom happened because the cash flow from the subsidiaries was large, they had usually raised additional funds locally rather than cut back on other investment or dividends.

An essential point from this is that the subsidiary managers usually have much more voice in the capital budgeting process than may appear on the face of it. Because they generally initiate a project, because they are closer to and possess most of the relevant information on the project, and also because often much of the assessment is based on non-quantitative criteria (e.g. company internal politics), local management has, in practice, considerable scope to get the projects they want. This appeared to be especially prevalent in subsidiaries that were financially self-sufficient.

In most companies the type of information required, the general procedures followed, and the way the system operated seem to differ very little whether for foreign subsidiaries or for the domestic company. The main points of contrast arise over the effect of taxation and the special risks which come from operating across national frontiers.

4.3 Control activities

We attempted earlier on to distinguish between planning activities and control activities, and suggested that it was difficult because of the similarity and interrelationships between them. But given this reservation, our discussion up to this point has been more concerned with planning activities. As we see them in this context, control activities relate to the process which measures how well the plans are being carried out, and which signals corrective action to be taken. This is achieved mainly by a feedback of information—mostly financial—through a series of reports. By comparison of actual performance against the plan and by measuring and analysing any deviations, trouble spots can be pinpointed and corrective action taken. This process takes place at both subsidiary and higher levels in the organisation.[18] As soon as subsidiary management is aware that operations are not going according to plan, it should initiate remedial action. Indeed, the ability to appraise and correct deviations from plans is an important measure of subsidiary management's performance, and is a crucial factor in the delegation of authority. Generally, when the subsidiary reports operating results to head office, its explanations of variations will indicate the corrective measures that have been taken. Thus, head office can make its own evaluation of the situation, and provide support, or take other action that it judges appropriate. These are essentially control activities, but they can lead to further planning such as the revised forecasts that we discussed above.

For the control to be effective, the operating results must be reported in a way that variances can be easily analysed. Equally essential, the reporting must be made quickly after the event. Many of the American companies we studied required estimates of key operating data such as sales, gross and net profits, cash balances, and perhaps major variances from budget to be reported via telex or cable within one to three days after the close of the period. Detailed reports would often be required by the end of the first week following the end of the preceding period. Some companies reported only sales figures in detail on a monthly basis, while others reported their complete operating results, that is income statement and balance sheet with supporting schedules. Income statements would generally be broken down by product line, and by customer—for example domestic sales, export sales, affiliate sales. Most reports were presented in the same format as the operating plan in order to facilitate comparisons of actual against plan, and often also actual against the previous year's results. In a few companies, only actual results were reported by the subsidiary. These data were fed into a computer at regional headquarters or head office which had been programmed to print out the final reports to show actual results against budget, the results of the year to date and last year, and even signal significant deviations from plans. These were companies demanding an enormous quantity of data in a minimum of time, and the only way this was feasible was by computerising this stage of the system. A serious defect in this latter arrangement was that the subsidiary management were fearful that they were being denied the possibility to vet their own results prior to submission and review by a higher authority.

At the other extreme, the method of control which one company used for its smaller foreign operations was exceedingly simple. Each subsidiary had two local bank accounts—one for receipts and one for expenditure. The subsidiary manager had control over, and could draw cheques upon, the expenditure account. Headquarters had control over the receipts account, and thus could monitor closely the amount of funds available to the subsidiary. This was backed by a cash balance report and cash forecast which (sometimes with the bank's help) were air-mailed each month to the parent company. This system had been traditionally used by the company because of the inability to obtain adequately trained local management in some of its far-flung operations in the developing countries.

Almost all the companies we saw reported their complete results at least on a quarterly basis. In the American-owned companies this was needed, if for no other reason, to be able to prepare the quarterly consolidations of the group's financial results to comply with US stock market regulations. This imposes a detailed analysis of intracompany receivables and payables, and in order to work properly, calls for fairly strict procedures. For example, to avoid the possibility of double-counting, some companies instruct their subsidiaries not to make cash remittances or invoice shipments during the last few days of each quarter unless absolutely necessary. A further precaution entails subsidiaries mailing a statement of their intra-company receivables to the affiliates concerned for reconciliation purposes. Various other types of routine reports were used. These included copies of the minutes of the meetings held by the local board of directors and management committees. They also included regular or *ad hoc* reports on the general economic situation in the host country, on marketing prospects, on competitor activity, on production or personnel problems, and on a number of other areas of interest.

In general, the complaints expressed by subsidiary management, such as those described in chapter 2, were more directed towards the control aspect of the overall process than towards the planning side, although in many ways planning is more difficult and certainly more time consuming. Perhaps this is not surprising. For in the follow-up process of control, the results of planning miscalculations come home to roost as it were, and the necessity to explain mistakes, no matter where the cause lies, is not a particularly enjoyable exercise for most people. Of course, this is not the only reason, perhaps not even the main one. As we have pointed out earlier, the necessity to report frequently to higher authority is often felt by subsidiary management to be a reflection on their ability. In any event, it is often burdensome, because many reports required by head office are of only marginal value to the subsidiary management in its own tasks. Often they were considered to be irrelevant to the internal control of the sub-sidiary. Furthermore, it is sometimes thought by subsidiary management that the reports are not read at head office in any case, and therefore, in addition to everything else, much of their effort is a waste of time. Grumbled one manager, 'No one ever seems to pay any attention to you if everything is going well—but just let things go badly and do you catch hell!' At the other end, of course, management at head office considers that their demands for reports are completely justified in order to keep adequately informed—and to permit their support if necessary when problems arise.

In most companies, although the subsidiaries were required to cable or mail more or less detailed reports, only exceptional items were followed up. The view of a senior American company official was one we heard often repeated: 'We don't try to run their day-to-day operations, but exercise our control by exception.' This, ironically, is perhaps one of the major reasons that cause subsidiary management to feel their reports are not looked at. For if head office is only interested in significant deviations from plan, and if these are accompanied by an adequate explanation from the subsidiary management, there is probably little need for head office comment. Although in the company mentioned above it was claimed that they exercised their control by exception, very detailed reports were nevertheless required of the subsidiaries. The following were reported on monthly: balance sheet and income statement (there were 149 items on these two reports), capital

F*

projects status, sources and uses of funds, market share, order backlog, salaried personnel numbers, inventory turnover, estimated capacity utilised, and others. In addition, certain key items such as sales, profits, and cash balances were forecast monthly for the following month. Each quarter, the annual plans were extended by three months so that the company always had twelve months 'visibility'. In the view of the company official mentioned above, the principal justification for this detail was that it imposed a discipline on subsidiary managers which might not have been achieved otherwise.[19] The fact that they might be asked for explanations by the parent company was more likely to ensure that they would take immediate corrective action—or at least be prepared to give a satisfactory answer.

In one respect this is the way a control system is intended to work, by self-control. Head office expects local management to evaluate its own performance and take corrective action if required; the detailed reports permit the centre to make its own judgment, and the expectation of this evaluation is thought to contribute to the subsidiary management's effectiveness.[20] This belief was reflected by the following comments:

A subsidiary manager commenting on a detailed quarterly report on local market developments, competition and results of the preceding quarter: 'This is a damned good exercise to remind myself of what is happening.' A subsidiary managing director to company headquarters: 'The financial returns made to central accounting involve only copies of documents already indispensible to the proper running of the Italian group. Their compilation by due date is thus doubly useful in *ensuring timely local control.*'

The demand for information which is of little or no use in their local operations is found particularly irksome by many subsidiaries. Nevertheless, this is a need that is increasing as operations are becoming more integrated along national and regional lines. To be effective, integration requires detailed planning, frequent feedback of operating results, and quick response when necessary to meet changes in operating conditions. This puts a premium on accurate and timely information being furnished to a control centre such as a regional headquarters. Often the information required is of a different form than the subsidiary uses internally, for to be of use in logistical decisions it must relate to the specific products concerned. The problem arises because typically plans and controls are built up and operated through the formal organisational structure of the company, generally by cost or profit centre, from the lowest unit up to the largest. Thus, at subsidiary level, departmental and plant planning and control information has been consolidated to reflect the overall operations of the subsidiary as a responsibility centre. Moreover, it is as a responsibility centre that the performance of the subsidiary and its management are frequently judged. In companies whose product line is homogeneous (type A), or where subsidiaries are specialised along product lines (type C), the planning and control system automatically generates product information that can be used by regional management for taking logistical decisions. However, in a multiproduct company where several product divisions operate under the aegis of a single corporate shell (type B) matters become more complicated.

The problem is that the subsidiaries typically generate information as a corporate entity whereas the product divisions need it broken down by product or major product group. In consequence, a double flow of information must be produced, the one superimposed on the other. The product information is used basically for planning and coordination of the integrated operations at regional level. At the subsidiary—the responsibility centre—information is used mainly for internal control and evaluation purposes.

Product-line information is often in considerable detail—for example, a complete income statement plus selected balance sheet and other information. Naturally this requires costs to be identified with and allocated to the appropriate products, in addition to the internal control need for allocating them to the respective responsibility centre. In some companies, the system is designed to provide this information automatically. In other words, subsidiary plans are built up by products which are in turn consolidated for the subsidiary. Although this is satisfactory for subsidiary to regional headquarters purposes, it is not always suitable for the internal control needs of the subsidiary, and an additional set of plans is required. It thus amounts to a substantial amount of extra work for subsidiary management, who tend to view the procedure as having little relevance to their own operation. Some companies have tried to ease the subsidiaries' task by moving the responsibility for product information to regional headquarters. There analysts will attempt to recast the subsidiaries' plans and reports in order to generate product information. Such data would necessarily have more limited value, for it could not be as detailed as when prepared by the subsidiary. The need for this information is evident. The best way to provide it is a problem that companies still struggle with.

4.4 Measurement of performance

The final element in a planning and control system is the measurement of how well the subsidiary and its management perform. The purpose of measuring performance is twofold. One is to determine the future allocation of resources to the subsidiary, even to decide whether or not it should be abandoned. This is a process in making comparisons to assess the relative advantages of using various resources in various activities, such as investing in subsidiary A rather than in B, or exporting from the domestic division rather than from the foreign subsidiary. The other purpose of measuring subsidiary performance is to facilitate the coordination, scheduling, or re-scheduling of a group of interdependent activities. Where an original plan integrated a number of such activities into a coherent and coordinated whole, the performance of each component must be measured periodically against the plan; and when there are deviations, the other parts must be adjusted to take them into account. Both these purposes are, of course, part of the planning process which we discussed above.

There are a number of other purposes in measuring the performance of subsidiary management. The following quotation includes most of them.[21]

1. It directs top management's supervision and assistance to where it is most needed and where it will be most productive.
2. It shapes the future executive team by indicating whom to promote, whom to retain and whom to remove.
3. It directs the activity of executives toward high scores on the aspects of performance on which they are measured and judged.
4. It gives job satisfaction directly by letting the executive know how he is doing.
5. It provides the objective, factual foundation for sound incentive compensation.

Performance can be measured in many ways including profits. These can be expressed either in terms of profitability such as a return on investment or on sales, or in terms of growth, or both. Other measures of performance included growth of sales and market share, both of which are considered of especial importance in the consumer goods industries, productivity, labour relations, personnel development, public relations, and perhaps others.[22] The ability to plan effectively is sometimes another measure. But, if we accept that the main objective of companies is long-term profits, or maximisation of the firm's net present worth,[23] then performance must, in the end, be judged by this measure.[24] The difficulty is, however, that much of what management does only begins to pay off in the future, and thus can be misleading if measured in terms of current profits. Of course, some elements—growth of sales and market share, and productivity—can at least be expressed in quantitative terms, if not directly in terms of profits. On the other hand, performance in achieving good labour relations, public relations, and personnel development, for example, are difficult to measure except in qualitative terms, for the payoff cannot be precisely determined until some future date, if at all. Somewhat the same argument can also apply to research and development, advertising, quality control and maintenance. Expenditure on these items will cut into current profits, and the results will not be shown until later. For this reason, current profits probably can never be used as the sole criterion of performance; nevertheless because, in the long run, it is profits that count, and for reasons of expediency, they are still generally the most explicit if not important measure.

In whatever terms performance is assessed, there still remains the crucial problem of selecting the appropriate levels against which measurements will be made. This is often crystallised in the question of whether to use a fixed or a flexible budget, as the major yardstick of performance,[25] or a specified profit ratio such as the rate of return. There are conflicting schools of thought on this problem which, it will be recalled, we touched on earlier.[26] From a standpoint of equity, the flexible budget—or revised plan—would seem much more satisfactory than a rigid standard. There would appear little justice in penalising a manager for not living up to his original plan if his failure was caused by events not under his control—such as a shift in the general economic situation. It is precisely this situation that is often recognised as the principal weakness of return on investment and other such rigid measures of performance.[27] On the other hand, the problem can be viewed differently by top management, and, as we suggested above, many of the companies we studied used the original plan or a specified profit ratio as a way of maintaining pressure on the subsidiary's management. However, most also revised their plans, especially for purposes of internal control and adjusting other activities to the new operating conditions. Consequently, it was not at all clear from our conversations with company officials which yardstick was given the most weight in the appraisal of their performance. Undoubtedly it is based on a mixture of several; this seems to be an area warranting further study.

Foreign subsidiaries are, in spite of the pressures to centralisation already noted, generally regarded as profit centres for purposes of performance measurement.[28] From the standpoint of the group the goals of the individual operating units—the subsidiaries or divisions—should not conflict with those of the overall organisation.[29] It is therefore intended that the system by which performance is measured and rewarded should not encourage a subsidiary to increase its profits at the expense of those of the whole company. The crux of the problem goes back to the use of profits as a measure of performance. We saw above that there are weaknesses in this measure. Current profits do not adequately take into account management's performance in various other aspects of its job, and that for this reason other more qualitative indices of performance are also used. There is a further, more serious complication in the use of this yardstick where there are intracompany transfers of goods and services, for the pricing of these is obviously a major determinant of subsidiary profits. Likewise, if a subsidiary were set up as an expense centre and only its inputs were expressed in monetary terms, the pricing of intracompany purchases could be an important factor in its costs.

Determining the price for an intracompany transfer is more difficult than appears at first glance. In some types of transfers, the most commonly accepted solution is to price goods on an 'arm's-length' basis, that is at the market price if there is an established market or at the price which would be charged to an outsider. There are, however, other categories of transfers where an arm's-length price cannot be meaningfully determined. Certain components, subassemblies, semimanufactures, patents, technical knowhow and so on are often not sold to outsiders. In these situations prices are usually based on a formula such as: local manufacturing cost plus a standard markup to cover overheads and profit, cost of the most efficient production unit of the group plus a standard markup, or by negotiation. At best subjective judgments are involved, and attempts to construct an artificial price as a substitute almost invariably end in an arbitrary allocation of costs or revenues between operating units. The result is that the true profits of the subsidiary can easily be obscured and thus its performance altered.

If the subsidiary's plan provided the yardstick for measuring its performance then, in theory at least, it would appear to be irrelevant at what level transfer prices were set. The effect of arbitarily constructed transfer prices on profits would be taken into account in the plan, and any distortion of profits which might result would not be an indication of either poor or good performance. Unfortunately, however, there seems to be some evidence that managers do not respond to planned achievement in this way if the following views are representative:

> Any observer of transfer price disputes in industry will agree that absolute profit levels are important to the managers. They will argue to get a price reduced (or raised, if they are on the selling side) with as much vigour as they exert in inter-firm bargaining. This may be due to an unconscious bias in the reward structure, but whatever its source it militates against any administered transfer pricing scheme that results in prices that are widely regarded as unfair or biased.[30]

> Despite years of budgetary indoctrination, managers still seem motivated to seek absolute dollar results; comparisons with budget do not have the same psychological force. . . .[31]

This is one of the inherent weaknesses of decentralisation. For if managers are judged by absolute profit returns there is always the danger that the subsidiaries will pursue goals which conflict with overall corporate interests.

In domestic operations, the distortion of profits caused by defects in the transfer price system is probably not unduly serious, for in the absence of a market-based price, artificially constructed transfer prices can usually be made acceptable to those whose performance will be affected by them. These would generally be cost-based prices determined by some standardised formula—standard cost plus a fixed markup to cover profit, direct manufacturing costs, and so on. Whatever the method used, the presumption is that transfer prices have been built up according to a logical set of rules prescribed by corporate management which are designed to motivate those in the subsidiaries to act in accordance with the goals of the corporation.

In multinational operations, on the other hand, transfer prices are frequently constructed to achieve certain corporate goals which may or may not mean the maximisation of a particular subsidiary's profit performance. There is often no attempt made to approximate an arm's-length price. In fact if a price based on the market or on cost is available, it is often not used. The purposes of deliberately manipulating transfer prices on intracompany sales of goods and services are discussed elsewhere; the overall result is that the profits of an overseas subsidiary are frequently meaningless as an indication of its performance. Yet, as we have suggested, the profit yardstick has a powerful attraction. The problem plagues management in these companies, and no solution appears completely satisfactory. There are a number of opinions on how best to deal with the difficulties.

One view holds that every attempt should be made to approximate as closely as possible in the subsidiary conditions which would be faced by an independent market entity. Transactions should normally be based on real market prices if they exist. In the absence of this, a cost-based price is constructed perhaps using the same formula applied to similar domestic transactions, although adjusted for duties and various other costs. The principal advantage of this approach is that it avoids creating the numerous management problems that arise when profits are distorted. Companies which follow this policy believe that the possible tax or other advantages accruing to the corporation from manipulating transfer prices are not worth the trouble caused.

One reason for this is that it makes it more difficult still to judge the performance of the subsidiary. 'If we fiddled our transfer prices, we'd never know if an operation pays or not,' commented one executive. Another said: 'We got in such a muddle, management-wise, we came to the conclusion that operation on an arm's-length basis was the only satisfactory way to price. Otherwise we do not know who is doing well and who is making a mess of things.' Another reason is that management in the affiliates or parent company divisions which are exporting at a low transfer price may object to what is in effect subsidising another organisation in which they have only a marginal interest. To add to their annoyance, proper allowance may not be given by head office for the lower margins which result. In this situation, management in the subsidiary which benefits from the advantageous transfer prices may forget or even be ignorant of the fact that they are being subsidised, and be dismayed when subsequent readjustments bring the price back to normal. This was expressed in one company by 'once you start mucking with prices, it is damned hard to get back to normal, once the exercise is over'. It was also felt to be a danger that low prices would be passed on, and when and if transfer prices came back to normal, margins would be squeezed to where 'they cannot sell any more'.

Another approach advocates keeping what amounts to two sets of accounts. One set records the official accounts which are used for tax, finance and various other local purposes. The other set of accounts is used for management control purposes. Therefore, discretionary pricing practices will be recorded on the official accounts, and profits may or may not be distorted according to the circumstances. The other set of accounts records adjusted transfer prices—as if intracompany transactions had been made at arm's length, or constructed under a formula which would be considered fair or unbiased by management. Performance is judged on these results. A variant of this practice is the credit back or credit forward system. This might be used where a subsidiary is exporting at a lower than arm's-length price to an affiliate. A memorandum account records the differences for evaluation purposes. One of the most obvious drawbacks of both these approaches is their complexity and cost.

The other method already mentioned, that of taking account of any transfer price manipulations in the budget, is widely used. Management's performance is measured against planned results—even if a loss were intended. Indeed to budget a loss in an overseas subsidiary is by no means a rare procedure. In such an event the performance of the subsidiary as an economic entity can only be measured in terms of its contribution to consolidated results, and this means by conforming to the budget. Many of the companies we studied appeared to follow this practice, in spite of the fundamental drawback which we noted earlier—that budgeted goals do not have the same psychological impact as absolute profits in motivating managers. There is the further alternative of abandoning the profit centre concept, and considering the subsidiary only as a cost centre, or relating physical output to monetary input as a measure of performance. But in one sense this begs the question because under such a system performance is still based on planned rather than absolute results. In any case, it would normally only be used for control of a manufacturing unit whose sales went to affiliated concerns. There are other drawbacks to the budgeted performance approach. For example, the transfer prices which were used as the basis of the annual plan might, because of changed circumstances, have to be altered during the year. Where the original budget was used as a performance yardstick, companies expressed the view that there was always the danger that the subsequent change would not be taken into consideration when operating results came up for review. The point was made, albeit rather obliquely, by the managing director of a United States-owned company in Britain:

If . . . the parent company determines on a particular course of action which may offer no advantage, financial or otherwise, perhaps it could even prove detrimental to the UK subsidiary, nevertheless the UK subsidiary must go along with the parent company's wishes. . . . That is not to say, of course, that if the parent company chooses to withdraw or utilise UK subsidiary funds elsewhere within the organisation in the best interests of the whole group the effect of such action should be overlooked or disregarded when measuring the subsidiary's subsequent performance. When year end comparisons come to be made, it is surprising how easily financial manoeuvres of this kind can be overlooked.[32]

Although such oversight is certainly irksome to the subsidiary management, it is probably an occupational hazard in multinational business that has to be accepted. In this regard, the overseas director of a British company thought that 'a foreign manager, if he is worth a damn, should realise that such operations are part of the game. Of course, it is up to us to tell him what is going on, and to take it into account when we review his business.'

A fourth and final approach is to disregard the effects of transfer price aberrations. In part, this is avoiding the problem because, as we have seen, it seems very likely that an appreciable amount of job satisfaction is derived from achieving what managers consider reasonable profits in absolute terms. It can, however, be argued, as in the view we saw expressed above, that if the subsidiary manager 'is worth a damn' he should realise the purpose of such operations. But even if this attitude is accepted, there remains the difficulty of judging the performance of the subsidiary as an entity. If the profits reported are meaningless, not only is its efficiency obscured, but it becomes impossible to allocate resources on the basis of sound economics. A case in point was the French subsidiary of a large German firm. Although the subsidiary consistently made a profit, it was found almost impossible to discover how much this was due to its efficiency, and how much to favourable transfer prices, and whether this profit was satisfactory or not. The parent company's organisation was such that no internal transfer prices had been calculated for intermediates. Goods were invoiced to the French company at the lowest prices that could be managed without running into difficulty with the customs authorities. The French manager was convinced that he was running an efficient business. It turned out later after a laborious investigation that he was not. Gains in efficiency are often much more valuable than the savings which might be made from schemes for shifting profits through discretionary pricing.

The problem of measuring the performance of foreign subsidiaries is complicated by more than merely the effect of arbitrary transfer prices. There are differences in methods of depreciating fixed assets, in wage rates, in interest rates and other costs, in taxation, and in the presence of price controls and other government regulations. These can cumulatively make intracompany comparisons difficult if not impossible. Some firms try to get round this impasse by reconstructing the income statement to compensate for differences in the local operating environments, or by using other non-profit measures of performance, or both. Examples of the ways taken to solve this problem by two of the companies in our sample are as follows:

In one company three results were measured. These were: first, an adjusted profit-to-sales ratio. Profit was calculated before local taxes, but after adding back depreciation, interest charges, amortisation of goodwill, and royalties and fees. Second was asset turnover, that is assets divided by sales. Assets were defined as net assets less cash and plus accumulated depreciation and capitalised rents. The third measurement was sales growth. The company had felt the need to try to compare the performance of its various subsidiaries and was experimenting with these criteria. They emphasised, however, that it was an experiment and recognised the difficulties in such an exercise. For this reason, it was limited to their European subsidiaries which were all relatively new, so that differences in manufacturing plant were comparatively small. Also the environmental conditions were believed to be similar enough not to distort the results excessively.

In another company, it was thought that the profits of subsidiaries were affected by too many variables which were not under the control of local management, and therefore that it would be a nonsense to use them as a measure of their success. This company used various other criteria, one of the most important of which was a measure of manufacturing efficiency. The relative efficiency of various key processes in each subsidiary in the group was compared to a calculated optimum practice. Adjustments were made to take into consideration local operating conditions, and the final result was presented in graphic form. Efficiency was expected to be improved over time, and effectiveness in achieving this goal played an essential part in the evaluation process.

Many companies follow variations of such methods when they consider profit performance to be an unsuitable measure. Growth in sales and market share, and maintenance of good relations with the local business community and government in the host country were other measures that were considered important. Inevitably, indeed, either with or without a valid profit yardstick to use, performance can become subject to non-objective appraisal. In the final analysis, it is a combination of all these factors that is taken into consideration. But, if any of them could be said to dominate, it is some measure of profit and growth.

4.5 Summary

The principles, the procedures, and the general problems of planning and control appear to be fundamentally the same whether a company operates in one national environment or in many. The apparatus of plans, forecasts, budgets and reports needed to give direction to, and assure coordination and control of, the organisation's activities satisfies the same basic requirements at home and abroad. The difficulties of measuring the performance of an overseas or domestic unit are in principle alike.

This being said, there are nevertheless special problems involved in multinational operations which can make the planning and control process more complicated and difficult than in a purely domestic organisation. These arise from a number of sources, and for several reasons.

First of all, the sheer distance between the headquarters and the foreign subsidiary is a factor in conditioning the type of control that can be exercised. With the advent of high-speed messages, more efficient means to process data, and travel by jet aircraft, the problem of remoteness has been overcome and it has become practical to supplement and support the capacities of local management through more or less elaborate systems of plans and control. The rapid feedback of information in this context permits the parent company to follow closely the foreign operations, and intervene and reinforce local management if it appears necessary or desirable.

This does not mean that distance is no longer a factor in the control of foreign subsidiaries—it is merely a less constricting one. On the other hand, faster communications, however achieved, are usually expensive, and in the case of the very small subsidiary, the greater cost of a closer control may not be worth while. Further, while distance *per se* is, in general, no longer the major determinant of the type of control that can be exercised over foreign subsidiaries, as long as there remain substantial differences in the cultural, educational, and linguistic backgrounds of the subsidiary and headquarters managements, communication is less than perfect and a confidence 'gap' seems bound to persist between them. Matters that are taken for granted by one party may need to be made explicit to the other; words are frequently misunderstood and nuances lost. We have suggested earlier that this tends to produce *close* group relationships, and its effect on the control system is to create a demand for explicit and detailed information.

Secondly, the effect of differences in the tax systems between countries, and the special risks associated with foreign investments are two distinct problems which are peculiar to multinational operations. Their impact on planning and control is felt in two principal ways.

One of these is a tendency to centralise decisions, especially in the area of finance. Because financial decisions in one subsidiary can impinge on those elsewhere, authority must be pushed upwards in the company to where an overall view can be obtained. One example, we shall see, consists of decisions over remittances of earnings. The method and timing of payments that may seem most sensible from the subsidiary's point of view may prove to be the opposite for the company as a whole because of the additional taxes on foreign earnings that may be assessed by the home country. Another example concerns the composition of the subsidiary's liabilities where certain policies can provide the parent concern with more flexibility in transferring funds. The objective is generally to further the interests of the group—to provide finance, reduce risks, avoid taxes, and so on—and this calls for policies which may not necessarily always benefit the subsidiary. Transfer pricing provides another example. In most cases, these are matters which cannot be satisfactorily delegated to the subsidiary, but must be decided by the central authority. Furthermore they impose a need for detailed, explicit, frequent, and rapid flows of information between units of the company if they are to be operative.

The effect of taxes and risk also makes it more difficult, and sometimes nearly impossible, to measure the performance of a foreign subsidiary. Tax- and risk-minimising schemes can distort the profits of a subsidiary to such a degree that they are virtually meaningless as an indication of its efficiency. The ramifications are confusing to follow in a domestic operation, but they become even worse in the multinational company. In the search for a solution, complexity is the byword.

Thus the tendency identified in the last chapter towards centralisation, in spite of protestations to the contrary is confirmed by this study of the actual methods of financial control. While a generalisation cannot be made to fit all companies, there seems to be a tendency for many to bring their foreign subsidiaries under a more *close* rather than a more *open* system of control. The increasing need for the integration of the operations of many companies is an important factor that pushes in this direction. But even where this is not so, improvements in communications and data processing techniques have made closer control feasible. This greater scope, added to the growing interest and skill in planning and control as ways of improving management's efficiency and effectiveness, is leading companies to extend their authority downwards into the local operation. We shall see in a later chapter that this creates as its counterpart a strong desire, and perhaps also the need, for complete ownership control.

The personalities

5.1 Roles in the multinational company

The discussion so far has been mainly concerned with the behaviour of the multinational firm in terms of technical influences—finance, organisation, and control. The more subtle aspects of managerial behaviour, such as the relationship between personality types and company structure, are outside the scope of this book.[1] The concern of this chapter is to grapple with a few problems best understood in terms of the way the individual fits into the organisation. The word 'role' is appropriate here and is usually used of the activities assumed to be attached to a particular position; relationships that these activities demand are called 'role relationships'. As an example, one of the features of promotion in any organisation is that the higher position is likely to carry with it more roles that have to be played simultaneously, and with them a more complex set of role relationships. Some of the roles which may have to be performed by the foreign manager have been isolated. The list includes such potentially conflicting positions as 'management's representative' and 'member of local business', or 'resident in a foreign country' and 'foreign citizen'.[2] Whether at home or abroad, the role of international executive may conflict with other parts a manager has to play. We have already seen that one problem of a geographical organisation is that the international executive may become divorced from other parts of the company. In the C type company the individual has to perform more roles simultaneously, with even more scope for conflict.

Another problem is that operations across frontiers will increase the complexity of the role relations which in any case exist for the senior executive. If conflict arises for him because he has to perform different and at times inconsistent roles ('wear two hats', as he usually says) at the same time, the next issue is that these roles involve relationships with many different groups of people. The bundles of relationships that result are usually called the *role-set*. This has been defined as 'the complement of role relationships which persons have by virtue of occupying a particular social status'.[3] There are factors making for disorder in the role-set which increase with the seniority of the status. One major factor in this disorder is the range of interests involved. At the lower levels of a hierarchy, the role-set is relatively small—comprising relationships with colleagues, immediate subordinates and immediate superiors with perhaps people of similar rank from customers and suppliers. The role-set of more senior executives will include a higher proportion of representative people—government, employees, other companies, the trade unions, and so on. They will represent a whole range of conflicting pressures. To these the multinational company will add a further complication that superiors, subordinates, customers, suppliers, and colleagues may belong to several different nationalities. But the role-set is not usually as complicated as might appear because a number of mechanisms operate to simplify it. The first is the simple fact that some members have priority over others—and fixing where the priorities lie is one of the skills required by the international manager. The second is that different members of the role-set have different degrees of power to enforce their point of view. The third is that some members of the role-set may make allowances for the demands of others, and realise that the person at the centre is a victim of this conflict. The fourth is lack of observability; some members of the role-set may not know what is happening. The fifth is the support the executive may get in coping with his role-set from others in the same position, for instance his professional society or institute. The sixth is the reduction of the role-set by cutting out one member. Figure 5.1 gives some elements in the role-set of the chief executive of a foreign subsidiary.

Of the mechanisms listed above, the last one is unlikely to be available to the chief executive; indeed, his role-set will be even more complex than suggested here. If the company is wholly owned, then 'shareholders' and 'parent company' will be the same. For an executive at headquarters with some overseas responsibility, the role-set will be complicated by the inclusion of several nationalities, and this can only be reduced if the firm withdraws from overseas. The fifth mechanism is also likely to be of only limited use. There is no *Guild of International Managers* to attend to his problems, although naturally he will have the usual professional support within the country where he is operating. The first two mechanisms may work in reverse. For the manager's priorities may work along some links, and the power may be with others. This may complicate the role-set problems still further. In addition, there is a sense in which many of the problems between companies and countries, outlined in chapter 10, arise because managers have tried to simplify their role-sets by paying too little attention to the concerns of the host country. On the other hand, the manager who is sensitive to these concerns, may attempt to limit his role-set by paying too little attention to the experience and requirements of head office. This leaves mechanisms three and four to assist the executive in the multinational firm. The fourth will be especially important, for the executive can resolve some of his problems just because members of his role-set do not understand the whole of his activities. This applies, of course, to the parent company among others; and this may well account for some of the strong opposition to the reporting systems. This was confirmed by managers of

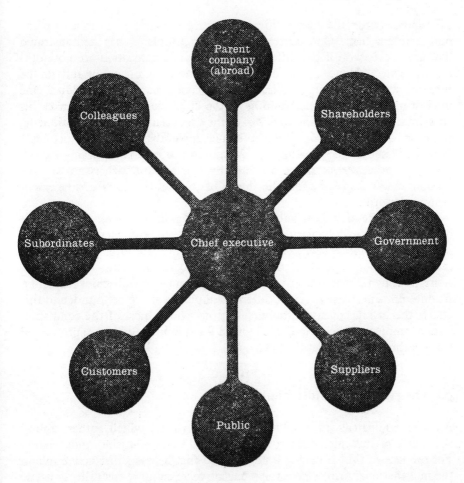

Fig. 5.1 The role-set of the chief executive of a foreign subsidiary

subsidiaries when they spoke about controlling their own independence by limiting the information that went to headquarters. Problems which can be analysed in role-set terms were sometimes anticipated, but they usually arose in totally unexpected situations. The most interesting of these is what we call the *buffer situation* (see para. 5.3 below). This is found among top managers of a national subsidiary, the group with the most complex role-set that the multinational company can provide. As explained below, they represent a foreign system to their subordinates who may be their fellow-countrymen, and are responsible for the operations to their superiors who are foreigners. This was found to be an exceptionally uneasy position, and the term *buffer situation* is used to describe it.

Another problem that has featured in this study is the securing of greater cohesion between the many different segments which go to make up the multinational firm. One writer on business problems has demonstrated how these can arise if the different parts of the organisation are not sufficiently related.[4] Hence the means used to promote some sense of unity in the firm are worth examining. These may be conscious or unconscious. One interesting example is the position of the chief executive who makes his contribution to the welding together of the organisation by the mystique he produces around himself. But the whole apparatus which has just been described under the heading of 'communications' is relevant—travel, meetings, procedures, and so on. Equally relevant are such issues as promotion across frontiers, and the image of the headquarters' management around the firm.

Finally succession is a subject which is significant here, for the role of the successor may be variously interpreted as promoting a change or promoting greater integration. Change and integration are often considered as inconsistent, but in practice the multinational company needs both at once. For it lives by innovation, and hence needs people who will achieve stability. At different times, as we show, different emphases are to be found, and this affects the making of appointments. On the whole, most of the companies in our sample were conscious of the need for stability, and hence promotion from within was the usual policy.

5.2 The significant individual

An anthropological study of the myths and rituals which gather around the figure of the chief executive would surely be a valuable undertaking. For the lack of this, it may still be assumed that he has a distinctive role in the multinational firm. The foreign executive, even more than the domestic one, understands the company most easily in personal terms; and the chief executive will often provide the terms. Sometimes he will come through as a legendary character, jolting the firm on to a new and distinctive path; sometimes he will come through as a stereotype, what the foreigner expects of one of his nationality. In some companies, the leader has consciously been built up into a legendary figure as a cohesive force within the firm and to counter the dangers of the stereotype. 'Know Mr X and you will know this company', the subsidiary manager is apt to say. He will then describe some exploit of the chief executive and speak of his influence in terms which might be called 'endearing abuse'. Part of the legend is usually some reorganisation of the company, often described as a 'shake-up'. But the legend must not be too remote; he must drop from the skies into the various parts of his empire, and not too infrequently.[5] One company specifically said that foreign managers had been integrated into the company by the way the methods and the philosophy of the chairman had 'rubbed off' on to them.

Besides integration and stimulus, reorganisation is one of the main functions for which the leader of the company is cast. His name may be identified with a drastic reorganisation along lines which are said to be his special interest. In fact his range of choice is more circumscribed than the myths generally suggest. This leads us to consider certain problems of succession and to link what is already known on this subject with the organisational outlines described in this study.[6] Specifically, the new chief has first to assert himself as against his predecessor, to establish his legitimacy and his authority. He can do this by a no change policy—'things will go on as before'. He can also do this by a policy of considerable change either in a more authoritarian or a more participative direction. It should be noted that autocracy and participation are not synonymous with *open* and *close* as these words are used in chapter 3. There can be a considerable degree of participation or consultation at each level of the hierarchy, but yet the oversight of the subsidiary can be *close*.[7] In any event, the participation occurs within some frame of reference; it does not extend to fundamental questions about the purpose of the firm. Equally there may be considerable autocracy at the top, but the foreign subsidiary may be left alone and an *open* relationship may develop. There are correspondences here; in other words, autocracy and *closeness* are often found together, but the connection is by no means invariable. Indeed, the intentions of the chief executive may not actually take effect lower down. We have seen earlier examples of how functional executives may be operating a system that seems *close* to the subsidiary although the intention of the main board is that it shall be *open*.

The chief executive's discretion is finally limited by the fact that his ideas have to be given organisational expression; and as far as the multinational firm is concerned, once it is multiproduct the organisation will develop into the B, C, or D types described in chapter 2. Since it will already correspond to one of these types, unless it is just emerging from the single-product A type, the choice is limited to one or two possibilities. One pattern of decision-making is sketched out in fig. 5.2.

A further limit on the discretion of the chief executive will be the special circumstances preceding his appointment. He may well have been chosen because his opinions or character were thought to fit the needs of the company at the time.[8] However, in such circumstances, there may be a self-reinforcing effect whereby if an individual fits a situation, he is liable to overfit it. Thus a man picked for his known ability to axe superfluous personnel may turn out too ruthless, while a man selected when a relaxation is considered desirable may prove too permissive. This tendency to overfit is a factor in making further reorganisation necessary. The powerful character is liable to prefer personalised rather than group management at all points in the organisation. But this may well prove inadequate and give rise to further changes. As an example, some form of group management may become necessary[9] because a communications centre requires competence

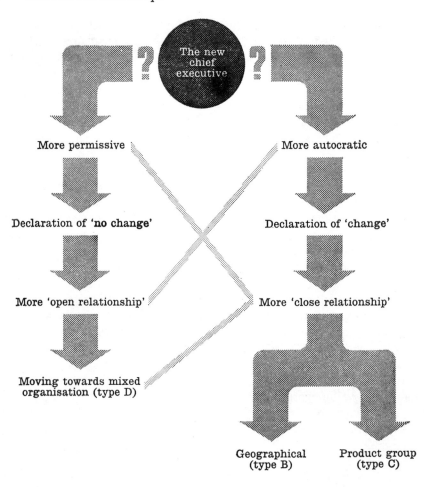

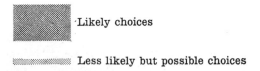
·Likely choices

Less likely but possible choices

Fig. 5.2 Constraints on the choices facing the newly appointed executive

and resources that are seldom found in one person. So the next reorganisation includes a growth in manpower. It is even more difficult in an
international than in a domestic organisation to draw the line between
adequate and inflated resources; hence the growth is likely to go on too long
and spark off a fresh reduction. The mutual interplay between the personalities and the structure can produce frequent reorganisations. In companies
where subsidiary management talked about the firm in terms of personalities,

there was often evidence of rapid short-term growth. It does seem as if the effect of the outstanding character is to produce this short-term rapid growth, where the development of more formal methods builds in a longer-term stability. In this connection there is a danger of frittering away human resources for short-term advantage by a doctrinaire authoritarianism.[10]

The method of recruitment to the board or management committees is another personal influence on the formulation of policy. Recruitment can be from the founding family. This is, of course, unusual in the multi-national firm but by no means unknown even in the largest of them. It has been suggested that a family firm, in the light of contemporary prejudices, may well be so self-conscious about its liabilities that it fails to realise its assets.[11] Among multinational companies this can only be mentioned as a suspicion. There was no evidence among the companies investigated that the continuing family links in a firm were either assets or liabilities overseas. It was the character of the reigning monarch, not a family tradition, which registered with the foreign subsidiary. The two most usual areas of recruitment for the firms studied were among functional specialists and product-group managers. For the larger firms, indeed, these two were almost the only areas of recruitment, except for the occasional director brought in from outside. The smaller firms, growing rapidly in the international field, and lacking sufficient managerial resources, were more likely to recruit top management from outside. Apart from this there seemed to be no identifiable regularity at all in the areas of recruitment. Some companies which were almost completely product group oriented, yet reported that most of their top management had come up through the functional services. Many companies, as might be expected, recruited from the product group and specialist areas equally. The only noticeable peculiarity that could be identified was that companies which did recruit mainly from the product group management were apt to speak about the problem of turning managers into directors. The busy product group manager, who had spent most of his life in line management, was said to face particular difficulties when he became a director. As a manager running a product group, his main concern has been with day-to-day decisions and he finds the transition to policy making and planning a difficult one. This may be less of a problem to the executive recruited from a functional service department who may have been used to considering overall corporate policy. Where this difficulty is recognised by the firm, written regulations may limit the activities of the policy-forming executives, for their too active intervention in routine affairs will be incompatible with the doctrine of individual responsibility for their subordinates.

A final word should be said on this subject of individual responsibility. We have already demonstrated the strong pressures towards greater centralisation in the multinational company. These pressures have further been seen to operate at the same time as greater emphasis is being put on individual responsibility. For instance, it is possible that management at home may acquire greater independence at the price of greater interference abroad. One firm with new products, a board recruited from the functional services, and a large overseas group, reported that reorganisation had moved the main centres of dispute from the home country to the foreign units. This is an example of moving the point of tension without removing it. Further, the development of the so-called recognised informal element in the organisation increases the independence of the individual executive, and the demands that the job makes upon him. Indeed, this repersonalised bureaucracy appears to modify the tendency to greater specialisation. There is a sort of specialisation belt that the executive passes through, perhaps early in his career, and from which he emerges into a world that makes more varied demands. At this stage a corrective to the early specialisation may well be needed. The international company gives scope for these developments. But there is also likely to be a widening of the gap between the home country management and that in the host country whose horizons are narrower. This gap is likely to be further increased when executives from the host countries are brought to the head office.

5.3 The buffer situation

Another area where conflict is likely to arise we have called the *buffer situation*. Such a situation was observed in the British subsidiary of an American company; it was also noted in foreign subsidiaries of British companies as well, which suggests that the situation does not depend on any particular national cultural features. The company in which it was first traced had a product group organisation worldwide (C type). This had the effect of producing several subsidiaries in some countries, but in these they had also an overarching national organisation. The top management of the national organisation in one particular country expressed considerable unease at their position. They described great difficulties of communication, and they considered themselves the 'Cinderella' of the concern. They were able to list the specific problems which resulted. On the other hand, the product group managers were very satisfied indeed. As unanimously as their superiors found major problems in the organisation, they could find nothing wrong with it. Cautiously and with circumspection some of the problems outlined by their superiors were put to the product group managers, separately and in private. Again the unanimity was impressive—no doubt such problems did arise in some organisations, but they could not possibly arise in this one. They were even able to explain in some detail how the procedures of their company made such problems impossible. There was a complete and dramatic contradiction here which could not be completely described without breaking people's confidences; but the details show a black-and-white case of two groups of managers each giving completely opposite accounts of the same company, the dissatisfaction being in the higher ranks, not in the lower.

A number of reasons suggest themselves for the unease of the higher rank, and these can be grouped into three sets of circumstances. When these three combine, a buffer situation can be expected to arise. The first of these is the situation where a national management is set up which cuts across the normal product-group organisation of the company. Managers in this position will find themselves as intruders in the set-up. Normal problems of communication will be intensified for them because their role does not appear to be a logical one. Their subordinates will tend to bypass them. A second situation is that of national managers who have to channel through to their subordinates messages which they know will cause resentment. They may well share this resentment because they regard the instructions as showing a lack of sensitivity to their local conditions. This is the kind of circumstance in which they become acutely aware that they are representing an alien system to the fellow-countrymen they are managing. Finally there will be a similar problem the other way round. Upward communication will pass through this national management, but in a form unacceptable to their foreign superiors. So there will be also difficulties over messages that way.

One example was found of a group which included both local nationals and expatriates expressing the problems of a buffer situation. In this case the expatriates had identified themselves with the host country. Normally the difficulties will arise where people find themselves representing a foreign management to their subordinates, although their own background and experience lead them to identify themselves with their local subordinates.

Anthropologists have identified similar problems in the role of the village headman in a colonial society.[12] This official represented the authority of a superior power to members of small communities of which he was otherwise himself a full member. The position in the firm is not of course the same; the headman was at the bottom of the hierarchy, and in that sense all the more closely identified with the people he ruled. But the top management of the national subsidiaries, where they are local nationals themselves, are representatives of the local organisation and at the same time agents of a foreign authority. As with the village headman, they find themselves in a situation around which a cluster of problems collect; and these problems do not exist, or are much milder in their impact, in other contexts. The buffer situation applies to managers who absorb the shocks which come in messages from outside before passing the messages on to their subordinates. This necessary activity may make them uneasy with head office, and this unease is increased by a tendency on the part of the latter to exaggerate both the discretion limits and the promotion prospects of the national management. The buffer situation works the other way too. For subordinate management in the subsidiary may misinterpret the firm's rules and procedures, and the national headquarters relays messages in a form suitable for head office to read. They soften the opposition of the subordinates to the international standards and practices which appear irrelevant in the particular country. 'They seem to forget', the national management complain of their superiors after doing their best to help 'them' to forget, 'that our fellow-countrymen are not like theirs.' They, the most senior national managers, may well be seeking less control from overseas, but more control over their own operating units. This creates tensions, especially where the managers of these units have strong international contacts.

Global promotion schemes may mitigate these problems, but at the expense of other objectives of the company such as the executive's identification with the host country. Other global policies are likely to increase the problems. Indeed it can be said that the acceptance and efficient operation of such policies may depend on the finding of other ways of reducing the problems at the buffer. The difficulties, especially the organisational problems such as the subordinates who consistently bypass the prescribed channels of communication, arise usually in the C type company; but at least one example was found in an A type firm. The problems of the B type company are many, but this particular geographical organisation does not seem so liable to the characteristic buffer problems.

One reason why global policies increase the difficulties is that they reduce the meaningful activity available to managers in the situation described. If, for instance, the managers concerned have been promoted from the active management of a product group, they now find themselves relieved of immediate day-to-day responsibilities and in a position to devote more of their time to thinking. But what should they think about? If many areas of policy are settled at head office, the mere application of decisions taken elsewhere in the group may well prove less than absorbing. They are also, we have said already, in a position that is anomalous in their particular type of organisation. Hence a considerable uncertainty about their role can be added to their other discomforts. Figure 5.3 illustrates the position with messages being absorbed by the national managements and passed on in a much modified form.

Two further problems should be mentioned in connection with this buffer position, although they can arise independently of it. One was that product group managers from head office, when they visited the country, would be liable to talk mainly to the product group management there. In so doing they might well give the impression that the national management was unimportant. An incautious word can convince subordinate managers in the host country that their future careers depended on head office, and that the national management were in an even more anomalous position than they were. This was said in more than one firm, and arose where any form of geographical management was alien to the company. The role of the national management, already difficult, could thus be further undermined.

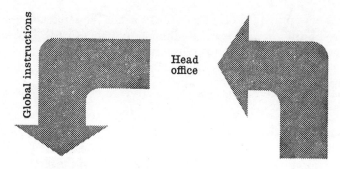

National management

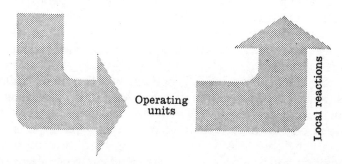

Fig. 5.3 The *buffer* situation

The other subject made more difficult by the buffer situation was that of intersubsidiary relations. It is possible for, and may be in the interest of, one national subsidiary to make problems in its dealings with another. A fertile area for these to arise is over transfer of goods and services at other than arm's-length prices. Unless there is someone at head office with considerable knowledge of local laws on these matters, the national subsidiary has a means of keeping discretion in its own hands by pleading that head office instructions are a breach of the law. One local company used some legal excuse not to transfer some materials at a price below normal to another national firm in the same group. Although the amount of cash involved would not have shown in their books, it would have meant the difference between a loss and a profit to the latter, a much smaller concern. Their opposition, arising out of a buffer situation, caused them to exercise what discretion was left to them. In another case, there was a blockage in the flow of technical information between subsidiaries for much the same kind of reasons.

As a final point, we found that sometimes, in explaining their role, executives at a regional centre will describe themselves as *buffers* between head office and the national subsidiaries. But the concept of the buffer situation does not apply to them at all. There is not the same ambiguity in their position, nor do they normally fill it on a permanent basis. There may be problems of communications for those in a regional centre, but they are not the same as those at the buffer whose characteristic problems have been discussed above.

5.4 Appraisal and stimulus

Studies of organisation structure have stressed the significance of appraisal in understanding organisational behaviour.[13] These have shown how appraisal, limited to certain aspects of a person's job, will change the objectives of the organisation to come into line with the appraisal rather than the reverse. As explained in chapter 1, enquiries were made about how subsidiary performances were judged. That questions about appraisal proved easy to answer showed that the subject was much on the minds of the executives concerned.

The most common method of appraisal was the simple collection of statistics, mainly financial, of the type discussed in the preceding chapter, but some of the most successful modern techniques depend for their effectiveness on face-to-face confrontation. This applies, for instance, to 'management by objectives' in which managers in consultation with their superiors discuss their objectives.[14] This increasingly popular method was mentioned by several companies, but not often across frontiers. It may well be that some firms hesitated to establish the machinery to do this, and that others in any case considered it incompatible with the type of system in which they were operating. In cases where management by objective was mentioned, it was taken right down to first-line supervisory levels, at least in intention. This was a case of a new management technique limiting the autonomy of the subsidiary, for the decision to use the technique was taken in the parent company. It should be added that in one firm which used this technique in the home country, but hesitated to enforce its use abroad, the appraisal methods used in one of its subsidiaries were very vague. A watered-down version of methods used in the parent firm was considered suitable for the host country, but seemed to have a poor effect on performance.

Management by objective generally involves a number of senior executives from both the subsidiary and the head office. In one American firm, the vice-president in charge of the particular product group would come over to take the chair at a series of meetings at which each overseas manager in turn would make a presentation. After doing this the manager would be subjected, in front of his fellow-managers, to some searching questions on all aspects of his work. Confrontation was seen to be an important element in the scheme. The appraisal technique used by another firm was to bring the chief executive of each foreign subsidiary to head office periodically for a series of conferences. In this firm the subsidiary manager came alone and was expected to answer for all aspects of his business. He had to face executives from all the different central services of the company in sessions which went on for a fortnight, with the managing director of the parent firm in the chair. This latter took the view that in the years during which these sessions had been held there had not been any abnormal results. The manager of the subsidiary which was performing well by other tests came through satisfactorily on this one.

An interesting problem arising out of appraisal methods is the effect these can have on the collection of information. One example which was mentioned concerned the reporting of lost business. In the firm concerned, the product promotion staff at head office were conducting a study of lost business and using this in development work. The collection of reports on this proved naturally difficult at home, but almost impossible abroad where sales managers would not believe that they were not being asked to hang themselves. Appraisal by objectives determined as the result of a direct confrontation between the manager and his superior would no doubt have helped to overcome this problem. Indeed in one of the companies that had introduced this it was specifically mentioned that the flow of information had improved, primarily because managers were less afraid of reporting their failures.

Naturally the significance of the appraisal system is likely to depend on the strength of the manager's position, and this in turn will depend partly on how *close* is his relationship with head office, and partly on whether there is any form of international promotion. One of the problems of the multinational company is that there may be few tangible rewards possible for subsidiary managers who perform well. Ironically it is those who use the *open* relationship most wholeheartedly who rob themselves of a *calculative* stimulus—they have no scheme for promotion beyond the subsidiary and limited scope for salary increases. They have even less scope for removing the unsuccessful executive abroad, and probably none at all if he is supported by his colleagues. But in any case, even with the closest of relationships, there are limits to the action that a company can take over a bad performance. For the subsidiary will be a legal entity in the host country, and the management may even have some legal protection. So, in general, it may be concluded that if satisfactory appraisal is a problem, it is also difficult to make the consequence of the appraisal convincing. There will inevitably be examples of subsidiaries continuing to perform in ways considered unsatisfactory by the parent company, and this fact must be set against what has been said about the general trend to a closer relationship.

The relationship between profit and appraisal has been discussed at length in the previous chapter. We only need to repeat here that several local companies mentioned bewilderment as to how their reports were judged, especially if straight profitability was not the criterion. The arguments against profitability were more often used at head office than in the subsidiary, although used out of consideration for the management of the latter. A manager from headquarters would say, 'We cannot judge them just on their profits, because we have developed policies which make it harder for them to make profits.' The local management would be likely to object to these policies as interference (no matter how they were being appraised) and hence prefer that profit should be the criterion. They were inclined to regard any other consideration as irrelevant and unjustified. 'We turn in a handsome return on the investment they put in here so why should we have to answer so many questions? It's all red tape apart from the profit figures.'

One subsidiary chief executive took a different view. He was, as it were, suspended between two companies. Both were foreign, and the holding was fifty-fifty. So long as the results were satisfactory, one of the companies reacted to the subsidiary's report with only an acknowledgement. In contrast, the other examined the reports in detail. Brought up in the former company, this particular manager expressed his admiration for the latter. He found this firm criticised even a good result if there appeared to be bad planning involved, and he personally approved of this. The joint venture mentioned was in a special situation for it has a captive market for a large proportion of its products. Where this was not the case, a company might consider market-share a suitable criterion. The rise or fall of the subsidiary's share of its domestic market was indeed mentioned by one or two firms as the most significant method of appraisal. But obviously this method has its limitations. Apart from the danger of ignoring costs, it has the possible drawback of concentrating attention on the more easily saleable but perhaps less profitable products.

The more complex methods of appraisal typically stimulate informal links in the organisation. If global promotion is a possibility, there is the tendency already mentioned to forge links with the head office executive charged with the collection of information from the different reporting product lines. If it is not, there is still the tendency to look for assistance and to develop informal lines of communication for this purpose. The distinction between nurture and discipline in the role of officials at head office is illuminating here. It may well be that the more elaborate the appraisal system, the more it becomes an entirely disciplinary system— whatever the intention. The links develop to produce a system of nurture which the company's organisation is failing to provide.

Alongside appraisal as a stimulus to the individual manager is the reciprocal stimulus which the manager brings to the firm. This is an area where the international company should have advantages. There should be available personal resources to provide stimuli to new ideas, and for the formulation of plans. The actual abilities available varied from company to company, some alleging a total lack of stimulus from their subsidiaries. Even more varied were the responses to stimuli, and the means used to make the plans effective. The ways in which the organisation causes blocks in communications, discussed in chapter 2, are obviously crucial here. Equally, global promotion policies, which may improve communications, may also have the effect of concentrating ability still more at the centre—a subtle form of brain drain.

Stimulus for new ideas for a company may come from inside or outside. Inside stimulus comes from the ideas, experience or research of any of the firm's departments; it may also come from special efforts such as suggestion schemes, projects, interchange of personnel. The larger firm has evidently more possibilities of damming or drying up the flow. This danger appears especially strong in international companies, where stimuli may be blocked by the length of the communications, problems of understanding across frontiers, and the absorption of much of the organisation in coordinating rather than innovating; and possibly there may be an attitude of—'We are overseas because of our knowledge rather than to acquire anybody else's.' Often a preoccupation with coordination brings about the general slowdown of the company. Such phrase as 'decisions in one unit are influenced by the implications of such decisions for other units' indicate a cautious attitude which may slow down the decision-making for the whole group. This outlook affects the unavoidable problems of long-distance consultation. One of these is that decisions cannot be discussed informally over a long period. Extra vigour in a well-organised small company may well be understood in terms of extra scope for internal stimuli. The position is reversed in regard to external stimuli. These may come from market studies, reports on or from competitors, general awareness of what is going on. Here the international company has a clear advantage. It has listening posts all over the world. The nature of the distinction between internal and external stimuli, and the peculiar position of the international company in relation to these, make for concentration on methods of collection and processing of information.

One firm reported that after a period of very rapid expansion abroad inexperienced managers working at full stretch did not stimulate new ideas, and left their superiors isolated. Such a situation can be exacerbated overseas, where the company has no roots. So there is much to show that there are difficulties in building the role of 'stimulator' into the overseas management, although this is so often described as one of the main advantages of an international company. Some companies have given considerable thought to this, and the development of a more cohesive system of management may well be one means of overcoming it.

'Management by objective' has already been mentioned as a technique which may be proving relevant here. So is long-range planning. In one company, however, strong local resistance to involvement in planning procedures had resulted in a shortening of the projections. Another company, sensitive to the pressures on the subsidiary, made long-term projections at home, but limited the demands on the foreign operation to those required by the exigencies of a particular operation, normally four years at the most. This limited the demands for information. Detailed planning for their foreign companies started abroad and was largely the sum of the local plans. Opportunistic rather than strategic, this company's planning was arranged as far as possible so as not to be a strong centralising force. Further the planning structures were not separated from existing departments, so that all managers had an active part to play. Environmental factors were carefully incorporated in the four-year plans. These included such matters as the general economic climate of the country under consideration, and likely government action there, the development of the market and the supply situation, and also the availability of labour. All of this was the business of the local company, with headquarters underpinning and assisting the research effort. In this company the planning was used in pursuance of an *open* relationship—the subsidiary was appraised on the quality of its planning in an attempt to force it to stand on its own feet. But this was very rare. The opposite extreme was exemplified by another firm, which broke up a foreign subsidiary on the grounds that it was sabotaging the global plans of the concern. The national legal entity was maintained, but within it the marketing director became completely independent, reporting directly to head office; the managing director was left in charge of the production side only.

Naturally the most elaborate planning was confined to the larger companies, but the degree of sophistication was apt to be limited by a considerable degree of optimism, despite statements to the effect that plans should take account of future probabilities. Statements of targets often seemed to consist of arbitrary percentage increases based on past growth. Some dynamic small companies, on the other hand, were without elaborate planning methods, yet seemed to have more clearcut and less haphazard targets. Thus planning procedures give an interesting example of the *open* and *close* relationship. If a company makes plans centrally and then splits them down the line to the subsidiaries, this would suggest a close relationship; but if done within some contractual system involving full discussion at each level, a considerable measure of independence can still be indicated. The reverse process, where the company's plans are the sum of the plans of the operating units, may be a sign of an open relationship; this also fosters the role of stimulator within the subsidiary, but may conflict with international strategies. However, the fullest use of global planning opportunities fits neither alternative. One thing is clear, that some companies tend to take away from local management much of their part in planning but to continue to appraise them on their skilfulness in this area. This inconsistency is only likely to be overcome by a further move towards contractual management.

5.5 The international executive

'Complete identification' with the host country was how the chairman of one firm described his objective in considering overseas appointments. If managers had to be expatriates, then they must be capable of making this identification. Whether expatriate or not, they must be able to promote what he called a 'two-way traffic' with their environment. This would include accepting stimulus from head office as well as adapting to local conditions. But other companies did not see the role of the foreign manager in such clearcut terms. Questions about this would be answered in different ways following different assumptions about his role. If the expatriate manager was regarded as a temporary officer, building up or reorganising the company abroad until local management was ready to take over, then expectations would be different than if he were regarded simply as an agent of head office, keeping the local operation in line with global policies of the group. The latter view is seldom stated in quite that form, but many expatriates are clearly abroad for that purpose. In such case 'complete identification' is more likely to be a worry than a wish at headquarters; it is more likely to be called 'going native', a phrase that is frequently used in articles about international business, but seldom so explicitly by the executives themselves.

From the point of view of the expatriate manager himself the international company creates a number of problems. These include a constant uprooting and absence from the centre of power. He may also find himself in an ambiguous position as between headquarters and the local operation. This is made more difficult by the question of understanding across frontiers, which includes problems of knowing what instructions can or cannot be given in any particular country.[15]

For the local national in the host country there are advantages in the multinational company with its prestige, its stability, its wide-ranging activities and perhaps its liberal personnel policies. But his is also likely to be a permanently subordinate position. Most of the companies had a policy of promoting local personnel to local executive positions,[16] but hardly any appointed local nationals to their main board; indeed there are difficulties about this in some countries. This fact would seem to deny to head office its most substantial means of control. Subsidiary management may be stimulated by monetary rewards and various non-cash benefits, and these are crucial up to a point; but ultimately they are probably not as powerful incentives as promotion. A policy that limits advancement encourages disaffection. In the long run local nationals are likely to be offered the same career opportunities as those in the parent company management. In the words of the English managing director of an American-owned subsidiary in the United Kingdom:

It seems to me that the British manager of an American-owned firm in this country is more restricted than his American counterpart and this applies whether he happens to be serving in his own country or over here. Quite naturally the ambitious United States citizen is entitled to feel that on the basis of merit the way to the top of the parent organisation is open to him. The United Kingdom citizen on the other hand may seldom feel that he has the same scope, no matter how good his results may be. It is here that there is a sharp distinction between the subsidiary of a British company and that of an American, for it is not unusual nowadays for the directors of the main board of British companies to be recruited from the boards of their subsidiaries. As British managers of United States subsidiaries are usually expected to be particularly dynamic and, in the American sense of the word, aggressive personalities, this limitation of scope can be difficult to swallow.[17]

However, a new type of international executive has been gradually emerging over the last twenty years, and this represents a third stage in the development of the international executive. The first stage was when all key positions overseas were held by expatriates, although this did not necessarily mean that there could not be a titular foreign chief executive. The second stage is that of the taking over of the key positions by local nationals. Even so there may be certain positions reserved to nationals from the home country. In some firms this would apply to the finance director;[18] in other companies there may be expatriate technical managers. Where these are in subordinate positions there tend to be problems and uncertainties. At best, the role of the subordinate expatriate is a delicate one. Is he really part of the local management or is he an agent of the parent company? This is the sort of question that is raised.

This stage of local management was the point which about two-thirds of the companies said they had reached, but some of them still had a high proportion of expatriate managers in key positions. The building up of an entirely local management was favoured as appeasing local feeling, aiding the recruitment of able foreigners, saving the expense of expatriate managers and for other reasons. But it produces problems of cohesion in the company and of the best use of resources, and may even rob the local national of the opportunities of foreign service. So the third stage has been coming into existence and with it the new type of international executive mentioned above. This is the international grade of management. It is now possible to meet a man who says: 'This is my first senior appointment in my own country.' There are some personal pressures involved, and some men pull out of the international grade for family reasons, but more companies are moving into this stage.[19] One company already has more foreigners in head office than expatriates in all its foreign subsidiaries put together. In an extreme case the consequences of not producing an international management grade were that a company had to close some of its overseas offices until there were sufficient managers with experience of the company to fill them.

Three companies, each with a considerable technological base, told us how they brought in complete teams of experts from the home country to set up new subsidiaries. In each case these were withdrawn as local managers were trained on the spot in both the technology and the methods of the company. One of these companies was of the type D described in chapter 2. In this case the withdrawal was assisted and underpinned by the geographical organisation. The other was a type C firm, product group organised at home and abroad. In this case the timing of the withdrawal was much more difficult. In fact in one subsidiary this was done too quickly, and experts from the home country had to return because of technical problems. Two of the companies reported difficulties which confirmed the role problems of expatriates in subordinate positions suggested above. In their view the satisfactory relationship which had been established before they had been repatriated was impossible to reestablish on their return. This particular situation was clearly an example of one of the problem areas, and one that was likely to apply in this form mainly to the C type company.

Several issues arose over global promotion in general and the international grade of management in particular. One was that for all the emphasis that is put on experience with the firm, where the local company management is given the final decision in making its own appointments it is likely to rate this experience *below* other qualifications. So the subsidiary is likely to appoint the man who has a proven record or who interviews best, and to disregard experience with the firm or even the parent company's management development policy. There were differences of practice on this, and some companies are increasing their efforts to ensure that their affiliates do comply with general appointments' policies, but this was a subject on which the subsidiaries themselves resolutely took an independent line in many of the firms investigated. Another issue applies mainly to the developing countries, and is that when a man reaches the international grade his value has increased so much that the company is likely to lose him. This can apply to all development of local nationals in such countries. A period at the head office of an international company is a very marketable qualification for a high governmental post in his own country. Then again there is the predictable problem of salary.[20] Most companies pay by the standards of the host country with special allowances for expatriates wherever they come from. For some companies this was a change of policy that resulted from the development of the international grade. Previously, when all expatriates came from the home country, they had been paid salaries according to home country standards. This had become more difficult when expatriate management came from several countries, and so host country salaries began to prevail. This further increased the tendency towards local management throughout the company, for it naturally became even harder to recruit home nationals for long periods overseas. This was one of the reasons for the self-accelerating process noticeable in the development of international management. With the general problem of salaries went also the problem of executive bonuses and share options in companies which had them. Where foreign managers were included in such schemes they would be likely to be so much 'in the know' about the company generally that they would have to share on equal terms with home managers.

The whole question of the employment and payment of foreign executives well illustrates the concept of problem-centred decision-making.[21] For company after company reported swings of policy produced by the sudden conviction that there were problems overseas concerned with management personnel. Indeed such a conviction gives rise to sudden reactions which, in the same company, would be avoided over domestic problems on the grounds that they were likely to produce too much of an upheaval. The rapid withdrawal and return of expatriate experts was one example of this; one company cited the sudden repatriation of two-thirds of the managers from the home country in one part of the world where heavy losses of local personnel had been noted. The sudden promotion of the local managers was intended to hold them and overrode all other considerations. This action proved successful—the newly promoted managers performed well in the short term at any rate—and so was repeated in other parts of the world.

Yet another problem for the expatriate manager is his future with the firm. Some companies attempt to build in an escape hatch for the man who fails abroad, recognising how difficult it may be to isolate the particular qualities required for the foreign post. One example of this was in a company which guaranteed an executive going abroad for the first time a similar post back home if he had to return prematurely. Most firms, however, gave no such guarantee and a man was expected to settle down in the foreign country. His frustration in the organisation might be compensated by the advantages of the life abroad, or he might have to leave the company to return home. One firm made this explicit in the following terms: 'If you succeed you may be promoted to headquarters as a member of the foreign department. You probably will not join the domestic operations. Except for this possibility, you are embarking on a career abroad until retirement.'[22]

A problem of a more elementary nature is language. This should not go without mention if only to refer in passing to one company which organised its first conference for all senior managers, but did not invite those who could not talk English. Linguistic ability is one of the subjects that ranks more highly in discussion of desirable qualifications than among criteria for an actual appointment. The one problem mentioned frequently in connection with language was the misunderstanding that arose when foreign managers exaggerated their understanding of reports and other documents. On the whole, managers seem to acquire considerable ability at coping in countries where they do not understand the language. They may rely to a great degree on multilingual secretaries, and the availability of such is often mentioned in discussing the siting of offices. Where secretaries who are able to write the official language of the company are not available, then multilingual managers may find themselves tied to their desks laboriously producing their own reports. In this case a head office demand for reports in the company language can produce a considerable grievance.[23]

With regard to personal considerations, obviously international tensions must affect global promotion policies, and most companies are sensitive to this. Even so, things can go wrong and one company reported the misfortunes of a manager transferred from his native country to another just before war broke out between the two. This situation may be harder to avoid than appears; if he had not been transferred, and war had not broken out, the failure to promote him would have been represented as discrimination. Another example of the personal demands which can be placed on an international manager was in a company operating in an area of revolution. This firm kept expatriates working in their plant long after it was economic to do so, and in spite of hardship and danger, to convince the local population (and anyone else who might be watching) that they did not lightly walk out on their commitments, and were prepared to restart if the situation changed. Such environmental factors condition the frame of reference of the international executive, as do the ability or otherwise of the firm to negotiate its environment.[24]

During the summer of 1966 advertisements were appearing in newspapers in several European countries for employees in one particular subsidiary of an international firm. These advertisements said, in effect, that the nationality of the applicant was unimportant, but he must speak at least two languages—those of the home and host countries. Seldom is the importance of nationality belittled publicly in this way. On the contrary, as we have seen, the current trend is towards an exaggerated respect for nationalism; but the pressures the other way have also been noted, and are illustrated by this example. Skill and knowledge form a stronger bond than nationality. If nationality is less important than is often suggested distance seems to be more important. These days much is said about the 'air age' and the telephone, and indeed no one doubts that it takes less time to get across Europe than it does to get across London, but the two journeys are not yet done with the same facility. What the multinational company still lacks is easy communication. You cannot, yet, wander into a colleague's office or meet him casually in the corridor if there are several hundred miles and an international frontier between your offices. The international company has difficulty in providing facilities for the regular informal chat. This adds an element of formality to its processes. Where the less formal arrangements are found there is constant travel. It is not surprising, therefore, to find that the companies which reported somebody like an outstanding leader also reported the most travel. While there was one company which notably combined formal procedures with constant personal contact, it is a safe generalisation that the reverse is normal.

Another reason why the overseas operation cannot be treated in the same way as an operating unit in the home country is because of the legal implications arising from the fact that it is generally a subsidiary—a legal entity —rather than a division. This combines with the fact that appointment to top management in the subsidiary is likely to be more permanent than that of general manager of an operating unit at home. The result is that the subsidiary management form a group which plays a part in the organisation for which there was no reliable precedent before the foreign business developed. This is not to overlook the difference that exists in most companies between the legal and the operating structure; it is to say that subsidiary management can use the legal situation to support their case for different treatment if they so wish.

Finally we have seen that some firms now investing abroad are large and complex organisations, and an intimate knowledge of how the firm works is an essential qualification for effective managers. Not only do they need to know the procedures and policies of the parent organisation, but they also need to know the limits of their discretion as subsidiary managers. In the view of several to whom we talked, a close understanding of the methods and personalities at headquarters was necessary for the smooth functioning of the organisation. To attain this takes time and experience with the company which the foreign national needs to acquire whatever his prior qualifications. The process can be helped by a scheme of management development going beyond the local subsidiary, and including opportunities of working for a period in head office or in another affiliate. The relevance and importance of this to the control process should not be underestimated, for it is the managers who form the effective link between one company and another. Their knowledge, attitudes and influence mainly determine the efficiency of the subsidiary. Without their cooperation it cannot be an operative part of the group.

In some firms, therefore, the disadvantages of an expatriate manager are felt to be outweighed by the advantages. On this subject one executive said:

Our own practice in the companies we have established is to send out one of our own people, as opposed to recruiting a man locally. Finding the right man is not of course easy because, in the case of European countries, a good knowledge of the language is necessary and it is obviously difficult to find this combined with the necessary managerial experience. In our opinion though, it is more important to have a man whom you know, who knows the business, rather than to recruit a local man and train him up. Communication is made very much easier, particularly bearing in mind in the early stages when overseas close liaison with the sponsoring company is necessary, hence a man on the spot who knows to whom to go for all the many things he wants is at great advantage over a locally recruited manager.[25]

As we saw earlier, this is not the only view but it shows one reason why expatriate managers survive in spite of all the forces against them.

5.6 Other considerations

In the course of this discussion on role problems, it has become apparent that there is sometimes a connection between the resolving of a role problem, such as that of executive succession or nationality, and the establishment of cohesion among the ranks of managers in the firm. The system of appraisal also can be used to improve links within the company, especially where a method which forces face-to-face confrontation is used. The general consideration of personal contact within an international company is a significant one. For instance, the practice with regard to meetings varies greatly from company to company, between those which have a considerable network of regular meetings and those that only bring people together for *ad hoc* gatherings to discuss specific problems. 'We do not need to travel long distances to tell one another that we have nothing to report', was one point of view, whose opposite was: 'The most valuable meetings are precisely those where the agenda is thin.'

Clearly there are different concepts of the purposes of the meetings involved here. The former view is concerned simply with the solving of the immediate problem, the latter with the building up of a unified management throughout the company, a 'cohesion' which could facilitate more informal methods of control. Similarly with visiting, this could be on a planned basis to enable regular contact, or it could be *ad hoc* for the purpose of solving immediate problems. In one company, for instance, either the chief executive or his deputy was always on tour, while the other held the fort at headquarters. In another there were regular conferences in each trading area. To these come the head office staffs concerned with the product groups in that area and the managements from the local subsidiaries. These conferences made detailed plans for the region as well as being intended to forge closer personal links within the firm. They also provided a training ground for less experienced managers who were thus sucked into the system. The word 'sucked' is appropriate here for the company, which appeared to have a considerable international cohesion with a system that was not too close. The local operation was described as 'revolving in its own orbit', but the pull towards the centre was very strong.

One use made of regional centres was to organise regular meetings for subsidiaries in their regions. In one American firm managers from the larger subsidiaries were brought into monthly conferences at the regional headquarters, and these conferences were attended by the President of the company. Typically the conferences lasted three days, of which one was spent examining company matters in general, and the other the affairs of specific product groups. Another firm used its European centre similarly with numerous regular meetings, such as a twice-yearly conference for local finance directors. Thus some companies built up strongly cohesive groups of managers, who came to know one another well. As another example, a British firm reported a regular visit from the chief executive and a senior functional manager to each subsidiary each year. In this company the managing directors of the subsidiaries came to head office once in two years, and the exact time between the visits had been the subject of considerable thought. Another British company had been at pains to build up a team of executives around the world who would know each other well. This was intended to produce a 'system of consultation combined with delegation of responsibility over a wide area, with the result that rapid decisions are made at all levels'.

This was also the objective of other companies which consciously set out to establish personal links across frontiers; but in some complaints were heard on the amount of time managers spent away from their desks, and the heavy load of coordination as opposed to constructive activity. Another company ensured the constant meeting of executives from different countries by setting up international committees for a number of purposes; one of these was an international council on which sat the chief executives of the larger subsidiaries. They had gone further than most we saw in developing what has earlier been described as contractual management. This firm also brought together, twice a year, up and coming managers from all over the world, for a course which included discussions with members of the board.

We have already indicated that the growth of wider expectations by the overseas management is both met and fostered by the development of an 'international grade'. It can therefore be expected that the drawing power of the centre, always strong for the expatriate manager, will become stronger for the foreign executive as well. Both are likely to make statements in the form of 'absence does not make the heart grow fonder', and wish to keep frequent contact with head office. Hence calculations made about the number of times a manager should be brought to the centre may well have to be made for foreigners as well as for expatriates. Growing feeling on this subject was observed when visiting subsidiaries. This can be expected to weaken the authority of the national managements and to contribute to the problems of the buffer situation. The authority of the local management is weakened because subordinates no longer depend on them for career prospects which are seen more and more in international terms. At a time when companies are showing greater sensitivity to local differences, this development is one that is likely to produce impatience with these differences.

In considering a manager's expectations the prestige of belonging to a company whose stock is safer than that of many governments must not be overlooked. This and other factors are producing new group patterns, so that the expatriate and the foreign manager can no longer necessarily be set against one another. There may well be some from each group working for policies which internationalise the company more. This may be expected to affect the pressures on the organisation of the company as a whole, indeed may well have influenced the coming into existence of the D type organisation. For there has always been a group at head office of returned expatriates, among whom some have developed a strong respect for local customs. These are the ones who gravitate most readily towards international divisions. They are natural allies for the foreign manager, if he sees his career in purely local terms. Once he begins to see his career in international terms his attitude on this subject is likely to change. He becomes less keen for his national subsidiary to be treated as a special case.

Foreign managers with international expectations may then form a pressure group against emphasising concern for national differences, and international avenues of promotion will become very important. Indeed, if the company has not yet developed these, this is considered a grievance and a cause for increasing turnover among managers.[26] Thus role relations and the role-set are becoming less affected by international frontiers; and this combines with their greatly increased complexity in the D type organisation. The pressures just discussed can be seen in terms of a changing pattern of relationships within this role-set. The pressures of this changing pattern are at present being met by techniques such as 'job enlargement'. This phrase and others such as 'management development' can be interpreted in terms of these role problems. They may also be seen as the organisation's method of meeting the exaggerated expectations built up during recruitment in a competitive labour market. The greater expectations lead to the more complex organisation needed to fulfil them and supply the necessary motivation. This, in turn, produces the complex set of role relations, expressed in such ways as multidirectional reporting and the blurring of the distinction between staff and line. ('Our function alternates between the advisory and the mandatory according to the performance of any given subsidiary,' said one regional product manager.) This in turn produces the pressures towards personal cohesiveness just described. 'Knowing head office', or 'knowing the company' were phrases which constantly recurred in conversations discussing the essential requirements of the foreign manager.

These 'requirements' have been examined in this chapter in the light of the needs of the elaborate organisations under discussion. Some of the companies in our sample face their managers with very exacting demands; they also place them in positions of some delicacy and potential conflict. As we have seen, the international nature of the organisation itself gives the executive a complicated role to play. The problems that have been mentioned here include the network of relationships known as the role-set.

We have seen how difficult it is to reduce this, and how any reductions may themselves produce new problems. We have also seen the influence of particular situations, such as that described as the *buffer situation*. On the other hand the same firms are experimenting with new patterns of management, and in particular with new means of appraisal. These seem to allow a greater freedom for the individual to make his own contribution by fitting the organisation to him rather than the other way round; and this is occurring within the greater centralisation shown in the previous chapters.

PART II
Financial policies and practices

The complex nature of the finances of multinational companies present problems in setting out a discussion of their financial policies and practices. Funds are usually available to such firms in a number of different locations, and in a variety of forms. Similarly, they have a number of means available to them to transfer funds within the group. Thus, as an example, a bank loan made to one national subsidiary of a group may be re-loaned to a fellow subsidiary in another country, or even used to pay dividends to the shareholders of the parent company. In the larger organisations the relationships are obscure, and it would usually be impossible to establish any direct or meaningful link between specific sources and uses of funds. As a starting point, we have decided to focus our discussion primarily on what takes place at the level of the subsidiary in the multinational company.

Finance available to foreign subsidiaries may be classified under two broad headings according to where it originates. These are: (1) local sources of finance—the cash flow generated from the subsidiary's operations, and the external finance obtained in the host country; and (2) foreign sources of finance—those obtained outside the host country.

We shall see in more detail below that the bulk of the funds employed by subsidiaries to finance their various needs are from local sources.[1] The largest single source of funds is from their cash flow, consisting of the retained earnings and depreciation allowances; this provides on average about 60 per cent of their financial needs. The second largest source of funds is what we have termed local external finance. This includes funds raised through the sale of securities, borrowings from financial institutions or other organisations, grants from governmental or regional authorities, and increases in trade credit, tax liabilities, and various other items. From an individual subsidiary's point of view, both these categories of funds are of 'local' origin; on the other hand, these funds can become a foreign and external source to the group, and thereby enter the corporate pool of capital. This happens when the subsidiary grants trade credit or makes loans to affiliated companies in other countries, or remits earnings to the parent company.

Normally a small proportion of a subsidiary's funds originates from foreign sources, that is, from outside its own country. Often these funds are channelled directly through the parent company, but they may arrive via affiliated companies. Essentially of three types, foreign external finance appears on the subsidiaries' accounts as: (1) issued capital; (2) intracompany loans; (3) intracompany trade credit. The origins of this category of funds are manifold, and a

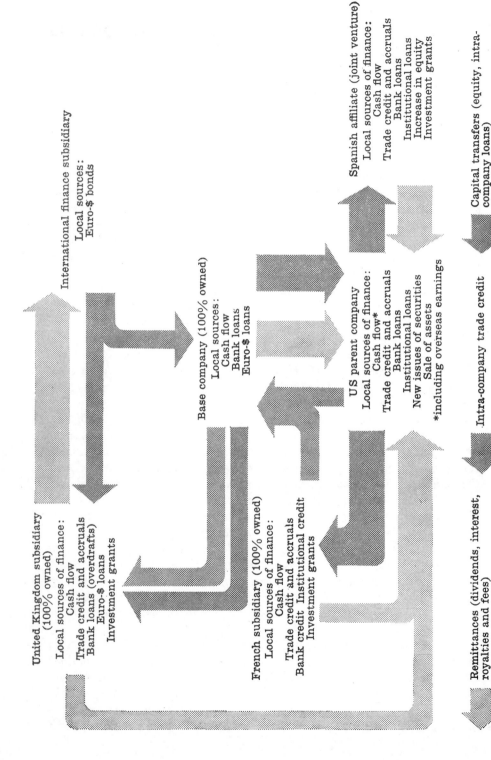

United Kingdom subsidiary
(100% owned)
Local sources of finance:
Cash flow
Trade credit and accruals
Bank loans (overdrafts)
Euro-$ loans
Investment grants

International finance subsidiary

Local sources:
Euro-$ bonds

Base company (100% owned)

Local sources of finance:
Cash flow
Bank loans
Euro-$ loans

French subsidiary (100% owned)
Local sources of finance:
Cash flow
Trade credit and accruals
Bank credit Institutional credit
Investment grants

US parent company
Local sources of finance:
Cash flow*
Trade credit and accruals
Bank loans
Institutional loans
New issues of securities
Sale of assets
*including overseas earnings

Spanish affiliate (joint venture)
Local sources of finance:
Cash flow
Trade credit and accruals
Bank loans
Institutional loans
Increase in equity
Investment grants

Capital transfers (equity, intracompany loans)

Intra-company trade credit

Remittances (dividends, interest,
royalties and fees)

reflection of the parent company's methods and policy of finance, and its attitude towards foreign investment. They might be part of the parent company's cash flow, or the sale of securities or other sources of finance in the home country. Funds could also arise from overseas sources—that is, from a third country. These might include the proceeds from the sale of Eurodollar bonds placed in international markets, and borrowings from overseas financial institutions. Foreign external finance could also include funds provided by affiliated companies in a third country—either supplied directly as a loan or trade credit, or indirectly as remitted earnings and other payments.

There are four principal ways to transfer funds within a multinational group. These are: (1) charges against income such as interest, royalties, management and various technical service fees; (2) after tax payments, namely dividends; (3) capital transfers in the form of subscription to equity capital, and extension and repayment of intracompany loans, including trade credit; (4) the transfer price mechanism involving the discretionary pricing of intracompany transfers of goods and services at a higher or lower amount than for value received. Besides providing a means to transfer funds, charges against income and the transfer price mechanism (see (1) and (4) above) can also furnish a way to shift profits between members of the group. This possibility has also led to the creation of the base company[2] which, located in a low-tax or low-risk country, can sometimes be used to siphon off profits, or to help finance group needs, or both.

This brief introduction suggests the extent to which the finance of different national subsidiaries in multinational groups can be interrelated and complex. This is brought out in more detail by fig. II.1 which in schematic form shows some of the sources and flows of funds in a hypothetical multinational company. Some of these are straightforward. Capital is transferred from the parent company to the subsidiaries, and dividends and other remittances are returned. However, some intracompany trade is routed through the base company, allowing it to accumulate funds (and profits) by varying the credit terms and prices on these transactions. Thus we see in this example that funds and profits are being transferred from the French subsidiary via the base company to its United Kingdom affiliate. The base company is also transferring funds to the parent in the form of remittances and loans. Besides this, there is an international finance subsidiary which is lending the proceeds of a Eurodollar bond issue to the United Kingdom subsidiary. Although all of these flows would probably not be occurring simultaneously, the diagram shows that funds can have their origin at various levels of the organisation—and can arise and be transferred in many different ways and forms.

To what extent can these funds be considered to belong to a single corporate pool of capital? Theoretically, the multinational company should be able to obtain funds where capital is the most readily obtainable and the least costly, and from there move it about the company wherever required. However, in

Introduction to Part II.1 Schematic flow of funds within a multinational company *practice such a goal is difficult to achieve for at least two reasons. First, to make such a goal operative implies thorough and detailed planning and control over the subsidiaries' financial operations—which as a consequence necessarily reduces their autonomy, and can have a high administrative and behavioural cost. Secondly, there are various officially imposed constraints on both the movement of funds to and from most countries, and on the proper reporting of profits. Therefore, funds and earnings can only be transferred freely within certain limits. We will return to look at these problems in more detail in the two chapters which follow.*

Arguments in support of international business have often cited the profitable investment of capital as one of the chief benefits accruing to the host country. The statistics published on direct investment made overseas by American, British and other companies are indeed impressive and show the magnitude of these flows. During recent years the extent of this investment has been one of the factors creating serious balance-of-payments problems for some of the investing countries (and also perhaps certain problems of a different sort for the recipient countries). Much has been written on this problem, and it is a subject in which we are only indirectly concerned in this study. However, from our data it appears that, at least in the highly developed industrialised countries of Western Europe, and in the United Kingdom in particular, once the initial investment has been made and the subsidiary begins to get established, it is typically able to obtain sufficient local finance and the direction of the capital flows tends to reverse.

As we suggested earlier, the bulk of foreign subsidiaries' finance, in the aggregate, is from local sources—from within the host country. This is brought out by the data shown in fig. II.2 below. The percentages shown are after payment of dividends and other types of remittances to the parent company. Indeed, if dividends had not been paid, the 115 foreign subsidiaries in the United Kingdom would have had more than enough (111 per cent) local finance to meet all of their investment needs. A much larger sample of US-owned manufacturing subsidiaries in Europe, which includes a mixture of both new and long-established firms, could have financed some 98 per cent of their investment from funds obtained in Europe if they had not paid dividends.

From fig. II.2 it can also be noted that funds from the parent or affiliated companies have supplied a relatively modest proportion of the subsidiaries' total needs, especially those of the American-owned. This is especially striking when compared to the amount of earnings they have remitted during the period. Over the eight years from 1960 to 1967, outflow of capital in the form of dividends made by the 115 foreign subsidiaries was over $1\frac{1}{2}$ times the inflow of funds from their overseas parent and affiliated companies;[3] for the US-owned subsidiaries in this group the ratio was nearly $3\frac{1}{2}$ to 1. Other data covering the European subsidiaries of American companies from 1960 to 1965 confirm this with out-flows exceeding inflows by about 25 per cent.[4] It should be noted that we are speaking of capital which is a source of funds to the subsidiary, excluding that

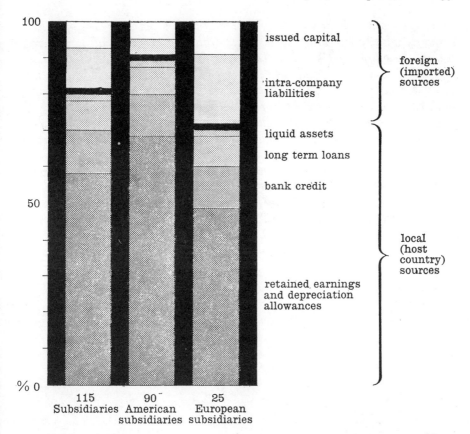

100

issued capital

·intra-company
liabilities

} foreign
(imported)
sources

liquid assets

long term loans

bank credit

50

local
(host
country)
sources

retained earnings
and depreciation
allowances

% 0

115   90⁻   25
Subsidiaries American   European
         subsidiaries subsidiaries

Introduction to Part II.2 Sources of finance for foreign subsidiaries in the United Kingdom, 1960–67

which might have been used to purchase the company originally or to take up an outstanding interest from minority shareholders. If we look at individual subsidiary behaviour in this respect, we find that almost two-thirds of those in the sample had a net outflow of funds to their parent or affiliates during the period. And this does not include other payments such as royalties, fees or interest which in some subsidiaries can be very large sums indeed. The significance of this—at least from a balance-of-payments standpoint—is that, once they are established, foreign subsidiaries tend to be net exporters of capital.[5] One might also conclude that controls over investment such as those recently introduced by the United States and France, and those long in effect in the United Kingdom will not impossibly handicap the development of foreign operations.

    The financial policies and practices we shall discuss in this section are, for the most part, decisions of head office. Policies are designed to achieve the goals of the parent organisation—though these may conflict with those of the host country, or even with the subsidiary's goals. If these policies are to be operative, authority must be pushed upwards and centralised at a point where an overall view of the entire group's activity can be obtained, the key variables evaluated, and decisions taken. Logically this can be only at head office; and, in fact, this was the case in virtually all the companies studied. While the subsidiary management might be invited—indeed, expected—to make their recommendations, the final decisions on most financial questions rest almost always with the parent company. This is a feature of the increasing centralisation that we have already noticed.

As a final note of introduction, we want to emphasise that no generalisations can be made in this area without qualifications. The policies and practices adopted by multinational companies to finance their foreign subsidiaries are too numerous, too complex, and too much in a state of change to be compressed into a few sentences. Their striking characteristic is diversity. Management has shown no lack of imagination or ingenuity in seizing the opportunities and in facing the risks of foreign investment.

6

Internal finance

6.1 Introduction

The largest single source of funds to companies is almost always their cash flow—that is, net profits after tax and provisions for depreciation. This source provided the foreign subsidiaries in our sample £1,080 million before payment of dividends, or over two-thirds of all funds used by them between 1960 and 1967. The ratio was somewhat higher for the group of American-owned companies in the sample whose cash flow represented over three-quarters of their total financial resources. As a comparison, cash flow provided some £12,020 million or about 69 per cent of the total finance of British quoted companies in manufacturing during the same period.

Just under two-thirds of this cash flow was reinvested by the subsidiaries in our sample, a slightly smaller percentage than that ploughed back by the quoted companies in the United Kingdom. From the data in table 6.1 below, one can see that this reinvested portion of cash flow—which we shall henceforth call internal finance—provided about three-fifths of the investment needs of companies operating in the United Kingdom.[1] It will be noted also that a very large proportion of the investment in fixed assets by the companies in our sample was financed from internally generated sources. Compared to the rate achieved by private industry in several European countries where a ratio of 65 to 70 per cent has been averaged during most of the same period, the record of the foreign subsidiaries has been impressive.[2] Also of note on table 6.1, funds arising from depreciation were substantially larger than retained earnings and comprised over 60 per cent of internal finance. Looking at it another way, depreciation provisions financed a little over one-third of gross investment, and retained earnings a little under one-fourth.

A somewhat similar picture emerges when the performance of individual subsidiaries is analysed. From a total of 914 subsidiary years of funds flows studied, internal finance provided over 100 per cent of total investment needs in one out of every three years; it supplied more than half of total investment needs in three out of every five years.

The extent to which subsidiaries are able to rely on internal finance depends on a combination of three factors: their rate of growth; their

Table 6.1 Internal finance

	1960–67 115 foreign subsidiaries in the UK £m	%	1960–67 British quoted companies £m	%	1960–65 American-owned subsidiaries in Europe £m	%
Internal finance of which:	724		8491		2220	
Retained earnings	283	39	3304	39	807	36
Depreciation	441	61	5187	61	1413	64
Net investment of which:	1225		13,779		4000ᵃ	
Fixed assets	823	67	10,910	79	2800	70
Net working capital	402	33	2869	21	1200	30
Internal finance as a % of net investment		59		62		56
Internal finance as a % of investment in fixed assets		88		78		79

Note. Data covering American-owned subsidiaries in Europe has been adapted from figures appearing in *Survey of Current Business*, November 1965 and October 1963. Dollars have been converted to sterling at the rate of £1 = $2.40.

a. Net investment is the sum of fixed assets and net working capital. The latter has been calculated by subtracting an inferred current liabilities figure (equal to one-half of the *funds from abroad* which was given in the original data) from the sum of inventories, receivables and other uses of funds.

Table 6.2 Relation of growth of assets to internal finance (115 foreign subsidiaries in the United Kingdom, annual averages 1960–67)

Internal finance (% of net investment)	Average annual rate of growth of net assets				
	less than 10% p.a.	10% to 15% p.a.	15% to 22% p.a.	more than 22% p.a.	Total
1. Less than 40	6	4	8	11	29
2. 40 to 61	3	8	10	8	29
3. 61 to 83	11	7	5	6	29
4. More than 83	10	8	6	4	28
Total	30	27	29	29	115

profitability; and their remittance policy. Taken individually, the effect of growth on internal finance was more apparent than the other two factors. From the data on table 6.2, for example, one can note that subsidiaries growing most rapidly tended to finance less from internal sources, although there were a few exceptions.

Among these, the four which grew more than 22 per cent p.a. and also relied heavily on internal finance (more than 83 per cent) showed the following growth, profitability, and dividend payout ratios for the 1960–67 period:

	Growth—average p.a. increase in net assets	*Profitability— net profit as a % of total assets*	*Dividends— % of net profits*
	%		
Subsidiary US-39	39	24·2	75
Subsidiary US-48	41	13·3	2
Subsidiary US-53	29	11·7	4
Subsidiary US-76	22	23·7	76

From this it might be concluded that the ability of the subsidiaries to meet investment needs from internal sources of finance declines as their rate of growth increases, unless profits are unusually high, or dividends (and other remittances) are relatively modest—and sometimes a combination of both. Of these three factors, perhaps none comes more completely within management's control than remittance policy. It is to a discussion of the main determinants of this policy that we now turn.

6.2 Remittance Policies

OVERALL CONSIDERATIONS

Studies of dividend policies of companies quoted on a stock exchange have shown that usually a good deal of importance is attached to what was done in the past, modestly modified by future hopes. In practice the majority favour payment of a stable dividend which bears a more or less constant relationship to expected *long-term* profits. This means that the amount of dividend paid will not be increased until management is reasonably sure that an increase in earnings is permanent. Conversely, a given dividend rate will be maintained in the face of falling profits until it becomes clear that an earnings recovery will not be soon in coming. Therefore, while this may cause the *payout ratio* (dividends expressed as a percentage of current profit) to vary in the short term with fluctuations in earnings, over the long term a more or less fixed percentage is aimed for. In British industrial companies this ratio has been around 50 per cent during recent years;[3] in American companies, it tends to move from plateau to plateau, and during the 1960–64 period averaged around two-thirds of earnings. For a number of reasons, stable, modest dividends seem to be valued more highly by shareholders than unstable, liberal dividends; and mindful of such a shareholder preference, a primary consideration of most companies is to maintain a stable and consistent pattern of payments.[4]

In the case of foreign subsidiaries, while it is difficult to generalise, maintenance of a stable dividend—that is, stable in terms of long-term profits, of what was paid in the past, or with regard to nominal capital—appears to be a much less important requirement. Somewhat less than a fifth of the wholly-owned subsidiaries in our sample could be said to pursue anything approaching a constant policy; indeed, in the great majority, the pattern of dividend payments was highly erratic. We may take, for example, the record of distributions made by a United Kingdom based, wholly-owned American subsidiary which produces office equipment and computers;[5] it is typical of the majority of foreign subsidiaries:

Year ended 30 November	Dividend payments (gross)	
	Amount (£000)	% of issued capital
1956	608·6	1521·5
1957	747·8	131·2
1958–60	nil	nil
1961	3324·2	583·2
1962	1399·4	245·5
1963	nil	nil
1964	1012·3	177·6
1965	nil	nil
1966	3596·1	630·9

Further, from the data in table 6.3 below, we see that, quite the reverse of the usual practice of quoted companies, dividend payments by subsidiaries appear to be fairly sensitive to short-term changes in profits. Among the 483 subsidiary years in which those in our sample paid cash dividends, a stable dividend was paid in seventy instances (15 per cent of the time) whereas the profit was stable within ±10 per cent of the previous year in 141 instances (or 29 per cent of the time). A similar test of dividend stability in British quoted companies showed a stable dividend 62 per cent of the time when profits were 'stable' only 28 per cent of the time.[6] Subsidiaries in our sample also tended to raise or lower dividends much more in response to changes in profit than did the British quoted companies in the above-mentioned study. Whereas the subsidiaries raised dividends in more than two out of every

Table 6.3 Relation of changes in dividend payments to changes in profits (only wholly-owned subsidiaries paying cash dividends)

Annual profit change	Annual dividend change			
	Raised	Unchanged	Lowered	Subsidiary years
$\geq$ 10% increase	149	28	36	213
Stable within $\pm$ 10%	72	19	50	141
$\geq$ 10% decrease	47	23	59	129
Total subsidiary years	268	70	145	483

three occasions that profits increased, the quoted companies raised them on only a little more than one out of three occasions; a cut in dividends coincided with a drop in profits about half the time for the subsidiaries, but only in one out of every four occasions for the quoted companies. Fifteen per cent of the subsidiaries paid no dividends at all during the eight years covered, and over a quarter of them paid a cash dividend in no more than one out of the eight years. This can be compared to only about 7 to 8 per cent not paying dividends in a sample of over 1,500 American companies, and most of this small proportion were also not making profits.

However, if the pattern of dividend payments of foreign subsidiaries is unlike that of quoted companies, dividends nevertheless absorb a large and in the aggregate similar proportion of earnings. From the data in table 6.4 we can see that despite a certain diversity between the various groups, subsidiaries have paid out between 40 and 60 per cent of their earnings as dividends during recent years. Subsidiaries, unlike quoted companies for the most part, use other means besides dividends to remit earnings to their owners. One might argue whether these other means—royalties, fees, interest, and trade—should be properly considered a remittance of earnings, for, in principle, they constitute payment for specific services or goods received by the subsidiary. But since many of these have no easily determined market value, companies have considerable latitude to charge the subsidiaries with more (or less) than the fair arm's-length value of the contribution. Indeed, since they are a before-tax charge against profits, and often are not subject to withholding tax, some companies have ample incentive to substitute these returns for dividends. Moreover, in some instances, they may be easier to remit than dividends.[7] But with regard to what actually happens, as noted elsewhere in this study and by others, the evidence is vague if not contradictory. Many companies tend to look on royalties and fees as marginal income. The cost of the research and development which went into developing the patent or process was already covered

Table 6.4 Dividend payments by selected groups of foreign subsidiaries (dividends expressed as a percentage of current earnings)

	1960	1961	1962	1963	1964	1965	1966	1967	8-year average
1. US-owned subsidiaries (manufacturing)	%	%	%	%	%	%	%	%	%
Total worldwide	47	60	57	43	48	54	53	58	54
Common Market only	44	55	69	50	57	86	61	73	59
United Kingdom only	54	68	66	50	56	49	58	61	60
2. UK-owned subsidiaries (all industries)									
Total worldwide	46	51	46	45	47	41	40	42	45
North America only	46	48	51	56	53	50	40	39	45
Western Europe only	58	42	60	56	73	58	56	56	57
3. European-owned subsidiaries (all industries)									
US only	53	41	44	47	29	32	52	42	43
UK only	36	109	47	46	44	37	44	44	51
4. 115 foreign subsidiaries in the United Kingdom	58	80	65	51	60	46	53	49	58

Sources. Data covering US-owned subsidiaries and foreign-owned subsidiaries in the United States have been adapted from figures published in various issues of *Survey of Current Business*. Data covering UK-owned subsidiaries overseas and European-owned subsidiaries in the United Kingdom have been adapted from figures published in the *Board of Trade Journal* annually on overseas investment.

by the domestic sales of the product and, in the words of one executive, royalties paid by the subsidiary were 'pure gravy'. In some subsidiaries, management felt that the charges were fair; they might be even less than on an arm's-length basis.[8] Others complained that they were being over-charged. On balance, it was our impression that most companies consider royalties, fees and other types of payments to be either a substitute for, or supplement to, dividends as a means of remitting earnings. In any case, at least for American and British subsidiaries, dividends represent the principal method used to remit earnings. During the 1961–67 period, US-owned subsidiaries in Europe remitted almost double the amount in dividends as in royalties and fees, although these latter payments have seen a more regular and rapid growth, probably because they are keyed to sales rather than to profits. British-owned subsidiaries in Europe returned almost four times more in dividends than royalties or fees during a similar period.[9] For both American and British companies, remittances in the form of interest have been only a small fraction of dividends or royalties.

Policies pertaining to the disposition of subsidiaries' earnings are influenced by a number of factors, and a list of them might run as follows:

1. The effects of taxation on the various types of payments, and on their timing;

2. The attitude of management in the parent company towards exchange risks and other hazards associated with doing business in a foreign environment;
3. The need for finance in the subsidiary;
4. The needs of the parent company for funds;
5. The degree of local autonomy or presence of a minority shareholder group in the subsidiary;[10]
6. Regulations concerning remittances of earnings imposed on the parent company by the home country.

While generally all these factors receive some consideration, some companies place greater emphasis on certain of them than on others, and even in a particular company priorities will change over a period of time. This being said, it was our impression that tax considerations, attitudes towards risk, and the investment needs of the subsidiary are given especial attention by most companies.

INFLUENCES OF TAXES ON REMITTANCES

In a study made in 1967 of remittance practices in thirty American corporations with European subsidiaries, it was reported that a quarter of them assigned 'the highest importance to the tax consideration'. Between 40 and 50 per cent of the companies interviewed paid 'considerable' attention to the tax effect on these decisions; in other words, it was either the most important or of equal importance to all other factors being weighed. Some companies are continually probing and searching for new schemes to reduce their taxes, and go to great length to minimise their impact on the repatriation of earnings. In some cases, this includes developing computer programmes to work out the optimum payments mix.[11] But, obviously, a substantial proportion of companies do not regard the minimisation of taxes as of such concern, and some merely look on them as a 'cost of doing business'. In one company it was said that 'the tax picture changes so rapidly' that it was not worth while to accord it a very high priority when determining remittance policy.

Which is the more rational approach? If significant tax differentials exist between the various countries in which the corporation operates, efforts to minimise taxes by substituting other types of payments for dividends may pay off in increased profits. The scope for this is diminishing, however, for there is a strong tendency among the industrialised countries at least to equalise the effective tax burdens and eliminate or reduce differentials which formerly existed. But even the presence of a differential does not necessarily create the means to avoid taxes. In many countries, the income received by a corporation from its foreign subsidiaries is subject to the full rate of domestic tax even though this income may have already been taxed to the subsidiary by the host country. Normally double taxation is avoided through the provisions of bilateral tax treaties between countries. In addition to these provisions, or instead of them, unilateral tax relief may be available in the home country. In some of these, notably the United States and the United Kingdom, the parent company receives a credit for the foreign taxes paid by the subsidiary which it can apply against the relevant domestic taxes on the same earnings. There are certain special provisions made in the case of some of the developing countries which tend to increase the amount of the credit available to the parent—the objective being to help encourage foreign investment in those areas. Some countries permit the excess credits which arise in cases where foreign taxes are higher than domestic rates to be applied against other foreign income earned that year, or to be carried forward or back to use in other years.[12]

As we have noted, dividends are almost always subject to more taxes than other types of payments *prior to their receipt by the parent company*, for they are paid out of taxed income and usually are further subject to a withholding tax imposed by the host country as well. But if these other payments escape most or all taxation in the host country, it follows that they also provide correspondingly little or no tax credit which can be applied by the parent company against the taxes it will have to pay when it receives this income. By substituting royalties and fees for dividends, taxes are not necessarily minimised, but merely shifted from one country to another. Where the total effective tax rate of the subsidiary was less than that of the parent company, there is no tax advantage in substituting other types of payments for dividends. If the taxes are not paid by the subsidiary in the host country, then they will be paid by the parent company when remitted. Where the subsidiary's tax rate is higher, the advantages of substituting other forms of payments depend on whether or not the excess credits can be applied against other foreign income. If, as is the case in the United Kingdom, the credits are computed separately for each country (the per country limitation), the parent company cannot use the excess credits and it would appear to be sensible to try to remit as much earnings as possible by some other means than dividends.[13] On the other hand, US companies can calculate the credits on a combined basis for all the foreign income (interest payments excluded). In this case, if the excess credits can be fully applied, there is no tax advantage from substitution. Therefore as a general rule we can say that the only time there is a tax advantage in substituting other payment schemes for dividends is when the parent company is taxed at a lower effective rate than the subsidiary, and is unable to use any excess tax credit which might arise. This is perhaps the most typical situation.

Because of the incidence of withholding and other taxes on remittances, it is usually more advantageous for a subsidiary to reinvest its earnings directly if it needs finance than it is to remit them and then have to ask the parent company for fresh capital to be returned. However, there are certain circumstances where repatriation of earnings followed by their return could result in a lower overall tax bill. This might arise if the remittance would provide excess tax credits which could be used to offset tax liabilities from other foreign income, providing, of course, that the parent company could compute its credits on an overall basis. This situation is not frequent, and companies normally find they have relatively little possibility to use their excess credits. As a result, companies try by various devices to shift their earnings in order to hold down the taxes on their foreign income to at least the domestic rate. This attempt is euphemistically called 'tax planning'.

Not all countries use the credit method to provide tax relief on foreign source income. In some, notably the so-called tax haven countries, but also in France and Italy and others, foreign dividend income is totally or partially exempted from domestic taxation, or subject to a reduced rate (although this does not necessarily apply to other payments). In countries where none of the above methods for providing tax relief are used, foreign taxes can generally be at least deducted as an expense from domestic earnings.

Taxes can also cause variations in the timing of remittances such as when the applicable tax rates are scheduled to be changed. Such a situation occurred, for example, in France during 1968 when many US-owned subsidiaries were instructed to delay dividend payments in order to take advantage of a reduction in the withholding tax rate from 15 to 5 per cent which came about as a result of a change in the bilateral tax treaty between France and the United States. However, the sudden uncertainty created by the general strike and social disorders in France during May 1968 caught many of these companies by surprise. This triggered a sudden wave of payments as the risk factor abruptly replaced taxes as the primary consideration in their decisions concerning dividends.

- Complications sometimes arise over remittances of royalties, fees, and other payments where the tax authorities suspect them of being substituted for dividends or otherwise used in such a way that taxes are avoided. Thus the parent company may be assessed with an additional tax if the authorities believed that, say, loans to its subsidiaries did not bear a realistic rate of interest. A slightly different problem may be encountered by the newly established subsidiary which for lack of funds is unable to remit royalties, fees, or interest owed to the parent company. In such circumstances, the parent could elect not to charge its subsidiary for these services until the latter's cash flow could support them. However, there is a danger that when payments were started, the local authorities could argue that they had not been paid previously, and thus were a disguised dividend subject to withholding tax, and so forth. In order to avoid such risk, many firms allow these charges to accrue as intracompany liabilities from the outset, even though they are aware that actual payment may not be made for a long time. Certain difficulties can arise with this practice. A British-owned subsidiary in France which had suffered losses since its beginning neither paid nor accrued royalties on parent company patents and processes it was using. The management believed that if these charges were accrued, they would appear on the parent company's accounts as an intracompany advance which the Bank of England might ask to be repatriated. If this happened, it would be expensive, for to return the funds to France when they were needed, the francs would have to be purchased on the investment dollar market at a costly premium.

Another type of tax problem arises over the reporting of foreign earnings that are *reinvested* by the subsidiaries. It will be recalled that generally additional taxes must be paid when earnings are remitted, and this raises the question whether or not foreign earnings (which remain overseas) that are included in the parent company's consolidated financial statements should take into account the additional taxes which will eventually have to be paid. If they are deferred, reported profits will be exaggerated, and this can have a favourable effect on the market value of the parent company's shares. This assumes that the shareholders will put some value on unremitted earnings, though this does not imply that they will value them as highly as repatriated earnings.[14] The conservative approach would be to set up a reserve account for future taxation, and make a charge against the foreign earnings *as if* they were repatriated.[15] Such an approach would help to avoid a break in the earnings' growth at some future point when remittances were started. This can be a material problem for companies if the foreign earnings in question are large in proportion to the overall earnings of the corporation. One company in our sample was in a dilemma over this matter. They had been consolidating the earnings of two very profitable subsidiaries which because they were located in a development zone paid very little local taxes. These subsidiaries were approaching a position in which they could start remitting earnings to the parent company; but if they did so, the consolidated profit was likely to drop due to the incremental taxes[16] (in the absence of offsetting higher profits) by over 20 per cent.

The discussion and examples above show some of the complexity of the problems encountered when determining the tax implications of the various methods of payment. While companies may not always obtain tax savings by substituting one form of remittance for another or by changing the timing of these flows, a company that fails to examine the detailed implications of its particular situation does so at its peril.

INFLUENCE OF RISK ON REMITTANCES

For many companies, the attitude of their management towards risk is the overriding determinant of their subsidiaries' remittance policies; and there are probably times when this is the most important consideration of every company. Operating in a foreign country normally brings commercial risks of a degree and kind quite unlike the usual types with which managers are familiar, and even the familiar ones are more difficult to evaluate. Differences in the economic, legal, and social institutions, and in language and culture complicate and delay their understanding of foreign business environments. Distances are greater; communications are often slower and less dependable; movement may be restricted by prejudice and lack of understanding. In these circumstances, certainty of judgment, sureness of touch, and ease of execution are hard to come by. It is no wonder that businessmen complain sometimes about not having the feel for foreign operations that they have at home. Caution is a natural reaction.

We cannot follow now all the repercussions of these uncertainties. In financial matters it seems to be the exchange risk that preoccupies management most. This came out of interviews with company executives, and in the analysis of our data. It has also come out in the findings of others. Briefly stated, it amounts to a fear of loss both from fluctuation of exchange rates, and from restrictions on the repatriation of earnings and capital—dangers which generally go hand in hand, and are far from being remote even in the most highly industrialised countries.

Memories are still fresh in the minds of many international businessmen of the severe restrictions prevalent in most European countries during the early postwar years of recovery. In many countries, these controls have been removed or greatly relaxed, but for those with long experience in foreign operations, the spectre persists. Indeed, events in the United Kingdom and France in the latter 1960s are enough to show that the fear is well founded. The past and the possible future are reflected in the remittance policies of some companies. Hence, some will still seek formal agreements with the exchange control authorities even in the host countries of Europe to assure the repatriation of earnings from their investments. Other companies feel it politic to maintain continual and stable remittances. The view put forth below by the Treasurer of IBM World Trade Corporation was echoed in several companies we interviewed:

> Once a company establishes a profit policy which is accepted by the host country, this policy should be a continuing one. The best policy would provide for remitting some profit, no matter how small an amount, if for no other reason than to establish a precedent. This should be done even if the parent company has to return this amount to the subsidiary as a capital contribution or loan.[17]

However, such considerations seem to be more relevant to the developing countries than to the industrialised nations of Europe. Indeed, relatively few companies appear to have pursued such a policy (that is, to maintain a stable payment pattern) for their European subsidiaries—a little more than a sixth of those in our sample, and about a quarter of the companies observed in another study.[18]

A common rule of thumb used by some firms to protect themselves against exchange losses is to not allow their subsidiaries to accumulate surplus cash, and this practice causes some subsidiaries to pay out most earnings each year. In the study of thirty American companies cited above, it was reported that a number of them (one-sixth) directed their European subsidiaries to remit from 90 to 100 per cent of their earnings each year 'in order to minimise the possibilities of exchange loss and any uncertainty about how much control we have over these funds', as one manager explained.[19] Our sample of British-based subsidiaries showed a similar pattern. During the period reviewed, 13 per cent of the 115 subsidiaries remitted over 90 per cent of earnings, and a quarter of them remitted over 70 per cent. In 1964 and 1965 when devaluation by the United Kingdom was widely felt to be imminent, the reaction of subsidiaries to this threat was interesting. Close to 30 per cent of those which had paid no dividends during the previous three or four years did so then. Twenty-five out of the 115 remitted *over 100 per cent* of their earnings, i.e. by paying dividends out of accumulated profits. In a few cases, virtually all of the retained earnings were remitted.[20]

As an example of what often takes place in these cases, we were told by the finance director in one of the American-owned subsidiaries we interviewed in Britain that, normally, they would determine the amount of the annual dividend remittance at year's end when the operating results were known. However, when in 1964 it was felt that the risk of devaluation had become serious, the parent company directed them to pay interim dividends. These, added to the subsequent year-end remittance, totalled about 130 per cent of that year's earnings. This executive had first joined the company during a previous sterling crisis, and at that time had been instructed to take the same action. One of the first letters which he had received from his superior in New York had contained a checklist of 'points which we are sure you will have already considered', namely, the various measures he was to take to minimise the company's exposure to exchange loss. Such checklists were referred to by several of the companies we studied.

If the response to the risk of exchange loss was an increased outflow of earnings, it would seem to follow that this would be accompanied by a reduction in the subsidiaries' stock of liquid assets. In 1960, as a group, the 115 subsidiaries in our sample held 9·4 per cent of their assets in the form of cash and government securities. By 1967 this ratio had declined to 3·7 per cent.[21] In 1960 nearly as many of the subsidiaries held large cash reserves (defined here as over 10 per cent of their total assets) as those which held only negligible amounts. The picture changed during the period and in 1967 only about 15 per cent of them had liquid assets exceeding 10 per cent of total assets. Although the accumulated cash reserves were used by some of them during the period to help finance large remittances—those which paid out the largest portion of their earnings tended to reduce their cash reserves more than those making more modest returns—this was not the only reason. Many were growing rapidly and drew on previously accumulated cash reserves as well as on other means of finance. In addition, their earnings tended to drop off, particularly during the last two or three years of the 1960–67 period. Nevertheless, a number of subsidiaries, by the use of supplier credit, bank loans, and a substantial cash flow, managed not only to remit most of their earnings while continuing at the same time to invest heavily, but also were maintaining relatively large amounts of liquid assets to finance future expansion—and perhaps also future dividends.

There are, of course, other ways that companies can protect themselves against losses from fluctuating exchange rates and restrictions on repatriation of earnings. These include matching financial assets in the subsidiary with local financial liabilities, providing intracompany loans instead of equity where possible, not capitalising reinvested earnings (so that dividends can be paid out of reserves), and through the transfer price mechanism. We shall look at these in some detail in a subsequent section.

INFLUENCE OF FINANCIAL NEEDS ON REMITTANCES

In some companies, the investment requirements of the subsidiary take precedence—even to the point that dividends might not be paid at all, earnings being totally reinvested. This appears to be a fairly normal practice during the early stages in a subsidiary's development where typically investment needs are large, and local borrowing facilities are not yet well established. It will be recalled that about 15 per cent of the subsidiaries in our sample paid no dividends during any year over the period reviewed, and another 10 per cent paid dividends in only one of the eight years. In all but three or four cases these were relatively new firms, a large majority of them were expanding extremely rapidly, and several were operating at a loss, at least for several years. Under such conditions, it is not difficult to understand why the needs of the subsidiary were given a priority over remittances. A few companies continued this policy after the initial build-up. An executive of an American-owned subsidiary in the United Kingdom expressed this as 'head office expects us to stand on our own two feet', and proudly added that 'they neither send us any capital nor do we remit any dividends'.[22] This meant, in effect, that their growth would be geared to what finance could be generated from operations or borrowed locally. A policy of reinvesting all earnings would seem to make good sense if the rate of return of the subsidiary were higher than that of the parent company. While the sample is too small to draw any firm conclusions, it is interesting to note that two-thirds of the subsidiaries which paid a dividend in only one year or not at all during the period (but obviously which *did* make profits) showed a greater return on their capital (net worth and intracompany liabilities) than the parent concern.

H

Such an approach might also be interpreted as another indication of the importance given to the risk factor by some managements with regard to their foreign operations. A parent company would sooner risk a subsidiary's earnings in new projects than provide it with additional fresh capital from the corporate coffers[23]—an attitude which can be likened to the gambler who is prepared to reinvest his winnings in new bets, but will not take any new money out of his pocket.[24]

Pursuit of an investment-oriented policy by a subsidiary that was nevertheless remitting earnings could be expected to cause the size of the dividend payments to fluctuate from year to year depending upon prior claims on its cash flow, and also upon its ability to raise funds locally or from other sources. An example of this can be illustrated by the case of a large British consumer goods company which had been operating overseas for many years. The financial director explained that 'for us, the first requirement is meeting the overseas companies' needs'. They are market-oriented, and if there is a market they are expected to make the most of it, including finding the funds necessary to finance new production capacity. Afterwards, they meet head office's need for dividends.' He added, however, that they were able to pursue such an approach and still repatriate a relatively large amount of earnings in the aggregate because they had many foreign subsidiaries, and their investment needs were not large or frequent.

Given this approach, an increase or decrease (provided they are significant) from one year to another in a subsidiary's rate of investment could be expected to have an inverse effect on the amount of dividend that could be paid. In practice this relationship appears to be more direct when investment is reduced than when it is increased; that is, companies seem to be more inclined to raise their dividend payments when their rate of investment drops off than reduce dividends when investment needs increase.

Table 6.5 Relation of changes in investment to changes in dividend payments (only subsidiaries paying dividends during period)

	Change in investment rate*		
Dividend change	Large increase	Large decrease	Subsidiary years
Dividend cut	73	55	128
Dividend unchanged	29	20	49
Dividend raised	96	96	192
Subsidiary years	198	171	369

* Large increase or decrease in investment rate defined as a ± 50 per cent change from the level of previous year.

It will be observed in table 6.5 that where investment in fixed assets and working capital was sharply increased, dividends were raised more often than they were reduced. Subsidiaries were able to do this by drawing on their cash reserves or by borrowing locally in some cases; in others, the parent company provided finance.[25] It should be noted that there were some unusual considerations which undoubtedly entered into many of the decisions; during part of the period, in 1964 and 1965 especially, companies anticipated devaluation of sterling, and in consequence many stepped up their remittances while at the same time continuing their investment programmes. Also, a change in the US tax rate caused some of them to alter their pattern of payments; both factors could tend to obscure the relationship between investment and dividend payments.

There emerges a picture of increasing complexity where the effect of taxation, attitudes towards risk, and the financial requirements of the subsidiary can lead to a variety of different payment schemes and patterns. But if these are perhaps the most important factors which influence the disposition of earnings of foreign subsidiaries, as we have already noted, there are other considerations which bear on, and which may even dominate, these decisions.

OTHER INFLUENCES ON REMITTANCES

In cases where the parent company pays out a large proportion of earnings to its shareholders, it follows that, in general, a relatively large and regular flow of earnings would be required from its overseas subsidiaries, at least in the aggregate. In other words, the dividend policy of the parent company would reflect on and determine the level of appropriation of the subsidiaries' earnings, perhaps even on a *pro rata* basis. There is some evidence to support this. In the aggregate, British quoted (parent) companies and their foreign subsidiaries paid out fairly close to the same percentage of earnings—52 per cent and 45 per cent respectively on average between 1960 and 1967.[26] American corporations, in the aggregate, paid out a larger proportion of earnings (about 66 per cent) than the whole of their overseas subsidiaries (54 per cent) during the same period. Part of this difference might be attributed to the large increase in US investment during this time, that is, a relatively large number of new and rapidly growing subsidiaries whose internal needs for funds prohibited the payment of much in dividends; part of it might be laid to other forms of remittances in lieu of dividends. Looking at the individual company practice, while there was considerable diversity of experience, large payout ratios in the parent company tended to be associated with large payout ratios in the subsidiary. In about two-thirds of the cases where the parent company paid out 50 per cent or more of earnings, their subsidiary did likewise. Where the parent company paid little or no cash dividends (although in several cases a stock dividend was paid) the subsidiaries also tended to pay little or no dividends.[27] Some of this apparent similarity is no doubt due to coincidence, but there is nevertheless a certain logic for the parent company to meet its own dividend requirements (especially if they are large) from a *pro rata* appropriation of the earnings of all units, foreign as well as domestic, of the corporation. Such a policy seems inevitable in the long run, particularly where the foreign operations comprise a significant proportion of the corporation's overall activities.

A policy of maintaining a regular flow of dividends can help reinforce control over a subsidiary, particularly where this makes it dependent on the parent for additional finance. Indeed, this provides a simple straightforward method of control which is relatively easy to administer. Another factor which can influence remittance policy is pressure from the home government. As an example, the Bank of England tries to get British companies to repatriate about two-thirds of their subsidiaries' earnings—although, judging from the Board of Trade statistics shown in table 6.4, this objective has not been reached.[28] The motive for this rate of repatriation is, of course, to improve the British balance of payments. American companies are also subject to government efforts in this direction in order to achieve similar ends.

6.3 The transfer price mechanism

The setting of transfer prices provides the multinational company with an additional means of transferring funds and earnings in the pursuit of its various corporate objectives. It operates by the arbitrary pricing of intra-company transfers of goods and services at a higher or lower figure than for the value received—what might be called the 'fair' or 'normal' price. The concept is necessarily imprecise in many instances. At best, there is a considerable amount of subjectivity involved, and consequently, management's choice of a 'fair' price can lie between rather broad limits. Nevertheless, however uncertain the 'fair' price may be on occasions, the practical implications of manipulating prices are obvious.

Transfer prices are frequently used to minimise the corporation's overall tax burden. To illustrate, let us take the situation where a British company was exporting to its American subsidiary. At the time of writing this (1969), British companies were subject to a 45 per cent corporation tax on profits; US companies' profits were taxed at over 50 per cent. Under such a tax differential, it would appear to make good sense to try to increase the profits of the parent company at the expense of the subsidiary by pricing the exported goods as high as possible.[29] An obvious limitation, however, would be the tariff on the imported goods. Raising the export price will increase the customs valuation and a larger duty would have to be paid on entry than otherwise. At its worst, the result could leave the subsidiary with insufficient margin to operate profitably, or risk pricing itself out of the market. In the opposite situation where the subsidiary is taxed at a lower effective rate than the parent company, the objective would be to export the goods at as low a price as practical.

The transfer price mechanism can also limit exchange losses where chronic inflation or balance of payments difficulties are a continued threat. Often where countries are suffering from such economic problems, dividends and other remittances are restricted, and transfer prices may provide the only means for the investor to repatriate earnings. Intracompany transfers of goods and services to the subsidiary in question would be marked up in price; alternatively its exports to affiliated companies would be priced as low as possible. Even if, as a result of this pricing, earnings were increased in a country with a higher tax rate, this might well be better than having profits blocked, or eroded away by a continual depreciation of the local currency. This device can operate even where intracompany trading is virtually nil. For example, one of the companies interviewed had extensive investments in Africa and South-east Asia. It periodically found that it could not repatriate the earnings of certain subsidiaries. Although there was little or no trading with these subsidiaries, the manufacturing plant was of a unique and complicated design available only from the parent company. Thus when explaining that they had not received a dividend from a couple of subsidiaries for a number of years, the financial director added: 'but do they ever pay through the nose when they have a mechanical breakdown!'

In addition to the use of transfer prices to shift profits for tax purposes and to alleviate exchange losses, companies also use them for other purposes. First, they are fixed in some situations to provide finance to a foreign subsidary, especially during the start-up period. Imports from the parent or affiliated companies are priced low to give the new subsidiary both a competitive advantage and, all things being equal, a greater profit margin. Thus, it is expected, the subsidiary can sooner 'stand on its own feet'—as it is frequently expressed—by being allowed to accumulate profits earned by this means. A similar approach is sometimes used when a subsidiary has losses which could not otherwise be carried forward against taxes.

Secondly, another purpose might be to understate profits in circumstances in which a high rate of earnings might induce customers or the local authorities to ask for a price reduction, or the labour unions to ask for wage increases. Several of the companies interviewed believed it politic to keep profits of certain subsidiaries at modest levels—generally where employee representatives had access to the accounts or where there was a profit-sharing plan. The threat of government intervention to reduce prices is also real as the pharmaceutical industry in a number of countries has found, and as Kodak, Procter & Gamble, and Unilever discovered in the United Kingdom. Whether these companies had much scope to shift profits, much less whether they would have explored such a policy, need not be considered. It is the example of a high rate of profit attracting attention and inviting investigation that is important. In countries where there is a risk that large profits might be regarded as exploitive and arouse political emotions, it would seem in the company's best interest to allay local anxieties by shifting a portion of earnings to another affiliate. This might be most subtly accomplished by transfer prices.

Thirdly, among the various objections to joint ventures, one frequently raised by many companies was the necessity to share earnings with foreign partners—especially where the parent company believed that it has contributed more than its fair share to the development and success of a subsidiary. This reluctance gives a parent company an incentive to shift profits to itself or to a wholly-owned subsidiary, and even where it does not elect to do this, it is often suspect. Foreign partners, on the other hand, seek transfer prices that increase the earnings and dividends from their investment. In such circumstances conflicts are bound to arise. A common solution is to use arm's-length prices such as would be charged to a distributor, or failing that—typically in cases involving semifinished goods and components—a price based on manufacturing cost plus a formula markup. Whatever the method adopted, it needs to be agreed upon when the joint venture is set up.

Companies emphasised in our interviews the opportunities of transfer pricing mentioned above. They also pointed out that, like many good things, it also entailed numerous drawbacks and constraints: it could be expensive to administer; it could cause the company to run foul of the tax and customs authorities at home and overseas; perhaps worst of all, as we described earlier, it could have serious repercussions on management, and on the company's control system.

In any of the stratagems mentioned above, the company's scope is, in practice, limited by the income tax and customs authorities. Much of the taxation of foreign business activity covers new ground, and the law has often developed in an *ad hoc* fashion to plug loopholes in existing legislation. In general, it is exceedingly complex and difficult to apply to the continually changing problems which arise in international operations. Tax officials are often insufficient in number to cope with the volume of work, and find themselves facing situations for which they are not adequately trained or experienced. In such circumstances, rulings can be arbitrary and may be unreliable as precedents for a company to follow in the future. Consequently many companies find themselves time after time embroiled in disputes over tax matters of various descriptions.

Where exports to subsidiaries are suspected of being priced too low, companies can come under fire on the grounds that they are avoiding income taxes. In the United States, the Internal Revenue Service has the power to reallocate income among members of a corporate group.[30] The threat is both particular and general. As an example of a particular matter with which the tax authorities are prepared to concern themselves, one could cite the question of whether research and development expenditure should be recovered in the transfer price or through a royalty based on turnover. As an example of the general position we might take the fact that in the United States the burden of proof is put on the company to demonstrate that the method of transfer pricing is reasonable. But the criteria which will be used to judge the 'reasonableness' of the transfer price are vague, and attempts to use former rulings as guidelines have not always been successful. In the United Kingdom, besides the Inland Revenue, the exchange control authorities also can have a say in the matter when it is suspected that a company is exporting capital via a low transfer price to an overseas subsidiary.[31]

The customs authorities can also be expected to challenge transfer prices where they believe that companies are attempting to escape paying the full amount of duties required. In our interviews, executives told us that they almost always had problems with the customs officials who questioned prices at which they invoiced shipments to their subsidiaries. Where the customs officials have refused to accept the invoiced price, the duty valuation has been raised to what is considered appropriate—by as much as 100 per cent in some cases we were told, though usually the increased assessment was smaller, from 10 to 30 per cent. There are often few guidelines in this area either. One executive in the French subsiding of a large group complained that 'We never know where we stand with the *douane*. Sometimes they let the things come in, the next time they'll slap a 25 per cent mark-up on the invoice.' In another company, we were told that it was futile to argue with customs. They just paid the additional duty and put up with it. 'Otherwise,' this executive explained, 'they're liable to tie up the goods in customs forever when we need them in the plant.'

It is somewhat ironic that it was at customs where many disputes over transfer prices occurred, for from the interviews it appeared that avoidance of duties was one of the lesser reasons for manipulating prices. For example, one company told us that it has had disputes with both the Canadian and Australian authorities over prices on exports to its affiliates in those countries. In both cases, it was claimed, the motive for invoicing at a low price was to help finance their subsidiaries since capital exports were virtually impossible from the United Kingdom (the exports were from the company's affiliates in Europe). The Australians alleged that an attempt was being made to avoid duties, and went so far as to dispatch someone from the local consulate to check over the company's books and cost records. The Canadians believed that the company was dumping, and insisted on a higher duty valuation. Here, too, the company's cost records were audited, which might imply that they would be willing to accept a transfer price based on cost. Whether or not these examples are typical, they demonstrate some of the external constraints on a company's discretion in these matters. In general, the company has to prove to the tax inspectors' satisfaction that the prices which it puts on the transaction are justified.

Given the opportunities to shift funds and profits by use of the transfer price mechanism, how important an instrument is it to multinational companies in practice? We gained the impression, though it needs further testing that, for operations in Europe and North America, it is less useful than is often believed as a means to avoid taxes, particularly for US companies.[32] This is because in order to produce any real tax savings, there would have to be an optimum combination of substantial tax differentials between countries, adequate profit margins, and perhaps low customs duties. Further, as was pointed out above, unless the parent company's tax burden is less than that of the foreign subsidiary, any tax advantage arises mainly from the fact that taxes are deferred, not reduced. Although most American companies admitted that they had at one time juggled their transfer prices in the hope of avoiding taxes, they claimed that they have abandoned such practices in Europe. The principal exceptions were for transactions with certain of the less developed countries whose tax rates were extremely high (India and Pakistan were frequently mentioned—their tax rates on distributed profits are 70 per cent or more). In these cases, they would try to siphon off some of the profit from the ultimate sale either in the parent company or in an affiliate such as a trading company in a low-tax country. The case of British companies was different. While few executives admitted that they tried to shift profits between the various units of the group, they appeared to have some incentive to do so. Since the UK tax rate on earnings is 45 per cent, and since British companies are not allowed to apply excess tax credits from one country to earnings from another, their earnings from overseas investments are almost always taxed at over the domestic rate. Under such conditions, it would at least make good sense to shift as much profit as possible to the parent company or to an overseas base company which enjoyed low taxes. A similar argument could be made for the Swiss international groups.

Nevertheless, given the narrowing tax differentials and the many external and internal complications which arise from discretionary pricing, many companies questioned seriously whether there was enough in it to be worth while. In the purely domestic company the problems surrounding transfer pricing are complex and difficult enough, but with the added complexity of foreign operations, they can take a quantum leap in magnitude. If they are to be used to shift earnings or funds about the group, the expected gain needs to be large for the extra trouble to be justified.[33]

6.4 Conclusion

If we try to generalise, we may say that policies concerning the use of subsidiaries' earnings could be placed somewhere between two opposite poles:

1. *A remittance-oriented approach*—that is, dividends and other methods of payments take precedence, with the investment needs of the subsidiary treated as a residual. From the subsidiary's standpoint, this would in many cases imply a rather rigidly sustained policy of appropriating a certain proportion of its earnings each year; it might mean maintaining a continual flow of payments in the face of fluctuating earnings; it might entail payments out of reserves; it might mean deliberately keeping its earnings to a minimum by means of inflated prices on transfers of goods and services to it from the parent and affiliated companies. In any event, considerations other than the investment needs of the subsidiary would be preponderant.

2. *An investment-oriented approach*—that is, the investment needs of the subsidiary have first call on earnings, and the residual is available for remittance. From the subsidiary's point of view, this would be the more flexible approach; indeed, where the subsidiary earned a higher return on its capital than the parent company, it would be the most rational, other considerations notwithstanding.

In practice it would be rare to find company policies that could be labelled so. neatly. First of all, there is considerable evidence that many companies pursue elements of both approaches simultaneously. They would obtain a regular flow of earnings in the form of royalties and fees, interest, or possibly by means of transfer prices, and would adjust the level of dividend payments to current investment needs in the subsidiary, or for other reasons. Probably the majority of the subsidiaries in our sample fall into this category. Secondly, companies may take different approaches to the problem in each subsidiary. If it were essential in a particular country to maintain a regular flow of dividends to ensure future repatriation, then this would be the most appropriate policy to adopt. In countries where this was irrelevant a more flexible approach would perhaps be more suitable. Tax considerations may make it advantageous to repatriate dividends from one subsidiary, royalties and fees from another, and use transfer prices in a third to realise its earnings. Thirdly, a company may change its policy over time with respect to a given subsidiary, moving from an *investment-oriented* approach during the development period to a *remittance-oriented* approach as the subsidiary matures and has less need for finance or is able to obtain adequate funds locally. There are also circumstances where the parent company has little choice but to take a fairly rigid approach and repatriate a regular and perhaps large flow of earnings from its overseas investments.

H*

In view of these considerations, probably the best that can be said is that companies approach the reinvestment or remittance decision in different ways at different times and under different conditions. Whether one approach is more rational or otherwise superior to the other can only be determined in the context of a particular company's operations and requirements.

External finance

7.1 Local external finance

The second largest source of funds used by foreign subsidiaries after their cash flow is found in the various types of finance available locally in the host country. These take a wide variety of forms, ranging from the short to the long term, from debt to equity, and also include such items as capital grants and subsidies from local official agencies, leasing, factoring and other special types of finance.[1] The bulk of this consists of relatively short-term obligations—trade credit and tax accruals, and bank credit.

In discussing this kind of finance we must necessarily refer to the special arrangements of particular countries. The traditions, policies and practices of financial institutions and businesses are predominantly national in form and outlook. It would indeed be of great interest to make a country-by-country analysis of capital markets, banking systems, trade credit terms, investment subsidies, and so forth. But this is clearly too vast a subject to be encompassed in this study. There is, besides, a considerable literature on these subjects, and we have included a number of references in our bibliography. We shall therefore limit ourselves to indicating rather than exhaustively describing these differences.

Our emphasis is on company behaviour. Consequently, we shall mainly be concerned with the attitudes of executives towards local debt and other sources of capital which are available within the country where they are based, but which require formal negotiation with a lender in order to be obtained. The spontaneous sources of credit, those which arise more or less automatically as a result of being in business, will only be touched on briefly.[2]

SPONTANEOUS CREDIT

This source—mainly composed of trade credit, deferred taxes, and miscellaneous accrued liabilities—tends to vary in amount with changes in business activity. As a firm's production rises, trade credit is likely to rise also, more or less proportionally. Tax accruals are more closely related to profits, although in some countries there may be a time lag because of the nature of the tax system. Trade credit can also vary as a result of management policy. For example, suppliers might be paid immediately to benefit from cash discounts if the company were highly liquid. Conversely, companies in financial difficulty or otherwise short of cash might try to obtain longer payment terms from suppliers. In general, however, companies will tend to conform to the usual terms of trade in their industry. The forces of custom are strong and there is the danger that deviation from the norm may be interpreted as a sign that all is not well. Because of this, it is unlikely that subsidiaries can do much to stretch trade credit to help finance their needs. Moreover, companies also grant trade credit to their own customers, and for most this use of funds easily outweighs the amount of trade credit received. In our sample, only a small handful of the subsidiaries received more trade credit than they gave during the period 1960–67.

LOCAL SOURCES OF DEBT

For the subsidiaries in our sample, local borrowing of all types amounted to slightly over 19 per cent of their combined total assets in 1967. This ratio is slightly less than the proportion of debt carried by British quoted companies during the same period, but appears to be significantly greater than that for subsidiaries in the Reddaway study, although the data are not entirely comparable. For both the subsidiaries in our sample and the British quoted companies, the ratio of indebtedness increased by more than two-thirds that of the beginning of the period. As a source of finance, the subsidiaries relied on borrowing to about the same extent as the quoted companies— over one-fifth of their total funds obtained between 1960 and 1967.

What factors determine the extent to which local debt is used by foreign subsidiaries? Obviously, the need for finance is one element, and this, as we have seen, depends on such things as their rate of investment, profitability, and retention of earnings. A small number of subsidiaries in our sample— about one-eighth of the total—used no debt at all during the years studied. With only one exception these were all very profitable, and most were able to finance the bulk of their requirements from internally generated funds. Another, perhaps the most important, factor is the cost and availability of local credit facilities. In some countries local credit is scarce, and this, aggravated on occasion by government monetary policy, tends to raise interest rates. Of course, interest rates are not necessarily always higher in the host country than those at home. Although this has been generally true for United States investors, those based in other countries—Italy and Germany, for example—have found overseas interest rates frequently lower than those at home. Table 7.1 gives an indication of the range of interest rates for various categories of credit to prime borrowers during recent years. Besides being more expensive, local debt facilities may be restricted to certain uses or even denied to foreign subsidiaries by the authorities in the host country. Nevertheless, both cost and availability of local debt are usually relative considerations which are measured in terms of the subsidiary's alternative sources of finance—funds from the parent company. These can be used as a supplement or substitute where local debt is not available in the amounts required, or deemed to be too expensive.

Table 7.1 Interest rates and yields on loans to prime borrowers in Europe and North America

	Average rate of interest p.a. *1961–69*	
Short-term bank loans	*low*	*high*
(*a*) Domestic currencies	%	%
US dollars*	5·30	10·00
British pounds	4·50	9·00
Canadian dollars	5·50	8·50
German marks	6·00	9·00
French francs	5·85	9·75
Italian lira	7·50	8·25
Dutch guilders	5·50	8·50
Swiss francs	5·50	6·50
(*b*) Eurodollars	4·38	12·19

	Average yield p.a. 1965–69	
Long-term corporate bonds and notes	*low*	*high*
(a) Domestic currency issues	%	%
US dollars	4·73	7·74
British pounds	7·22	10·85
Canadian dollars	6·05	9·10
German marks	6·97	8·20
French francs	7·22	8·65
Italian lira	6·60	8·41
Dutch guilders	6·36	8·60
Swiss francs	4·58	5·55
(b) Eurodollar issues		
European companies	6·18	8·23
US companies	5·96	8·10
Convertibles	4·25	6·00

Source. Morgan Guaranty Trust Company, *The Financing of Business with Euro-dollars*, New York 1967, table 4, p. 27; table 6, p. 29, and *World Financial Markets*, New York, 1969, tables iv and v.

* US short-term bank loan interest has been computed assuming a 15 per cent compensating balance must be maintained. This has the effect of increasing the nominal rate by about 18 per cent.

What constitutes an acceptable cost of local debt varies between companies and over time. Although domestic interest rates, the liquidity of the company, and its perceived cost of capital all have an influence, the attitude of its management towards exchange risk appears to be a major factor. Many companies try to have the financial assets—debtors, cash balances, and marketable securities—of their subsidiaries matched or exceeded by liabilities denominated in the local currency. To the extent that this is achieved, the parent company is afforded protection against exchange loss from inflation or devaluation (it may even be able to realise a windfall gain). But this may be costly where local interest rates are high. Normally, most companies will be prepared to let their subsidiaries borrow in the host country at a higher rate of interest than they would need to pay at home—this premium being considered a worthwhile additional cost for the protection it would give against a possible exchange loss. Perception of such risks varies over time with the course of events in a particular country, and therefore management can be expected to attach a greater premium to local debt when future convertibility of the local currency is in doubt. This undoubtedly goes a long way towards explaining the spectacular increase in the use of local debt—mainly bank overdraft—by foreign subsidiaries in the United Kingdom in 1964 and 1965. Those in our sample increased their bank borrowing during those years at well over twice the rate as shown by the British quoted companies.

From table 7.2 it can be seen that the number of subsidiaries which used local debt in 1964, 1965, and 1966 also increased markedly over the previous three years. Many which had used no debt up to then borrowed relatively large sums between 1964 and 1966. Fear of devaluation by the United Kingdom prompted them to borrow locally in order to repay intracompany loans or increase or speed up payment of dividends, and in some cases both. And where many subsidiaries had been financing their investment needs with funds from their parent, they now substituted bank overdrafts and long-term loans. A similar reaction by foreign subsidiaries was seen in France in May 1968 following the general strikes and the resulting economic uncertainties.

There may be other factors which have a bearing on the use of local debt by foreign subsidiaries. It is possible that the management of some parent companies have an aversion to debt on rather intangible grounds, and thus exclude it as a source of finance. However, apart from an allusion to the desirability of 'a clean balance sheet', i.e. no debt, by one company treasurer, we found little evidence of this attitude.

In some companies, the parent management take the view that local debt stimulates the performance of subsidiary managers because it makes them more acutely aware of the cost of finance than if they were furnished with intracompany funds.[3] That this opinion is sometimes confirmed by those in the subsidiary can be illustrated by the following case. After the investment

Table 7.2 Use of local debt by foreign subsidiaries (long-, medium-, and short-term loans from all sources)

Year	*I* *Number of subsidi-* *ary years local* *debt was increased*	*2* *Total subsidiary* *years analysed*	*Relative fre-* *quency of local* *borrowing (col. I* *divided by col. 2)* %
1960	39	112	35
1961	51	113	45
1962	51	114	45
1963	53	115	46
1964	73	115	64
1965	83	115	72
1966	84	115	73
1967	68	115	59
Total for period	502	914	55

restrictions announced by the US government in January 1968, the French subsidiary of an American company was instructed by head office to borrow locally in order to repay a sizeable intracompany loan. The manager of the subsidiary was dismayed by the prospect of having to pay interest on this loan, and seemed quite unconvinced by the suggestion that the cost (real or imputed) to the parent company of the intracompany loan could well have been higher. His reaction was simply, 'my profits are all shot to hell'.

A parent company has sometimes an incentive to use local debt to im-prove the attractiveness of a project overseas by increasing the return on funds which it commits from its own resources.[4] Since, in many instances, additional debt incurred abroad has little or no effect on the overall capacity of the parent company to incur debt in its own country, this introduction of an element of gearing into the capital structure of the subsidiary has obvious merits.

Long-term debt

In most countries, and also in the United Kingdom, foreign subsidiaries have had somewhat limited recourse to local sources of medium- and long-term debt. The figures shown in table 7.3 illustrate this.

Taken as a whole, subsidiaries carried a substantially lower percentage of long-term debt in their financial structure than the quoted companies which operated under the same conditions. This trend persists, for during the period 1960 to 1967, the subsidiaries continued to raise proportionately less finance in this form than the quoted companies. Likewise, though they were operating in a different environment, the foreign subsidiaries of British parentage seemed also to use relatively less long-term debt in most countries.[5]

Table 7.3 Use of long-term debt by foreign subsidiaries (aggregated data)

	British quoted companies		115 subsidiaries in the United Kingdom	
	1960	*1967*	*1959*	*1967*
Gearing (% of long-term debt to total capital and liabilities)	8·3	13·6	7·1	8·6[a]
	1960–67		*1960–67*	
Long-term debt as a source of finance (% of investment in net assets)	14·3		8·3[b]	

a. The mean of the ratios of long-term debt to total capital and liabilities for each of the 115 subsidiaries was in 1959 2·2 per cent; in 1967 6·4 per cent.
b. The mean of the ratios of long-term debt as a source of finance for each of the 115 subsidiaries was 7·7 per cent between 1960 and 1967.

Close to half of the subsidiaries in our sample (54 out of 115) had long-term debt outstanding during at least part of the period covered by the analysis; forty-eight of these raised long-term debt during the period, and most for the first time. There were more fast growing subsidiaries among this group than on the average (two-thirds grew at a rate of 15 per cent or more per annum whereas about half of the total sample grew at this rate). Perhaps reflecting this larger need for funds, these subsidiaries also tended to borrow more frequently and in larger amounts from the local banks than did the average. However, whereas they used somewhat less intracompany debt than on average, they made relatively more use of equity capital. This shows a certain consistency, for in spite of the fact that long-term debt and equity capital usually come from completely different sources, they are normally prompted by the same need in the subsidiary: to finance investments of a permanent nature. If debt cannot cover the whole of this need the parent company can be expected to provide the balance as equity.

Besides, permission to borrow local long-term funds may be contingent on additional equity being invested by the parent company.

Many subsidiaries did not specify the type of debt instrument in their accounts, nor give much information about the terms. However, relatively few subsidiaries have been able to raise funds by a public issue of debentures,[6] and this allows us to deduce that the bulk of these loans has been private placements such as a loan from an insurance company or a pension fund, or a loan from a bank. The latter would probably be on medium term, say, three to five years, perhaps from the London branch of a foreign bank, and would be likely to be based on Eurodollars.

Why have foreign subsidiaries used considerably less long-term debt than quoted companies? One reason is that many subsidiaries are relatively unknown to local credit institutions, and do not have the necessary credit standing to qualify for such credits. Almost three-fourths of those which had raised long-term debt were larger than the average subsidiary in our sample, that is, with total assets of over £8½ million sterling. Besides this, most were long established and included some of the best-known names in British industry. Their size and the confidence established through years of association with banks and other institutions enabled them to tap sources of long-term capital that were not available to smaller, relatively new, and hence unknown subsidiaries—even where the parent company itself might be well known. There are cases, of course, where the parent company arranges financing through the local branch of its home (i.e. a foreign) bank, or when it provides a local bank with the necessary guarantees.

Another main reason why foreign subsidiaries have generally not made greater use of long-term debt is that they have been subject to discrimination by the local authorities who have been reluctant to give them permission to raise capital in this form, on the grounds that these are permanent funds which should be supplied by the parent company. This 'discrimination' appears to stem more from the local government's preoccupation with the country's balance of payments or lack of investment capital, and often both, than from any xenophobia. It is difficult to generalise on such matters, for conditions differ from country to country as well as over time. But some discrimination has been and still is an obstacle for the foreign investor in most countries. Probably only the USA, Canada and Germany among the major countries can be viewed as exceptions. Even in Switzerland long-term issues are closely regulated, but rather more to keep down interest rates than for other reasons.

In the United Kingdom, in particular, the principal concern has been the chronic balance-of-payments deficits, and controls over borrowing by foreign subsidiaries have been directed at protecting or increasing the country's reserves of foreign exchange more than anything else.[7] The general rule is that foreign subsidiaries should finance investment in fixed assets from funds provided by the parent company. In practice, as our figures mentioned earlier seem to indicate, the attitude of the British authorities, just as in the case of the repatriation of earnings, is reasonably flexible and pragmatic. Here again, each case is considered on its own merits, and though the authorities do not make known the criteria upon which their decisions are based, subsidiaries which export a large proportion of their turnover, or invest in regional development areas probably stand the best chance of having their requests met. Furthermore, permission to borrow long-term funds is often accompanied by certain constraints on the subsidiary's financial operations.

As one example of these, there may be restrictions imposed on dividend remittances. One subsidiary in our sample had the following note added to its accounts for 1962:

> When the £1,500,000 6¾% Debenture Stock was issued, an undertaking was given that, without prior reference to the Bank of England, [the company] will not distribute more than 50% of the available profits in respect of each of the financial years ending in December 1962 and 1963, and not more than 60% of such profits in respect of each of the financial years ending in December 1964, 1965 and 1966 . . .

Apparently permission was forthcoming, for this subsidiary paid out 55 per cent of stated earnings as dividends in 1962, none in 1963, but almost 80 per cent in 1964, 1965 and 1966. The motive behind the Bank of England requirements obviously is to discourage subsidiaries from using local debt to finance the remittance of 'excessive' amounts of their earnings which could be used for investment purposes. The control is not all-embracing in this respect. Another subsidiary which, in 1964, raised £1·8 million in long-term debt and an additional £900,000 in bank overdraft, paid out almost £3 million in dividends that year. Whatever the motives of the subsidiary (probably to beat the expected devaluation), such practice would seem to be shortsighted, and in the long run could lead to tighter controls on local borrowings by foreign subsidiaries. This case notwithstanding, most subsidiaries which had borrowed long-term funds followed a relatively modest remittance policy.

As another condition of raising long-term debt, the authorities may require that a portion of intracompany loans or earned surplus be capitalised. The reason is similar to that above—to prevent the proceeds of the loan from being used to remit funds (or at least to make it more difficult to do so). An interesting case suggesting such policy was the issue of £2 million of 8 per cent debenture stock by Burroughs Machines Ltd, the wholly-owned subsidiary of Burroughs Corporation, USA. Just prior to making the new issue, in September 1966, Burroughs increased its issued share capital from £570,000 to £5,000,000. This was accomplished by capitalising £1,572,814 of reserves, and by converting £2,857,186 of intracompany loans into share capital.[8] Therefore, where issued share capital had formerly represented only about 3 per cent of total assets, the operation brought this ratio up to over 26 per cent and reduced greatly its indebtedness to the parent company. Since Burroughs was undertaking a major investment programme, it was unlikely that it would have used the funds to repatriate capital to the US. Nevertheless, the fact that the loan and its reserves were capitalised seems to indicate that the Bank of England made it a prior condition to the issue.

As an alternative requirement for prospective borrowers, the authorities may insist that a proportion of the permanent capital be brought in from foreign sources, perhaps on a *pro rata* basis to match the long-term funds raised locally.[9] In some situations, the subsidiary may be allowed to borrow locally in proportion to the amount of local shareholder interest, with the consequence that, the greater the percentage of foreign ownership, the less can be borrowed in the host country.

In certain other countries, the obstacles encountered by foreign subsidiaries wanting to raise long-term debt have been more prompted by a relative scarcity of long-term funds than by currency problems. This has been the case of France during most of the period after 1958, although exchange difficulties once again became serious as a result of the May 1968 disorders and the ensuing economic uncertainties. If official controls over the French market for long-term funds have been somewhat relaxed over the years, it is still not easily accessible to a foreign subsidiary. Practically no foreign subsidiary has issued debentures (*emprunts obligataires*) in the French market during recent years—IBM France being an exception. And again in this case, as with Burroughs in the United Kingdom, IBM has been a major exporter and has invested heavily in the development areas. Investors in France have long been reluctant to subscribe to bond issues, and under these conditions the authorities do not seem prepared to allow foreign companies to compete with domestic borrowers for the capital that is available. The prospects of change could be summed up by the remark of a highly placed French banker: 'I doubt if we'll ever see the day that General Motors or DuPont compete with Citroën or St Gobain [for capital in our markets].'

On the other hand, in France as well as in Italy, Belgium and other countries, foreign subsidiaries can often obtain a term loan from one of the semi-public credit institutions under conditions comparable to those demanded of a domestic borrower. In France, this institution is the Crédit National which is the main source of term credit to the private industriel sector.[10] Comparable institutions in other countries, such as the Istituto Mobiliare Italiano in Italy and the Société Nationale du Crédit Industriel in Belgium, appear also to loan to foreign subsidiaries on the same terms as their domestic customers.[11] In practice, the criteria for granting these loans are—as in the United Kingdom—closely tied to the subsidiary's export record and the location of the investment in an area of high unemployment. The nationality of the parent company is held to be less important.[12]

Another important consideration for this type of loan, especially in France, appears to be the security that can be offered. If, as there is ample reason to suspect, lenders lay great stress when reviewing a loan application on the solvency and credit standing of the borrower, then the foreign subsidiary may sometimes actually have an advantage over local borrowers. Where the parent company provides a guarantee, there is little risk to the lender, and this tends to make the loan more attractive.[13] Even in 1964 and 1965 when there was a highly emotional and hostile attitude in France towards foreign investment, the Crédit National, which might be presumed to reflect closely official policy, continued to loan to foreign subsidiaries. According to a prominent French official closely associated with this financial institution, foreign subsidiaries putting up an approved project, and supplying ample guarantees have been permitted a more liberal debt–equity ratio than would be typical for most domestic borrowers. His personal feelings on the matter were reflected by: 'C'est déplorable, mais hélas, c'est comme ça!' But to ask otherwise could be, in effect, to ask the lender to turn away good credit risks in order to accept the poorer ones.

In summary, foreign subsidiaries appear to be somewhat at a disadvantage compared to domestic companies in raising long-term debt in the domestic capital markets of most countries. This is especially the case for a public issue of debt securities where generally the public authorities have been reluctant to allow them in the queue for new issues. On the other hand, there is a much more liberal attitude with regard to term loans from financial institutions—providing that the loan is to be used to finance a project considered to be in the national interest. In view of this, it is probably safe to say that if a subsidiary is to borrow on long term, the funds will have to be used to finance investment in an area of regional development, or to expand export capacity. Besides this, the subsidiary's discretion to remit dividends or to repay an intracompany loan may be limited. These are not insurmountable obstacles, however, for in practice, even in the United Kingdom during a period of exceptionally tight control on lending to foreign subsidiaries, those in our sample raised about 21 per cent of their external finance as long-term debt—a not insignificant source.[14]

Short-term bank credit

Short-term borrowing from banks—overdrafts, advances, and discounted trade bills[15]—furnish foreign subsidiaries with a sizeable part of their external finance. Table 7.4 provides an aggregate measure of this for our sample of subsidiaries, using British quoted companies as a yardstick for comparison.

Table 7.4 Use of bank credit in the United Kingdom by selected groups of companies (aggregated data)

	115 subsidiaries in the United Kingdom		*British quoted companies*	
	1959	*1967*	*1960*	*1967*
Bank credit as a % of total assets	3·9	10·7	3·8	6·3
	1960–67		*1960–67*	
Bank credit as a source of finance (% of investment in net assets)	12·7[a]		7·5	

a. The mean of the ratios of bank credit to total sources of funds for the 115 subsidiaries was 14·3 per cent.

While quoted companies were, relatively speaking, larger users of long-term debt, the subsidiaries have been much the larger users of short-term bank credit, especially in 1960, 1964, and 1965 where it accounted for almost a quarter of the total funds used. Tables 7.5 and 7.6 provide additional measure of the change in the use of bank credit by the subsidiaries

Table 7.5 Bank borrowing by foreign subsidiaries

Year	*1* *Number of subsidiary years bank credit increased*	*2* *Total subsidiary years analysed*	*Relative frequency of bank borrowing (col. 1/col. 2)* %
1960	33	112	29
1961	41	113	36
1962	39	114	34
1963	42	115	37
1964	61	115	53
1965	63	115	55
1966	59	115	51
1967	50	115	44
Total for period	388	914	43

during the 1960–67 period. There would have been probably more of an increase between 1964 and 1967 but for the fact that many subsidiaries were able to raise relatively more long-term debt then than during previous years.

There was a considerable diversity of experience among the many subsidiaries in our sample with regard to the extent they were indebted to the banks. The data in table 7.6 is of particular interest in showing the wide range in the amount of bank credit that individual subsidiaries have used—a variation obscured by the aggregated figures in table 7.4—and brings out even more clearly their shift to use more local debt during the eight years analysed.

A major reason for the increased use of bank credit during the latter part of the period was the attempt by many companies to hedge against an anticipated devaluation of sterling. This resulted in subsidiaries relying on local debt to finance new investment to a much greater extent than they had in the past. Besides this, of the subsidiaries which had the most bank debt outstanding in 1967 (those in the 3rd and 4th quartiles in table 7.6), more than half decreased their intracompany indebtedness during the previous

Table 7.6 Bank indebtedness of foreign subsidiaries[16] (individual subsidiary experience)

	1st quartile range	2nd quartile range	3rd quartile range	4th quartile range
Number of subsidiaries	29	29	29	28
Bank credit as a % of total assets:				
1. Beginning balance sheets	0	0	0 to 1·9	1·9 to 54·1
2. Ending balance sheets	0 to 0·5	0·5 to 8·6	8·6 to 21·0	21·0 to 43·5

Note. 'Beginning balance sheets' were in all but three cases for 1959. 'Ending balance sheets' were in all cases for 1967.

three or four years. For many the amount that was reduced, i.e. remitted to the parent or an affiliate, was substantial. One subsidiary, for example, completely repaid its intracompany loans which had been standing at over £3 million. To offset this large repatriation of capital, and to be able to maintain a high rate of investment, bank loans were increased by more than three times to almost £5 million. So as not to overdo it, the subsidiary did not pay a dividend that year.

On the other hand, increases in bank credit in order to remit larger dividends were less frequent. While a number of those which paid exceptionally large dividends in 1964 and 1965 also borrowed heavily from the banks, this did not appear to be the general rule. Indeed, those which borrowed the most from the banks seemed to pursue a more modest dividend policy than the group which showed relatively little bank indebtedness. In some instances this may have been due to the banks placing restrictions on dividends as a condition for the loan. But most of the explanation is that the majority of the subsidiaries who borrowed heavily from the banks were expanding rapidly and needed the funds to finance investment—not to increase dividends.

We asked bankers and subsidiary officials whether there was any discrimination against requests for bank credit from foreign subsidiaries such as generally appeared to be the case in long-term debt. The answer in most cases was: *usually not.*

First, many agreed that foreign subsidiaries may in fact have an advantage over a local company in obtaining bank credit. Among the criteria used by bankers to decide on a loan request, the security offered by the borrower is often the most important. If the parent company (or sometimes a third party such as a foreign bank) will provide sufficient guarantees, there is little risk attached to lending to a subsidiary, even if it is not creditworthy in its own right. The typical example of this situation is the newly established and yet unprofitable subsidiary which obtains finance from local banks where a domestic company (without such parental backing) would not.

Secondly, even under conditions where there are certain restrictions on the use of bank credit by subsidiaries, they seldom pose serious problems to the company concerned. Traditionally, bank credit in most countries is intended to meet short-term working capital requirements which are self-liquidating. This is the case in the United Kingdom where, at least in principle, banks are supposed to limit foreign subsidiaries to loans for such purposes. However, for both domestic companies and foreign subsidiaries bank loans are often not self-liquidating, and thus tend to become more or less permanent finance—though subject to periodic review. Further, they are frequently used to provide temporary 'bridging' finance which is normally intended to be funded with more permanent funds as soon as they can be suitably arranged. In practice, therefore, bank credit is put to such flexible and diverse use that even if it were not intended by the lender to finance investment in fixed assets, much less the repatriation of earnings and capital, it may often be used indirectly for such purposes. For example, of the 388 occasions that subsidiaries in our sample increased their bank borrowings, over two-thirds coincided with an increase in fixed assets which, it appeared, could not have been financed in any other way; similarly, in 150 subsidiary years (almost 45 per cent of the time) where intracompany debt was reduced, and in 110 subsidiary years (or over one out of every three years) where dividends were increased, bank credit was called upon. Generally, such borrowing was only temporary, and the loans were subsequently reduced as funds were generated from internal sources, or other finance was arranged. It is unlikely that the subsidiary manager, when negotiating loans, would indicate to the bank that the loan would be used for anything but conventional purposes. In the United Kingdom, for instance, this would usually mean for financing working capital needs. And it would generally be possible to comply with the letter of the agreement, if not the spirit, by arguing that an apparently 'unauthorised' use of the loan (such as remittance of dividends) was in fact financed out of cash flow and not by the loan. Moreover, control of bank lending to foreign subsidiaries is normally delegated to and administered by the banks themselves, and their relationship to the individual borrower is perhaps the most important factor in whether or not a loan will be granted. Even where discriminatory control of credit to foreign subsidiaries is the policy of the central banking authorities, it is difficult to make it effective without an elaborate administrative apparatus.[17] When the subsidiary is important to the economy of the local region, and a major client, the bank can be expected in most circumstances to try to meet its requests for funds.

Summing up, bank credit provides a flexible and an important source of finance to the foreign subsidiary. As primarily a temporary source of finance to subsidiaries, it finds its counterpart in the intracompany loan. A main advantage of bank credit over the intracompany loan is the protection against exchange loss that it can provide. From our analysis of subsidiary operations in the United Kingdom, there is a strong reason to conclude that this can provide a powerful incentive for its use. A disadvantage of bank credit may in some cases be its cost, though in North America and in Europe interest rate differentials have been relatively small, and the extra cost may often be marginal. Other possible disadvantages can be: restrictions placed on the subsidiary's use of bank credit; a demand by the bank for a guarantee which the parent may be reluctant to provide; the risk that the credit facilities may be reduced or withdrawn as a result of official policy. In any case, by providing almost one-third of the external finance of subsidiaries, it has proven to be a major source of funds.

OTHER LOCAL SOURCES OF FINANCE

Many countries—France, Belgium, Italy, the United Kingdom, and others—have been actively promoting regional development designed to foster industrial growth and modernisation in areas which suffer from chronic unemployment. At the same time they have been trying to discourage further expansion in large industrial centres that are becoming increasingly congested. To implement programmes of this kind, various incentives are offered to firms which will invest in the designated areas.

These vary from country to country, and even within countries, according to the severity of unemployment, general economic conditions, and other factors. They include a range of direct investment grants, tax concessions and allowances, interest subsidies and other benefits. For some investors, these can be important sources of finance: grants can run as high as 40 to 45 per cent of the investment in fixed assets; tax holidays and special depreciation allowances can increase cash flow by 50 to 100 per cent—sometimes more; cash flow can also be increased by interest-free or low-interest rate loans, or reduced rates for public utilities. In some instances subsidiaries may be permitted long-term credit facilities which would otherwise not be available.

There are often special dangers in store for foreign companies which invest in the development areas. Even though the benefits may appear to make the project especially attractive, the foreign investors' lack of detailed knowledge of local conditions makes it particularly difficult to judge objectively the opportunities available. Problems concerning personnel seem to be one of the major difficulties encountered. Existing company personnel are often reluctant to move to a development area, and indigenous labour is often unskilled or must be retrained. Besides this, distances to markets or from sources of supply may increase costs; communication may be poor; the climate and other features of the area may be disagreeable. Investors may have little choice in the matter, for in many instances a foreign subsidiary will not be permitted to locate or expand anywhere but in such development areas. This is very often the case in France.

In the United Kingdom we examined one instance where the subsidiary had been told in effect by the Board of Trade to build their new plant in the north of England or Scotland, or not at all. The management of the subsidiary took the view that the capital grant and possible loans were hardship payments rather than incentives. Their principal markets were in the south of England, and higher costs of transport made the venture less profitable than if it had been sited near London. Another company got itself into serious difficulty in France. Investment grants were tied to the number of new jobs created, and this led them to build what proved initially to be excess capacity. Further, they encountered severe and costly problems in recruiting and training management and operating personnel. The repercussions were so serious that the parent company felt itself obliged to explain the situation to the shareholders.[18] From our discussions with company officials we received the impression that while some subsidiaries have had very successful experiences investing in the development areas, the overall record has been mixed. The attitude of most managers was that there were more disadvantages than advantages, and few indicated that they would invest in such areas unless they either had to or there were some other special circumstances (besides the grants and subsidies) which made it advisable.

Leasing, factoring, and hire purchase provide other methods by which subsidiaries can obtain local finance. In general, subsidiaries have access to them on the same terms as local companies. However, since these are all relatively expensive means of finance, they are only of interest to the subsidiary in special situations—as a last resort for example, when the parent company is unable or unwilling to remit funds, and local bank credit is insufficient or unavailable. One of these methods, the leasing of industrial equipment, is of particular, though in the United Kingdom perhaps only historic, interest, and merits a few additional words.

The relative attractiveness of leasing compared to other methods of finance depends a lot on the particular tax structure of a country. Many have provisions for investment allowances whereby a company is permitted to write off for tax purposes amounts in excess of the original purchase price of new plant and equipment. This has the effect of reducing taxes on earnings and thus increases the cash flow and the net return on the investment. However, this allowance goes to the purchaser of the assets—the leasing company in this case. Since the company using the equipment, the lessee, is not entitled to the allowance, this form of finance is generally much more costly than debt or other capital, and has achieved only limited success. Benefiting from the allowances themselves, the leasing companies in some instances have been able to charge very low rates of interest on these contracts; in the United Kingdom, the effective rates were ranging from 2 to 3 per cent p.a. when the bank rate was between 4 and 5 per cent. Nevertheless, in spite of such low rates, few companies found it an attractive proposition because of the loss of the allowances which could substantially reduce their tax liabilities. However, in certain conditions, leasing can be attractive and cheap. For example, the foreign subsidiary which is operating at a loss, or which has insufficient profits to take full advantage of the allowances, may find leasing to be a very suitable source of finance.

7.2 Foreign external finance

Foreign external finance consists of funds received by a subsidiary from sources outside of its host country—these normally being the parent or an affiliated company—in the form of issued equity capital and intracompany debt. Not all of this finance necessarily represents a transfer of cash. A portion or even all of a subsidiary's equity may have been issued to the parent in exchange for a contribution in kind, such as machinery, or rights or patents or knowhow. Much intracompany debt arises from a receipt of inventory 'on loan'; it also may arise from a dividend declared but not paid, or from accrued charges for services received such as royalties, fees, or interest. To complicate the picture further, a subsidiary may also receive finance from its parent through the transfer price mechanism on intracompany transactions of goods and services. While this will not show up directly on the accounts, it operates indirectly by increasing the subsidiary's cash flow.[19]

Our analysis indicates that funds from the parent company have been a significant, but in the aggregate not a major source of finance for foreign subsidiaries. Taken as a whole, those in our sample received about 18 per cent of their total finance between 1960 and 1967 from contributions to equity and increases in intracompany debt—a smaller source than local debt. However, if this source of finance was not large in aggregate terms, it was nevertheless frequently called upon by the subsidiaries—on average in almost two out of every three subsidiary years analysed. Most of it was in the form of intracompany debt, for equity capital was used in less than one subsidiary year out of fifteen on average. Looking at it in terms of each subsidiary, over three-fourths of them increased intracompany debt during the period under review whereas less than one-third received equity funds. Furthermore, there was considerable diversity in the extent to which parent company funds were used by subsidiaries. For several, especially those which were making a loss, these funds were virtually their only source of finance. As a group, almost 40 per cent of the finance used by the European-owned subsidiaries was from this source; by comparison, the American-owned used relatively little—about 10 per cent of their total sources.

What factors influence the use of parent company funds to finance foreign subsidiary operations? This question has largely been answered already in the section on local debt finance. We argued there that the most important factors determining the use of local debt instead of, or in addition to, parent company funds were: (1) the amount of need for external finance; (2) the relative cost and availability of local debt; and (3) the perception of risk from exchange loss by the management of the parent company. Our conclusion was that, generally speaking, company policy was to endeavour to have the subsidiaries finance themselves as much as possible from local sources—unless the cost of doing so would be excessive. This last consideration seldom seemed to be a factor in operations in Europe and North America where interest rate differentials have been relatively narrow; besides, the protection against exchange loss gained by the use of local debt was generally worth the extra cost, if any.

But regardless of what the companies would prefer to do, it is evident that there are frequent occasions when local sources of finance are either insufficient, inappropriate, or simply unavailable to meet subsidiary requirements. When a subsidiary is first established or purchased, at least a minimum of its initial capital needs will have to be provided by the parent company.[20] In our sample of subsidiaries in the United Kingdom, those that relied most heavily on parent company funds tended to be among the smallest, least profitable, and fastest expanding. Typically these might be expected to be relatively new and without a strong local credit standing. In such circumstances, or where local sources of credit were scarce—during a credit squeeze, for example—the parent company would have to provide supplementary or substitute finance, or risk endangering the future success of its investment.

Herein lies an important advantage of the foreign subsidiary over its domestic competition, which is usually limited to the local financial markets for capital: the ability to call on supplementary finance if necessary. Thus not only can a foreign subsidiary often minimise the impact of local credit restrictions, but it can also be kept alive during difficult economic periods or when it is trying to break into a new market by infusions of capital from its parent or affiliates.[21]

Once the need for parent company funds has been established, what factors determine whether they will be provided as equity or as intra-company debt? Several might be listed: local regulations and customs; the length of time the funds will be needed; tax considerations; attitudes towards risk and other intangibles. Perhaps most important is the amount of flexibility the company feels it must have to shift funds between the various organisations in the group. Though this turns on tax considerations and attitudes towards risk, it also is a reflection of the level of financial integration that has been reached in the effort to manage a common pool of corporate funds.

First, at least a minimum of the parent company funds required to establish a new foreign subsidiary will have to be supplied in the form of equity. In some circumstances, this will be spelled out by the local regulations, generally in terms of a minimum capital sum. Where local credit facilities are to be used, the banks will usually insist on a certain minimum ratio of equity to total capital. However, they are flexible in their requirements, and each case is judged on its own merits. Where a company seeks to keep its equity contribution to a minimum, and this appears to be rather typical, the banks will generally ask for a guarantee, or alternatively require intracompany loans to be subordinated to the local debt. In some countries, tax or exchange control regulations may favour an equity contribution over loans. India and New Zealand, for example, levy additional taxes on profits which exceed a certain proportion of issued capital. Other countries limit dividend payments to some ratio of issued capital. Thus the treasurer of a British company told us that while they usually remitted funds from London as intracompany loans, they reversed their policy in cases such as the above and provided equity.

Secondly, beyond any constraints imposed by local regulations, the permanence of the need for funds is an important determinant of whether equity or intracompany loans are used. Where the need is felt to be temporary, companies frequently prefer to use an intracompany loan. An example of such an occasion was provided by one of the subsidiaries which we interviewed. It had used intracompany trade credit to finance the construction of a new factory during a period when bank credit was restricted by the authorities as part of an attempt to halt excessive demand in the economy. A sizeable portion of this subsidiary's turnover consisted of equipment imported from its parent and affiliated companies with whom it maintained a large current trade account. This account was allowed to go unpaid temporarily in order to provide the needed funds. Since the funds were needed for only a year or so, they had decided against equity. If, as sometimes happens, the funds proved to be needed rather more permanently, the subsidiary could have always capitalised them at any time by converting them into equity.

What companies consider to be a 'permanent' need in this context naturally varies a great deal. Where a relatively rapid payback is projected, and especially where the subsidiary is expected to be able to finance a substantial part of its needs from local sources, it seems reasonable for a parent company to consider very little of its investment as a permanent commitment. In such cases, it could make good sense to have as much as possible of its initial stake in the form of intracompany loans—in other words, the subsidiary should be undercapitalised. One might question the rationale behind such policy. After all, capital invested in the form of intracompany debt is also subject to the same sort of risks as is equity; from the point of view of the parent company, the investment still represents a use of resources no matter in what form the funds are committed. Nevertheless, such a policy can have several advantages.

One of the main advantages of substituting intracompany debt for equity is that it can often reduce the impact of taxation, and thereby increase the return on investment to the parent company. As surplus funds accumulate in the subsidiary, they can be used to repay the loan principal. Since this is considered a return of capital, there are normally no withholding taxes levied by the host country, nor any additional taxes when received by the parent company.[22] The potential savings would be greater if the subsidiary's effective tax rate were less than that of the parent; it could also be argued that they would be greater to the extent that the cash funds were derived from tax-free income, that is depreciation. If instead, the subsidiary were financed with equity, any funds repatriated would have to be paid out of current or previous earnings which have been taxed; they would also be subject to a withholding tax in most cases, and possibly even an additional tax upon receipt by the parent company. The amount repatriated could be reduced by half or more. The advantages of substituting debt for equity have been noted by several writers.[23]

The use of debt in subsidiaries also permits the withdrawal of earnings in the form of interest. This can benefit foreign investors for at least two reasons. First of all, as was noted earlier, there may be a tax advantage in substituting intracompany debt for equity if remittance of interest results in a lower overall tax burden to the parent company than dividends. Although it is impossible to generalise because of the wide range of terms in the various bilateral tax treaties that govern these matters, and also because of the effect of a possible subsequent taxation of foreign income when it is received by the parent company, it is clear that taxes can often have an important influence on the type of remittances, and hence, on the capital structure of foreign subsidiaries.

In some situations there may also be certain political advantages in repatriating earnings in the form of interest rather than dividends. In many countries, the less developed in particular, dividend payments are still somewhat of a *bête noire*, and can lead to charges of exploitation, and other difficulties. As it has been put in another study 'the benefits of foreign investment are often ignored, all attention being directed to the price paid, that is, the remittance of dividends'.[24] For somewhat similar reasons, there may be occasions when it would be advisable to understate the subsidiary's profits. To accomplish these objectives, the substitution of parent company loans for equity could be a sensible course of action. The stimulus of the necessity to meet loan requirements has been pointed out earlier with regard to bank loans, and a similar pressure can be sometimes felt by subsidiary management even in the case of the obligations of intracompany loans (at any rate, where the terms were formalised and called for interest to be paid and repayment according to a schedule).[25]

Another major advantage of financing subsidiaries with intracompany loans instead of equity is that it provides greater flexibility, or in other words, greater ability to shift funds between the subsidiary and other members of the corporate group. This can be valuable for two reasons.

Many multinational companies have attempted, some with more success than others, to integrate all or part of their overseas financial operations. They think of and try to manage the funds belonging to the various foreign subsidiaries of the group as if they formed part of a common pool of capital. The measure of success of such an exercise is the speed and efficiency with which funds can be moved about the group. However, when operating across national frontiers, differences in the currency, tax, and legal systems of each country make it a difficult goal to realise. To take a common situation, one subsidiary of a group may have accumulated surplus cash funds, while another is expanding and in need of funds. The problem is to get the surplus cash to where it is needed as quickly and cheaply as possible. Though the funds belong to the same group in one sense, they cannot be transferred without justification. One solution would be for the cash-rich subsidiary to pay a dividend to the parent company which would then remit the necessary funds to the subsidiary in need. As pointed out above, some companies have such a policy and require their subsidiaries to remit all funds in excess to their current investment requirements. But this can be expensive because of withholding taxes, and may perhaps run into difficulties with exchange controls.

The alternative solution would be to have financed the subsidiaries so that they maintained a substantial proportion of intracompany debt in their capital structure. The cash-rich subsidiary would then repay its loan to the parent (or sometimes a base or holding company) which would in turn loan the proceeds to the subsidiary in need. Such an operation would normally not be taxed,[26] nor as frowned upon by the exchange control authorities as a remittance of dividends. In some circumstances, the cash-rich subsidiary could make the loan direct to its fellow subsidiary, but this might be more difficult to justify because of exchange control or fiscal implications. Where there is a sufficient volume of intracompany trading, the same end is achieved by altering the terms of payment. Such practices as described above are commonly used by the international oil companies and others whose finances are highly integrated. There are obvious limitations to such devices, but they can go a long way towards providing the necessary flexibility to operate a common pool of funds.

The flexibility provided by intracompany loans can also help to reduce exchange loss. Over the long run, as the rash of devaluations in November 1967 demonstrated, such losses are probably inevitable even for operations in the industrialised countries, and no doubt should be counted as one of the costs of international business. However, in the short run, there are precautions which a management can take to minimise these hazards. Thus where a subsidiary's capital structure includes intracompany debt, the parent company can reduce its 'exposure' to one-time exchange losses such as devaluation by the timely repayment or reduction of the amount owed. This assumes, of course, that local finance is available to replace the intracompany funds which are to be withdrawn. As noted elsewhere when discussing the question of short-term bank credit, this practice was widespread in the United Kingdom during 1964 and 1965 when sterling came under pressure. If account is taken of all the methods of repatriation used, almost 60 per cent of the subsidiaries in our sample substantially reduced their exposure to exchange loss by reducing their liabilities to parent and affiliated companies (or by increasing their intracompany assets). For many subsidiaries, this represented the major use of funds in 1964 and again in 1967. As a group, the American-owned subsidiaries in particular repaid £25·5 million in 1964, a sum which comprised over 20 per cent of their total use of funds that year, and represented over half of their aggregate dividend remittances. Virtually the same thing happened in 1967. The actions of two subsidiaries were especially interesting and worth illustrating.

One subsidiary, established before World War II, had received most of its initial capital from the parent company in the form of an intracompany loan. At the time of the 1949 devaluation in the United Kingdom, the loan had stood at roughly £3·5 million, representing an investment by the parent company of approximately $17 million at the former rate of exchange of $4.86 to the pound. At the new rate of $2.80 to the pound resulting from the devaluation, the parent company suffered an exchange 'loss' of over $7 million. The company apparently had learned its lesson from the experience as can be deduced from the changes in the following balance sheet items between 1963 and 1965:

	1963	*1964*	*1965*
Liabilities to parent and fellow subsidiaries	£3,350,000	£785,000	nil
Bank loans	£1,725,000	£3,265,000	£4,675,000

By 1966, the subsidiary's investment programme required additional funds, and the parent company returned some £125,000; in addition, the subsidiary was able to fund part of its bank loan by raising £3 million in medium-term debt. Another subsidiary repaid almost £6 million in intracompany debts, most of which was financed by an increased overdraft. 'We had to play it safe, you know,' explained the subsidiary manager. Besides these, there were a number of other subsidiaries in 1964 and 1965 which replaced intracompany loans in amounts of over £1 million by increased overdrafts.

Changing the credit terms on intracompany trade is another way to hedge against one-time exchange losses. The illustration in fig. 7.1, involving trade between three subsidiaries of an integrated US-owned company, each located in a different European country, may be taken as a typical example of how this operates. The British subsidiary imports semi-finished products from its Dutch affiliate for further processing and distribution. Part of the British subsidiary's output is exported to its German affiliate, and the rest is sold in the British home market. Normal trade credit terms on all transactions is sixty days. Figure 7.1 shows the flow and volume of this trade expressed in pounds sterling.

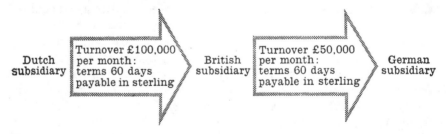

Fig. 7.1 Flow and volume of trade to illustrate table 7.7

Given this pattern of trade, the effect of the 1967 devaluation of sterling on certain balance sheet items of each company is shown in table 7.7, when (1) no hedging took place, and (2) substantial hedging took place. The effect has been translated into terms of exchange loss or gain in local currency for each subsidiary, and in US dollars for the parent company.

Taxes and incremental interest expense have been omitted to simplify the illustrations.

Table 7.7 Effect of hedging against exchange loss

		Intra-company assets	Intra-company liabilities	Exchange Gains and losses Local currency	Exchange Gains and losses US dollars
No hedging					
(a) before devaluation					
British subsidiary	(£)	100,000	200,000	—	—
Dutch subsidiary	(H.fl.)	2,020,000	—	—	—
German subsidiary	(DM)	—	1,125,000	—	—
(b) after devaluation					
British subsidiary	(£)	100,000	200,000	—	—
Dutch subsidiary	(H.fl.)	1,730,000	—	− 290,000	− 80,500
German subsidiary	(DM)	—	960,000	+ 165,000	+ 41,250
Net exchange loss:					$39,250
*Hedging**					
(a) before devaluation					
British subsidiary	(£)	200,000	—	—	—
Dutch subsidiary	(H.fl.)	—	—	—	—
German subsidiary	(DM)	—	2,250,000	—	—
(b) after devaluation					
British subsidiary	(£)	200,000	—	—	—
Dutch subsidiary	(H.fl.)	—	—	—	—
German subsidiary	(DM)	—	1,920,000	+ 330,000	+ 85,000
Net exchange gain:					$85,000

*The hedging was accomplished by giving the German subsidiary four months' rather than two months' terms, and paying the Dutch subsidiary C.O.D.
Exchange rates before devaluation used above were:
£1 = 11.25 DM, 10.1 florins, $2.80;
after devaluation £1 = 9.60 DM, 8.65 florins, $2.40.

Referring to the figures in table 7.7 we see that without hedging, the parent company's net exposure to exchange loss was approximately $39,000. The Dutch subsidiary would be paid in sterling which would after devaluation yield some 14·3 per cent fewer florins upon conversion than before, producing an exchange loss of about H.fl. 290,000. The German subsidiary, on the other hand, would have an exchange gain of DM 165,000, for it would be able to buy sterling 14·3 per cent cheaper to pay for the goods imported. If the currencies used for invoicing were reversed, then the exchange gains and losses would have been incurred by the British subsidiary.

The hedging operation in the example consisted of directing the British subsidiary to give its German affiliate 120 days to pay, and to reduce its liabilities to the Dutch affiliate to zero, i.e. to pay for its imports C.O.D. Such tactics would produce an exchange gain of DM 330,000 for the German subsidiary, or $85,000 from the standpoint of the parent company.

Other instances of this type of hedging were reported in the British press during the 1964–65 devaluation scare. Two examples were the following:

> Prestige, the kitchenware group, has been instructed by its parent, Ekco products of Chicago, to pay all outgoing service and royalty accounts immediately, while the nine overseas Ekco and Prestige subsidiaries who buy from Britain have been given permission to delay payment, instead of pumping money into a country whose currency has been under pressure.

> Addressograph-Multigraph in the UK, now settles all transactions with its US parent on a thirty-day basis, instead of the previous ninety days— though they do this reluctantly, as they want maximum credit for expansion here.[27]

The obvious goal of such actions is to move as much 'hard' currency as possible out of the country and convert it before devaluation. Though it is easier to visualise this where liabilities are being repaid, allowing longer credit terms on exports to fellow subsidiaries amounts to the same thing. In the example above, the German subsidiary is being financed by sterling, in other words, by the additional credit it receives from its British affiliate.

Hedging has its costs. The British subsidiary in our example would have to find an additional £300,000 to carry the extra £100,000 trade credit given its German affiliate and to reduce to zero the £200,000 owed to the Dutch affiliate. This is a problem that requires making a judgment— or perhaps making a bet would be closer to the truth—on whether the risk of devaluation is worth the added cost.[28] In the case of wholly-owned subsidiaries, the answer is probably yes, providing that interest rates are not excessive and the risk is felt to be relatively shortlived. However, where there are local shareholders in the subsidiary (such as the Prestige Group mentioned above) one might wonder how they benefit from the hedging which we have described. If local borrowing is required, its cost can only reduce the profits which would otherwise be available for dividends or expansion. In effect, the interests of the minority are subordinated to those of the majority shareholder—the parent company.

Apart from the additional financial costs which may be required to support these measures, there are sometimes other constraints. In the United Kingdom, for example, payment for exports cannot exceed six months after shipment without permission from the exchange control authorities. Moreover, the exchange control authorities are sometimes on the lookout for subsidiaries which have used overdrafts to finance extended terms on exports to affiliated companies.

Companies also improve their flexibility by maintaining a low ratio of issued capital to earned surplus in the financial structure of their foreign subsidiaries. This means that as profits are earned and reinvested in the subsidiary, they are left as earned surplus (revenue reserves in the accounts of British companies) and are not capitalised. While the distinction may seem to be insignificant, it is an important one. Once profits are capitalised, they are permanently committed to the subsidiary; an occasional extra-ordinary dividend out of accumulated earnings has gone.

It will be recalled that in 1964 and 1965, almost a fifth of the subsidiaries in our sample dipped into their reserves to pay an especially large dividend—that is, one which exceeded their current earnings. One subsidiary, for example, whose profits had been running at about £700,000 annually, appropriated £3 million in dividends in 1964. Those were not typical years, for as we have already noted, many subsidiaries increased their remittances for fear of devaluation or for tax reasons. But this need not be the only motive for wanting to remit an unusually large dividend during a particular year. The parent company may be in need of funds, and a subsidiary with surplus cash reserves or ample borrowing capacity may be in the best position to supply them. Again, several subsidiaries in our sample tem-porarily suspended dividends in order to plough back all earnings to finance expansion. After the financial need had been satisfied and surplus funds became available, a portion of past earnings were released as an extraordinary dividend.

Many of the subsidiaries in our sample started off relatively 'poor' with the bulk of funds from the parent company provided in the form of intra-company loans. As they expanded, their financial needs were met first out of cash flows and local borrowing. Where additional funds were required from the parent company, they were provided as loans, and not as equity. Retained earnings were left in the earned surplus account and not capita-lised. As a consequence, many subsidiaries have developed and prospered over a long period of years with no more issued capital than when they were first founded. In a third of the subsidiaries, issued capital amounted to less than 10 per cent of total assets, and in about half of these, it was less than 5 per cent. In contrast, the issued capital and capital reserves in the British quoted companies amounted to over 25 per cent of total assets. There were a number of subsidiaries where issued capital was less than 1 per cent of total assets. One in particular, whose total assets amounted to almost £12 million, showed issued capital of only £1000. The number of formally undercapitalised subsidiaries would have been considerably larger had not several capitalised a portion of their reserves during the period. It should be emphasised that it does not necessarily follow that a small proportion of issued capital in a subsidiary's financial structure also implies a small proportion of net worth to total assets, in other words, that it is heavily indebted. In fact, there was almost no perceptible relationship between the two. Several of the subsidiaries whose balance sheets showed a very large proportion of equity funds had only a very small percentage of them in the form of issued capital, and in others, the reverse was true (they had in general been making losses).

In spite of the increased flexibility, some companies believe that there are advantages in not minimising the issued capital. In the case of a quoted company, there is usually good reason to capitalise reserves from time to time in order to make a scrip issue. The reduction in the market price of each share and consequent improvement in their marketability often increases the value of the total holding. Exactly the same considerations are relevant for a subsidiary where it has a group of local shareholders whose shares are traded on a stock exchange. Nevertheless, there are other reasons why a wholly owned subsidiary (i.e. one whose shares are *not* traded on a stock exchange) may find it politic to capitalise its reserves periodically. By doing so, retained earnings are permanently committed to the enterprise and provide an overt demonstration of faith in the local economy and regard for its interest. Somewhat similar motives have inspired some subsidiaries to capitalise reserves in order to maintain an appropriate ratio between issued capital and future dividend remittances.

In many countries, dividend appropriations are commonly expressed in terms of a percentage of the nominal value of the issued share capital. If, over a period of time, this ratio increases substantially and gets out of line with the usually accepted practices of firms in a particular country or industry, some managements fear that the subsidiary could become subject to criticism from, for instance, the local financial press. Moreover, it is thought that where a justification is needed, exchange control authorities more readily approve an increase in dividends remitted to the parent company if the appropriation represents a reasonable percentage on capital. In this view, a return of 10 to 20 per cent on issued capital would 'look' much better than a spectacular return of, say, 75 to 100 per cent or more (an astronomical return of over 250,000 per cent in the case of the subsidiary mentioned above with the £1,000 in issued capital). Several subsidiaries in our sample appeared to accept this approach, and capitalised reserves to maintain an approximately constant ratio between dividends and issued capital. Another frequent reason was noted earlier in connection with the borrowing of local funds. Bankers in both London and Paris pointed out that not infrequently their clients had been required by the Bank of England and the Crédit National to 'freeze' a portion of their earned surplus by capitalising it before their loan applications would be approved.

Up to now our discussion of equity capital has been restricted to ordinary shares (common stock in the United States, *action ordinaire* in France, etc.). A small minority of the subsidiaries in our sample—14 out of the 115—had also preference shares (preferred stock) outstanding during some of the period. Half of these were quoted subsidiaries, among which three were gradually redeeming their preference capital and two others completely retired the outstanding shares during the period covered by the analysis.[29] Only one subsidiary made an issue during the period. An additional measure of how seldom this financial instrument is used by subsidiaries is given by the fact that such shares only amounted to 1·5 per cent of total capital and liabilities in 1959, and 0·7 per cent in 1967; this compares with 5·6 per cent and 2·8 per cent for the British quoted companies in the respective years. As is apparent from these figures, even among this latter group, the use of preference shares had declined during recent years and they have seldom amounted to more than 2 or 3 per cent of the annual new capital issues made since 1955 in the United Kingdom. Their tax disadvantages account in part for their unpopularity. Dividends must be paid out of earnings after tax, whereas interest payments on long-term debt are deductible for tax purposes. This drawback has been compounded by the Corporation Tax. As a financial instrument, preference shares are in some ways a substitute for loan capital, and it has been suggested in other studies that they were often issued by companies who would have had difficulty raising capital from other sources.[30] In foreign subsidiary finance, the intracompany loan is the counterpart of the preference share. As shown above, intracompany debt is a substitute for local debt when the latter is not available or appropriate. However, in the case where an intracompany loan's repayment might be construed as a 'constructive dividend', it has been suggested that a redeemable preference share might provide a satisfactory alternative. Most of the outstanding preference shares are relics from the subsidiaries' pre-acquisition days. Some companies permitted these shares to remain in the hands of the general public; others bought out the former shareholders' interest, although the shares were not retired.

FINANCIAL STRUCTURE

The overall effect of the various methods of finance on the subsidiaries' financial structure can best be appreciated in the perspective of a series of ratios. First of all, we can see from table 7.8 that the subsidiaries have substantially less working capital than the British quoted companies in the same industrial group; in some cases it is negative.

In spite of a substantially higher level of short-term indebtedness in the subsidiaries, it does not necessarily mean that there is more risk attached or that lenders are in a less secure position than in the case of the quoted companies. Often the parent company will guarantee the subsidiary's debt obligations; and the intracompany debt is generally subordinated to all other liabilities.

Secondly, the wide diversity of practice observed among the 115 subsidiaries in our sample is brought out by the financial ratios in table 7.9. In the summary below, the following medians, quartiles, and ranges can be

Table 7.8 Ratios of liquidity (current assets divided by current liabilities)

Company classification	Median	Quartiles		Range
Food manufacturing				
16 subsidiaries	1·34	1·09	1·86	0·71 to 3·06
8 quoted companies	1·64	1·30	1·76	n.a.
Chemicals and drugs				
34 subsidiaries	1·31	1·03	1·74	0·60 to 2·53
28 quoted companies	1·63	1·36	2·11	n.a.
Machinery				
21 subsidiaries	1·70	1·24	2·30	0·91 to 4·41
58 quoted companies	1·93	1·70	2·35	n.a.
Electrical/electronic				
18 subsidiaries	1·39	1·07	1·61	0·48 to 2·06
11 quoted companies	1·80	1·64	2·75	n.a.

Note. Intracompany liabilities have been included as a current liability. Source for quoted companies: Dun & Bradstreet, *Business Ratios*, London, Summer 1968, table 3, p. 33.

Table 7.9 Selected financial ratios in 1967 (per cent of total assets)

Type of finance	Median	Quartiles		Range
Ordinary shares	17·5	8·5	29·4	0·009 to 61·7
Owners' equity	45·8	36·0	60·4	(20·1) to 84·8
Long-term debt	0·0	0·0	10·3	0·0 to 49·0
Bank credit	8·6	0·5	21·0	0·0 to 43·5
Intracompany liabilities	6·7	1·6	13·6	0·0 to 83·5

noted. Additional and more detailed financial data covering the sample appear in Appendix II.

7.3 Special-purpose subsidiaries

An integral part of the financial strategy of many multinational companies is the various special-purpose subsidiaries. These are of two main types: the base company (which can be either a holding company or a service company,[31] or both); and the international finance subsidiary.

BASE COMPANIES

The holding type of base company, as its name implies, is designed to hold ownership in the equity of other companies, in particular, the overseas subsidiaries of an international group. The service company is designed to act as the intermediary for intracompany sales of the group, and may also administer its licensing operations, management services, finances, and other functions. In practice, the base company may be organised to act both as a holding and a service company, and may also be a sort of overseas head office with responsibility to coordinate regional marketing, production, finance and other functions of the group. Thus, the base company can have a rather broad range of corporate activities.

This notwithstanding, a primary purpose of these companies has been to provide a group with a means to avoid or defer taxes. As a result, they are generally set up in one of the so-called tax-haven countries such as Switzerland, Liechtenstein, Panama, the Bahamas, or the Netherlands Antilles. In the case of the holding companies, the tax advantage arises in situations where the overall tax rate on income received from the group's foreign subsidiaries is less than the rate suffered by the parent company. For example, a subsidiary which is subject to an effective tax rate of 35 per cent may remit dividends to its Swiss holding company. These are taxed in Switzerland at, say, 5 per cent, leaving 61·75 per cent of the original earnings to be used for other group purposes. If the dividends had been routed directly to the parent company which was taxed at, say, 50 per cent, the group would of course be left with only half of the original profits. In such schemes, the additional taxes probably have to be paid when the earnings are eventually repatriated.[32]

In the case of the service company, taxes, besides being deferred, can also often be reduced. The typical service company is used to channel the intracompany transactions of the group as they flow from the point of production to the point of final sale. Although the transfers are invoiced through the service company, the goods themselves are shipped direct to their destination. Thus, if the British subsidiary of an international group were to ship goods to its German affiliate, the covering paperwork would show that the British company had sold to the service company in, for instance, Switzerland, which in turn had resold the merchandise to the German company. This device provides a group with additional flexibility to shift funds and profits. By manipulating the terms of the intracompany sales that are routed through it, that is by importing at a low price and exporting at a high price, profits can be siphoned off and allowed to accrue in the service company. A tax deferral (from the parent company's viewpoint) is achieved in the same manner as described above for the holding company. A tax reduction may also be achieved if one of the subsidiaries involved in the transactions is taxed at a higher overall rate than the parent company. In that case, goods would be invoiced to the high-tax subsidiary at prices which would tend to shift the bulk of the profit to the base company.

Apart from the tax incentives for operating a base company, there may be other financial motives. By altering the payment terms on intracompany trade credit, funds can be temporarily transferred to provide short-term finance, and additional flexibility as was pointed out in a more restricted sense when discussing devaluation. For example, subsidiaries with surplus cash or which can borrow cheaply from their local banks may be instructed to accept longer payment terms if they were exporting to the base company, or pay more quickly if they were importing from it. The funds which would accumulate could then be loaned to a third affiliate. Alternatively, if the base company has other sources of finance, it can funnel these to one or both of the subsidiaries. According to the treasurer of one large integrated company, this advantage in itself justifies operating a base company.

INTERNATIONAL FINANCE SUBSIDIARIES

The international finance subsidiary has as its main function the floating of long-term bond issues on the international capital market. What distinguishes international issues from those on a national capital market is, first, that they are sold mostly outside the country of the borrower;[33] secondly, that they are denominated in a widely accepted international currency—dollars, Deutsche marks, units of account, Swiss francs—sometimes but not necessarily different from that of the borrower; thirdly, that the issuing group generally consists of an international consortium of banks; and fourthly, the subscribers, although firm data are lacking, are also at least international. International bond issues in their present form are a relatively new development in finance, for prior to the announcement of the US interest equalisation tax in July 1963 and its subsequent enactment the following year, the great bulk of these issues was made in New York, though many of them were subscribed in large part by nonresidents of the United States. The shift of these issues to Europe since then has resulted in a rapid development of a truly international market where none formerly existed. This was given a strong impetus by the US programme to improve its balance of payments. Since 1965 a substantial number of American multinational companies have looked to this market for funds to finance their overseas operations.

The investors in this market are primarily wealthy individuals from all parts of the world, though perhaps the bulk of them operate from Switzerland. Because these investors insist that payments of interest and principal should be free of withholding taxes, the issue is normally made by a subsidiary domiciled in countries which accord the necessary tax privileges—the Netherlands Antilles, the United States,[34] and formerly Luxembourg. Non-US companies normally chose a Luxembourg or Netherlands Antilles holding company for the issue. However, tax considerations have made the US or sometimes the Netherlands Antilles holding company more suitable for American companies, mainly because Luxembourg companies are not covered by the double-taxation treaties with other countries. Consequently, when the Luxembourg holding company loaned the proceeds of the issue to an operating subsidiary, interest payments would be subject to the maximum rate. A US finance subsidiary, on the other hand, can benefit from the double-taxation treaties concluded with other countries on the same basis as any other United States company. In addition, losses can be set against other US domestic income.

While most issues have been denominated in US dollars, a growing number of them have been in Deutschmarks, and also a few in units of account or other international currencies. US companies have on some occasions made issues in marks, usually where the funds are to be used in Germany. Since repayment would be in marks and from presumably German profits, this had provided certain protection against exchange loss.

A substantial number of the issues has been convertible into the ordinary shares of the parent company, especially in 1968 when they accounted for over one-half of new issues of Eurobonds. In terms of interest rates, convertible loans have been cheaper than straight-interest issues, though they entail a certain amount of dilution eventually. They have run about $4\frac{1}{4}$ to $6\frac{1}{2}$ per cent compared to $5\frac{3}{4}$ to over 9 per cent for those without the convertible feature. In principle, this type of loan can also provide the company with a means of enlarging its foreign ownership; in practice, it remains to be seen whether the investors will retain the shares after conversion.

That the amount of capital raised is large and growing is shown in the figures below.

Table 7.10 Eurobond issues

Type of borrower	$ million equivalent				
	1965	*1966*	*1967*	*1968*	*1969*
US corporations	358	454	562	2046	1062
Non-US companies	393	467	1014	931	1515
Governments and international institutions	253	219	423	525	678
Total issues	1004	1140	1999	3502	3235

Source. Morgan Guaranty Trust Company, *World Financial Markets*, 16 December 1969.

The international bond market has been used mainly by large, well-known borrowers. Most issues have been in the range of $15 million to $30 million, and it is rare to see one for under $10 million. There are some interesting aspects to the market—companies such as Nabisco or Olivetti or ITT can borrow at better terms than, for example, the Finnish, New Zealand, or Belgian governments. The reasons for such quirks have been attributed mainly to 'imperfections' in the market—the preferences of the investors

1*

who somehow see more glamour and perhaps less risk in the big companies than in some of the smaller countries of the world.

It has been said that the multinational company provides a catalyst for closer and better economic ties between countries. The international bond market in Europe, arising out of a situation created by foreign investment and nurtured by the demand for capital caused by its growth, provides solid support for this statement.[35]

PART III

Performance, motives and the environment

This part contains four subjects which illustrate significant aspects of performance and decision-making in the multinational company. Thus chapter 8 outlines some of the achievements of such firms, and should be read in conjunction with the following chapter which analyses the reasons given for the move or the further development abroad. This chapter looks back to chapters 3 and 4 in linking the strategy pursued to the relationships that develop between the home and the foreign units. There is also a brief examination of the reasons for failure.

Chapter 10 glances at the vexed question of relationships between companies and countries. These include the problems of the foreign company with government and public opinions both at home and abroad. These are examined as part of the environmental constraints within which the company is working, not in the context of a discussion of national points of view. These are only considered here inasmuch as they affect company policies. One aspect of the relationship between companies and countries is the question of ownership. Local participation in local subsidiaries, and the lack of it, is discussed in chapter 11.

Growth and profitability of direct investment abroad

8.1 UK and US direct investment overseas in manufacturing

In the opening lines of this book, reference was made to the magnitude of foreign investment and to its rapid growth during the past twenty years. Although this has been well documented elsewhere, it is of interest to recall a few of the main statistics covering this development.[1] Measured first in terms of net book value, American and British direct investment overseas in all countries has been growing respectively at a compound rate of about 9 per cent and 6 per cent annually since 1957. At the end of 1968, the value of total American overseas investment reached £27,000 million; by the end of 1967, total British direct investment overseas, not counting that in petroleum, approached £4700 million. Earnings and income from these investments have also increased substantially during this period. In 1968 American-owned foreign investments earned over £2900 million, and provided some £2600 million to their owners in the form of dividends, interest, royalties, and other payments. And the most recent data covering British overseas investments showed that in 1967 their total earnings amounted to about £438 million, and dividends, interest, royalties and other payments exceeded £310 million.

What are the implications of this investment? For many countries, foreign investment represents a significant and growing proportion of the total investment in the private sector of their economy. Indeed, in some, the industries with the most promise of future growth are becoming dominated by foreign-owned or controlled companies. This is a development which is giving rise to a spreading malaise in government and other circles in these countries, and one which we will look at more closely in chapters 10 and 11.

In this chapter, we want to explore but two aspects of foreign direct investment—its rate of growth, and its profitability. We shall begin by briefly considering the overall performance of American and British overseas investment in manufacturing industries based on published data,[2] and then narrow our scope to look in more detail at the performance of our sample of 115 foreign subsidiaries operating in the United Kingdom.

Growth and profitability of American and British direct investments overseas in manufacturing over the past eight years is shown in figs. 8.1 and

8.2. Among the most interesting features of this data, we might note the following:

1. Total US direct investment overseas in manufacturing is about four times larger than the comparable British stake. In continental Europe it is 7·5 times larger. Although not shown on fig. 8.1, British investment in American manufacturing is only about one-fifth that of American investment in the United Kingdom.

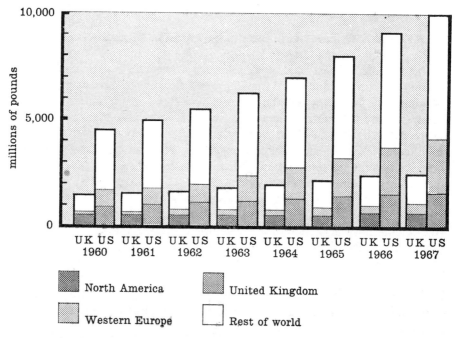

Fig. 8.1 Book values 1960–67: direct foreign manufacturing investment by United Kingdom and United States companies at the end of each year

2. Investment by American companies in overseas manufacturing has been growing at a faster rate than that attained by British companies. Worldwide this has been respectively at a compound rate of about 12 per cent per year compared to just under 8 per cent. A greater difference can be noted in continental Europe where the rate of increase in American investment in manufacturing has averaged about 20 per cent per year compared to about 11 per cent for British investment.

3. The profitability of American investment has tended to decrease over the period reviewed, especially in continental Europe and in the United Kingdom. On the other hand the profitability of British investment overseas, although lower than that enjoyed by American investments, has tended to increase overall, and especially in North American manufacturing. In

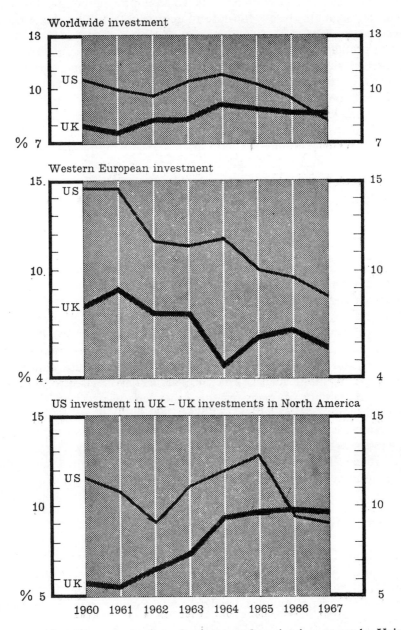

Fig. 8.2 Profitability 1960–67: direct foreign manufacturing investment by United Kingdom and United States companies (earnings after taxes divided by book value)

Europe the most recent years have shown an improving profitability, but it is still substantially below the rate of return obtained by the American investments.

4. The profitability of American investment overseas has until 1967 been consistently above that of domestic investment in the United States where the average rate of return has been of the order of a little over 9 per cent. For British companies, the picture is slightly different; the rate of return on United Kingdom investment overseas has tended to average about that on domestic British investment—higher in some years, and lower in others. The lure of higher profits has been often given as the primary motivation for investing overseas. Although the evidence above would tend to support this argument in the case of the American investments, it does not hold up in the light of the data covering the British. We shall suggest in the next chapter that there are other generally more powerful motives for overseas investment.

There are a number of reasons for the trends noted in the average rate of return from these investments. At least part of the decrease in the profitability of American investment can be attributed to the rapid growth of the investment base, and perhaps especially to the relatively large number of totally new investments that were made. Generally, there is a considerable time lag between when the initial investment outlay is made and when it begins to earn profits.[3] Besides this the effects of increased competition in many industries, and also poorer trading conditions brought about by attempts of some governments to manage their economies have tended to reduce the former profitability of many of the American investments. Of course, profitability is also affected by the general efficiency of companies, and by such things as intracompany transactions, and accounting methods; for some overseas ventures, there will be in addition currency depreciation or devaluation or both to affect profits. We will return to explore some of these factors in more detail in the case study which follows.

8.2 Foreign investment in the UK

The analysis of the accounts of our sample of 115 foreign-owned subsidiaries in the United Kingdom reveals some interesting data on their growth and profitability and it provides us with the opportunity to study these performance characteristics in more detail than was possible from the aggregated data shown above.

GROWTH

We have defined growth, for our purposes here, as the rate of increase in the *net operating assets*[4] of the subsidiary. On this basis, between the end of

1959 and 1967, the subsidiaries' growth ranged from a compound rate of only 1 per cent p.a. to a little over 100 per cent p.a.[5] The median rate was 15·3 per cent for the 115 subsidiaries, the lower quartile 9·9 per cent, and the upper quartile 22·1 per cent. In other words, half of the subsidiaries in our sample were doubling their net operating assets about every 4·8 years, on average, and a quarter of them doubling net operating assets every 3·5 years on average.

Chemicals, pharmaceuticals, electrical engineering and electronics, and office equipment manufacturers were the industries which showed the largest percentage of fast-growing subsidiaries, with close to two-thirds expanding at more than the median rate. Inasmuch as these are considered to be growth industries, this should not be surprising. Their rate of growth is particularly impressive when compared to a sample of British quoted companies in similar industries. While the two sets of data are not strictly comparable, the order of magnitude is considerably over 2 to 1 in favour of the subsidiaries.[6]

Overall, there appeared relatively little association between the subsidiaries' rate of growth and size. There were more that were fast growing among the groups of small and medium-large subsidiaries; and there were slightly fewer that were fast growing among the group of large subsidiaries.[7] However, the differences were not striking enough to be able to suggest the effect of size on their growth rates. This seems to run counter to the usual pattern expected in the growth of a firm. In her study of company growth, Penrose wrote:

> There is a maximum rate at which each individual firm can grow under given circumstances. If we consider only firms for which these circumstances are extremely favourable, we should expect the rate of growth of the medium-sized and moderately large firms to be higher than that of the very new and very small firms and higher also than that of the very large firms.[8]

In a foreign subsidiary, the 'favourable circumstances' for growth are not all of its own making. This means that, unlike an independent company, a foreign subsidiary is affected by various advantages and constraints which are due to its association with the parent or affiliated companies. Thus in its initial stages of development a small foreign subsidiary is not likely to suffer from a lack of resources; finance, management, and technical knowhow can be made available by the parent. On the other hand it may be set up to produce a specific range of products, or to sell to particular markets, or both, and in this sense may be effectively limited in size. Of course, its market opportunities need not be thought of as necessarily restricting because the link-up with a multinational group can often provide it with greater markets than would have been possible for an independent company.

Because of these rather special circumstances, it is difficult to apply the same argument to the subsidiaries as to independent companies.

Another claim which is also hard to substantiate for subsidiaries is that growth and profitability are positively correlated. The view that a high rate of profit would stimulate—or be necessary for—a high rate of investment has a certain commonsense appeal, and was indeed invoked by Kodak Limited to defend its high rate of profit before the Monopolies Commission's investigation of its pricing policy in 1966. Kodak argued that 'a high rate of growth can only be financed in the long run by a well-organised company maintaining a healthy level of profits', and that 'this is why it is usual for companies which are undergoing a high rate of growth to achieve a rate of return which is higher than the average'. To support their contention, Kodak presented to the Commission schedules based on published data which showed that 'companies whose net assets increased in value by fifty per cent or more over the years 1958–60 generally achieved a higher rate of return on capital than the rest'.[9] In a study of a number of British companies in the food and electrical manufacturing industries, it was found that there was a significant correlation between average rate of growth and profitability. The author took the view, however, that 'the relationship between profits and growth is not a causal one, but rather that both growth and profitability are reflections of the character of the firm'.[10]

But for whatever reason, we found very little correlation between growth and profitability for the subsidiaries in our sample. A scatter diagram, on which the profitability of each subsidiary had been plotted against its rate of growth, showed nearly complete randomness—a shotgun-like pattern.[11] There are several possible explanations for this which shall be explored below.

PROFITABILITY

One of the intriguing questions raised by our study of foreign-owned subsidiaries is how to explain the higher rate of profits they achieved compared to a sample of British quoted companies which, for the most part, we can assume operate in the same business environment. In 1960 the foreign subsidiaries, as a group, earned a 7·3 per cent return on total assets, compared to 6·1 per cent for the quoted companies; in 1967, the respective rates of return were 5·6 per cent and 4·2 per cent. The American-owned subsidiaries, as a group, were more profitable, enjoying a return of 8·4 per cent in 1960, and 6·7 per cent in 1967.[12] The diversity of the subsidiaries' average[13] profitability during the 196ᴄ–67 period was striking, ranging from a − 10·7 per cent rate of return (or more exactly—*rate of loss*) up to a high of 24·7 per cent. The median return was 6·6 per cent, the lower quartile 3·5 per cent, and the upper quartile 10·2 per cent.[14]

Although it has declined considerably during the 1960s, the relatively higher profitability that American-owned subsidiaries have for years enjoyed has been the object of much discussion among some circles in the United Kingdom.[15] Various hypotheses have been advanced to explain this better performance, but one is led to conclude that there are a number of factors at work.

One explanation is that assets in each group of companies were valued on a different basis. The source of our data covering the quoted companies was based on published accounts, and it is generally believed that for this purpose companies value their fixed assets on the basis of historical cost.[16] The subsidiaries in our sample also generally used historical costs for valuing fixed assets shown in their accounts, although some of them had been revalued during the period of our review. Thus it appears doubtful from this evidence whether the method of valuation was sufficiently different for the two groups materially to affect profitability.

A much more plausible—and popular—explanation of the foreign subsidiaries' higher rate of profit is that they are not bearing their full share of expenses for research and development, technical knowhow, and other corporate resources from which they benefit. It is impossible to prove or disprove this premise without virtually a subsidiary-by-subsidiary inquiry, and this is a subject in which most display considerable reticence. There is evidence both in support of, and against, this argument. For example, in submitting evidence before the Monopolies Commission, Procter and Gamble Limited argued that 'the amount of the technical service fee paid its American parent [1·5 per cent of net sales] would be higher if such an arrangement came to be negotiated between strangers at arm's length. Each 1 per cent difference would affect the return on capital by 4 per cent'.[17] As another example, Kodak Limited paid a total annual royalty of 3 per cent on net sales. This consisted of 1·5 per cent payable under patents granted by the parent company, and another 1·5 per cent in respect of technical knowhow. However, until 1962 these services were made available by the parent company without charge to the British subsidiary.[18] Kodak explained this to the Monopolies Commission in arguing that:

> the major part of the cost of research is borne by the parent company. . . . Further, if Kodak [Limited] were not a member of the Eastman Kodak Group, the cost to it per unit of the research and development required to produce goods of comparable quality would be immeasurably greater than it is . . . [and] by debiting it only with *its proportion* of the parent company's current expenditure on research and development, the parent company is allowing Kodak [Limited] to retain, for the financing of future development, some part of the benefits of the world-wide organisation which it [the parent company] has created.[19]

In other words, Kodak was arguing that its profits were higher than they would be if it were bearing the full cost of research and development needed to support its operations. This is a view shared by many.[20]

Part of the reason that subsidiaries are not charged with more of the corporate general expenses is that they sometimes may be difficult to justify. Many of the expenses incurred by the parent company for, say, research and development, are not immediately and directly assignable to the subsidiary. Take, for example, a corporation which manufactures and sells business machinery ranging from relatively simple equipment such as typewriters and accounting machines to the most complex and advanced computer systems. If the activities of the subsidiary were restricted mainly to the typewriters and accounting machines, it would probably not find the local fiscal authorities sympathetic towards attempts to allocate expenditure incurred by the parent in the development of the computers until they were part of the subsidiary's activity. Consequently, the subsidiary could only directly contribute to the financing of this future development from which it may eventually benefit by remitting dividends. Therefore, to the extent that the subsidiary's share of corporate research and development expenditure is deferred in this manner, its profits will always tend to be overstated, and comparisons with domestic companies in the same business, or even with its parent (whose profits reflect total research and development expenditure usually, whether successful or not), are bound to be distorted. Probably most subsidiaries are assessed with some sort of royalty payments for use of patents or for technical services, but few details appeared on the individual accounts that we studied to confirm this. One authority found during the mid-1950s that nearly half the US-owned subsidiaries in Britain made some sort of payment of this type. He noted a gradual movement by the parent companies to take payment in this form, since subsidiaries were reinvesting a large portion of their profits rather than remitting them as dividends.[21] But if the cases of Procter and Gamble, Kodak, and others are anywhere near being typical, and royalties paid only represent a portion of the true value or cost of the services received, then the rates of profits achieved by foreign subsidiaries are certainly overstated. We did encounter a few examples where the subsidiary management felt that they were being overcharged for services and products from the parent company. Such practice would of course tend to understate profitability. Profits could also be affected by the interest paid on intracompany loans.[22]

Another plausible explanation is that the foreign subsidiaries are more efficient than independent domestic companies, and this is directly reflected in a higher-than-average profitability.[23] Indeed, the firm which expands overseas is generally more dynamic than the average company, and it is also apt to be larger and more profitable than most. Certainly many of the firms among those interviewed were using what might be considered sophisticated management techniques if this is any measure of efficiency. But this is only part of the answer. Many of the most profitable subsidiaries were exploiting a complicated and advanced technology whose development had been perfected before being launched on to the British market, and the benefit derived from this accumulated experience was a prime factor in their ability to earn high profits. This appears to be especially true of the chemical industry as well as of the pharmaceutical industry, electronics, and office machinery manufacturing. Kodak claimed this in defence of its dominant position in the colour film market in the United Kingdom, stating that:

> Its position has only been achieved and held by the [Eastman Kodak] group's ability to offer products that have been and are better than those of its competitors and by constant improvement in services and standards of processing. These products and improvements reflect the skill and heavy investment of the group in research over many years and also the accumulated manufacturing knowhow which has enabled consistent high quality in volume production and processing to be secured.[24]

Similarly, Procter and Gamble Limited argued that its dominant and highly profitable position in the household detergents market in the United Kingdom was because 'it is an efficient company and part of an efficient organisation . . . and the benefits of the parent company's financial resources, manufacturing knowhow, technical developments and experience in marketing techniques have been of great significance'.[25] Firms in our sample such as Kodak and Procter and Gamble, along with others, had near monopoly positions in their sector because of this technical superiority, or because of the nature of the industry.

Another factor tending to boost profitability is specialisation. A substantial number of foreign subsidiaries concentrate on only a narrow range of products—those with the highest margins of profits—and do not attempt to manufacture other lines. In contrast, it has been said of, as an example, Imperial Chemical Industries in Great Britain that manufacture of certain products which yielded relatively low profits was nevertheless continued 'in the national interest'. If ICI did not produce these products (certain heavy chemicals), they would have had to be imported at the expense of an additional drain on foreign exchange. For reasons such as these, or because of tradition, or even for more irrational reasons, a domestic company may find it more difficult to abandon certain product lines or markets than might a foreign subsidiary whose major decisions are likely to be taken by a more coolly objective, distant parent company less influenced by the local environment.

While the sample of foreign subsidiaries was more profitable than the British quoted companies, there was a greater differential between the ninety American- and the twenty-five European-owned subsidiaries in the group. This is brought out by the data appearing in table 8.1. Someone who is accustomed to the rather broad discretionary procedures permitted to the accounting profession in most countries on the continent in Europe would probably dismiss such striking differences in the rate of profit as meaningless, no more than the result of a deliberate, conservative policy of management to understate profits. We have assumed this not to be the case under British accounting practice, and we have taken the figures shown on the accounts at their face value. However, there are at least two or three other explanations which bear a brief examination.

Table 8.1 Comparative rate of profits: United States and European-owned subsidiaries (net profit after tax divided by total assets)

	1960	1961	1962	1963	1964	1965	1966	1967	8-year average*
	%	%	%	%	%	%	%	%	%
First quartile									
25 European subsidiaries	3·8	1·2	1·2	1·7	3·0	2·5	1·0	1·4	2·5
90 American subsidiaries	5·9	3·4	3·7	4·6	5·6	5·0	3·2	3·4	4·4
Median									
25 European subsidiaries	5·3	4·1	2·8	3·8	4·0	4·1	2·9	2·5	3·1
90 American subsidiaries	9·8	8·2	7·4	8·2	8·2	8·2	6·2	6·3	7·8
Third quartile									
25 European subsidiaries	7·4	7·0	5·8	6·1	6·1	7·4	5·3	6·2	5·5
90 American subsidiaries	13·5	12·2	10·8	10·8	10·9	12·2	10·9	9·0	10·9

*Eight-year average refers to the median and quartile values of the means of the annual rates of return on total assets of each subsidiary.

First of all, one may argue that the sample of European subsidiaries is too small to be representative; a larger sample would be desirable. However, the number of European-owned manufacturing subsidiaries in the United Kingdom is not large, and those which have been included in our sample comprise most of the largest and best known.

Secondly, American-owned subsidiaries may be more efficient than those of European parentage. If this were so, it would be for much the same kinds of reasons that we suggested they were more efficient than British quoted companies. These include superior results from research and development, better technical knowhow, especially in production and marketing, greater financial resources, more effective management methods, and so forth. While this is a convenient answer, it seems hard to believe that this is the main reason in view of the success of many of the European parent companies in their own countries.

Finally, and we feel that this must be the most likely answer in the case of a number of the European subsidiaries, their profitability may be understated—not because of the skill of their accountants, but for reasons of (1) their capital structure which has the effect of significantly reducing profits after tax, and (2) their pricing policies on intracompany transfers. As evidence, in support of the first cause, the nine Swiss-owned subsidiaries were notable for having a large proportion of intracompany liabilities in their financial structure, the group averaging 23 per cent in 1959 and 37 per cent in 1967. The tax differential between Switzerland and the United Kingdom provides greater incentive for a Swiss company to repatriate earnings as interest and royalties (which under the terms of the bilateral tax treaty between the two countries has not been subject to withholding tax) than there would be for, say, an American company. The reason is that remittances to an American parent company, whatever the form, would be ultimately taxed at least at the full American rate, and the prevailing tax differential between the countries did not give much incentive to substitute one type of payment for another. The Swiss companies, on the other hand, rather than suffer British taxes on earnings remitted as dividends have, it appears, structured their subsidiaries' capital so as to remit as much as possible in the form of interest. The net effect of such policy, assuming that our evidence is representative, is to reduce materially reported net profits. Besides this, other evidence suggests that the profits of at least the Swiss-owned pharmaceutical subsidiaries are lower as a result of arbitrary pricing of material imported from their parent companies for use in their manufacturing.[26] Together, these practices go a long way towards explaining the low rate of profits earned by some of the European subsidiaries.

To conclude, taking the data at its face value suggests that the subsidiaries overall have achieved an impressive performance. Both their rate of growth and profitability have been consistently substantially above that achieved by the British quoted companies. Moreover, this can be mostly attributed to the success of the American-owned firms. However, an adequate explanation for the reasons of their success is less clear. While greater efficiency, technical superiority, and good management are important factors, there is strong evidence that the subsidiaries' reported profits are an inadequate index of their true performance. We have already seen in earlier chapters that, for various reasons of policy, companies frequently have an incentive to understate or overstate the results of a particular subsidiary. The usual assumption that companies will want to maximise profits may not be always valid at the level of the subsidiary. For, although corporate entities in the legal and accounting sense of the word, their economic performance may often only have meaning when considered within the context of the entire multinational group. This is a characteristic of the foreign subsidiary that creates special problems for the analyst, and bears keeping in mind whenever their growth and profitability are appraised.

Strategic considerations in the move abroad[1]

9.1 Why operate abroad?

Some companies have operated abroad for generations. A straight question as to why they went abroad would hardly be relevant to managers who have inherited a century or more of foreign expertise. Nevertheless these companies are just the ones where the reason for the operation is simple and clear—their business is concerned with raw materials that are scarce or unobtainable at home. Such companies are by their nature multinational, but the actual decision-making process leading to the original investment abroad can only be guessed at. Although nowadays these particular firms may well be diversified, they started with *natural resources* as their main business and this title has therefore been used to describe their origins. There are other concerns, too, which are necessarily multinational, such as shipping and air lines. Transport crosses frontiers and raw materials ignore them; these are among the industry groups which are committed to activities in more than one country. But most of the firms we investigated were in a business with no such necessity, and this chapter examines the range of reasons given.

Two specially interesting points emerged from questioning about the motives for the foreign operation. One was that, for all the talk about plans and strategies, the actual decision often arose from some chance, almost freakish event. Thus some firms reported approaches from foreign business men, others anti-trust suits, and yet others mentioned taking over a company which already had interests in other countries. Among the most common were personal influences of one sort or another. For instance, managers in one firm said that the only clear policy decision on record was *not* to manufacture abroad. This was based on the opinion that their goods were of a quality that would be permanently competitive across any barriers and foreign manufacture could only reduce the return on investment. Nevertheless this firm now has several factories around the world. Each was sanctioned as an exceptional breach of the policy; but those who campaigned for these developments found themselves powerfully supported when evidence came to light that customers were beginning to go international. This development had not been anticipated because in this particular industry the suppliers were the large firms, and the customers much smaller. However when the customer-companies did go international their demands became more exacting.

In addition to evidences of these almost casual routes to foreign operations, the other interesting point was that the majority of firms cited defensive reasons for the move. Under questioning they did not usually see themselves as aggressive entrepreneurs, merchant adventurers looking for fresh fields to conquer. As with their financial policies, their general commercial policies were apt to be described in defensive terms. They went abroad, they asserted, to protect markets or to provide greater security for their shareholders. Apart from a few exceptional firms, risk-taking, both personal and corporate, was reduced to a minimum in spite of publicity statements to the opposite effect. If there were no such things as tariff barriers or transport costs, we were repeatedly told, most companies would not be multinational. Other writers have drawn attention to this essentially defensive character of the decision to go abroad. One of these, after emphasising the threat to exports, goes on to stress the extra security of a global spread of manufacture—'parlaying one's bets', he calls it.[2] He suggests that this type of caution is a feature of American firms. No doubt this suggestion is made because a number of European firms are multinational in origin, but it remains that most of the European companies included in this present study also gave defensive reasons.

These defensive reasons may be the clinching arguments in a process of discussion. They are the points which loom largest in responses to questions, but other aspects of the thinking behind the decisions are more difficult to unravel. There are the more personal reasons already mentioned. There are also the political pressures, the factors operating within the companies' politics, which influence the decision. It is possible to identify certain managerial groups which themselves constitute pressures towards foreign operations, and some which urge opposite policies. The activities of these groups have already been examined in the chapters on organisation and power relationships. So it can now be suggested as a likely hypothesis that those forces in the company which press for manufacture abroad also press for this to be undertaken in a decentralised manner. Those groups, on the other hand, which strive against the move abroad in the first place, are the ones which press for a centralised approach when this move actually happens. Their instinct is to treat the foreign as if it were an extension of the domestic operation.

Finally the personal pressures are reinforced by a climate of opinion among businessmen about the possibilities of making money overseas, especially if the spread is large enough to offset losses in one region by windfalls in another. The facts about profitability in foreign subsidiaries collected in our last chapter tend to bear out this opinion. It would seem that if the company has an executive group with skills and commitments towards foreign operations, then it will respond to pressures such as market protection by developing overseas manufacture. Otherwise it may well respond in other ways. Table 9.1 sets out the overt reasons for the move overseas. The organisational and personal pressures which, it has just been suggested, settle the argument one way or the other are harder to identify. The fact is that every company has, as it were, a potential overseas management in its export department. It may well be suspected that a company damages this department if it refuses to consider manufacture abroad at a suitable stage. The people most skilled in foreign trade are likely to gravitate towards the firms which give most scope to the talents and skills they develop. These will be firms which are at least open-minded about supporting their export effort with assembly and manufacture where needed to overcome obvious frustrations. Such 'open-mindedness' will mean in practice that the export department, or some other management group, is liable to grow strong enough to press for this move abroad. Hence the motives that are listed on the table will grow into powerful arguments. If, on the other hand, this sort of development has not occurred, the company may lose those with international expertise, and thus become less likely to develop abroad in the future.

Table 9.1, then, summarises the decision-making which is discussed more fully in the rest of this chapter. This table distinguishes between the defensive and the more aggressive strategies, and shows that there are quite a number of the latter in spite of what has just been said. However, in interviews it is the former that are mentioned more often, the aggressive much less frequently. The distinction is drawn between motives which are essentially concerned with preserving existing business—protecting markets or preserving dividends—and those which involve a change of direction and a search for new opportunities. There are some reasons for foreign manufacture which do not fit either of these categories; these are called *other pressures* and listed separately. They include some environmental influences towards the development of manufacture in another country and one example is that of measures taken by governments to attract foreign investment. But these other pressures also include those internal to the company, the pressure groups which actually use the other arguments and propose and push the multinational strategies.

The second column of the table discusses the significance of the different pressures. The difficulties of a more precise weighting are explained at the foot of the table, but it should be noted that among the categories mentioned less frequently there may be included some very powerful reasons, which had yet gone unnoticed or unacknowledged in companies where they applied. For a different reason there is a problem about giving weightings to government action to encourage foreign business. The importance of what might be called the negative influence of government action—tariff barriers and import controls—are freely stated. There seems to be some reluctance,

Table 9.1 Why foreign operations?

1 The reasons	*2* The frequency with which this reason was mentioned (symbols explained at the foot of the table)	*3* The corresponding expansion strategies and relationships (see pp. 68–74)
I. DEFENSIVE STRATEGIES A company is operating abroad to defend its existing business as a result of:		
1.1. Government action in establishing or increasing:		
a. tariff barriers	A	Marketing, *open*
b. import controls	D	
c. legislation (at home or abroad) against monopolies or trade agreements	C	
1.2. Demands for local manufacture and other problems of nationalism in overseas markets	B	Marketing, *open*
1.3. Transport costs and delays	A	Marketing, *open*
1.4. Difficulties with agents, and licensees	B	Marketing, *open*
	C	Manufacturing, *close*
1.5. Troubles with after-sales service and other technical difficulties abroad	C	Manufacturing, *close* or marketing, *open*
1.6. The need to protect patents	C	Manufacturing, *close*
1.7. The need to ensure supplies of raw materials and components	B	Natural resources, *close*
1.8. The need to go international when competitors, suppliers or customers do so	B	Marketing, *open*

Table 9.1 (cont.)

1 The reasons	2 The frequency with which this reason was mentioned (symbols explained at the foot of the table)	3 The corresponding expansion strategies and relationships (see pp. 68–74)
1.9. The need to protect shareholders at home from trade recessions at home by:		
a. a geographical spread	C	⎰ Manufacturing, *close*, or
b. product group diversification (which may involve geographical as well)	D	⎱ Investment, *open*
2. AGGRESSIVE STRATEGIES 2.1. The search for: More profitable uses for underemployed resources at home in:		
a. capital and equipment	B	Investment, *open*, or Manufacturing, *close*
b. personnel	D	Natural resources, *close*, or Manufacturing, *close*
c. knowhow	C	Manufacturing, *close*
2.2. The more effective use of opportunities by the development of global plans and strategies for resources and markets	C	Marketing, *open*, or Manufacturing, *close*
2.3. Access to foreign knowledge or methods	D	Natural resources, *close*
2.4. The need to expand, when this can only be abroad, and the possibility of escaping from constraints at home	D E	

3. OTHER PRESSURES
3.1. Influence of governments, for example:

a. by general encouragement to foreign investment	E	Marketing, *open*
b. tax concessions	D	
c. cheap loans	D	
d. grants or guarantees	D	
e. buildings	E	
3.2. Influence of other companies, e.g. approach for knowhow	C	Manufacturing, *close*
3.3. Internal to company, such as pressure groups advocating overseas manufacture because of the expertise and insights of members	C	

Note on the frequency (col. 2): It has proved impossible to give a weighting to the different pressures in the form of: '2.2 was reported by sixteen companies'. Apart from the smallness of the sample, supplemented in this case by printed accounts, the main reason for this impossibility is the problem of defining a company opinion. If Company X is said to report a certain motive, who for this purpose is company X?—The chairman? The managing director? A majority of the board? The public relations officer? The official historian? Or who? Hence the following symbols have been used to represent as accurately as possible the weight given to the different motives: A. This motive was mentioned by virtually everyone questioned or reported in every company to which it was applicable at all; for instance under heading 1.1 companies exporting manufactured goods and under 2.2 companies importing scarce raw materials. B. Mentioned in some form or other by executives in over half the companies investigated or reported. C. Mentioned by executives in less than half, but more than two, of the firms. D. Mentioned once or twice only. E. Not mentioned at all in companies questioned, but referred to in the literature.

however, to acknowledge positive influences. Executives are apt to say that government incentives to business change so frequently that it is impossible for a company to base plans on them. However, in some cases the behaviour of the company throws in doubt the correctness of belittling positive government incentives. For instance in countries which adopt measures to attract business to areas where unemployment is endemic, there is often a concentration of foreign companies in just those areas.[3] This suggests, contrary to what their executives say, that multinational companies are responsive to government incentives; and that, therefore, a weighting based on the interview results would be unreliable. The fact that they often establish plants in problem areas is a contribution that foreign companies make to local economies.

The third column of the table refers back to chapter 3, and gives the expansion strategies and initial relations mentioned there beside the motives to which they correspond. It should be emphasised that these 'correspondences' are only the initial result of the move abroad; the relationships then become liable to the dialectical process described in chapter 3. But at least this table suggests some of the clusters of motives which collect around the various strategies, and which are then influenced by the personal and social pressures which we have examined. The motives provide, it could be said, the economic substrata for the social analysis of the behaviour of the organisation.

9.2 Defensive strategies

The most common reason given for the move abroad, then, is the protection of an existing market. A principal threat to a developing export trade is action by the foreign government to foster local industry and to conserve currency by tariff barriers or import controls. The threat can be overcome by the establishment of local manufacture; and so it can be said that it is obstacles to trade, not the reverse, that produce multinational firms.[4] Even where tariffs are not increasing, these reasons can apply as they still give an advantage to local manufacture which may thus be enabled to knock out imports as it grows more efficient, or becomes better able to cope with demand.

The emphasis on such threats may be exaggerated by companies where there is a balance-of-payments problem in the home country, for they have difficulties over the export of capital. Nevertheless in manufacturing firms, the advantages of large-scale production alone give support to emphatic statements that, if all trade was free and unimpeded, companies would be much more reluctant to disperse their manufacture. One company reported four stages in the decision to set up a manufacturing plant overseas. The first was to assess the present selling success, and the second to find out the present tariff position. Then the likely future effects of tariffs would be assessed, and fourthly the advantages of mass manufacture at home would be balanced against the expense of smaller runs abroad.[5] Another firm took the view that 'if there were no tariff barriers, import duties or national feelings, all manufacture would be done at home'. Many companies considered that, while some local production was necessary, the more sophisticated and costly parts could still be made at home and exported. There was less likely to be an import duty on these, unless local manufacturers had developed something sufficiently similar. It should be said that just as the raising of tariff barriers can be a powerful motive for starting production abroad, the subsequent lowering of these barriers can increase the attraction of foreign production. For this lowering can make it possible for a company once started in a particular country to consider sales in neighbouring countries. American firms both in the European Economic Community and in the Latin American Free Trade Area have found this. Direct import controls are another threat to a market which can be avoided by local production. Indeed these considerations not only influence a company towards the move abroad, but in some cases make a quick decision vital. Some countries may not be able to support more than one firm in a given industry, and the first one in will be given protection. In any case once local manufacture has become viable, someone is bound to start it. The other government intervention listed under defensive motives is legislation against monopolies and trading agreements. Anti-trust suits are, of course, specifically American, although legislation to produce similar results is increasing in Europe and especially in the Common Market countries. Nevertheless European as well as American firms mentioned the break-up of agreements in the United States or with American companies as stimulating developments abroad.

In addition to actual legislation designed to foster local industry, various nationalistic pressures may threaten foreign goods in a country and suggest local manufacture. These pressures include the placing of contracts by both government and private agencies and the adoption of local standards. At certain times and for certain consumer goods, the foreign product may be fashionable; but a market built up in this way is vulnerable and manufacture nearer the point of sale may become a necessity. Problems of transport are a similar factor, and one that was mentioned by most respondents. Problems of transport may particularly point to a decision to manufacture the lighter, specialised equipment at home, and the rest locally. One example was a small engineering company in the early stages of growth abroad. Starting from the production of one piece of specialised equipment, this company had developed into allied product lines. At the time of the enquiry this firm only had one manufacturing unit overseas; this was in Australia, where the transport saving was obvious enough. The manufacturing company grew out of a marketing subsidiary, and it was thought likely that others would develop in the same way.[6] The same firm was building a factory in the European Common Market. Press reports had praised its robust selling in the Common Market countries; but the expenses of transport and the delays involved had proved so frustrating as to impel this new venture. Another small company made specialised electronic equipment which was usually carried by air, as rapid delivery and minimal handling were essential. Naturally the expense of air transport made manufacture nearer the market viable as soon as sales began to climb.

Thus both transport costs and transport delays were frequently mentioned. Less frequently, but sometimes forcefully, stated were problems with agents. Many companies that are not multinational in the present sense have been establishing marketing subsidiaries overseas to avoid problems with agents, and some have done this by buying the agents themselves. The role of the foreign business agent is a study of its own;[7] but one important problem is the cost of the agents' commission, and another is how to get an adequate return on the other expenses involved. For the company has to inject effort into the area, and the agent's initiative may be minimal.

Another difficulty of a similar kind, also mentioned by a limited number of firms, was with after-sales and other forms of technical service. Once some measure of local manufacture was established, there was a base for a more effective maintenance and advisory service in the country concerned. In some branches of engineering this could be a crucial consideration. Another technical issue which constitutes a defensive motive for going abroad is the protection of patents. Nationalistic outlooks in many countries produce bias against foreign business; but foreign patents registered and used in the country are enforced. Thus both tariff barriers and patent laws suggest local manufacture—the nationalism of the one combines with internationalism of the other. The protection of patents may be vital to a technically oriented firm, where a large research outlay can so easily be dissipated. Obviously it is impossible to have a subsidiary in every country, but some companies aim at world coverage—that is, usually, coverage of the non-communist world, although increasingly licensing agreements are being made with eastern countries—through agents and licensees in countries where direct manufacture is impossible. Other companies use foreign subsidiaries to grant and police licences in their areas of the world. With some companies registering numerous new inventions each year, the marketing and protection of these inventions becomes of increasing concern.

The seventh motive listed as defensive is the need to ensure supplies of raw materials. Wherever materials or components are scarce, there is a tendency for companies to buy up their suppliers. Whether or not this constitutes a pressure to operations abroad obviously depends on the kind of material. But the pressure is becoming increasingly common. The result is a form of vertical integration, for the company now manufactures numerous stages of its product from primary material to consumer article. This vertical integration brings its own difficulties. Undertaken to reduce the company's exposure in one direction, that of dependence on suppliers who may prove unreliable, it leads to exposure in another, that of over-dependence on one type of business. A slump in one part becomes a slump in the whole in a vertically integrated concern. Hence further defensive expansion is likely. The other difficulty about vertical integration across frontiers is that it can reduce rather than increase the possibilities of a global strategy. For the manufacturing units in the group find themselves committed to certain suppliers to the exclusion of others. So this type of integration is unpopular with production managers who find themselves no longer able to shop around. As part of a policy to leave them to stand on their own feet, many firms will allow purchasing outside the group; but managers usually said that they regarded this permission as theoretical. At least they would have to give a very compelling reason for buying outside. Vertical integration may well be a route to multinational operations, or at least an extension of them. It also produces problems within the company which may lead to further commitments abroad.

A pressure of a totally different character which has been mentioned already is the growing internationalism of so many industries. Historically, some firms reported, they were finally moved to go multinational when other firms in similar or related businesses did so. These other firms could be competitors, customers or suppliers, or even all three; but it was the information that customers were going multinational which had the most influence in making a company decide to do the same.

The last two groups of defensive pressures consist of the search for greater security for shareholders. The strategic consideration here is to even out fluctuations in profits, so that the company can achieve the normal over-riding objective of a steadily rising dividend (see above pp. 159–63). Diversification helps to achieve this purpose in two ways. One is a greater geographical spread, which by definition means operating in more than one country. The aim here is that a recession in one country should be matched by a boom in another, thus cushioning the impact of the former by the latter. The other form of diversification is by the addition of new products or services. This will not necessarily produce foreign operations, but in some cases does have this effect. An example is when a company that is already multinational is bought in the process of diversification.

Both these routes to expansion are intended to provide a cushion against setbacks in the home country, or in any market that is important to the company. One company, which achieved geographical and product group diversification at the same time, regarded the former as a means of insulating shareholders against temporary setbacks in the economy of the home country. The chairman of another company has recorded that: 'It has long been our policy to expand our overseas subsidiary companies at a rate at least as great as we expand in Great Britain, thus keeping us abreast of world developments wherever they arise and at the same time providing us with the security of a widespread international business.'[8]

In addition to problems caused by the economic condition of a particular country, any company involved with capital goods might face a temporary shortage of work in one of their markets. So geographical spread and product diversification could be especially powerful motives with such companies. As one put it, if a huge contract was out for tender only one company would secure it. Hence operating in several countries reduced the chances that the company would be without contracts at any given time. If this medium-sized company took this view, so did one of the largest studied. This latter company manufactured in more than twenty-five countries, and was constantly reassessing the risks involved in any particular area. Product diversification had been undertaken in order to underpin the geographical spread. This diversification was into products which appeared to develop logically from existing lines, and included a move into service industries; these services also were operated internationally. Naturally diversification into new lines or services is easier for the large companies,[9] many of whom achieve product group and geographical expansion at the same time. The organisational problems that this produces have already been discussed, and are the principal factors producing organisational change.

9.3 Aggressive strategies

'If you could be a fly on the board-room ceiling, I think you might be surprised at the number of times a surplus of funds and managerial talent was a major factor in setting a company off on the diversification trail.'[10] This quotation expresses one spur to an aggressive strategy on foreign manufacture. Among the limited number of companies that mentioned underemployed resources, the main emphasis was technical. Firms were looking for more effective ways of using any technical superiority they might have, and for spreading the cost of research. This superiority may be of an actual marketable invention, or it may be of a manufacturing technique. It may also be of management methods, and the realisation that the methods a company has evolved will put it immediately in a favourable position in another country can be significant impetus towards moving there. However, this can also have its dangers, especially if local reactions to the new methods are incorrectly anticipated.

Some firms mentioned overseas operations as a more profitable use of their capital,[11] and we have already suggested that the evidence of the last chapter supports this. Among the many reasons for this profitability was the occasional opportunity to buy a sound small company at an attractive price. Indeed one firm, currently looking for acquisitions abroad as a profitable use of its resources, reported approaches by companies unable to finance their expansion plans.[12] Other firms found limited use for their resources at home and were impelled into foreign operations when they realised this. Very few companies indeed actually mentioned underemployed personnel resources. On the contrary the problem of recruiting adequate managers was one of the factors which made for caution in embarking on projects abroad. However, where a firm had built up a capable management team, then it had also recruited people who would be likely and able to use the other arguments effectively. To this extent managerial resources could be the least mentioned but ultimately most significant element. Indeed an aggressive strategy implies staff of a calibre to think out and implement such policies. One particular way in which the underemployment of the resources of personnel arises is when a company is heavily committed in export trade with some part of the world. The achievement of this trading success will have meant building up a team of specialists in that part of the world— experts in everything from the local market to the local language. The very existence of this team will produce a lobby towards further expansion in the area concerned, and the skills acquired are likely to be underemployed.

The phrase *underemployed resources* can also refer to machinery. For example a company which has re-equipped at home may be able to use the displaced machinery abroad. A relatively small company with a limited spread overseas reported that underemployed resources both at home and abroad had led to overseas developments. This company had started abroad entirely with marketing organisations, and some of these had grown into production. The advantage of buying a firm using similar machinery and then rationalising production was also mentioned; and so was the development of a subsidiary from marketing to assembly and servicing, and from there to manufacture. Thus the realisation that a company has a potential that is not being fully used either at home or abroad can constitute a pressure towards expansion overseas.

The second group of aggressive strategies is the search for a global policy, and the various special opportunities which encourage such a search. Again this was not often mentioned by the managers questioned, not nearly as often as they should have mentioned it to judge by what has been written on the subject. Articles in several journals advocate global strategies in terms that are admittedly often glowing rather than specific. The development of such policies seems to depend on the exercise within the firm of management groups committed to promoting and operating the techniques involved. But once such people are recruited they constitute a pressure to ever more sophisticated policy formation, to the consternation of existing management in small subsidiaries abroad.

Global strategies do, of course, include so many activities that any attempt to be specific is apt to appear naïve or even absurd; but among those that should be mentioned are considerations as to where a product can be manufactured most cheaply. The whole question of rationalisation across frontiers has been discussed already,[13] but this is a point on which the aggressive firm neatly reverses the responses suggested by those adopting defensive strategies. For it becomes possible to make calculations about the theoretically ideal site for the manufacture of any particular product taking into account all the costs of production and transport, and all the constraints on trade. Whether and how such a calculation is implemented will also depend on the available personnel, and their outlooks.

Along with the use of the company's resources abroad goes the search for other benefits from the host countries. A foreign subsidiary can be a 'listening post', sensitive to local conditions and having access to research and other sources of knowledge in the country concerned. The importance of this aspect of the affiliate's role can offset some problems and expenses. Hence companies argue that even an unprofitable national subsidiary can produce overall benefits to the firm. Unless this is to be regarded as special pleading in all circumstances, it bears out what has already been said about the difficulties of profit appraisal of the foreign operation.

The development of an aggressive strategy will take account, therefore, of many considerations about the availability and cost of resources in various parts of the world. These include materials, capital, knowledge and labour. Indeed increasing foreign manufacture in low labour cost countries, in some cases in spite of political risks, is occurring and is naturally forcing up wages in those countries. But there are other detailed issues where worldwide strategies can produce local opportunities. For instance there is the winning of government contracts, particularly in defence equipment. These are likely to be awarded to a company which can show at least a proportion of local manufacture. Indeed a multinational company is in a particularly strong position here. Skilful organisation can give it the best of both worlds, for it can combine the foreign knowhow that governments often require with the local manufacture that they insist upon.

Another example is the case of aid programmes to developing countries. In some cases a loan from some western country may be 'tied'; it may be a condition of the loan that contracts are placed in the lending country. Thus a company with its head office in country A may be negotiating for a contract with the government of country B. But country B proposes to finance the project with a loan from country C, which insists that the contract goes to a company with its registration. The company in country A must, therefore, have a subsidiary in country C in order to win the contract; it may also need one in country B which will favour a local firm if only in order to conserve currency. In this case at least a three-cornered spread is needed for this one contract. Reasons of patriotism and national security may be other factors that weigh with the host country.

Noticing bargains overseas should also be listed as an aggressive strategy. Once a company has started operations abroad, it finds itself in a position of looking for suitable companies to purchase for a number of reasons. In addition to finding firms which will be a profitable use of resources for a company which has already got foreign experience, the purchase of an existing organisation can be a cheap and rapid way of increasing capacity in any part of the world. This applies especially in developed countries with high site values and an overpressed building industry. This type of motive can lead to joint ventures and is discussed again in the next chapter. Another result can be expansion into some countries where a significant, if difficult to measure, return will be the ability of the subsidiary to gain access to the local technology. This may only apply in a limited number of circumstances, but appeals to companies looking for long-term expansion.

A number of pressures to expansion, sometimes apparently for its own sake, make up the final group of aggressive strategies. There is a widespread view that to stand still is to decline. Some companies reported that they had originally gone overseas in order to continue to grow since their domestic and export markets had reached their maximum possible size. They might, for instance, already dominate the home market and any further expansion would cause their government to intervene; or alternatively their competitors might be in a position to block further developments at home. So a sense of 'expand or go under' would involve building up the foreign operations.

A company which mentioned this type of motive first went overseas as part of a rapid expansion by acquisition. The management regarded the move abroad as a logical development of their growth; but they had actually expanded into the foreign operations by buying a company which already had foreign subsidiaries. The parent company put great score by careful planning. The chairman spoke about 'out-thinking' his competitors, by which he meant a carefully planned expansion designed to balance one product against another, and one geographical area against another. Thus, unlike some firms in the same original business, this company was insulated against recessions in any one of its product groups. This expansion involved a limited territorial spread and a limited vertical product spread, much of which was achieved by the purchase of firms with which the company already traded. Such a development overseas—by intention, as a step in a calculated advance, and yet by a route which could have produced the same result without the intention—is an interesting and not uncommon model of the operation of aggressive policies. Other examples are the noticing of profitable opportunities abroad. These opportunities may lie in the chance to introduce a product in a new market in which for some reason local manufacture was necessary from the start; or it might arise from the chance to buy a company which was especially relevant to the present stage in the firm's growth. Another company reported profitable opportunities as a reason for their wide spread overseas. Their product was one which came into demand as countries developed. In appraising prospects in a developing country, they would set the political risk against potential growth, which could be huge. In general the aim to take worldwide advantage of their inventions and products was crucial to their policy development.

Among the less tangible motives are power,[14] prestige and the reputation of the firm. The position of power that a company may be able to establish for itself is significant, especially in a developing country. Some companies have been able to establish close working relationships with governments who have accorded them a unique position in return for the import of capital and the development of local industry. Similar activities in the home country might have been frowned on as monopolistic. At home the company might play a very small part in the nation's economy. In the host country its role might be very significant indeed. While abuse of this power can bring threats of nationalisation, the country concerned is likely to be itself frightened of a threat by the firm to withdraw.

In concluding this section on aggressive strategies, it should be said that there are signs that regional as well as global programmes are increasingly being advocated. The development of common markets and free trade areas has stimulated this. In some companies such policies entered into their active considerations. These were mainly firms which already had long-range planning departments, probably with a marketing emphasis. The advantages of regional planning strategies are being stressed by some consultancy firms and so are likely to become more generally accepted. There can be no doubt that the multinational company has special opportunities for developing aggressive global or regional policies. The fact that more has not been done about this already is surprising.

9.4 Other pressures towards foreign operations

The other pressures, like the defensive strategies, list first the influence of government activity on the decision-making process in the company. But there is a difference in the way firms respond. The negative effects of government action in tariff barriers and import controls are widely said to be the principal reason for the move abroad. The positive influences are less often acknowledged.[15] But many countries keep trade missions and information centres open abroad to encourage foreign investment. Inducements offered, sometimes only to firms which will settle in areas of unemployment, include tax concessions, cheap loans, grants, guarantees or buildings to rent. In some cases this may be backed by considerable publicity. Government agencies may put their services at the disposal of foreign investors, and may encourage national companies to forge links with those from other countries. In addition to that of government inducements, another influence on the decision to go abroad is that of foreign firms themselves. This was mentioned occasionally as when a company had been approached by a foreign firm in the same business with a view to some form of amalgamation which would enable a pooling of resources.

One company said that the initiative towards new developments always came this way. At first their response had been to sell knowhow. But this proved unsatisfactory as the business of the licensee increased rapidly, and he gained benefits from the development which could have gone to the firm itself. Hence developed the policy of buying shares in the foreign company, sometimes with the cash payment made for the manufacturing rights. This was both a profitable use of the resources acquired, and ensured that the parent company had a continuing share in the profits gained from its invention. In some cases a further development occurred. For the company found that, if they had a 30 per cent share in a firm in a foreign country, they often put more than 30 per cent of the development and sales effort in that area. In addition they stopped exporting there. So it was logical to build up a larger holding until the one-time licensee had become a subsidiary. All this firm's overseas' companies had developed in this way except one. This exception was a wouldbe licensee about whose prospects under existing management the company had serious doubts, and they bought them outright instead of selling them knowhow.

Underlying much of this discussion have been the personal factors in the formation of policy. The pressures exerted by different groups of managers with different backgrounds and primary interests constantly came out in this investigation. These pressures are, for instance, influential in promoting the organisation and reorganisation discussed earlier in this book. There the groups are mainly those identified with either product group or geographical management or the central services. The pressure for manufacture abroad comes, as we have seen, from the export department with its specialists in foreign affairs. The product group managers usually resist this trend. The pressure groups that advocate developments abroad consist of those who have expertise in other countries and insight into other cultures. Without some internal pressures, it may well be suspected, the other pressures to the move abroad may not be powerful enough. This is why some companies do go overseas and others with similar opportunities, interests and resources do not.

Finally the advocates of the foreign venture will find their arguments reinforced by the climate of opinion already mentioned, and by the growth of centres of international business in cities like Geneva and Brussels. These centres have all the attendant facilities from experts in the relevant aspects of company law to multilingual secretaries, as well as ample provision for the leisure of the foreign executive and the education of his children. Hence they support the economic evidence by making the actual process of setting up the foreign operations less painful.

9.5 The abandonment of foreign operations

In the spring of 1967 an American company, General Tire and Rubber, abandoned its operations in the Netherlands. The huge losses which brought about this withdrawal were put down to over-optimism about the possibilities and lack of understanding of the problems of the area.[16] Among these latter was a closeknit relationship between existing firms in the business which made it difficult for the newcomer to achieve a satisfactory position. It may also be that the firm had appraised the possibilities by criteria and methods which are satisfactory for domestic expansion plans, but are just not satisfactory abroad. The following year the most drastic loss made by any of the world's biggest companies was made by the Celanese Corporation, and was almost entirely incurred in its subsidiaries in Italy, Canada and Britain. The largest part of this loss of £56,200,000 was in Sicily and was put down to a series of technical problems exacerbated by economic difficulties.[17] These chilling considerations introduce a brief discussion of the arguments against venturing abroad.

Many of the motives given for overseas operations have parallel disincentives. For instance overemployed resources may lead to a withdrawal. One small company found itself short of capital, and sold its French subsidiary. The defensive pressures to foreign operations also have their reverse side. For instance one company mentioned a foreign affiliate whose factory was now in 'mothballs' as they put it. This operation had been founded at a time of exchange difficulties with the country concerned. These made local manufacture advisable, but the project had never succeeded as the market had proved too small.

Among the most important dangers in the move abroad is that of too rapid growth. Whatever motives may impel a firm to take the first steps, most companies start with ideas such as that of the 'limited geographical spread'. But many find the commitment larger than expected, and have difficulties in fixing an upper limit in practice. The extra growth needed to achieve the original object of the expansion abroad may turn out expensive. There may be great rewards ultimately, but there is the immediate problem of coping with unexpected demands on available resources. The return on investment of established multinational companies may turn out to be higher outside the home country, but it is more difficult to assess the number of firms which have withdrawn from overseas operations because the growth proved too expensive. There is some evidence that this may have happened when other reasons—such as 'the political situation'—have been given. At least one celebrated example has occurred in recent years of a large company which became insolvent as a result of a too rapid development abroad was a major factor.

One structural issue that actually inhibits the move abroad is the position of the licensing department. This department has a vested interest in upholding its choice of licensee, and in defending his reputation.[18] Further, the agreements may have been made on the assumption that licensing arrangements would be long-term, and it may be difficult, or indeed impossible, to alter these. Another inhibiting factor is the sheer problem of establishing an industry in a new area. It has been said that 'an industrial complex tends to sustain itself'.[19] Setting up in a completely new region carries not only the budgeted expense of bringing in manpower and training others, it carries the unbudgeted expense of a total lack of the local facilities of an established area; there is, to take one small example, no engineers' club in which to talk over problems. This is the converse of what has been said earlier in this chapter about the growth of centres of international business.

Usually if a company withdraws from foreign operations, this happens early in its career abroad. Among the few examples of firms well established in foreign activities that had ceased to be international was one which had owned one of its subsidiaries for forty years. During that time the link had become tenuous and the parent company had not been very successful in its home country. The subsidiary came to regard the money sent to head office, which in any case was based on gross sales and not on profits, as a fee for services which were not being provided. It considered itself to be supporting an unprofitable central organisation, and increasingly asked what the fee was being paid for. Eventually the particular subsidiary took the initiative in arranging for a purchase of the shares and thus became independent. Other national subsidiaries did the same, and the group ceased to exist. In fact the only link left between the various companies is the name they all still carry, together with one of their products and some production and sales methods.

The vulnerability of marketing subsidiaries in a period of technological change is another risk. For example if a country ceased to use some product or raw material, a marketing organisation could not survive unless it rapidly grew into production. One company included in this research had faced a position in which its selling organisations could only be maintained where there were production interests as well. The world spread had been wide due to the marketing of a scarce raw material. Technical changes cut the market for this material. So the company now operates only in countries where the old subsidiaries had been enterprising enough to develop some productive activities. This company emphasised from its experience the importance of anticipating technical change as part of a global strategy.

Financial problems—currency restrictions, taxation difficulties—have caused some abandonment of foreign operations. The chairman of one British company mentioned the obstacles of taxation, Bank of England control and the cost of foreign currency, in addition to government exhortation against the export of capital. Nevertheless his company, like most of those questioned, considered some limited expansion abroad a necessary self-defence.

K*

If there are pressure groups within management for the move abroad, the converse is also true. The arguments against foreign operations are powerful to those most concerned with production, home marketing and sometimes finance. There are identifiable groups in most companies who represent opposition to the move abroad. This move disarranges the structure of the firm, and shifts the balance of power within it. Sometimes the resistance that builds up, while it does not succeed in preventing the move abroad, manages to distort the organisational changes required. The significance of the arguments against the move can be expected to depend on the relative strength of the rival groups.

Companies and countries

10.1 The multinational company and the home country government

The multinational company is involved in a love–hate relationship with governments and peoples at home and abroad. Massive public relations exercises are mounted to increase the love and reduce the hate, and these have not been unsuccessful. There are naturally many areas of mutual interest; but there are also considerable possibilities of economic and social conflict which are likely to get worse as the international firms get more powerful. It may well be that these companies will one day become large supranational organisations registered with the United Nations. Even now they seem able to bridge the divisions of the world more easily than political or religious organisations. One usually unstated advantage that these companies have for their own management is a certain independence of the constraints of national governments. Attempts to assert this independence, on the one hand, and to limit it on the other, lie behind many of the problems between companies and countries. Some of these problems concern relationships between the parent company and its own government at home. The firm is subject to the strong pressures to begin or to increase its investment abroad listed in chapter 9. Whatever may be the policy of the government, the firm is likely to assume that what is in its own interests will also be in the interests of the home country; and this will be in spite of the fact that companies are well aware in their own affairs that the interests of the whole often do not coincide with those of the parts. In the eyes of the government, the outflow of funds may appear to damage the national economy, at least in the short run. But the transfer of technical knowledge and manufacturing facilities will also appear to be against the national interest in certain circumstances. A realistic payback may appear to the countries concerned so long-term as to be almost a mirage.

American discussion of this subject usually assumes the need to encourage the free flow of capital, but that some limitation (preferably voluntary) is necessary when a balance-of-payments crisis threatens. European opinion tends to be less sure of the desirability of investment abroad. The ex-colonial countries have a longstanding stake in the developing nations, but this is generally discussed in the light of different criteria. Investment in another industrialised country, it is considered, can be appraised by economic considerations; social policies, however, are involved in considering action in developing areas. Nevertheless these countries represent huge potential markets. For British firms and the British economy, the economic considerations involved in overseas investment have been analysed in great detail by the Reddaway report already mentioned.[1] The report shows that the multinational firm brings advantages and disadvantages to the home country; it shows too the significance of the actual timing of the investment. Inasmuch as there is an area of conflict between the national government and multinational companies investing overseas, this is likely to become more intense as the size of these companies increases. Governments are bound to be more apprehensive if firms are able to export large amounts of capital at times when this can be damaging to the nation's currency. At the same time, the companies are themselves becoming more powerful and thus more able to find means of freeing themselves from governmental constraints. If they are big employers of labour then their threat to move a particular plant to another country will be taken seriously. The following quotation gives an example: 'This country is fighting for its economic life, and one of its chief weapons is Shell. It cannot afford to let that weapon go.'[2]

So there may well be areas of conflict between the company and its own government. The more international the company becomes, the more are problems likely to develop. For it is too much to expect that the global planning procedures of the firm will produce projects for new investment or integrated production which always coincide with the political interests of the government. Equally the problems should not be of a continuous nature, and there are identities of interest as well. The large multinational company may be a part of national prestige, it 'shows the flag' for the home country. In a sense it demonstrates the national ability to succeed. Hence it furthers national objectives. It may also use government facilities abroad, and perhaps contribute to these as well. Most companies seem to regard their relationships with their own governments as cooperative, although punctuated by occasional strong disagreements. With foreign governments there is a similar mixture, but the disagreements are more severe and complicated.

10.2 Cultural differences

Cultural differences between countries are frequently discussed, often in terms of other people's attitude to work, but are hard to identify with any precision. Accounts of problems between foreign companies and the people of the host country are apt to read like the difficulties the same people have with their own national minorities. One side claims to bring 'economic advantages', the other side alleges the destruction of its culture. Neither side talks directly to the other. To make this comparison is not to belittle the significance of the problems. There are always potential, sometimes even endemic, disputes between the foreign firm and its hosts, but these do not usually become critical at least in the industrialised countries. It must also be said that culture is changing all the time, and the problems of anticipating cultural change differ little from one country to another. Change, as it affects local nationals both as customers and as participants in a business organisation, is determined by wealth, technical innovation, the spread of education and other such influences which show remarkable similarities in different countries. Indeed some of the alleged cultural differences would appear to be no more than travellers' tales. Obviously the brash and insensitive manager abroad is likely to stumble across some obstinate problems which can be put down to the local culture, but he is likely to do the same at home.

Stereotypes of behaviour in other countries do seem able to survive experiences which demonstrate their falsity. What is certain is that the *mores* that attach to the management of people and the expectations which accompany promotion to different levels in the hierarchy are rapidly changing, and that the growth of industrialisation is producing similar changes everywhere. With consumption habits, also, the differences between countries are becoming less. International firms selling in one country products proved successful in another are influencing this change. There are some failures; but companies are reporting an increasing popularity of, for instance, international brands in consumer goods. One company mentioned developing countries in this connection. Their experience had been that local brands were popular when a country first became independent, but as the population became more sophisticated the sales of international brands increased. In general it would appear that more industrialisation, and the higher standard of living and the more widespread education that go with it, reduce differences between countries while increasing the diversity within a country.[3] International firms in the consumer field are themselves important contributors to this trend.

Many statements about cultural differences are based on national stereotypes which at best incompletely correspond with reality. Many firms have evidence of this in their intrafirm comparisons. Thus ideas that in some countries employees work harder than in others may well be contradicted by the firm's own productivity figures. If it is becoming axiomatic that labour effectiveness depends on management ability, these comparisons are certainly bearing out this axiom. One executive said in a company which had a long experience of foreign manufacture: 'We are all as lazy as we are allowed to be'; the social scientist might wish to add to this, 'or as energetic as we are allowed to be'. A number of differences are thus becoming less or indeed proving insubstantial, but this still leaves many which must be taken seriously.

Among these are different expectations both for managers and workmen on such matters as job security, different degrees of willingness and ability to travel, different ideas about the relationship between work and leisure. Some of these have been well documented. For instance, the composition of the labour force varies from country to country and to ignore this will upset any forecast. As usual the stage of industrialisation affects the difference more than national traditions. Thus greater industrialisation means fewer young people in the labour force, for they will remain in full-time education, but a great increase in the number of women seeking work outside the home. It also involves a lower proportion of manual to professional workers. The spread of education obviously changes job expectations and consumer habits. Cultural differences may also be detected among the so-called 'tension-reducing mechanisms', the procedures for dealing with industrial disputes. In one country there will be systematic bargaining procedures, in another country more paternalistic methods. The relative steepness of salary scales in different countries reflects different cultural backgrounds, and so does the relative position of different occupations on these scales.

Another difference is the degree of secrecy and openness which companies observe about the facts of their business. European firms are known to be more secretive than American, and some European countries seem to be more secretive than others. That secrecy in some issues is a matter of tradition rather than business necessity is shown by the way European companies will claim that it is absolutely necessary not to disclose facts which American firms have always published. Of course there are other factors involved in the matter of secrecy. On the one hand inside an organisation pressures often build up against the disclosure of information; on the other hand from outside the firm governments or stock exchanges may compel the publication of facts about the business. But, this admitted, there does seem a cultural difference between countries in the general attitude as to whether you reveal as much as you can or whether you conceal as much as you are allowed to.

Another issue on which there are national differences is that of government intervention. American managers abroad often remark on the need to adapt themselves to a situation in which the government plays a much larger role in the decision-making process than that to which they have been accustomed. Since head office executives in the United States may not understand the greater influence that European governments are likely to have, this is a possible cause of problems between them and subsidiary managers. National and regional planning in Britain and France is one example of a form of government action intended to affect business decisions, and requiring consultation.

One study of cultural differences contrasts employment practices in Japan with those in the West.[4] Among many significant statements about these differences, one is the assertion that 'the extent and nature of the involvement of the firm in the life of the worker are based on different assumptions as to the nature of the work relationship'. One suspects that these assumptions are changing in Japan, because the author tells us that they are much criticised there. However the practical consequences of these assumptions include such matters as stability of employment with high redundancy payments, little attachment of pay to productivity except sometimes in the form of a group bonus system, small differentials between managers and operators. All these are matters which are clearly changing in the West too, but in the opposite direction. Through greater awareness of the significance of the group, which social scientists have long been emphasising, the West will move nearer to the Japanese position as well as vice versa. For at the same time, no doubt, greater consciousness of the significance of the individual will move Japanese practice closer to that of the West. This is in no way to deny that at the moment there are significant differences which must influence policy. Nor is it to doubt the author's statement that 'American techniques fail to communicate successfully what it is they are trying to accomplish'. The same can happen in Europe. What is suggested is that the differences are transitory and should not be exaggerated. The problems are those of cross-national operations rather than cross-cultural as such.

The area where it would be expected that the sensitivity to local customs would be most important is that of labour relations. Up to a point this is obviously true, and true within a country as well as across frontiers. Skilled management takes account of the different customs of different industries and regions as well as countries. But this is not the whole story. For one thing, if local nationals do not like their customs flouted, they may be also sensitive to being treated as different. The patronising foreign firm may be worse than the insensitive one. Another point is perhaps more significant. This is that foreign methods of handling labour can make a great impact. For instance the more egalitarian customs of American managers can create a very high morale among European workers.[5] In general it can be said that workers in multinational firms may make rude remarks about their foreign bosses, but they show no more staying power in their invective than those who are employed by their own fellow-countrymen. Indeed, it may well be suspected that companies are handicapping themselves unnecessarily by being oversensitive to local culture, especially considering the reserves of voluntary support the international company has—assets of knowledge and prestige that may be frittered away by too much concern for local differences. On the other hand, the importing of liberal foreign labour policies may make the company unpopular with its fellow-employers. This points to the peculiar difficulty of a genuine integration in the local economy. The size, resources and technical efficiency of the international firm make it able to develop practices with regard to labour which other employers oppose. Moreover, the firm can transfer from one country to another experience and research in industrial relations, although it may be suspected that this is the least exploited of the average company's theoretical advantages.

However, in one company that has tried to pick up some of the results of studies in the social sciences and use them round the world, the chairman has said: 'Shifts in the social structure are leading us to carry out changes in the organisation of the production process in which increasing account is taken of the capacities and ambitions of the individual employee. In this connection we mention smaller working groups, changes in the traditional layout of work positions, enlarging the scope of certain jobs and giving people more responsibility.'[6]

While multinational firms may have different practices with regard to employees, much more different are likely to be the ways that workers' organisations respond to management. These will be based on ideas about the role of labour, the degree of cooperation that is traditional, and the methods of conducting industrial strife. The patterns of industrial conflict for different countries have been worked out, and some of the distinguishing factors isolated. These can be considered in terms of age and membership of the labour movement, the degree of acceptance of unions by employers, the political links of organised labour, and the involvement of the state in management–labour relations and other issues. How these vary between countries has been demonstrated and adds up to marked differences in practices to some of which the unions adhere tenaciously.

In a somewhat lighter vein, the penetration of most of the world by a symbol of American culture, Coca-Cola, has been documented by E. J. Kahn, who writes: 'The acceptability of Coca-Cola in any region is apt to depend on the region's political orientation towards the United States. For the last ten years or so, our foreign critics have taken to identifying the policies of our State Department with those of the Coca-Cola company.'[7] The brash, direct appeal of the United States consumer product advertising is not popular in some countries, although that is not to say it is ineffective. And in advertising styles can be seen some differences. Some advertising that is widely used in northern Europe cannot be used at all in other parts of Europe and Asia; or where it can be shown it gives an impression the opposite of that desired. But more interesting than different advertising styles or regulations is the general way in which the company approaches the business of putting itself on the map in the host country. In many situations the local culture is most favourable to the firm which keeps in the background, and promotes the product or the brand rather than the company. This implies long-term attention to fitting the company into the host country situation. Some pressures operate against this; for instance the effort may not be visible to the parent company. So the local manager may favour measures that run counter to the local culture but help to make an impression at the head office of his firm.[8]

Thus the cultural differences are growing less, but are likely to remain significant in some areas of behaviour for a long time to come. The significance is declining most rapidly in consumption and leisure activities, and appears to be most persistent in employment conditions and methods of management. Cultural differences, in other words, remain longer inside the workplace than outside.

10.3 The multinational company and the host country

Of which country, home or host, is the foreign subsidiary supposed to be a citizen? The host country, most firms would say; but their practices do not always bear out this answer. From reading the literature it would appear that this problem is more worrying to United States than to European firms, and maybe here lies a cultural difference. But no United States manager we met seemed much concerned with the ideological problems so often raised in the *Harvard Business Review* and elsewhere. No one, for instance, echoed the question: 'How far do you go in compromising the principles of a free economic system with socialistically inclined governments?'[9] Indeed company managements are concerned to keep a neutral stance at least in public, but a division of loyalties occurs in areas of political or ideological sensitivity. In recent years problems have especially occurred with United States firms operating abroad over trade with China. On the whole, European countries and companies of European origin are actively developing trade with eastern countries. Hence a European firm boasts of a trade success with China, which a United States firm would not even accept. This produces an acute clash of loyalties for the foreign subsidiaries of the latter, some examples of which are mentioned below.

However the ideological and practical problems are by no means confined to United States firms. The subsidiaries of British companies have been involved in problems in dealing with Rhodesia, for instance, and South Africa as well. A prime minister of this latter country is reported as having said: 'This matter of mother companies being able to compel their daughter undertakings in other countries to act according to instructions from the governments in the mother countries rather than to consider the policies of the governments in the countries where they trade certainly must make one think.'[10] In connection with Rhodesia, the opposite allegation—that companies do not enforce home country policy on foreign affiliates—has been made. For example a leader-writer in a British newspaper in 1967 wrote: 'British-based international companies are similarly untroubled. To maintain the level of their trade with Salisbury requires no more than a shuffle of subsidiaries.'[11]

In general, problems of nationality are less tangible but more explosive than many other problems. In opposition to all that can be said about economic advantages is set the combustible material of national autonomy. Because of this, the attitude of many a host country government is ambivalent. The advantages of foreign investment are clear and the foreign firm is not slow to emphasise them. Capital from abroad may be a much needed stimulus to the local economy. It helps the development of local industry and provides employment. With it come technical expertise and invention. One company claims that its huge and expensive research at headquarters is feeding inventions into sixty different countries. Indeed, as has been noticed, the ability to sell technical innovations and the desire to protect its inventions is crucial to the life of the multinational company. In one American firm which manufactured advanced electronic equipment, 95 per cent of all products manufactured in Europe had been developed in the United States; the other 5 per cent were invented in Europe and represented a reverse flow. The German statesman, Ludwig Erhard, has been quoted as saying: 'Along with American capital goes plenty of knowhow and the spirit of competition which will doubtless benefit German industry.'[12] In an underdeveloped country the multinational firm can start the growth of industry.[13] The introduction of new food technologies is another aspect of this subject which is sometimes mentioned, as is the general raising of health and living standards.

With regard to the integration of foreign firms into the local economies, the efforts of W. R. Grace in founding new industries in Peru have been documented. So has the sustained policy of the United Fruit Company to improve relations with its host countries in Central and South America.[14] Again the chairman of a large British company which has been overseas for 150 years has gone on record as saying: 'I doubt if big business can be loved or liked anywhere. But I believe that we could at least be understood and I hope respected—and worthy of respect.'[15] This sums up much of what could be said on this subject, except to add that some companies appear to be more concerned with being 'loved' than being 'respected', and much public relations labour is expended in this cause.

One of the snags of the propaganda exercise is that the multinational company is impelled to demonstrate that it contributes to the economy of the host country, at the same time it will be demonstrating its beneficial effects for the home country. While there may be truth in both propositions, it requires some optimism to be able to assume that the transfer of funds between the two countries is in the best interests of both countries and of the company at the same time. American firms have been also particularly concerned to rebut charges that they do not contribute to the local economy, while at the same time taking measures to protect themselves against devaluation where currencies are weak, and demonstrating that their activities do not harm the American economy either. It is claimed that, whatever is said about the mobility of foreign capital and its tendency to make local financial crises worse, the foreign manufacturing company has a vested interest in stability. Violent currency fluctuations are a nightmare for such a firm. It is also claimed that the foreign company imports capital that does not need a quick return. But there are other kinds of advantage that the multinational firm can bring. It is less committed than the national company to the business centres of the host country, and thus can more easily establish a plant in an area of unemployment. This is one example of a social benefit. Other claims include contributions to local education, especially technical, and to such matters as the reduction of atmospheric pollution.

To what extent statements made for public. relations reasons in fact correspond with the realities of policy formation may well be doubted.[16] The existence within the company, however, of a pressure group with genuine international sympathies has already been mentioned and is a factor here. No doubt the influence of such a group is more powerful in some companies than in others. Companies can also point to measures to ensure that they are sensitive to the views of the host country, for instance by recalling managers who have fallen foul of local opinion. But, we have seen, there are substantial reasons for operating abroad which are obviously worth equivalent efforts to be able to remain there. While, in a small country, a foreign company may be in a powerful position and able to use its ability to leave as a threat, in most countries the international firm is threatened as well as threatening. Valuable assets have been confiscated, and in some cases the commandeered plant has become a competitor in world markets. Trade agreements may eventually produce compensation for investments taken over, either to be run by the state or a local firm, but the compensation is likely to seem inadequate.

There are, then, dangers for the company as well as advantages for the host country. The most interesting problems lie in the general field of 'citizenship', but there are also difficulties when it is seen that a significant part of a country's economy is subject to decisions taken abroad. Naturally the foreign subsidiary is fully subject to the laws of the country in which it operates, and answerable to the taxation authorities of that country; but there may well be circumstances in which it is caught between the laws of two countries. For instance in 1940 a United States Bank with a branch in Paris was ordered to place a proportion of its reserves in government stocks under a wartime emergency measure. But the United States Government held that if the bank complied with this instruction it would be breaking the Neutrality Act by investing in the securities of a country at war. The lawsuit which resulted from this situation was never resolved because it was still in progress when the Germans occupied Paris. Such dramatic clashes are rare, but are most likely to occur in connection with trading policies as is demonstrated below.

The magnitude of foreign investment, particularly that made by United States companies, has created a great deal of worry among Europeans and others in the industrialised world. This fear—phrases like 'neocolonialism' have been used—has been the subject of numerous conferences, studies, articles in the press, as well as pronouncements and debates in political and business circles. One contribution to the debate which has made a considerable impact is *Le Défi américain*. The first chapter of this book begins with a warning: 'Fifteen years from now, it is quite possible that the third greatest industrial power in the world, after the United States and Russia, will not be Europe, but American investment in Europe.'[17] While the book was not altogether against foreign investment, it sharpened European concern over the increasing size of this phenomenon. It helped to turn a vague discomfort into a sense of threat.

In some quarters the threat is considered a serious problem. A special report to the United States Chamber of Commerce included the following warning:

> The US economic presence in Europe is moving into an increasingly hazardous era in which European public acceptance is diminishing while US investment exposure steadily increases. US business is, by and large, unprepared, inadequately informed and insufficiently aware of this historical trend and its possible portents. The question of foreign investment climate in Europe may be the most important single problem in the Atlantic Community. . . . Certain Europeans in politically strategic places are becoming more manifestly nervous about what they view as dangerous long-range economic consequences for Europe resulting from continued expansion of US investment and production facilities in Europe. . . . US business faces increasingly urgent public relations and corporate communications challenges and they are growing. . . . In many cases new company programmes must be launched. In some cases, this will involve a virtual revolution in company public affairs, public relations, and foreign government operating concepts overseas.[18]

However unlikely it may appear now, it is not impossible that these sentiments could in the future lead to various legal and economic restrictions, and degenerate into a destructive round of retaliatory measures and counter-measures between the host and the investing countries. Fear of economic domination is at the bottom of the present unease. Specifically there are fears that foreign investment will gain a monopolistic position in the market where the existing local industry is not strong enough to resist the increased competition. Another worry is that important decisions taken outside the host country may be detrimental to its national interest, and further fears are that the influx of capital may create or worsen an inflationary situation, while the long-term balance of payments suffers from the eventual repatriation of profits earned by the investment.

It seems unlikely that any government can see as desirable or even tolerable a situation in which key sections of its economy fall under the control of foreign interests. But this is exactly what has been taking place in some countries in Europe; it is a problem which has vexed the Canadians for years. Table 10.1 gives some indication of this development in Germany, France and Canada.[19]

Table 10.1 Estimated foreign participation in certain industries in Germany, France, and Canada

Industry	Total foreign		PARTICIPATION US	UK	EEC	Others
Germany 1965 (% of nominal capital)						
Petroleum	85		43	25	31	1
Chemicals, rubber, etc.	16		37	11	28	24
Non-electrical engineering and vehicles	26	of	69	3	4	24
Food, beverages, tobacco	43	which	24	14	39	23
Electrical engineering, instruments, optics, etc.	23		54	3	30	13
All industries *1968 data*	19		44	10	26	20
France 1963 (% of turnover)						
Petroleum	60		33		n.a.	n.a.
Chemicals and related	23		52		17	30
—pharmaceuticals	17		n.a.		n.a.	n.a.
—detergents	58		n.a.		n.a.	n.a.
—synthetic rubber	100	of	n.a.		n.a.	n.a.
Tractors and agricultural equipment	+60	which	58		n.a.	n.a.
Telecommunication equipment	+50		42		n.a.	n.a.
Semi-conductors	n.a.		+25		n.a.	n.a.
Office machines	n.a.		75		n.a.	n.a.
Canada 1963 (% of voting control)						
Manufacturing	60		77			
Petroleum and natural gas	74		84			
Mining and smelting	59	of	88			
Railways	2	which	100			
Other utilities	4		100			
Total of above industries and merchandising	34		79			

Sources. Deutsche Bundesbank, *Monthly Report*, November 1966, pp. 23–4, and May 1969, pp. 22ff.
Ministère de l'Industrie, *Rapport sur les investissements étrangers dans l'industrie française*, 17 July 1965.
Watkins *et al.*, 1968, p. 422.

In the United Kingdom, the value of United States-owned companies alone amounted to roughly 11–12 per cent of the net asset value of all British quoted firms by 1964.[20] It has been estimated that, at the present growth rate this proportion will double by 1981. During 1964 the investment by United States-owned companies in plant and equipment represented also about 11–12 per cent of total fixed investment in Britain;[21] and, according to another source, United States investment runs much higher in certain industries.[22] In that year as a percentage of the total turnover of each industry, it amounted to over 40 per cent in petroleum, computers, tractors and agricultural machinery; in the automobile industry it was over 50 per cent and was substantial in several other industries.

The significance of these facts is clear. Foreign investment, and especially United States investment, has begun to occupy a dominant position in several key industries in each of these countries. Furthermore, these tend to be industries with the most promise of future growth. It seems unlikely that this development can continue indefinitely without some more serious reaction from the host countries than occurs at present.

One problem for the government of the host country is that it faces constraints in dealing with the foreign company which it does not face with domestic firms. One of these constraints is in the general area of international law. One writer, in referring to the opposition that the international firm encounters, has produced evidence in support of the view that the 'international law' on the subject may well play an ambiguous role. 'Western business', he writes, 'and the present political states have responded to this hostility and subsequent attack by erecting a theory of private international law seeking to justify and perpetuate the *status quo vis-à-vis* foreign-owned assets . . . so long as private international law thus recognises the validity and relevance of only one interest—that of the private property-owner—it is foredoomed to failure.'[23]

Another constraint is provided by trade agreements and the fear of reprisals from other countries as a result of any constraints that might be imposed on foreign business; this fear may well be increased if the firm has the support of a powerful government. Electoral implications make these constraints more irksome. There is always the possibility of gaining advantages in an election campaign by pointing out the disadvantages of foreign intervention in one's country; at the same time the prosperity the foreign firms bring also has electoral consequences. Hence it is possible to find examples of firms being both threatened and encouraged by the same government. In the following pages we record a few instances of actual problems between companies and countries.

In France there has been a prolonged debate for and against foreign investment. In 1964, for instance, ministerial statements declared that foreign ownership of French industry had gone too far. But the need for capital and technical resources from outside was clearly felt, for permits for foreign investment continued to be issued. In 1967 the French Government was even advertising for foreign investors. In 1966 press reports indicated that permits were getting easier rather than more difficult to obtain in spite of alarm at the high proportion of foreign ownership in certain industries. Thus an article in *France-Soir*[24] set out the fears and problems involved in allowing the economy to become 'colonised'; but this article also gave two compelling reasons for not preventing the import of foreign capital. One of these was that the country could not generate internally sufficient capital for the modernisation of its industry, and the other was that the rest of the Common Market countries were accepting foreign investment, and so France would be affected by the competition from these firms if she did not do the same. In fact the following year (1967) France, with 36·6 per cent of the population of the Common Market, actually received 22·6 per cent of United States investment in that area.

A dramatic issue which stirred up considerable controversy was that of Fruehauf and the lorries for China.[25] Fruehauf-France SA, a subsidiary of the Fruehauf Trailer Company of Detroit which owned a majority interest, was awarded a contract by Berliet, the French lorry manufacturer. The order was for lorries destined for China. In January 1965, shortly before delivery was due, the United States parent company ordered the cancellation of the contract. It was said later in the French courts that the reason for this action was intervention by the United States Government. After the cancellation had been confirmed, the management of Fruehauf-France resigned and asked the local Tribunal de Commerce to appoint an administrator to manage the company in accordance with French law. This was done and the action was upheld on appeal. The Appeal Court in Paris asserted that judicial interference in the internal affairs of a private business was only to be undertaken in extreme cases, but that this was such a case; for in this instance a French company had been given orders that would ruin it and cause unemployment for its workers, and these orders had been given on the instructions of a foreign government for reasons that were unconnected with business. Hence the court considered that intervention was justified and completion of the contract was ordered.

In neighbouring Belgium, on the other hand, great efforts have been made to encourage foreign firms to come to the country.[26] In recent years Brussels has come to house the European headquarters of many foreign companies. Another small country which has traditionally played the host to foreign business is Switzerland, and Geneva in particular contains the administrative centres of many companies. Indeed firms find many advantages in settling in this country—the banking and the tax systems, the availability of multilingual personnel, as well as personal advantages for foreign executives such as the climate and the international schools. However, a wave of xenophobia a few years ago, resulting from a relatively large and growing foreign population, led to legal changes. The changes in the immigration laws made it more difficult to get work permits and also compelled companies to reduce the number of foreign workers in their employment. These measures applied equally to domestic and foreign firms, but were clearly likely to cause more inconvenience to foreign firms. At the same time, as part of a campaign against inflation, fresh limits were placed on the import of capital.

It is interesting that, in Switzerland, laws against the immigration of people have been accompanied by measures to limit the immigration of capital. There sometimes does seem to be a connection between the two, although the reasons for this must surely have something to do with congruence of attitudes, a general prejudice against things foreign, as well as economic considerations. Countries which traditionally accept both foreign nationals and foreign capital introduce specific measures to control one or both of these when the flow becomes too great. Other countries start from the opposite assumption, and specific measures are required to relax control of immigration. This may well be another cultural difference that should be added to those already mentioned.

A country which has strictly limited the inflow of foreign capital is Japan. According to the *Financial Times* in 1964 only one wholly-owned subsidiary of a foreign firm in that country had been authorised in the previous ten years.[27] And this was during a period when foreign businesses were making great efforts to acquire manufacturing facilities within the country. The increase of opportunities for foreign operations in that country has come gradually as a result of international agreements, and with the movement of Japanese firms abroad.

As regards the United Kingdom, foreign investment is very large and for years grew more rapidly than in any other European country, although in proportion to population no faster than in Belgium. By law the Treasury must give permission for the import of foreign capital into the country, and sometimes conditions are attached to foreign takeovers. As with other countries there is a record of attempts to encourage foreign investment and to restrict it at the same time. An official effort to encourage more investment from abroad, and especially from the United States, was reported in the British press in October 1965. But at the same time, and frequently since, the dangers of foreign domination of the economy were argued.[28] One trenchant example of such argument is a book called *The American Takeover of Britain*, which states that there were '1,600 U.S.-owned subsidiaries, associated companies and branches operating in the United Kingdom at midsummer 1967'. This book describes the gradual absorption of British companies by American, and raises questions about the effect of this on British national policies. At the same time it is onesided and does less than justice to the advantages the foreign firms bring; and does not mention at all the huge amount of British investment in the United States. To counter charges about the effects on the British economy, the *American Economic Report* for April 1964 published figures showing that between 1961 and 1963 United States firms in Britain had increased their exports by 17 per cent, while the average for all British firms was 11 per cent. The same report showed that forty-two American companies brought new investment into the development areas during the same period, and listed the following contributions by these firms to the British economy: fresh capital, the purchase of British materials and services thus reducing imports, the training of managers in new fields pioneered by the United States, providing employment in the development areas, channelling American research into British industry. In a speech in Parliament in 1968 a member of the British Government, Mr Wedgwood Benn, is reported as saying:

> International companies own about 10 per cent of our industry and do about 20 per cent of our exports. Ford has had an £850 million net balance in exports in the last few years, and £200 million this year. We have done quite well out of the exports of these big international companies.[29]

The same speaker, however, went on to suggest that whatever economic advantages the firms might bring, there were some major problems. For as they developed, he said, 'national governments, including our own, will be reduced to the status of parish councils in dealing with the large corporations which will span the world'.

In the same debate, another speaker referred to rumours about plans for international rationalisation within the Ford motor company, and in particular to the transfer out of Britain of some of that company's manufacture. This ability to rationalise across frontiers is an obvious point at which company and country interests may conflict. Indeed such rationalisation is a delicate undertaking within a country, and much more so across frontiers. Nevertheless it is a clear possibility for the international firm, and enables more economical production.[30] Some examples of companies switching export markets from one country to another were discovered in this study, as were examples of firms which allowed national subsidiaries to compete freely with one another. One way of getting the advantages of international rationalisation, without causing so much damage to individual countries, is by setting up a system of bargaining between national subsidiaries and making them responsible for the rationalisation. As a result advantages can be gained, and political and economic developments anticipated, by arrangements which are at least not disadvantageous to any of the countries concerned. One company described elaborate arrangements for doing this.

The division of loyalties that can affect a national subsidiary comes into the news periodically in Britain, although less dramatically than in France. For instance, the United States Government objected to the British subsidiary of a United States electrical firm supplying equipment used in Viscount aircraft sold to China.[31]

In Britain, as in other countries, there is a body of opinion that is against foreign firms, but there are also those who take the opposite view and press the dangers of their withdrawal. Thus in 1964 a newspaper article showed that Britain's share of United States investment in Europe was beginning to decline.[32] This article listed the advantages that Britain gained from this investment as: the import of capital, higher export of goods, technical knowledge, improved management performance. An example of how foreign companies can aid development areas was given some years ago by the *Glasgow Herald Trade Review.*[33] This not only listed the concentration of American firms that had moved into the area; but also pointed out that they brought in modern technological industries and made the area less dependent on traditional occupations.

Germany is another country in which ambivalent opinions have been expressed on foreign investment. Press reports have given the views of German bankers who consider that United States firms have been investing too rapidly in the Common Market. They take the view that this not only provokes nationalistic reactions,[34] but is also damaging to the dollar and hence to the international monetary system.

Problems caused by United States trading policies are not confined to Europe, they also apply in Canada, where trade with China is encouraged. But for Canada many of the problems of the host country are exacerbated by the very high proportion of foreign investment in native industry. The last time the Canadian dollar was devalued, in 1962, one of the reasons was said to be the withdrawal of foreign capital. But now the main problem is the one of national sovereignty that many countries are finding. Nowhere are these problems set out with such clarity and fascinating detail as in a Canadian Government report on the subject.[35] This report gives a wealth of information on the extent and influence of foreign capital. It makes a number of points about the threat to national sovereignty; it also makes the opposite point that it is unlikely that liberal Canadian policies with regard to foreigners in general and foreign businesses in particular will change. A national policy of restricting foreign investment is made more unlikely by the federal constitution of the country. Hence national feelings and traditions are held to be powerful factors on both sides of this argument. A number of fiscal arrangements that have been made to encourage Canadian ownership of key businesses are listed, but significantly the main proposals of the report are concerned with safeguards for national sovereignty. These include some drastic measures to prevent foreign trading policies being imposed on subsidiaries. This is mainly a matter of trade with communist countries, which is encouraged in Canada. Among the proposals are the establishment of a state agency to trade with countries that foreign subsidiaries might avoid, and that any refusal to sell to this agency at current prices would be a criminal offence. Another group of proposals aims to prevent foreign courts concerned with anti-trust legislation collecting information from or giving instructions to firms registered in Canada.

Thus in country after country appears this theme of the need of foreign capital balanced by the fear of foreign domination. In an independent democratic country it would seem reasonable to expect that the fear of domination would be strong, and hence it is interesting that there is less overt opposition than there might be. This does not mean to say that there are not dangers for the company which could be headed off by measures designed to provide for national aspirations. The problem of ownership of multinational firms will be discussed at some length in the next chapter. From the discussion in the present chapter, it would appear that there are some legal measures that would safeguard national autonomy; but it is likely that international agreement would be needed to ensure that companies did not just invest in countries with the least safeguards. This legislation could enforce greater autonomy for the national organisation than exists at the moment. As long ago as 1960, an article appeared in the *Harvard Business Review* suggesting some considerations that would make foreign firms more acceptable. These were: not to pull out of a country once established there, not to expect a country to allow its economic institutions to become foreign dominated, not to intervene in the political affairs of the country but to participate in the economic and social life, to honour contracts and to treat local nationals as equals.[36] These comparatively simple points would appear to meet many of the stated objections to foreign business, but there remain possible areas of conflict of interest which must be accepted. These genuine conflicts are likely to be reinforced by emotional attitudes on both sides.

At the same time there are clearly forces working against nationalism, not least among local nationals in the foreign firm. One of these is the existence of an international management development scheme. It is likely that any legal attempts to make a national subsidiary more autonomous will be frustrated if the management are involved in a promotion ladder that runs outside the country. The discussion of such schemes, as well as of the problem of the two headquarters earlier in this book,[37] illustrates some of the forces at work here. Others have also been mentioned, such as the international character both of technology and of management techniques. These are generating outlooks inside the firm which are surely going to make some of the anxieties of national governments look petty and parochial. This can be seen not so much as a power conflict between governments and large companies, but as part of a general trend towards internationalism which is as real in the contemporary world as the revival of nationalism. No doubt international organisations will then be charged with the task of seeing that the activities of the companies are restricted where their interests clash with those of the international community as a whole. For the companies themselves it can be said that, while the flouting of national feelings may be dangerous, in the longer term measures which ignore the growth of internationalism can be even more harmful to the firm. The more able and ambitious personnel will gravitate to those companies with the greater international scope.

11

Ownership policies

11.1 General

One of the most persistent and controversial issues facing multinational companies concerns the ownership of their foreign subsidiaries. From one aspect, this is the question of whether a wholly-owned subsidiary or a jointly-owned subsidiary, typically with another company, is the more suitable form for foreign direct investment. From another aspect, to what extent should individual residents of the host country be permitted to share in the fortunes of local foreign-sponsored companies? Just as there is no single answer to many problems of management in multinational companies, there is no single answer to these questions either. In this chapter, we shall examine some of the major features that bear on the issue, and in particular those which can have an influence on a company's financial management. In keeping with the general theme of the study, most of the discussion will be devoted to ownership policies of companies operating in the industrialised countries in Europe and North America.[1]

We will begin by briefly considering the principal forms that foreign direct investment can take. It can be divided into three main categories depending upon the percentage of the subsidiary's equity that is held by the parent company. These are: wholly-owned subsidiaries (generally 95 per cent or more of the equity is owned by the parent company), majority participations (generally between 50 and 95 per cent of the equity is owned by the parent company), and minority participations (less than 50 per cent of the equity is owned by the parent company).[2] There is a rather blurred borderline area between the small minority participation and portfolio investment, but generally, the former is accompanied by a certain degree of management control such as, for example, the right to nominate a member of the board of directors. Data covering these ownership patterns in selected countries are given below in table 11.1. The statistics show clearly that there is a strong preference for foreign direct investment to take the form of wholly-owned subsidiaries, and where this is not so, the second choice is for majority participations in most circumstances. It should be noted, however, that the only available American information is old, and according to more recent sources, there is a growing trend, even in Europe, for new US ventures to be jointly owned.[3] Nevertheless, it is commonly believed

Table 11.1 Pattern of ownership classified according to the percentage of foreign ownership in subsidiaries (value in pounds sterling in millions)

Subsidiaries—location	Wholly-owned more than 95%		Majority 50% to 95%		Minority less than 50%	
UK-owned in developed countries[a]						
Sterling area		%		%		%
number	605	54	224	20	290	26
value	482	44	516	47	98	9
Non-sterling area						
number	975	57	269	16	471	27
value	645	49	546	42	128	9
USA manufacturing[b]						
value	275	94	13	4	3	1
Foreign-owned in the United Kingdom[a]						
US-owned (value)	946	75	185	15	132	10
Other nationalities (value)	446	70	171	27	23	3
Foreign-owned in Germany[c]						
number	3292	61	872	16	1211	23
value	1600	79	192	19	234	12
Foreign-owned in France[d]						
US-owned (number)	181	57	94	30	43	13
Other nationalities (number)	66	33	93	44	40	20
US-owned in Europe[e]						
number	2050	76	464	17	182	7
value	1320	76	358	21	50	3
US-owned in Canada[e]						
number	2301	83	331	12	133	5
value	2240	62	1040	29	321	9

(a) Based on data for large investing companies and appearing in 'Book Values of Overseas Investments', *Board of Trade Journal*, London, 26 January 1968, p. xiv and p. xx.
(b) Pizer and Warner 1962, pp. 38–9.
(c) Deutsche Bundesbank, 'Foreign Ownership in German Enterprises', *Monthly Report*, May 1969, pp. 22ff.
(d) Based on data covering 7,000 firms and appearing in *Les Liaisons Financières Françaises*, Paris, Société d'Editions Economiques et Financières, 1966.
(e) Pizer and Cutler 1960, p. 101.

Note. Definitions used in the above data are subject to minor variations according to source. The US Department of Commerce data appear to define wholly-owned as more than 95 per cent foreign-owned, and minority participation as from 50 to 25 per cent foreign-owned. The Deutsche Bundesbank data appear to consider wholly-owned as over 90 per cent foreign-owned, and minority participation as less than 50 per cent foreign-owned. The Board of Trade data seem to consider wholly-owned subsidiaries as more than 99 per cent owned. In practice, it would seem that normally a participation of less than 10 per cent would be more in the nature of a portfolio investment, and this probably has the effect of overstating the proportion of minority holdings in Germany. *Value* in the above data refers to book value (issued capital plus reserves) except for the German data where it refers to nominal value (issued capital) held by the foreign investor.

in Europe that a preference for wholly-owned or majority-owned subsidiaries is a peculiarly American trait. This view appears to receive support from the data in table 11.1; yet, from our discussions with executives during our field research, and from analysing other published material[4]—especially that covering the larger companies—it is difficult to substantiate any great difference in ownership policies between American and European companies, either in attitude or in fact. It may be that European companies do tend to enter into joint ventures more often than their American counterparts, but there are too little data available to establish the facts firmly.[5]

Joint ventures can be further classified according to the type of local investor. Again, these fall into three principal categories, namely, local private interest (generally a firm or group of firms, but also private individuals), local public interests (either the local government, or one of its agencies), and the general public. Under a strict definition of the term, only the first, and possibly the second of these should be considered as joint ventures—that is, companies whose management is shared on approximately equal terms by the local and foreign investors. Nevertheless, for purposes of this discussion, we shall use the term joint venture in a broader sense to refer to any foreign subsidiary in which local participation in its ownership is material. In Europe the most common type of joint venture has another company or group of companies as the local partner. It is relatively infrequent to find the local government as a partner, although government-owned financial institutions will frequently contribute loan capital to foreign subsidiaries. Further, there are not many joint ventures in Europe with participation by the general public. In the United Kingdom, for example, there are only a dozen or so foreign subsidiaries in which a portion of the ordinary shares is held by the general public and quoted on a stock exchange.[6] In the other European countries, as well as in the United States, this form of joint venture is not common.

Joint ventures in Europe arise mainly in two ways. Perhaps the most frequent route is where the foreign investor buys a share of an established local company. Examples of such associations in the United Kingdom include the recent purchase of a majority shareholding in the Rootes Motor Group by the Chrysler Corporation, American Tobacco's purchase of control in Gallaher, and the minority shareholdings taken in Smiths Food Group now taken over completely[7] by General Mills, and in United Glass by Owens-Illinois. These need not be only quoted companies; indeed the majority are not. The other principal type of joint venture is between companies when a totally new subsidiary is established. Rank-Xerox, the fifty-fifty jointly-owned subsidiary of the Rank Organisation and Xerox Corporation, and Kimberly-Clark Limited, the two-thirds–one-third jointly-owned subsidiary of the Kimberly-Clark Corporation and the Reed Paper Group, provide two examples of this type of association.

What are the determinants of ownership policy for foreign investments?

If we consider some of the factors which influence companies' choice in this matter, it will be seen that there are both advantages and disadvantages to either wholly-owned or jointly-owned subsidiaries. In most circumstances, management has a choice as to which form of holding it will adopt. But in certain countries, and in some sectors of many countries, there is legislation which directly or indirectly limits foreign investment to joint ventures. This is the case of Japan where, with rare exceptions, a foreign investor cannot have more than 50 per cent of the equity of a Japanese company. There are similar restrictions in some of the less developed countries such as India, for example. In Europe and in the United States there are also certain restrictions which bar foreign subsidiaries from some types of government contracts (usually military or otherwise associated with the national security), unless it can be demonstrated that the foreign influence or control is negligible. It may be also necessary to show that the foreign content of the products in question is under a specified percentage.[8] Generally speaking, however, management does have a choice when formulating ownership policies for investments in the industrialised countries. We will look first at the case *against* joint ventures.

11.2 Disadvantages of joint ventures

Most foreign investors prefer a wholly-owned subsidiary to a joint venture; indeed, the preponderance of this form of ownership control was clear from the data on table 11.1. Some companies will invest under no other conditions. Although a long list could no doubt be compiled of the arguments used by companies to justify and support this bias, it would probably boil down to two or three principal objections: conflicts of interest with the local partners over various aspects of management, a reluctance to disclose information to outsiders, and an unwillingness to share the earnings of the investment.

CONFLICTS OF INTEREST

By far the most frequently voiced objection to sharing the equity of a foreign subsidiary is fear of conflicts of interest that can arise. The growing tendency towards unification of markets and the rationalisation and integration of production and other functions on a regional, or even wider, basis means the concentration of manufacture in certain plants and the assignment of export markets on mainly economic criteria. Under such conditions, as already pointed out, the interdependence of the various subsidiaries of the group makes any attempt to measure their individual profitability a difficult if not arbitrary exercise. Often too, for tax or other reasons, a company's foreign business may best be structured so that more of the ultimate profits are taken in one subsidiary than in another. The problems that might be encountered by having local partners are obvious. In some circumstances the local partners might participate in a greater share of the overall earnings than their contribution warranted. The parent company, on the other hand, might be tempted to penalise the joint venture by, for example, diverting business to wholly-owned subsidiaries in the group, or by overpricing inward or underpricing outward transfers of goods and services. It is not difficult to see that either side can believe that the other receives greater benefits than he is entitled to. Where conflicts of this sort are likely to arise, it is thought better to stick to wholly-owned subsidiaries. One company's view on this problem is provided by the argument of the former chairman of General Motors:

> From an operational point of view, our overseas subsidiaries are as fully integrated in our overall operations as any division or plant in the United States. The fact that an overseas subsidiary is governed by the regulations of another sovereign nation does not alter this basic business relationship. Nor does the particular location of the operation in any way diminish the need for a coordinated approach to serving world markets. On the contrary, geographical dispersion makes the need for coordination even more compelling.
>
> The strategic importance of a unified ownership of operating units was recognised at a very early stage in the development of General Motors overseas. A policy of coordinated control could be expected to result in improved business efficiency only if it had as its counterpart a policy of unified ownership. And as we have accumulated worldwide operating experience, our view on unified ownership has been strongly reinforced.
>
> Full ownership of our overseas subsidiaries has permitted us to reach decisions involving these subsidiaries on the basis of sound business principles—on the same terms as our domestic divisions. This freedom to base our decisions on objective economic considerations has been valued so highly in General Motors that we have invested in new facilities, or maintained our investment in existing operations, only in those countries where national laws have been compatible with unified ownership.[9]

Of course conflicts of interest can easily arise whether there are integrated operations or not. One of the most frequent areas of dispute concerns reinvestment of earnings. A parent company is often willing to wait considerably longer for its return on investment than its local partners—especially if it enjoys royalties or fees from the investment, or exports to it. And besides being willing to delay dividends, we saw in chapter 6 that, for reasons of their own convenience, parent companies will vary the amount and timing of these payments within wide limits. Typically, the conflicts arise when the parent company wants to reinvest most of the earnings while the local partners want to distribute the bulk of them. Generally, these differences can be smoothed out and a compromise reached without undue difficulty if there are only a few local partners to deal with. But where the subsidiary is quoted on a local stock exchange and the general public holds a minority interest, it is in a much more inflexible position—both with regard to its dividend policy and other aspects of its financial policy.

Local investors, when considering a purchase of shares in a subsidiary (or any company for that matter), base their choice on such criteria as a sound financial structure, a good record of earnings, and a satisfactory dividend policy. Above all, they expect the subsidiary's operations to be conducted in a fair and orthodox manner. If the investor himself does not go through such a decision process, his brokers and some adviser probably does. Moreover, the decision is made with reference to alternative investment opportunities in the shares of other companies in the industry or in the general market.

In all these respects, the position of the quoted subsidiary is much like that of other quoted companies. But in one way it differs greatly. It has given a special hostage to fortune. One of the main reasons for wanting local shareholders, we shall argue below, is to counteract the onus of being considered foreign-owned, and it is this public relations aspect which can be damaged the most if it fails to conform to local financial orthodoxy. The financial press can be expected to make the most of what it considers unsatisfactory performance or unsuitable policies. The fact that the subsidiary is foreign-controlled only makes for better copy. Consequently, this class of subsidiary can be expected to pursue financial policies which resemble those of other companies quoted on the local stock exchange.

It will be recalled that in our sample of 115 foreign subsidiaries there were twelve firms which were quoted on the London Stock Exchange.[10] As a group, their financial structure departed considerably from that of the wholly-owned subsidiaries, resembling in many ways the average of the sample of British quoted companies we have used throughout our discussion as a yardstick for comparison. The position is shown in detail in table 11.2 below:

Table 11.2 Comparative financial structure in 1967 (percentage of total assets except for debt : equity ratio)

Company Group	Issued capital	Prefer- ence capital	Net worth	Long- term debt	Bank loans	Intra- company liabilities	Debt: equity ratio
	%	%	%	%	%	%	
12 quoted subsidiaries	25·9	1·3	57·3	10·6	5·2	5·3	0:74
103 wholly-owned subsidiaries	18·8	0·6	46·1	5·9	12·5	11·1	1·14
1235 British quoted companies in manufacturing	21·4	2·8	52·5	13·6	6·3	n.a.	0·91

L

Significantly, the quoted subsidiaries carried less debt than the wholly-owned group, especially short-term debt, and their net worth was substantially larger. Also, they had on average a much larger proportion of cash and marketable securities (11·7 per cent of total assets) than the wholly-owned subsidiaries (6·2 per cent). Much of this can probably be attributed to the fact they distributed relatively less of their earnings (48 per cent from 1960 to 1967) than the wholly-owned group (57 per cent) while their growth rate was lower and their profitability roughly the same. It seems likely that this performance, in combination with a conservative dividend policy 'imposed' by market conformity, led to their relatively high liquidity and low indebtedness. In other words, they had more cash than they knew what to do with. Such a situation would be much less likely to occur in a wholly-owned subsidiary where the parent company would generally increase repatriation of earnings for use elsewhere in the group if they were not needed locally.

Of all the measures of financial performance, it was their dividend policy that conformed the closest to the general stock market norms, and for the most part was marked by stable, gradually increasing payments. Out of ninety-five company-years observed, dividends were raised or held stable on seventy-nine occasions (83 per cent of the time).[11] Of the subsidiaries in this group which deviated from the general pattern, one was only founded at the beginning of the period reviewed and did not earn adequate profits to support a dividend until 1965 (British Enkalon). Another was taken over by the majority shareholder during the period, after which time it began to alter its apparent former policy (H. J. Enthoven). A third suffered persistent operating losses between 1964 and 1967 and stopped paying dividends (Black Clawson International). The other subsidiary which suspended its dividend was considered by one writer as 'the most shocking post-war United Kingdom example of an arrogant board imposing its dividend policy upon an unwilling minority'.[12] This firm, the Crown Cork Company Limited, suffered more bad publicity from its action than has perhaps any other foreign-affiliated company in the United Kingdom. The reason given by the company for suspending the dividend was that all available funds were needed to finance a diversification programme. The chronicle of events makes an interesting case study. Excerpts from press reports which have appeared periodically since the announcement that dividends would be stopped, include the following.

1 November 1963: . . . a decision like this would be difficult to justify in any circumstances; in those of the present case it is impossible to do so. First of all, Crown Cork is a subsidiary of a US company, Crown Cork International. Secondly, the last Crown Cork balance sheet showed loans to the holding company of £900,000. Thirdly, and even more weirdly, in September of this year, Crown Cork redeemed its £400,000 preference shares at a premium of 5s. a share. If cash is needed for expansion, the way to get it is not to starve the minority holders.[13]

12 November 1963: . . . The cessation of dividends is unfair to the minority holders (71·5 per cent of the equity is held by the US parent) and the Board is meant to represent all the shareholders. The amount involved is relatively small and so this devotion to 'primitive financing' by retentions alone is explicable only (though one hopes this is not the case) by a deplorable wish to squeeze out the minority.[14]

25 March 1964: . . . This sort of financing seems both stupid and unfair to the minority holders.[15]

25 April 1964: . . . Crown Cork is not going to be allowed to get away with its shabby treatment of minority shareholders scotfree . . .[16]

26 February 1965: Replying to a complaint in the Commons yesterday about the Crown Cork Company's refusal for the second year, to pay a dividend to British shareholders, Mr George Darling, Joint Minister of State, Board of Trade, said on present information there did not appear to be grounds for the appointment of an inspector under the Companies' Act to investigate the affairs of the company.[17]

In March 1966, the shareholders were given a glimmer of hope by Crown Cork's Managing Director. During a press conference he was reported as saying that:

. . . a distribution would be made [in 1966] barring any catastrophe . . . shareholders had previously been treated over-generously, while the company had suffered through bad operations with little money being channelled to development. . . . The final say on dividend policy naturally rested with the US parent company, . . . which had enlarged its holding of the British company from 75½ per cent to 77 per cent during 1965. . . . There was the possibility that the US company might eventually bid for the minority shares, but 'this is not on the cards at this stage'.[18]

Considering its previous stance, the press reaction was predictable.

17 March 1966: By the sound of it, the Board is not exactly going to lash out to compensate for three dividendless years—shareholders are thought to have been treated over-generously in the past. However, this is beside the point. For all the protestations at the time that the decision to use the whole of cash flow for capital expansion was not just a way of squeezing out the minority, it has had just this effect. Crown Cork has an entirely clean balance sheet with no form of gearing and no overdraft. Its financing policy may gladden the heart of the Bank of England and the Chancellor, but it is a dire warning to shareholders in companies who are contemplating partial deals with US firms.[19]

There was still no dividend by February 1967, and the press commentary was as harsh as ever.

> *27 February 1967:* There is no serious public company in the UK other than Crown Cork which has abandoned dividends to finance a capital programme with the balance sheet ungeared and the hope must be there will not be another.[20]

Next, the Treasury made a request and offered an opinion.

> *7 March 1967:* The firm, which has paid no dividends since 1962, invoked the British Treasury when it announced it would make no payment for 1966. Crown Cork said its decision was made 'after consultations with and in deference to the request of the Treasury'. Pressed to explain its stand, the Treasury said in a statement to the House of Commons today that it had told the company that it did not seem imperative to increase its distribution during a period of voluntary dividend stand-still . . .[21]

It is an understatement to say the policies Crown Cork pursued were not suitable for a quoted company. The best solution would have been for the parent company to buy out the minority shareholders.[22] As it was, the apparent indifference of the parent company to local sensitivities over this issue was harmful to the image of foreign subsidiaries in the United Kingdom. The statement of the British company's managing director that 'the final say on dividend policy naturally rested with the US parent company' implies that the parent knows best. The evidence presented above suggests they are wrong and that financial policies of this category of subsidiary need to reflect closely local practices and expectations. We have tried to point out the dangers to the *parent company* in not respecting local standards of behaviour. This does not necessarily imply that quoted subsidiaries are poor investments from the minority holders' point of view. The others in our sample increased their dividends over 15 per cent per year on average during the period reviewed—a record that must compare favourably with other companies in the market.

DISCLOSURE OF INFORMATION

Many of the practices used by multinational companies to avoid or defer taxes, to protect themselves against exchange losses, or to achieve other corporate objectives are neither feasible nor appropriate when there are local shareholders in the subsidiary. This is particularly so for quoted subsidiaries which are required to publish their accounts. To disclose financial information is at minimum a nuisance; where its financial policies deviate from local orthodoxy, their announcement can be embarrassing, as the experience of Crown Cork showed. On account of these factors, some flexibility in financial operations is lost, or at least seriously reduced. If the parent company is not prepared to accept this, then the joint venture form of investment should be avoided. The fact that most companies do exactly this is not surprising.

UNWILLINGNESS TO SHARE EARNINGS

A third and perhaps most compelling reason of all why investors are reluctant to enter into joint ventures is an unwillingness to share the earnings of a subsidiary which they have developed. This attitude is probably strongest in the technologically advanced industries where the parent company enjoys a monopoly or near-monopoly position. In such cases, there is often little real contribution that a local partner can make, and companies find it difficult to see any justification at all for sharing ownership. The typical attitude of businessmen could perhaps be summed up by the words of one executive who said, 'We do all the work and take all the risk; if it's a success why should we let the locals in on it? If it's a flop, they won't be interested. Either way, I can't see the point.'

OTHER DISADVANTAGES

There are a number of other disadvantages to joint ventures in some circumstances. American-owned companies are subject to special legal constraints, for example. Under US anti-trust legislation, the parent company can be liable to prosecution if its agreements with a foreign partner are held to be in restraint of trade. The taxation of foreign income is affected by the percentage of the equity in the subsidiary that is held by the US parent. Certain US government guarantees and other benefits are only applicable if the US holding is relatively large; however, this may work in reverse for host government benefits to the subsidiaries.

Even in the absence of any fundamental problems such as we have outlined above, many companies consider that too much time is wasted in settling petty disputes in joint ventures about whatever management problems that may be at hand. Frequently, these are due to differences in the approach to business between local management and head office, though they can arise just as easily in wholly-owned subsidiaries. But in the joint venture local management is provided with an additional excuse to question central authority. It brings into the power structure a managerial group whose autonomy can be given strong local support. As an official of the Ford Motor Company noted, local shareholders have been 'used as an umbrella to resist change. Local personnel will point to the minority shareholders when they want to argue against innovation.'[23]

At least from management's point of view, the case against joint ventures appears to be based on strong and rational arguments. We will now consider some of the arguments *for* sharing ownership of a foreign subsidiary.

11.3 Advantages of joint ventures

There are three principal areas in which benefits may be gained from a joint venture: (1) the managerial, technological, or productive; (2) the financial; and (3) what might broadly be called the political.

TECHNICAL RESOURCES

Where competitive conditions make speed an important factor in entering a foreign market, the joint venture may present the opportunity to acquire needed managerial, technological, or productive resources at a substantial savings in time and expense. Often the local partner can offer a trained sales organisation or labour force, or productive facilities to complement the special knowhow or financial resources or both of the foreign investor. The alternative is to create an entirely new organisation. Although in many cases events have shown that this would have been a better solution, the apparent advantages offered by investing in an existing firm lead many foreign investors to opt for a local partner. Frequently, the foreign investor has little choice, for the expense of going it alone in terms of management resources rules out any other decision.[24] But unless the partners are of comparable size and strength, such marriages of convenience are often shortlived, or at least full of strife. Sooner or later conflicts of interest arise and, external factors permitting, the foreign investor ends by either buying out his local partners or disinvesting. This occurs so frequently that one is led to conclude that joint ventures made on these grounds are generally little more than a temporary expedient to secure an entry into the market.

FINANCIAL CONSIDERATIONS

Financial considerations provide another rather similar reason for choosing a joint venture form of investment. For lack of finance a firm may not be able to expand into foreign markets under any other type of ownership. This may arise where rapid domestic growth absorbs the bulk of its available funds; it may result from restrictions over the export of capital coupled with either the inability or unwillingness to borrow from sources in the host country; or it may stem from a combination of rapid overseas expansion plus either a reluctance to risk its own capital, or simply a lack of funds in the amounts required to finance all the projects which it believes necessary for its position in the overseas markets. In such cases, the foreign investor may seek local partners who are willing to accept an assured market, knowhow, patent rights, or other assets as a substitute for cash in return for a share in the equity. Under such an arrangement, the local investors contribute at least a part of the cash required to finance the project. Besides enabling a foreign investor to stretch his financial resources, such a policy also provides a hedge against political risks by reducing the amount of capital at stake.[25] Numerous instances of companies adopting joint ventures as a means of economising capital were cited in the Friedmann and Kalmanoff study. This appeared to be less often an important motive for American companies than it was for those of other nationalities, especially in countries such as Japan and Italy.[26] Among the companies interviewed during our field research, one in particular made specific reference in its policy manuals to the financial arguments in favour of joint ventures in the developing countries. These were (1) the *need* to economise because of the twofold problem of rapid overseas growth and the near-impossibility of exporting capital from the United Kingdom; and (2) the *desire* to economise in order to lessen the risk of exchange loss.[27] Hence, they aimed at having a 'substantial' minority share of the equity capital held by the general public in these countries. Their policy was different for their European activities, where it was thought that regional integration of their operations, more adequate local sources of capital, and no general demand for local participation permitted them to adopt a policy of wholly-owned subsidiaries. The distinction between investment in Europe and elsewhere came up frequently during our interviews with companies. Since most of the industrialised countries have well-developed capital markets and financial institutions, local borrowing can often be used to provide all or most of the outside finance required, thereby making local equity capital rarely necessary. Furthermore, loss from fluctuating exchange rates or expropriation is less critical in the industrialised countries, certainly when compared to the developing countries. For these reasons, one is led to conclude that there is often little justification on strictly financial grounds for seeking local investors in countries in Europe or in North America.

Of the many businessmen and bankers who discussed this question with us, it was rare to find one who believed that companies would choose a joint venture for financial reasons alone. Their general consensus was that this would only be a minor consideration. A similar conclusion was reported by the Reddaway study which stated: 'It was almost always said by companies that minority holdings had not been used as a deliberate source of finance—although the possibility of their being so in the future was not excluded.'[28] Perhaps a small company, with neither sufficient internal sources of finance nor well enough known overseas to be able to borrow locally, might find it necessary to seek local investors. Even so, this is probably much more a problem which faces the relative newcomers to overseas operations. As we argued in chapter 7, once established, companies seem able to develop local sources of finance satisfactorily to meet their needs. It has not always been that way, and in the future a lack of finance may force some companies again to seek equity funds overseas by inviting local investors to take a minority holding in their subsidiaries, especially if the alternative is to risk their market position by cutting back on investment. In particular, with the continual deficits in the balance of payments run by the United States, the principal investor country, stricter controls over capital exports may again oblige some US companies to consider joint ventures for financial reasons. But so far, it has been mostly for other reasons that companies are motivated to invite local ownership in their foreign subsidiaries.

POLITICAL CONSIDERATIONS

During the discussions with companies, what we have called *political considerations* continually emerged as the principal reason for seeking local shareholders in a foreign investment. While this is a catch-all term, it reflects the belief that sooner or later some degree of local participation will be necessary if the investment is to remain viable. For example, it is often held that the joint venture form of foreign investment is less at the mercy of local chauvinistic feelings which might lead to various forms of discrimination, or at worst, to nationalisation or expropriation. While this seems to be the general view, experience has shown that at least in the less developed countries, joint ventures have not always fared better than wholly-owned subsidiaries in times of crisis.[29]

In Europe and in other industrialised parts of the world, the threat of discrimination against foreign investment exists. Company officials have become increasingly aware of this and frequently expressed concern about how it could affect their foreign operations through loss of markets, or through particular sanctions such as being denied access to local sources of capital, refused tax concessions and various subsidies otherwise available to local investors, and similar forms of restraint. During the past few years, these have rarely posed serious problems. But the attitudes towards foreign investment appear to be changing and, if they were to grow more unfriendly, the present threat of restrictions could turn into reality. That this is a real possibility was suggested above in the previous chapter. Indeed, in the way it chronicles increasing opposition to foreign investment in a number of countries, chapter 10 could be said to have already provided strong arguments for more joint investment for political reasons. However, it is also true that in normal times the doctrine of reciprocity serves to protect foreign investment. If, say, the French threatened discrimination against British investment in France, they would risk British retaliation against French interests in Britain. This, of course, ceases to apply in times of crisis such as war but in normal times it constitutes some brake on interference with foreign investors.

What are the implications of this growing national unease for company policy? Will the subsidiaries appear any less foreign if local investors are permitted to subscribe to a portion of their equity? If so, how large a local shareholding is required to achieve this goal? What type of local shareholders are most desirable? The answers given to these questions were often contradictory, and thus it is difficult to draw a firm conclusion.

One opinion was that a policy of local ownership was desirable and essential to maintain satisfactory public relations in the host country. Company officials holding this view expressed it in words such as the following:

> We want to feel a part of the local country, and local shareholders are one way to do this.

> Putting the shares on the market gave us a French image, and has paid off by the favourable press comments we have had.

> We feel it is important—particularly in the natural resource business where we are extracting the mineral wealth in other countries—that the local population should have an opportunity to invest in the undertakings for which we are responsible there.[30]

This belief has received considerable support from other sources in Europe. For example, a leading German paper wrote that if Ford and General Motors would sell a minority share in their German companies, 'this would make a great impression on the German public'.[31]

The call to participate in the ownership of multinational companies also comes from sources politically more strategically placed. One of the strongest statements of this position is the report on foreign ownership in Canadian industry which we cited earlier. Perhaps the most comprehensive and objective study yet produced by a host country, it presents a number of arguments why a share of the ownership of foreign subsidiaries should be made available to Canadian investors. After recognising the various reasons that companies had for persistently refusing to issue shares of their subsidiaries in Canada, the report went on to outline the Canadian viewpoint:

> But problems for the companies are one thing, considerations of national interest another. More disclosure and the opportunity to participate in profits earned by Canadian firms without respect to the ownership of the firms constitute benefits for Canadians. . . . A diminution in the parent's flexibility in dealing with the subsidiary *may* be in the national interest. . . . The prevalence of the wholly-owned subsidiary in Canada in the form of private companies, as well as the existence of Canadian-owned private companies, neither of which offer their shares to Canadians, means that the supply of publicly traded Canadian equities is less than it would otherwise be, and that the Canadian capital market for equities is not as fully developed as it would otherwise be. [Therefore] . . . the granting of incentives to firms to encourage the issue of common shares . . . [is] necessary. . . . The existence of minority shareholders in what would otherwise be private companies wholly-owned by a foreign parent

L*

would make the subsidiary a more distinct and separate entity. This can be expected to facilitate the decentralisation of decision-making within the multi-national enterprise and increase Canadian representation on boards of directors. In both respects, this facilitates the expression of private Canadian points of view through the presence of Canadian citizens as managers, directors and shareholders and may provide additional channels for the Canadian government for the exercise of its policy.

The report concluded that an objective of Canadian policy would be 'to take positive steps to encourage increased Canadian ownership and control of economic activity, in ways that will facilitate the achievement of greater national independence and continuing economic growth'.

One of the report's recommendations was that 'stronger incentives be considered to encourage large corporations, including foreign-owned subsidiaries, to offer their shares to Canadians, thereby increasing the supply of Canadian equities, facilitating disclosure, and providing levers for public regulation and for dealing with extraterritoriality.'[32] The report urged that while such a policy would have its costs, they were likely to be more than compensated by its long-range benefits. In sum, the multinational company was here to stay, and Canadian policy had to come to grips with this development.

A similar argument, though less encompassing, was used by a senior official in the Common Market Commission at a meeting on international business in Brussels. He maintained that it was unsatisfactory to deny European investors the opportunity to invest in what were among the most successful and fastest growing companies in Europe. He thought that no small part of the explanation of the continuing poor performance of the European stock markets (up to 1967) was the lack of a sufficient number of good companies available to investors. A public offering by some of the foreign-owned subsidiaries would provide a healthy stimulus to revive interest in this form of investment.

These are not opinions shared by all. Many of the bankers we interviewed expressed the view that past experience showed that the interests of minority shareholders were often ignored, and that in general such investments had proved to be unattractive. This appears to be a fairly widespread view in the United Kingdom, where experience with one subsidiary in particular has made the British investor very sceptical of minority shareholdings. With the financial press reminding investors that the example of Crown Cork 'is a dire warning to shareholders in companies who are contemplating partial deals with US firms', one might wonder how well a minority offering in a foreign subsidiary would be received in the United Kingdom.[33] In addition to this, government policy-makers may have doubts whether the use of host country capital to take up a minority interest in a subsidiary is the most efficient allocation of scarce resources—especially if these funds were, for example, used to cancel debt held by the parent company.

These various conflicting points of view show up again in the experience of two companies with large overseas interests, and further illustrate how hard it is to generalise on this issue.

To cite the case of Ford, one of its original reasons for selling a minority interest in the English company was to improve its local public image. Henry Ford Sr had been told that, 'as a purely American-owned company, with so much British propaganda against it, it [Ford of England] would never have the same chance for its merchandise as a company of which the British public were part and parcel'.[34] Similar considerations led shortly after to the offering of minority shareholdings in the other European subsidiaries. This action appeared to be successful from a financial standpoint, for the stock offerings met with such demand that the brokers had to ration the shares.[35] In spite of this, local participation in the subsidiaries did not always dispel the feeling that Ford was a foreign company—which was after all the main objective of the move.[36] Perhaps its name has always been too well known for it not to be taken for an American company, and there may have been other special factors as well. In any case, Ford eventually decided that whatever public relations benefits could be derived from having local shareholders were more than outweighed by the numerous disadvantages their presence created. And as events have shown, this action has not damaged Ford's market for automobiles in the United Kingdom or in Germany.

In another example, a large British company with extensive overseas investments had a policy of creating minority interests in certain subsidiaries for at least two reasons. First of all, explained the financial director, they did it 'as a sort of hedge against expropriation'. Secondly, in some instances, they had sold to the public primarily as a policy of disinvestment in a particular country. They believed that expansion in some markets was certainly limited, and that it was better to withdraw some of their capital in order to reinvest it elsewhere. However, the two reasons were interrelated because the examples that were cited were countries where the economic and political stability had been, and appeared likely to continue to be, in jeopardy. In fact, according to another official in this company, they sold shares in the subsidiaries in question to the local nationals in order to 'get their money out while the getting was good'.

But such a rationale was only relevant to investments in a developing or relatively unstable country. Indeed, the company's European and American subsidiaries, by far the largest of the group, were wholly-owned. 'We wouldn't think of inviting local investors in Europe or the United States,' we were told. 'After all, if Ford or Vauxhall can be 100 per cent owned by the Americans, we see no reason why the Americans should feel a need to acquire a portion of our US company.' The implication here was that their policy was based on reciprocity; since there was no general pressure in the US or Europe for national participation in the local subsidiaries, and only insignificant risk of political or economic instability, there was little to be gained by inviting local ownership.

In countries where they had sold a minority interest to local investors, their policy was to encourage as widespread a distribution as possible. This was explained by the financial director as: 'What we don't want is a large shareholder such as an insurance company, or a powerful local financial group, or local government. They all get enough out of us already.' Therefore, they attempted to encourage their local employees, suppliers, and customers to subscribe to the shares which were offered, reasoning that this would involve them more in the success of the local operation. Further, it was believed that a relatively large number of small shareholders would not normally try to interfere with management of the company. They claimed that the best indication of the advantages gained in public relations from having local shareholders was their experience in Brazil. Although less than 25 per cent of the Brazilian company was locally owned, articles in the press usually treated it as a purely domestic company, and indeed, rarely mentioned the fact that it was foreign-controlled. In a poll taken on the question of foreign ownership in Brazilian industry, over 80 per cent of those polled thought the company 100 per cent Brazilian. Management in the parent company thought that if this attitude could be attributed to the local shareholding, then the policy had achieved what they had intended.

For any major improvement in public relations to result from inviting local ownership in foreign subsidiaries, a number of conditions must be satisfied. First, an effective impact on local opinion depends on as wide a distribution of shares as possible among the investing public. This requirement will vary considerably between countries, in accordance with the development of the capital market and the savings habits of investors. Where investment in industrial securities is uncommon, as is generally the case in the developing countries, local shareholders are most likely to be found among a subsidiary's suppliers, customers, employees, and others closely involved with its business. Moreover, these are also the individuals most interested in its success. In these instances, probably only a relatively small proportion of the equity needs to be offered, thus reducing the risk of any loss of control. In countries, however, where the stock market is a popular means of investment, local shareholders will tend to be found much more among the general investing public, including the large institutional investors. As a consequence, enough shares must be made available to permit active and orderly trading. Judging from numerous examples of quoted subsidiaries in the United Kingdom and in France, it is likely that at least 25 per cent of the equity needs to be offered locally to achieve this goal.

Secondly, the attitude of the financial press must be favourable. It influences a public that extends far beyond the local shareholder group.[37] It sees its role as that of business critic, with the job of looking after the best interests of the community and in particular of protecting the shareholders in their relations with industry. In these circumstances, companies have to live up to local expectations of corporate behaviour or risk incurring unfavourable publicity.

But fundamentally, what is required is a strong desire on the part of the investing public to hold shares in foreign-owned subsidiaries, and it is not clear how widespread this demand actually is. Certainly in the United Kingdom, quoted subsidiaries have had a generally unfavourable press although, to be fair, this has been in connection with the policies and practices of only a few of them. On the continent, the demand appears to be stronger, but perhaps not as strong as it is in Canada, Australia, and some of the developing countries. Especially in the latter, it seems to be bound up with a need for national identity and wanting to be master in one's own house. Finally, it is doubtful whether local ownership is in itself sufficient to dispel the onus of being a foreign company.[38] Although it is often believed that this will create a strong local interest in the prosperity of the subsidiaries, other factors such as the policy of selection and promotion of local nationals to management positions, observance of local customs and business practices, cooperation with the local community and national authorities, and even choice of name are perhaps as important in gaining local identification.

11.4 Future policy

In summing up, it must be recognised that the ownership policies of multinational companies are a subject of critical importance. The emergence of this type of corporate entity as one of the major economic developments of this era is unmistakable, and its influence on national economies is pervasive and growing. There is at the same time an increasing interest in the host countries to take part in this growth. The problem, as it was put by the former chairman of General Motors, 'is to find ways to accomplish the objective of worldwide participation in the ownership of multinational businesses'.[39]

His solution was to encourage foreign ownership in the *parent company*, a proposal which has found considerable support among a number of US multinational companies which have arranged to list their shares on European stock exchanges.[40] This attempt to broaden foreign ownership may be furthered by the practice of many companies of issuing convertible bonds on the European capital market.[41]

The proposal would appear to be a better solution for the long term than for the immediate years to come. It is an inadequate answer now because the pressures for national independence are too strong to allow partici-pation in a remote and *foreign* company to be an acceptable alternative to participation in a *local* company. By investing in the local subsidiary, investors take a direct and visible part in the growth of *their* economy. The parent company might provide a better investment, more broadly based and less subject to local economic fluctuations. But by being given the opportunity to invest in the local subsidiary, local investors at least have a choice in how they dispose of their funds.[42]

There are costs in such a policy of local participation. For the host country, it could mean less tax income—from withholding taxes lost on dividends paid to the minority holdings, and from lower profits if intracompany pricing is altered to reflect a more accurate distribution of corporate costs; it could have an impact on its balance of payments if the proceeds of the sale to create a minority holding were repatriated; and it could possibly affect growth if the presence of a minority interest were a disincentive for the com-pany to invest further. For the companies, a minority interest complicates management, and especially so in the area of finance. Dividend policy is affected, not only with regard to the percentage of earnings that are distri-buted, but also in the timing and stability of their payment. Policies con-cerning financial structure, intracompany pricing, hedging against risks, and transfer of funds have to take into account the interests of the minority holding. As a result, flexibility is reduced, and with it, the ability to operate a corporate pool of funds. It is not surprising that from the heated argu-ments of some businessmen to the cool rationalisations of others like Donner, the attitude of most businessmen to local participation is critical.

Nevertheless, the forces for greater participation exist and are growing, and to deny them would seem a shortsighted policy that multinational companies can ill afford; the extra costs will have to be considered as one of the prices paid for doing business in a foreign country. In the concluding chapter we shall consider the possible alternatives that seem feasible for companies to adopt in order to respond to the desire for local participation, while not unduly jeopardising management efficiency.

12

The strategy of multinational enterprise

Some of the factors which shape the policies of multinational companies have now been identified. Among the most interesting are the clash of opposing forces in the decision-making process—the financial interests of the parent company against those of the subsidiary and perhaps the host country as well, the nationally minded against the internationally oriented groups in management, local autonomy against central control, and so on. Influenced by these and other conflicts, large and fast-growing companies are developing new types of structure and new methods of ensuring that the best use is made of their funds. We have glimpsed at the underlying social and financial mechanisms, and analysed their consequences for the various interests involved. It is now time to take a final look at the situations, conclusions and likely developments to which our information points.

12.1 Organisation and relationships

This book began with a discussion of the organisation of the multinational company in terms of its structure, the relationships between its component parts, and the roles of its executives. The main structural theme is the conflict between the three projections of the company—product group, geographical and central services. Reorganisations affecting the international side of the firm's operations can usually be put down to conflicts between these projections, and especially to the problems caused to the foreign operations by a thoroughgoing product group organisation at home. Each company stresses its own individuality, but in fact every firm examined could be classified under four main types for purposes of observing how the foreign operations fit into the organisation. Types A, B and C give priority in their overseas links to the central services, the geographical and the product groups respectively, while type D operates a sophisticated system which combines the three. The way in which the majority of the companies fit these types, sometimes through successive reorganisations, points to the limited options available to a firm which finds its present organisation unsatisfactory. In fact these options are more limited still, because type A normally only applies to the single-product firm, while type D is only possible with a large concern. Naturally there are many variations within these types, and firms in particular industries will have different emphases which are likely to be reflected in their affiliates—the mirror effect, we have called this. But with regard to the development of the four types, in our sample these are in no way related to the main industry group of the company or whether it is in consumer or capital goods.

Blocks in the communications systems have been seen to be a principal factor in causing structural change. Thus we have outlined in chapter 2 the characteristic problems that arise in a geographical organisation, in which the firm concentrates all its executives with foreign expertise or interest in an international division. This produces a block in communications at headquarters where the product group managers give minimum service to the foreign operations. Where, on the other hand, the organisation has a product group framework both at home and abroad, one common problem is a block in communications between the home and the foreign operations. The controls are likely to be *close* and thus the upward communication flow considerable to the point of being oppressive. But the downward communications are likely to be minimal. There will also be problems of coordination abroad where several product groups are operating in the same country.

As a result of these problems has arisen what is here called the type D organisation, in which a new pattern of relationships between the three projections is worked out. The essence of this arrangement is that there are strong international links in both the geographical and the product group projections, and probably in the central services as well. One projection will operate the 'hire-and-fire' link, the actual line relationship, but reporting will normally be along other projections. So the D type company talks about multi-reporting channels. The system is elaborate and expensive and only applicable, it would seem, to large firms. It arises partly from the impetus to clearer assertion of individual accountability, but only achieves this up to a point. It may well be suspected that another pattern will emerge eventually. The D type company accelerates the tendency noted in some businesses today of reversing one well-known feature of a bureaucratic organisation, the emphasis on the job over against the person. The very nature of the D type company is to produce a system where the job is to be fitted to the person, rather than the person to the job.

Our main propositions under the general heading of organisation are: *that the trend towards increasing emphasis on the product group projections of a company raises problems when that company goes abroad. Communications blocks arise from over-emphasis on either geographical or product group aspects of the organisation. Hence some companies are developing elaborate organisations with multiple reporting systems. These are producing what may be called a repersonalised bureaucracy.*

These influences affect the units of a multinational firm quite differently from those of a domestic one. The way they have been stated implies that the communications block can be removed by changes in the organisation, as it is to the structure rather than to the communications as such that the successful company turns its attention. Indeed one of the problems of the multinational company is that some conscious efforts to improve communications can produce great, even insupportable, pressures on the subsidiary —distorting its organisation and the direction of its managerial effort. This study has produced other evidence of the complicated and contradictory pressures which determine the relationships between head office and the foreign subsidiaries. Certain trends are clear. Whatever the origin or intentions of the company, the relationships oscillate between varying levels of centralisation. Technical considerations have been seen to reduce autonomy, while personal influences work the other way. The forces at work here were unravelled in chapter 3, while chapter 4 showed the financial control arrangements involved. A number of interesting points emerge.

The main themes of the discussion on the power systems can be summed up as showing a trend towards greater use of *voluntary*, that is non-financial, means of ensuring commitment on the part of the executive, while at the same time reducing the limits of his discretion. But this reduction, in its turn, is to be seen in the narrowing of his terms of reference rather than his personal autonomy. These trends are accompanied by two paradoxes, clearly indicated in our evidence although equally clearly eligible for further research. One of these is that *calculative* phrases are used for the means of achieving this *voluntary* commitment, and the other paradox is that decentralising theories are masking centralising facts. Another way of expressing the first paradox is that the language of self-interest is used of measures that turn out to have less self-interest than is claimed. One might suspect that it is just as well from the point of view of the companies that these two paradoxes go together. If what we have called the decentralising ideology did not act as a powerful brake on the centralising tendencies evident today, it would appear doubtful whether such a high level of talent and enthusiasm could be sustained in the foreign subsidiary. For, again in the light of our evidence, there seems to be a connection between a high degree of centralisation and a loss of local talent, and a reduction of purposeful activity among those who remain. And this reduction could make *voluntary* commitment meaningless while increasing the costliness of the foreign operation.

The actual degree of centralisation is described in general terms since no measure which gives a convincing precision in the relationships between head office and the foreign subsidiary is yet available. One factor to take into account is, of course, the declared policy of the company, and the way that that policy is translated into actual rules and regulations. These may specify in detail the way the foreign company administers its affairs; but they may, on the other hand, limit the amount of interference that head office executives are permitted. The rules may specifically say that on all but a few reserved decisions the head office can only advise the affiliate. If the official rules correspond with the realities, then a glance at the rule book should be a sufficient indication of the level of centralisation—that is in firms which have written regulations at all. But many other factors operate here. These have been outlined in chapter 3, where it is suggested that the relationships can be very *open* or very *close*, but in fact fluctuate around some standard arrangements called the *normal line*. The main factors involved in pressing both for and against more close links, it is suggested, are missed opportunities. But there are two principal antagonists in the power struggle, the managers in the foreign subsidiary and the functional managers in the parent company. The former can use the local differences, the local laws, the distance, the tax problems and suchlike as their weapons. So long as they operate successfully they can use these effectively; and, in spite of the increasingly close relationships that we record, it is possible to find firms where the regulations are unread by local management. The functional managers at head office, on the other hand, are busy promoting global policies; this involves the introduction of new techniques and the collection of increasing quantities of information. The promoting of these policies can reduce the autonomy of the local operation much more than the company intends.

Alongside the main trends in the relationships, issues of centralisation and control, a number of interesting secondary features appear. One of these is the problem examined earlier under the heading of organisation, where decentralisation by product group produces centralisation for the local national operation. For the purposes of this study, that is, more product group autonomy often means less autonomy for the national subsidiary. But, we have seen, some companies are very sensitive to national feeling and hence introduce features which are otherwise out of keeping with the logic of the organisation. As a consequence certain problems arise. One of these, called here the *buffer situation*, is discussed under the heading of personal issues. Another is the problems of the *two* or, in some cases, *three head-quarters*. This study unearthed a few examples of this, but one suspects it must be more common that our examples would suggest. For whenever a situation was discovered where this problem might arise, questions at the head office of the national subsidiary elicited responses which suggested its existence. Where it was possible to follow up these responses, the existence of this particular problem was established in the subsidiary. The likely situation is where a national subsidiary has a considerable autonomy and manages several plants in different product groups. As part of the 'consider-able autonomy', the local national headquarters will be the route for com-munications between the plant and the head office in the home country. For without this the autonomy would be largely illusory anyway. However, such an arrangement can be very unsatisfactory for the local experts, especially the technical ones. They are likely to attempt to bypass an arrangement which gives them a line of communication to people who share their nationality but not their specialist knowledge. The people with whom they wish to establish close links are in the parent company, and no doubt the wish is reciprocated. So they avoid the national headquarters, which the firm has established out of regard for local feeling, for the sake of the international headquarters. This is what is meant by the problems of the two headquarters, and it constitutes a pressure for a more close relationship that comes from abroad. The authority, and hence the autonomy, of the subsidiary is reduced as the international links are strengthened at subordinate level.

A decentralising factor, on the other hand, is the problem for which we have used the phrase *vicious circle*. This arises when instructions are issued to the subordinate without consultation, and without that subordinate seeing the reason for the order. This may spark off a number of reactions, such as efforts to evade or even sabotage the instructions. Examples of this, given in this book, include demands for information which seem irrelevant to the subsidiary or the circulation of comparative figures which the local managers regard as pillorying them unjustly. When the appropriate department at head office becomes aware of the evasion or sabotage, it will take steps to stop it by issuing fresh instructions or reformulating the rules. If these also come to the subsidiary without warning, fresh avoiding action is likely. This is the essence of the vicious circle. When no one realises what is happening a likely reaction at headquarters is to order more stringent measures of control. When the situation is understood there can be a pressure towards either some measure of decentralisation aimed at promoting voluntary cooperation; or there can be at least some move towards an agreed form of decision-making, called elsewhere in this study *contractual management*.

The other issue which seems worth a mention here is that of discipline and nurture in the relations between the centre and the affiliate. It became clear in discussions with subsidiary executives that in their eyes some 'friend in court' at a senior level in head office was desirable. This was an executive who provided a secure liaison for them at a high level, but also ensured the transmission of information that was needed for the efficient working of their unit. If the nurturing function of head office was being mainly provided by one individual, or perhaps by one department, it could also be true that another individual or department exercised the disciplinary function, in the eyes of the subsidiary. The fact that head office may not perceive that this is happening can mean that a reorganisation is carried out which alters the subtle balance between the nurture and the discipline. These changes may not seem to have any such significance to the head office executive, but they affect considerably the position of the subsidiary.

Finance tends to be the most highly integrated of the functional departments and is one for which special considerations often obtain as we have indicated earlier. These include the possibilities of economy of scale that can sometimes be gained by operating a corporate 'pool' of funds, together with possibilities for reducing taxes, minimising risks, and achieving various other financial objectives. Without a centralised control over these matters the danger of suboptimisation is high. Subsidiary management, either because of an inability to assess adequately the impact of its financial decisions on other parts of the organisation, or because of a conflict of interest, may try to maximise its own objectives without regard to those of the company as a whole. In general, this basic tendency towards centralisation in the area of finance finds its counterpart in the integration of other functional areas. This will be reinforced by the attempt of some companies to link together such operations as planning and reporting, production scheduling and inventory control for several subsidiaries within a regional or even wider area by means of a central computer.

Another important factor which influences the degree of centralisation or decentralisation is the amount of confidence placed in subsidiary management. The acquisition of the specific and detailed technical knowledge of a particular company that is required to do an effective job can be a lengthy process. And, however long this may be, it generally takes even longer to demonstrate this competence to one's superiors and gain their confidence. For this reason, companies may not be willing to delegate very substantial autonomy to local nationals until they have adequately proved themselves. The length of this probationary period may depend on such factors as the parent company management's experience and sophistication in foreign operations, the complexity of the technology and its rate of change, the rate of growth of the subsidiary, and the capabilities and motivation of the individuals in the subsidiary. In the shorter run, parent companies will probably maintain close supervision of their subsidiaries through comprehensive financial controls and the use of expatriate management in the key posts.

Finally, improvements in the methods of exercising control may lead to more centralisation. These have come about in two ways. At one level, better and more rapid means of communication allow the parent company to keep in close contact with the various units of the organisation. Whether it is by high-speed transportation, or by fast and dependable telephone, telex and postal communication, the flow of information can be maintained at a volume and regularity that was impracticable not long ago. Further, the introduction and use of computers make it feasible to process and interpret large masses of data which it used to be impossible to handle. On another level, improved techniques of planning, programming and budgeting have been developed, and have become widely used as a result of the forces of business necessity, management education and current fashion. As a result, where there is an opportunity to achieve economies of scale through closer integration of certain activities, it has often become technically feasible to effect it. In these circumstances, authority over more and more matters is moved upwards, whether this is justified or not.

Thus a number of propositions arise from considering the power and control systems, but principally: *that a decentralising ideology masks a centralising reality. The factors which create this situation include an increasing integration of multinational operations, an increasing speed of technological change, and the rapid development of global techniques, strategies and information collection.*

We have seen how the multinational firm is developing new structural patterns. One consequence of this is the strengthening of the individual as against the organisation; and another is the development of methods of communication that, although outside those prescribed, are carefully fostered. Both these trends are towards a more human organisation, and may be regarded as a *quid pro quo* for the greater centralisation. A man may have less discretion in a house that is more his own.

Among the personal problems of the international executive is a form of *role conflict.* By this is meant that he has to perform two or more incompatible roles at the same time. The conflict arises because he is a national manager in a host country while also being the representative of a foreign investor. This is a difficulty whatever his nationality; it can involve a severe strain when, for example, the movement of money out of the country or the transfer of production to another country is involved. In most companies, head office spoke about complete identification with the host country as their policy for managers abroad; but at the same time measures to make this 'complete identification' impossible were being implemented. Another problem for the foreign executive is interpreting messages between the foreign managers in the home country and his own subordinates in the host country. The *buffer situation,* as we have called it, is an uncomfortable position and especially where the existence of an overriding national management does not fit in to the product group system of the company. It can exist, however, in highly profitable firms. Part of the difficulty, it has been suggested, is the underemployment of the talents of the senior executives in the subsidiary. Some companies overcome this by part-time appointments to the direction of the local company; this has the further advantage of importing to the firm distinguished local citizens of the host country. In other circumstances it seems ironical that companies which are addicted to describing management as a 'scarce resource', tolerate a waste of this resource abroad. This is yet another of the paradoxes which can be identified in the multinational operation.

Apart from these problems, the foreign executive can be in a very strong position indeed. He has the prestige of working for an international firm, and the security of the national subsidiary. But he is subject to severe pressures in an organisation which may well seem big and amorphous, and in which the individual can easily be lost in spite of what has just been said about the humanising innovations. Hence it is not surprising to find that companies put considerable resources into promoting greater cohesion and stress the need for executives to know their way about the company. For this purpose there are intracompany conferences and much travel between home and host countries. From this also arises the stress put on actual experience inside the organisation, the developing of an instinct for knowing where to turn in any circumstances. Indeed some companies represent themselves as extraordinarily sensitive. For instance executives, who will ridicule a 'who does what' dispute in one of their factories, will at the same time blame the foreign official who causes friction inside head office by taking his problems to the wrong person. The process which this view implies can make the *recognised informal* procedures, about which we have written, more rigid than the formal ones.

Another factor which promotes cohesion in some large companies is the personality of the chief executive. In some firms his name is constantly mentioned, and every small shift in policy is ascribed to his personal preference. In other companies the name of the chief executive is not mentioned at all. We have already suggested that the foreign manager may be better able to understand the company in personal terms than in the light of any written description. Hence the ability of the company to project the personality of its chief throughout a large and varied organisation may be of great significance to the wellbeing of the firm, although at variance with contemporary emphasis on greater participation at every level. Nevertheless this latter feature is represented in the evidence in the form of what has been called *contractual management*. This covers two trends. One is that towards greater independence for managers and management groups within fixed limits of discretion; the other is the setting up of procedural arrangements for working out the details of policy-making. For example, a firm may decide that rationalisation across frontiers is desirable, but leave all decisions about this to a meeting of chief executives of foreign subsidiaries. Thus any rationalisation that was eventually agreed would be by negotiation between those affected. These negotiations, along with other similar issues, are much influenced by the management development policies of the company. Global promotion schemes, with accompanying concepts such as that of the 'international grade', are seen to be important in many ways. They contribute to the removal of some of the frustrations of the local executive; they breed an international outlook; they open up new lines of communication.

So we may conclude that: *considerable personal pressures are involved in the management of multinational companies and especially difficult is the position of national management in a product-organised firm. Global promotion is another issue with significant implications for the future.*

12.2 Finance

In turning to financial policies, we must bear in mind how they can be influenced by the different business environments in which the multi-national company operates. In some countries, taxes on profits are lower than in others. Risks of exchange loss, discrimination against foreign investors, and political or economic disorders vary among countries, even within relatively integrated trading groups such as the Common Market. Finance and the various factors of production differ in cost and availability from one country to another. In such circumstances, the multinational company is provided with strong incentives to shift profits about the group in order to try to maximise its earnings or minimise its risks, or both. Inevitably, this can give rise to conflict, for some of the benefits enjoyed by one part of the group are gained at the expense of another. Likewise, the share of some host countries in the earnings and other benefits provided by foreign investments is disproportionate to others. We saw that there are restrictions imposed by the company itself by its reluctance to jeopardise its management control through pursuing certain policies. However, as long as these incentives exist, it is naïve to think that companies will not attempt to take advantage of them. True, as national economies become more and more integrated, and as the tax and risk differentials between countries are narrowed, this cause of conflict will tend to be reduced. This evolution has been, and will continue to be, subject to fits and starts. The end is, of course, the disappearance of national economic boundaries, but this is not yet in sight. In the meantime, companies will continue to be American, or British, or Swedish, or French, and so on, and this means that they will try to maximise their earnings and ultimately to pay their dividends in terms of dollars, or sterling, or kroner, or francs. Given this situation, it is hard to see how conflict can be avoided.

The principal characteristic of their financial policy which we noted was the wide diversity in the sources of finance and the financial structure of subsidiaries, and in the means used to transfer their earnings and other corporate funds. This stems from a number of factors operating both at the subsidiary and at head office.

At the level of the parent company, tax considerations, cost and availability of alternative sources of finance, and attitudes towards risk are the principal factors which determine its policies concerning the finance of foreign subsidiaries.

Efforts to minimise the overall tax burden lead companies to substitute various payment schemes for dividends as a means of repatriating earnings; it leads them to use other devices such as discretionary pricing of intra-company transfers of goods and services, and base companies to shift earnings to low-tax countries; it leads them to plan carefully where and how ownership of their foreign investments is held. This being said, for most operations in Europe and North America the narrowing of the tax differentials between the various countries as well as a tightening up and stricter control of the regulations has greatly reduced the scope for avoiding taxes that companies once enjoyed. Nevertheless there is still a considerable way to go before real tax neutrality between countries is reached, and until then the impact of taxation on financial decisions in multinational companies cannot be neglected.

Another factor which bears on the parent company's decisions as to how subsidiaries are to be financed is the relative cost and availability of the various sources of funds at the group's disposal. In the early stages of a subsidiary's development, before it has established a strong local credit standing and while its needs are large, the parent company obviously has little choice in many cases but to provide more or less all of its needs. The same may be true where, because of local conditions, finance might not be otherwise available to an established subsidiary. Indeed, this support from the parent company can provide the subsidiary with an important advantage, for investment opportunities seldom need to be rejected or postponed because of lack of the necessary finance. But even when the subsidiary can raise money locally, and the parent company has a choice, it may still be able to raise capital more cheaply within its sphere of operations, or make use of its own or an affiliate's surplus cash. In such cases there can be an incentive to use these funds instead of those locally available to the subsidiary. To take fullest advantage of such opportunities it is important to structure the subsidiaries in such a way that funds can be easily transferred at a minimum of cost and inconvenience. As a result, subsidiaries are financed frequently by loans and advances from the parent company rather than by equity. Besides this, reinvested earnings are allowed to remain as earned surplus and are not transferred to a capital account. This means that the retained earnings are available for dividends, thus providing further flexibility to transfer funds.

Probably the most important single factor affecting group financial decisions is the attitude of parent company management towards exchange risks. This often leads companies to undercapitalise their foreign subsidiaries, and to borrow locally as much as possible—even if this means greater cost; additional finance from the parent company is put up in the form of loans rather than equity; complex devices are used to divert or siphon off profits from the high-risk areas; surplus cash is kept to a minimum in the subsidiary by a policy of systematically repatriating most of the earnings. The overall effect of these measures is to keep the company's own capital at risk to a minimum, and to provide it with as much flexibility as is practical to repatriate funds quickly if and when necessary. That companies are sensitive to exchange risks was noted from our data between 1964 and 1967 when large sums were repatriated from United Kingdom-based subsidiaries through increased dividends and changes in intracompany accounts. One of the main reasons why companies seem so sensitive to exchange risks, it has been suggested, is the extraordinary nature of the loss.[1] Since they appear on the financial accounts of the parent company, their impact on the management and on the shareholders may be greater than losses arising from, for example, commercial failures. The responsibility can be more clearly identified, and the ability to avoid or reduce loss from this source is normally within the means of companies that take the appropriate safeguards.[2] Failure to do so in most cases can be interpreted as negligence.

The subsidiary's needs for finance will vary according to its rate of growth, its profitability, and the disposition of its earnings. Over half of its finance, on average, comes from internal sources. Depending on the availability and cost of local finance, its credit standing, and the willingness of the parent company to provide a guarantee, the subsidiary will typically be able to meet all or most of its additional needs for funds by borrowing from sources in the host country—primarily the banks, and on short term. Any further finance will then be provided by the parent company as a loan or equity. In sum, the bulk of foreign subsidiaries' finance is from sources within the host country—its own cash flow, and the local credit.

As a result of all these considerations, financial policies and practices of foreign subsidiaries will generally bear little resemblance to those of companies quoted on a stock exchange. Compared to quoted companies, foreign subsidiaries typically have substantially more short-term debt, particularly if their intracompany liabilities are included; it is not unusual to find that they are technically insolvent with current liabilities exceeding current assets as can be seen from the detailed data in Appendix II. Another difference is dividend policy. In the quoted company, perhaps the principal characteristic is consistency and stability of payments. In contrast, a relatively large number of subsidiaries do not pay dividends, although some make payments of other kinds. Moreover, in the majority of cases, subsidiary remittances are seen to be anything but stable. It is not surprising that the financial policies and practices appropriate to quoted companies are seldom typical of those in wholly-owned subsidiaries. The subsidiaries do not have a local shareholder group to be considered; they generally do not have to publish their accounts; they can operate behind a cloak of anonymity. This does not necessarily imply that their methods are unethical, but it does mean that they can take decisions based on sound economic reasons and not worry about the impact on their public relations.

Thus *general policies and particularly financial policies in multinational companies are specifically designed to further the goals of the parent company, and only incidentally those of subsidiaries or host countries. Such a built-in bias is bound to create conflict between the different parts of the organisation, between the whole organisation and its home and host countries, and between the home and host countries themselves. Typical of such policies are the various schemes which are used to shift earnings from one country to another in order to avoid taxes, minimise risks, or achieve other objectives.*

The additional economic and political variables which come from operating in several environments produce financial policies different from and generally more complex than those typically found in domestic companies. The implications of this are that (1) normal standards of company behaviour with respect to disposition of earnings, sources of finance, structure of capital, pricing of intracompany transfers, liquidity, and so forth are not necessarily relevant to a foreign subsidiary; and (2) the performance of subsidiaries becomes difficult, if not impossible, to measure.

12.3 Performance and motive

Many of the companies which cooperated in this study have successful records and, in spite of the many difficulties recorded, normally achieve their objectives. There are obvious problems about collecting evidence on the failures, they may not even still exist. But, even making exaggerated allowances for this, the attractiveness of foreign investment for the companies themselves remains. It might be expected, indeed, that every firm with sufficient resources and a suitable line of business would be developing foreign subsidiaries. The fact is that only a minority of companies actually become multinational, and that this minority includes numerous small firms as well as some very large ones. No doubt this situation partly reflects inertia within the organisations; it also must surely represent the strength of the opposition inside the companies to this particular use of resources.

Those firms which are abroad include a number, especially European, which are there by the nature of their business—such as extractive industries, forestry products and tropical agriculture. Many of these date from colonial times. Of the rest, including most of the American multinational firms, the majority are in manufacturing for consumer and industrial markets, and give defensive reasons for the move abroad; these include the preservation of the markets against tariff barriers and transport costs and the reaction to legal problems.

Personal pressures are involved as well as financial ones, as we have seen. The development of trade in any part of the world, if done through the firm's own export department, involves also developing a sensitivity to the life of the region concerned. This 'sensitivity' is in fact a group of managers, and they are likely to be suggesting that the company's interests require local manufacture of at least part of the product. Firms operating through agents or licensees may be receiving contrary advice, if the executives who deal with these overseas representatives are supporting their choices. In this case it is probable that some specific difficulties with an agent provide the original stimulus to a process which eventually leads to local manufacture.[3]

Another contrary pressure is that of the production managers at home; for them foreign manufacture leads to a number of problems, especially the uneconomic use of their resources caused by the reduction of their production runs. Hence the decision to go abroad is subject to the lobbying of rival groups, among whom a strong and knowledgeable export department can be decisive.

Thus we conclude: *that under some circumstances foreign operations are more profitable than domestic. This provides one motive for such operations; the search for raw materials and scarce resources provides another. Apart from these, the main motives stated by companies are defensive—the protection of existing markets. There are personal pressures involved, with identifiable groups working both for and against the move abroad.*

12.4 Nationalism

The foregoing discussion contains a reminder that the nature of the firm's business is not such a dominant factor in the making of international arrangements for organisation and finance as might be expected. Another unanticipated point is that operations across frontiers as such prove to be more significant than any specific national differences. Although different countries react to the presence of international firms in different ways, the influences at work are similar. Thus most countries want foreign capital and knowhow to strengthen their economies, but oppose the increasing domination of key industries by foreign firms. Hence the love–hate relationship we have described. In this connection the growing internationalism of the firms, which includes the recruitment of local executives with international interests, may well affect their reactions to nationalism in the host country. Further, if the firms allow themselves to be pushed into closer accord with the aspirations of national governments in order to secure their markets, they may find this difficult to enforce on their own local executives. For the cadre of international executives will become cosmopolitan in outlook and less in step with nationalistic opinion in their country of origin. This tendency has also been noted among executives of other supranational organisations. [4] It means that companies will not resolve problems of relationships with countries simply by recruiting local executives; they may exacerbate them if the men they recruit are untypical of their countries.

At this point it should be said that there appears to be some *amplification process* at work in relationships across frontiers. The formidable communications systems which the firms have built up, as well as problems of style and language, seem to ensure that messages received are louder than those despatched. Head office whispers a request for information, the local concern receives a loud demand. The subsidiary murmurs a reminder of 'national differences', the headquarters hears a shout about a 'strange culture'. In this particular instance, the 'amplification', like the 'sensitivity' mentioned above, is the work of a group of managers at head office. This group includes men who have spent years abroad, gained a genuine respect for foreign methods, and come back as experts on local cultures. They typically staff international divisions where such exist, and press for them where they do not. They contribute an awareness of alien practices, but may make the company oversensitive to these practices.

If messages become exaggerated, so may responses. Problems overseas may stimulate reactions of a more sweeping nature than would be considered appropriate for domestic difficulties. These reactions and reorganisations can be expected to interfere with the development of satisfactory formal communications, and of the more delicate informal links. Thus if a subsidiary management complains of 'not knowing where it stands', this is not necessarily a demand for more written instructions. It may come from a desire for more informal links with the sources of nurture, discipline and stimulus.

Thus we have suggested that: *national differences as such are becoming less significant: it is the fact of international operations that is important rather than particular local differences. Nevertheless there are likely to be increasing problems in the future as the growing internationalism of the company executive becomes out of step with local national opinion.*

12.5 Ownership

Some implications of this fact of international operations are seen when the question of ownership is discussed. The attempt to maximise the advantages of operating in multiple business environments, and to minimise the disadvantages, has constituted a pressure towards wholly-owned subsidiaries. For it is patently easier to do this when there are no local shareholders to be considered on such matters as dividend policy, the allocation of markets, or the pricing of intracompany transfers.

The question that was raised in chapter 11 was whether this policy would continue in the future. We suggested that foreign investment in certain industries in Western Europe and Canada has grown to such an extent that the risk of an unfavourable political reaction in these countries could only be ignored at the companies' peril. Since foreign penetration is particularly strong in the technologically advanced and fast-growing industries, the facts suggest that there would be a growing pressure for local participation in this growth, and also for more voice in the operations of these industries. Companies have certainly been aware of this demand, and steps have been taken by some to satisfy it. One example is the listing of the parent company's shares on local stock exchanges. Other examples include the appointment of local nationals to senior management posts in subsidiaries, in regional headquarters, and occasionally in head office. Also included are local research and development programmes, and close cooperation with the local authorities in achieving national objectives like regional development and export sales. Indeed foreign companies are frequently more cooperative in this respect than local national business.

These measures may not be enough and, for foreign investment to remain viable, a more direct form of local involvement which could be achieved through joint ownership may well become essential. Most companies would appear to agree to this proposition in general terms for a policy of joint ownership is widespread in the developing countries as a means of reducing the risk of discrimination, investment restrictions, or other unfavourable reactions to foreign investment. The problem in Western Europe and Canada appears to be one of determining the degree of urgency of the need for more local participation.

This may well be more urgent than most companies seem to sense, and their long-range interests may be to take the appropriate steps to prepare their foreign investments for local participation at an earlier rather than a later date. By local participation, we mean a wide distribution of the subsidiaries' shares among the local investing public, not a joint venture with a local company. The objectives would be to have a wide local shareholder group in order to obtain as broad a support as possible for the prosperity of the subsidiary, and this would include listing the shares on the local stock exchange. However, such a policy would have some adverse consequences for the companies and to a certain extent for the home and host countries as well.

First, with regard to the implications on company policy, it is evident that the presence of local shareholders would bring a considerable loss in flexibility. In particular dividend policy and financial structure would have to conform more to local standards of financial orthodoxy. Also, the pricing of intracompany transfers of goods and services would have to be more on an arm's-length basis than in the absence of minority shareholders. Another effect would be that the subsidiaries would have more 'visibility' because of the disclosure requirements that usually are needed for stock exchange listing, and consequently poor performance—whether real or only apparent—of one subsidiary could no longer be buried in another in the group's consolidated reports to its shareholders.

How serious would these effects be? In the mature subsidiary it seems unlikely that they would cause major difficulties, although disclosure would be considered as at least an inconvenience. However, in a subsidiary undergoing rapid growth the problems would be somewhat more serious. With local shareholder interests to consider, it would not be advisable for the subsidiary to provide itself with finance by reducing dividend payments. To do so would risk the hostile reaction which was observed in connection with the Crown Cork Company in Britain, and thus defeat the purpose of local participation. On the other hand, the parent company might possibly be reluctant to loan funds to the subsidiary and share the benefits of these loans with local shareholders if they had not contributed *pro rata* to the loan. In theory, no doubt, the attractiveness of an intracompany loan to the parent company as the majority shareholder in such a case depends on three variables. The first is the parent company's own rate of return on investments; the second is the earnings expected in the subsidiary as a result of the loan; the third is the after-tax income from the subsidiary as a result of the loan and in the form of dividends, royalties and fees, and interest. However, in practice, as we have pointed out, the margin of error in predicting future benefits from foreign investment is such that this type of analysis is extremely difficult and hence considered often to be of doubtful value. In these circumstances, the company would probably be more likely to try to assess the alternative position: what would happen if the funds were not loaned? If the answer to this was that its existing investment was endangered by failure of the subsidiary to grow at the rate the market required, the company would be likely to invest without hesitation even with the deadweight of local shareholders.

Probably the most serious snags to local participation arise where subsidiary operations are integrated. In such firms there is often such interdependence among the subsidiaries in the group that it would be inappropriate, if not impossible, for them to try to achieve the degree of autonomy demanded by local participation. The tendency to sub-optimisation would be too strong if the interdependent group were not unified under a common ownership. While perhaps for a few companies this argument could be carried so far as to embrace the entire worldwide organisation,[5] most integrated operations do not extend beyond a regional trade area for any practical purposes. Thus it would not have to be the individual subsidiary that invited local participation, but perhaps a regional holding company which would represent a viable economic entity. There would, of course, be various tax and legal obstacles to be overcome. In particular, there would be the problem of where to domicile the holding company. On the other hand, there would probably be little or no additional administrative support required since regional management groups are already established for many companies.

There could, then, be two types of local shareholdings. Subsidiaries whose operations are essentially national in scope, such as consumer non-durable goods manufacturers and those with a large volume of government business, could issue their shares directly on local stock exchanges and could aim for national identification. The rest of the subsidiaries are those whose operations are integrated with other units of a group and are therefore regional in scope, typically makers of durable goods such as machinery, automotive equipment and cars, complex electrical and electronic products, and some chemicals. These might not themselves issue shares to local investors, but could produce a similar effect by a regional holding company.[6] The aim could be to achieve a regional identity, European for example.

The advantages to the companies of local participation are twofold. First, it provides them with much more local identity and in this way helps to reduce the risk that anti-foreign attitudes may grow to troublesome proportions. Secondly, it can give to the parent company, through the sale of a part of its shareholding, an opportunity to recover capital or even make a capital gain. This may not be an advantage under all circumstances. For instance foreign earnings might be valued by the parent company's market price in the same way as domestic earnings, with the shares selling at a higher price-earnings ratio than could be realised in a sale of a partial interest in the subsidiary. In this case the shareholders of the parent company could suffer a loss in their holdings. On the other hand, the reverse could also be true if there was a great deal of interest in the subsidiary and its shares were bid up to a multiple of earnings which exceeded those of the parent company.

The spinning off of minority interests in foreign subsidiaries also has certain implications for the host countries. One is on their balance of payments. The immediate, short-term, effect is a reduction in reserves to the extent that the proceeds from the sale of the minority interests are repatriated. In the case of a relatively small subsidiary, this clearly would not have a material impact on most countries in Europe. However, the cumulative effect of a number of large subsidiaries selling off minority interests within a relatively short period of time could be substantial. On the other hand, in the long run, the repatriation of earnings would be reduced by the proportion of local ownership in the subsidiary.

Another possible result of a minority interest in a foreign subsidiary is a decrease in its rate of growth if the parent company diverts its resources to other subsidiaries which are wholly owned. However, if a policy of inviting local participation is undertaken on the initiative of the company, it is unlikely that it will then deliberately undermine the future success of this policy. To do so would be contradictory and self-defeating. For the long-term political advantages of local participation to pay off, the interests of the subsidiaries would have to be respected. In addition to the probable long-term favourable effect on the host country's monetary reserves, compared to the alternative of a wholly owned subsidiary, other advantages of this policy include both the stimulation of local capital markets by increasing the supply of equities available and a greater assurance that the subsidiaries' policies will reflect local interests.

To sum up, for the multinational companies to invite local participation in their foreign investments is likely to result in both cost and benefit. The costs tend to be more serious in the short term. There would be the inconvenience of disclosure, less flexibility in financing the subsidiary or in using its excess funds elsewhere, and to the extent that the stock market multiplier of the parent company exceeded that of the local subsidiary (after adjusting profits for additional taxes and the like) there would also be a loss in the market valuation of the company; but this last should be only in the short term. It is necessary to emphasise the time element in this argument because the value of the company calculated over a longer time horizon should be greater where there is local participation on account of the lower risks which result from this policy. As noted earlier, companies appear to agree with this view with regard to their investments in the less developed countries; they are likely to come to a similar reasoning about their investments in the industrialised countries. Thus, *while the desire to enforce company-biased objectives and policies helps to explain the strong and compelling preference of most companies for wholly owned subsidiaries in the industrialised countries, this will sooner or later need to be reconciled with the rapidly growing demand for greater local participation in their ownership, and greater autonomy in their operations.*

Throughout this chapter likely future trends in the organising and financing of multinational companies have been indicated. Many of these are clear enough—a continuing increase in multinational business, *closer* relationships within the firm, more local equity participation, more international promotion schemes for managers, more subtle ways of securing their commitment and mutual interdependence in the different projections of the company, and so on. One factor, we suspect, would have loomed larger if this study had been carried out ten years later; this is the involvement of national governments, as well as supranational governmental agencies, in the development of the type of multinational operations that we have been describing. This involvement can come about in at least three ways, all of which exist at the moment; all of them, too, carry a suggestion of a rapid increase in the total number as well as in the individual sizes of the companies.[7] One is the influence of legislation to prevent companies from gaining too much power in any particular national economy. The necessary laws have existed for nearly a century in the United States; and developments known to have been influenced by anti-trust suits include, for instance the founding of British-American Tobacco, the move of Dupont into Europe and the establishment of British Petroleum in the United States. Other countries are adopting such legislation, as well as placing conditions on foreign investment within their territories. It is hard to believe that any country is going to be permanently without legislation which limits threats to national sovereignty from international business concerns. The second influence of governments is the reverse, namely the positive assistance by a government in the building up of international firms based on its territory. This can be done by state sponsorship of research, as witness state support for British-based electronic companies in the development of micro-circuitry.[8] It can also be done by state-assisted mergers, loans and so on.

The third means of government influence is the operation abroad of state-owned enterprises. Many airlines are already examples of this, as is the establishment of a Soviet bank in London. The British Steel Corporation and British Petroleum (partly state-owned) are further instances.

If governmental action is likely to be used to increase the actual number of international concerns, a much more speculative suggestion is the possibility of greater links between international companies and supranational organisations. The United Nations, for example, might establish its own facilities for registering companies, which would then cease to have any country of origin. Such companies would be able to make an entirely different approach to ownership, career prospects, and other questions discussed in this book. Needless to say there is no sign of this at the moment.

Some of the problems outlined in this study will undoubtedly succumb to technical change. Thus the problems caused to the foreign subsidiary by excessive information flow, and the development of sophisticated systems at head office, could be overcome by greater use of computers abroad. When reporting systems are 'on line', they should prove less burdensome to the local manager. But if, at the same time, he is not becoming more international himself, these developments may well be accompanied by more severe controls and more thoroughgoing measures to ensure accountability; for companies may increasingly fear that local concerns will go their own way despite global planning. The contractual management which we have seen developing is likely to include more convincing means of ending the contract.

Whatever may be the numbers and sizes of the multinational companies in the future, it is quite certain that they will handle a growing proportion of world trade. It is likely, too, that in spite of government activity these firms will promote internationalism both in managerial outlook and in consumer preferences; and this internationalism may provoke its own, in the current jargon, 'backlash'. The word 'complex' has been worked hard in this study, and indeed every aspect of the subject involves issues which interact to such an extent that considerable disentangling is required. In any study of human behaviour there is liable to be complexity but, in looking at multinational companies, there is reason to think that the high-water mark of complexity has already been reached in the financing as well as the organisational arrangements. With greater internationalism may go greater simplicity, as firms develop more standard international procedures. Among our hopes is that this book may contribute to the discussion and the formulation of these procedures.

M

The method and scope of the field research

The sample

The operation of the multinational company is here studied from the behavioural and the financial standpoints. This combination provides a suitable analysis of the management process at the policy-forming levels of the companies. The basic approach followed a path common to both disciplines: the development of a theoretical framework as a basis for the fieldwork, an interview programme, a documentary analysis, the drawing of conclusions and the drafting of a report. The companies put much documentation concerning their policies and organisation at our disposal; this was used to supplement and correct the information gained in the interviews. Documentary evidence from companies not actually visited was also used to confirm some of the processes identified in companies that were.

The fieldwork was done between the years 1964 and 1969, and the selection of companies was at first haphazard. The initial approach was made to firms where one of the authors had some personal contact. Since only a few of the most senior executives of the companies could provide the information required, and the interviews were bound to be demanding, this seemed an appropriate way to start. However, once this source of supply had been exhausted, other companies were approached on the basis of the extent of their global spread; that is to say, those with subsidiaries in the largest number of foreign countries. Some smaller companies were also investigated to check for differences. In the event, the refusal rate was no higher among the companies where there was no previous contact, and was only about 10 per cent of all the companies approached.

In total, over eighty manufacturing companies and thirty banks cooperated in some way in the research. About half the companies were investigated in some depth, and these provided a major part of the evidence for this study. These were mostly large companies. In terms of size, over 80 per cent had worldwide consolidated net assets valued at more than £50 million, 50 per cent over £200 million and 30 per cent over £500 million. The foreign subsidiaries which we interviewed were smaller. The actual figures were not available for all of them; but we estimate that their total assets varied from about £200,000 to over £90 million. The companies were located in seven European countries and in the United States, and were of nine different nationalities. Most of the firms belonged to manufacturing industries which included chemicals and related products, electrical equipment and electronics, machinery, office equipment and computers, paper, textiles, automotive components, food, drink and tobacco; mining and oil companies were also included.

Among the companies which we interviewed in some depth, over three hundred executives took part. About half of these were senior executives or members of the board of the parent company, or of a regional centre; the other half were senior executives in a foreign subsidiary. In addition, executives of some of the companies and most of the banks were interviewed by members of research groups directed by one of the authors. Discussions were also held with international accountants, management consultants, and with individual executives in some companies which had been unwilling to agree to take part formally. These last, in fact, accounted for most of the refusals. In this respect, executives in American-owned companies were usually more willing to discuss their operations frankly and in detail than were those in European-owned firms, and this was true whether they themselves were American or European. Senior executives in subsidiaries of American companies seemed to have more discretion in talking to us than their opposite numbers in European firms. The interviews were of considerable duration, usually two or three hours, and repeat interviews were sometimes possible.

In making a formal approach to companies, the following is an example of a letter that was sent:

I am writing to ask your cooperation in a major research project into the management process in international companies.

This project is being organised jointly between ourselves here in Manchester and the European Institute of Business Administration in Fontainebleau, with the support of the Organisation for Economic Cooperation and Development. I enclose a brief summary of our preliminary report, and would be grateful if you could spare the time to see me to discuss whether your company could contribute to this study.

The basic method of the research is by interview of senior executives of the company, both at home and abroad. We are, as I like to put it, trying to build up a picture by looking through different people's windows. Naturally we undertake that all the conversations will be confidential, and that no companies will be mentioned by name in the final report. Further any specific references to a company will be submitted back first to check for confidence and accuracy.

We are primarily concerned with the relationships between head office and the foreign subsidiary and how these work out in practice. We like to ask questions about organisation, finance, coordination, control, relationships with foreign countries and so on; and how these work in all the functions of the company. In addition to the interviews we ask for access to the relevant documents.

While we accept full responsibility for any report we produce and undertake not to occupy more of the time of any individual executive than is really necessary, we would very much like the work to be regarded as a joint venture between Industry and University—and a valuable example of realistic and fruitful cooperation.

In view of the guarantee of confidence, no companies are mentioned by name in this book. The only exception to this is in quotations from printed sources, and these do not necessarily refer to companies which have cooperated in the research.

The interviews

To lay claim to objectivity is not to deny that there is a problem here. For the nature of our investigation precluded the use of some of the techniques employed to correct subjective judgments. Participant observation, for instance, is clearly impossible in research of this type—you cannot join the board of a company for six months to observe it in action—and question-naires are not very welcome among policy-making executives. Nor are they necessarily sensitive enough to get the required information. Hence questioning and cross-questioning to a standard checklist was the way that most of the information was collected. This was rechecked by the written evidence and by what observation was possible, and these checks would lead back to further questioning. The interviews were semi-structured, and many of the executives spoke at length about the problems of their com-panies. But certain points were always raised about the organisation and the finance. Statements ascribed to a particular company have been cross-checked with more than one executive and referred back to the company again while the study was being written. This was felt to be the most appropriate way of collecting information for this particular subject. All the generalisations are the result of careful study of material gathered in several companies. It must be remembered, however, that this method has its limits.

Most of the material was received in a subjective form, and came from people who varied from the extremely self-critical on the one hand, to those who regarded any conversation as an opportunity for public relations on the other. Nevertheless, this information has been collected through a good deal of looking and listening around the offices of the companies. It has also been 'stared at', to use Freud's phrase. As far as possible attempts were made to arrange the 'interlocking of various research procedures'.[1] In the introduc-tory chapter we sketched out the behavioral presuppositions of this study. Although most of the existing work has been done on the lower levels of hierarchies, and hence it was far from obvious that this would be relevant, many of the models already developed have in fact proved to the point, and an attempt has been made to build on to them. In addition, a dialectical process has been noted in the decision-making to which justice must be done. This arises, for instance, in the context of pruning staff or simplifying some unit of the organisation. The pruning or the simplification is then found to damage the rest of the organisation in some way. The cuts are then restored, but never in quite the same form as they were before. From the facts collected, it would seem that some cyclical view of the company's development is appropriate. But the use of the word 'cyclical' here does not imply any biological analogy. For such analogies can be most misleading.[2] The cycle consists of the intended and the unintended consequences of decisions consciously, if not always rationally, taken.

In those companies which were investigated in some depth, relationships between several units of the organisation in different countries were looked at. This was carried out by means of the interviews already described, and study of the written material. One problem that has already been briefly discussed is how to identify the opinion of 'a company'.[3] We said there that precise statements about the motives for overseas operations were impossible because of this problem. A similar difficulty applies to some of the other issues we discuss, but even where a situation can be established and investigated in sufficient detail, there is the further problem of finding enough examples for any comparative analysis. Take, for instance, what we have called the *problem of the two headquarters*.[4] We found that wherever a self-sufficient national organisation was established with subordinate units in the host country, the tensions described would arise. We have found no exceptions to this, and sometimes feelings have been very strongly expressed indeed. Nevertheless we have found only a limited number of such situations, and the nature of the problem is such that we are unlikely ever to find enough to carry complete conviction.

For the financial data, the check-list consisted of questions about financing and appraising the overseas operations, and problems of ownership and control. But the questioning was not kept in watertight compartments. The following considerations affected the 'behavioral' questioning.

Studies of organisation behaviour as well as accounts of international firms both suggested that the most significant factor here would be relationships, including: methods of control and compliance structures,[5] centralisation and decentralisation,[6] style of management,[7] the effect of appraisal on policy-formation,[8] and other ingredients of decision-making.[9] Hence the initial questioning was about relationships, and in particular centralisation, to find out the specific influences on companies working across frontiers. However, early in the interviews it became clear that relationships and structure did not go together.[10] So eventually developed the threefold division of the questioning into structure (organisation), relationships (power, close to the financial concern over control), and role (the more personal aspects).

Among the issues specifically investigated were the interaction between the systems internal to the company and those external, centralisation and decentralisation, the influence of national differences.[11] In examining the processes of change in both relationships and organisation, some of the concepts developed by Cyert and March made a useful starting point.[12] Concepts like 'problemistic search' and the 'quasi-resolution of conflict' illuminated problems that came to light in the early interviews, especially the way policies had changed as a result of 'missed opportunities'. As we showed in chapter 3, questions about local autonomy could produce replies suggesting that opportunities were being wasted because either there was too little autonomy or too much. Examples of this were, in the former case, the loss of local talent, and in the latter the neglect of important management techniques. Hence some questioning was concentrated on this point. At head office this involved surveying the actual decision-making left to, or forced upon, the affiliate; and abroad one looked at the nature of the decisions made, and how those concerned knew that they could make them. These questions were normally asked of a range of officials, and their answers crosschecked. It was sometimes possible, in a guarded way, to crosscheck exact statements. This type of questioning elicited some of the specific situations described in this book, for instance the contrast between what the company expected of subsidiary management and what the local managers thought was required. It also came to light that the local management could regard different officials at head office as having different purposes—discipline and nurture as they have been called. Questions were introduced to find out more about this.

In the case of appraisal, the expectation was that there would be a close link between changes of policy in the subsidiary and the methods of appraisal used.[13] This proved to be the case, although the questioning in this section soon expanded to other influences, including personal relationships and the circulation of global comparisons. One particular question, asked of all the subsidiary managers, brought out a small number of interesting examples of the interplay between objectives and regulations. This was: Can you think of any examples of reformulation of policy at subsidiary level? And if so, why did it occur, and what happened as a result? The distinction between the formal and the informal aspects of the organisation was also introduced into the questioning.

Many writers on the large business organisation have mentioned problems of communication, the possible slowness and the likelihood of misunderstanding.[14] Others dwell on the effects of distortions in the information flow.[15] The starting-point for us was to see whether the expected problems of communication really did apply in the multinational company, and how they affected the formulation of policies. Another question was whether organisational distance had more effect than geographical.[16] It soon became apparent that the study of communications led into the general study of the organisation. This produced the beginnings of an outline of the types of organisation set out in chapter 2, and subsequent questioning was designed to check this outline. How do you set up a subsidiary overseas? Does it mirror head office organisation? Does it report to product group or geographical management? To whom do the various managers in this subsidiary report? What are the unofficial or informal lines of communication?[17] What are the usual arrangements for personal contact? Who goes, and how often? How is information collected, and how is it disseminated? One particular question that was added in the light of experience and that elicited some problems in the subsidiary was: 'Are you asked to supply information to head office which you do not require for your own purposes?'

Questions about the role problems of managers arose from expected difficulties between home and foreign operations, and especially the problems to be found in the *role-set* of the international executive.[18] As shown in chapter 5, the role-set problems proved even more severe than anticipated and in some ways that had not been expected. Among other problems under the heading of role Howe Martyn suggests that there is a likely conflict between those who have been abroad, and have gained a more intuitive understanding of the foreign operations, and those who have not. Another example of this might be between expatriate and local managers in the subsidiary. But there is a conflict of loyalties for the foreign manager himself, especially when he is charged with activities which are for the benefit of the whole company but against the interests of his subsidiary.

There were other subjects of questioning, such as the attention paid to the strategic and other considerations involved in the move abroad.[19] But the above list covers the main themes of the enquiries which provided the evidence on which this work is based.

The financial statements

In addition to the field research, an important part of our study was based on the detailed analysis of the financial statements of a relatively large number of companies operating in the United Kingdom and owned or controlled by foreign (non-resident) companies. These data were of particular importance to the portion of our study which deals with the capital structure of foreign subsidiaries, the sources of funds that have been used to finance their operations and growth, and the remittance of dividends. During our field research these were topics which did not lend themselves to discussion except in rather too general terms. If an adequate appraisal is to be finally made, figures covering a number of years must be studied in depth. This, obviously, was not feasible in a short visit to a company. Moreover, business-men were usually reluctant to speak on these matters with the frankness and precision needed to clarify completely their motives and actions.

There are certain limitations to the conclusions that can be drawn from these data, for company accounts are prepared once each year as of a given date, and do not reflect all the events which took place during the year. For example, a company whose activities are seasonal is likely not to choose as a reporting date that period of the year during which it is most heavily in-debted. Also, there is frequently a considerable amount of 'window dressing' that is done in order to improve the appearance of the balance sheet for publication or filing. Keeping these reservations in mind, the analysis provided nonetheless valuable data to complement and support the more general information which came out of the interviews with company officials.

Our analysis of financial accounts has been limited to the United King-dom. We have not made parallel studies of foreign-owned or -controlled subsidiaries in other countries in Europe, or elsewhere. The accounts of foreign subsidiaries are not readily available in other countries. Very few are quoted on a stock exchange. In France and Germany, for example, most subsidiaries take the legal form of the private limited company, that is, *Société à responsibilité limitée* and *Gesellschaft mit beschranker Haftung* respectively, and are not required to file their accounts for public inspection. Even companies adopting the equivalent status of a public company in these countries—the *Société anonyme* (SA) in France, and the *Aktien Gesellschaft* (AG) in Germany—have not been required until recently to file or publish their accounts unless they were quoted on a stock exchange. In Belgium, however, the *Sociétés anonymes*, even if not quoted, must publish their annual accounts in the *Journal Officiel*. Unfortunately these data proved to be of

M*

rather limited use because the accounts were not prepared in detail or uniformly except in the case of very few companies. Generally, the liabilities side of the balance sheet showed only two items: owners' equity and outside capital. Out of twenty-five foreign subsidiaries whose accounts were looked at, only one presented the accounts in any detail. Nevertheless, there is some other information available, albeit that this consists of the aggregated data of a large number of foreign subsidiaries. Thus, certain reference will be made to the statistics published by the US Department of Commerce[1] which covers American-owned companies operating in Europe, to the statistics published by the *Board of Trade Journal*,[2] and to the data appearing in the Reddaway Report[3] which cover a large sample of foreign subsidiaries belonging to British-owned companies.[4]

The analysis of financial data covers all or almost all of the period from 1959 to 1967 for 115 foreign-owned or -controlled subsidiaries based in the United Kingdom. Since a few of the subsidiaries were either established or reorganised during the period, some data were unavailable or defective. Where this is of relevance, note is made in the presentation of the statistics.

The selection of the subsidiaries for the sample was made according to the following criteria. First, it was decided to include only those in manufacturing industries, except automobiles. Subsidiaries of the international petroleum groups and primary metals were purposely excluded on the grounds that their size and, in the case of the petroleum companies, their rather highly integrated type of operations were such distinctive characteristics that they would unduly bias the analysis of the data. Secondly, given this initial selection, all subsidiaries were included in which we have obtained interviews, and also those in whose parent or affiliated companies we had interviews. The remaining subsidiaries in the sample were selected so as to include, as far as possible, the principal operating subsidiary of each of the large, well-known international groups. This was more difficult than it might appear. Some foreign investors have established many subsidiaries, some of which are not actively trading and others are for leasing, credit or other auxiliary purposes. In addition, the name of the subsidiary often bears no relation to that of the parent company. Given these problems, we believe the methods of selection was sufficiently unbiased to provide a representative sample.

One hundred and three of the subsidiaries were wholly owned, that is, the whole of the ordinary share capital of the subsidiary—with the exception of the directors' qualifying shares—was held by a foreign (non-resident) company. A number of them, however, had preference shares or loan stock outstanding and quoted on a British stock exchange. For the most part, they did not publish their accounts, and data covering this part of our sample consisted of the annual financial statements which had been filed with the Companies' Register to satisfy the requirements of the Companies Acts of

1948 and 1965. Twelve of the subsidiaries were public companies, at least for part of the period, that is to say, their ordinary share capital was quoted on a UK stock exchange. In each of these, which we shall refer to as 'quoted subsidiaries', the majority of the ordinary share capital was held by a foreign company. The source of data covering these concerns was mainly published information such as annual reports or Moodies' cards.

Eighty-nine of the subsidiaries were owned or controlled by United States companies, although ownership was in many cases routed through a holding company based in Switzerland, Panama, or elsewhere. Among the non-American subsidiaries, there was one Canadian-owned (for purposes of our analysis it has been included with the American-owned subsidiaries), and twenty-five owned or controlled by companies domiciled in Europe—four Dutch, nine Swiss, five Swedish, five French, one Belgian, and one Italian.

The subsidiaries varied greatly in size, ranging from about £400,000 in total assets for the smallest up to more than £150 million for the largest. As can be noted from the data below, the smallest 25 per cent of the subsidiaries accounted for only 4 per cent of the total assets of the group, whereas the largest 25 per cent made up almost two-thirds of the total assets.

Size of subsidiaries

Assets per subsidiary in 1967	*Proportion of subsidiaries* %	*Proportion of total assets* %
Less than £4·5 million	25·1	4·0
£4·5 million up to £8·6 million	24·3	10·8
£8·6 million up to £19·3 million	26·0	18·8
Over £19·3 million	24·6	66·4
	100·0	100·0

The subsidiaries were from several of the more technologically advanced and fast growing industries. These, together with the number of subsidiaries in each, appear on p. 308.

As a first step in the analysis, it seemed necessary to recast the balance sheet and income statement data for each subsidiary into a standardised form of presentation. This is shown in tables AII.1 and AII.2 below. For the purposes of our study and because of the practice of some subsidiaries of lumping certain items together, we have had to make a few minor interpretations of the figures. This primarily related to intracompany liabilities, but to a lesser extent the treatment of reserves and provisions posed minor problems. Notes explaining our terminology and methods appear in detail at the end of this appendix. Generally, we have expressed the data as financial ratios as it appeared that relationships would be more meaningful if shown in this manner.

Industry	Number of subsidiaries
Chemicals, including artificial fibres	16
Pharmaceuticals, including proprietary drugs and cosmetics	18
Food manufacturing	16
Electrical engineering and electronics, including precision instruments	10
Office machinery and computers	8
Machinery and machine tools	21
Miscellaneous manufacturing, including rubber, home appliances, household products, building materials, packaging materials, automotive components	26
	115

It is of considerable interest to provide some sort of yardsticks against which to contrast our data. For this purpose, we have selected aggregated data covering British quoted companies on the grounds that they are operating under similar environmental conditions regarding markets, finance, taxes, and so forth.[5] Thus we aggregated our data by adding together the accounts of each subsidiary, item by item, for the years 1959 and 1967. We have also included data covering the foreign subsidiaries of twenty-seven British companies as another measure.[6]

Although the presentation of data in tables AII.1 and AII.2 is useful in order to analyse the financial structure of companies, it mainly serves to record the cumulative results of past financial decisions. It does not show the flows of funds in and out of the companies during a given period of time. To bring this out, we prepared a sources and uses of funds statement for each subsidiary. The format used is shown by tables AII.3 and AII.4 below. These data are presented as a monetary aggregate for the eight-year period on table AII.3; they are also presented in the form of percentages of total uses of funds for the different categories of subsidiaries on table AII.4. The figures are net which means that an increase of, say, bank credit in some years may have been offset by decreases during the other years. On table AII.3 British quoted companies are used again as a standard of comparison. The data covering these include virtually all quoted companies in the United Kingdom in manufacturing.

Table AII.1 Balance sheet items and other selected financial data (*mean value for each financial ratio except profitability and dividend payout*)

Company group:	115 foreign subsidiaries in the UK		90 American subsidiaries in the UK[a]		25 European subsidiaries in the UK	
Year:	1959	1967	1959	1967	1959	1967
Total assets:	£757m	£1797m	£559m	£1311m	£198m	£486m
Assets	%	%	%	%	%	%
Net fixed assets	32·5	35·4	32·6	34·9	31·8	37·4
Current assets	67·5	64·6	67·4	65·1	68·2	62·6
(of which cash)	(10·7)	(4·4)	(10·9)	(4·5)	(9·3)	(4·2)
Total	100·0	100·0	100·0	100·0	100·0	100·0
Capital and liabilities	%	%	%	%	%	%
Ordinary shares	21·6	19·6	19·2	18·1	31·2	24·8
Preference shares	0·9	0·6	1·1	0·8	0·3	0·1
Reserves	27·2	27·1	28·5	29·9	22·5	16·9
Owners' equity	49·7	47·3	48·8	48·8	54·0	41·8
Long-term debt	2·2	6·4	2·0	6·1	3·2	7·6
Bank credit	3·6	11·7	3·9	12·2	2·3	10·0
Intracompany liabilities	15·3	10·5	14·6	7·2	18·2	22·5
Other liabilities	29·2	24·1	30·7	25·7	22·3	18·1
Total	100·0	100·0	100·0	100·0	100·0	100·0
Period:	1960–67		1960–67		1960–67	
Profitability (*median value* of net profit after taxes as a percentage of total assets)	6·6%		7·8%		3·1%	
Dividend payout (*median value* as a percentage of net profit after tax)	48%		51%		45%	

a. The sample of American-owned subsidiaries represents about 45 per cent of the value of all US investment in manufacturing industry in the UK measured in terms of book value at the end of 1967. Based on the book value of $3,877 million appearing in *Survey of Current Business*, October 1969, p. 28.

One of the more difficult tasks in attempting to interpret a large mass of data, such as is represented by these accounts, is to select a method of presentation that shows up the differences between companies as well as one that shows the characteristics of the group as a whole. This requirement is partially met by the method of presentation used in table AII.1, where each subsidiary in the different classifications received equal weight in arriving at the different values. However, there is an obvious danger using aggregated data of the type which appear on tables AII.2 to AII.4 to describe a heterogeneous group of companies because the characteristics of the smaller members of the sample are likely to be obscured by those of the larger. Indeed, we are more interested here in observing the individual

Table AII.2 Balance sheet and other selected financial data (aggregated data)

Companies: Year:	Foreign subsidiaries in the UK		British quoted companies		Foreign subsidiaries of 27 British firms 1955–64 annual averages[a]
	1959	1967	1960	1967	
Total assets:	£757m	£1797m	£14,731m	£21,886m	£1202m
Assets	%	%	%	%	%
Net fixed assets	36·0	39·8	45·0	46·3	34·3
Stocks	30·2	27·5	27·5	25·2	40·2
Intracompany assets	2·9	3·6	n.a.	n.a.	n.a.
Debtors	19·3	25·4	19·0	22·7	25·5
Cash, etc.	11·6	3·7	8·4	5·8	n.a.
Total	100·0	100·0	100·0	100·0	100·0
Capital and Liabilities	%	%	%	%	%
Ordinary shares	20·2	19·3	23·4	21·4	⎫
Preference shares	1·5	0·7	5·3	2·8	⎬ 45·8
Reserves	27·9	26·6	32·3	28·3	⎭
Owners' equity	49·6	46·6	64·5	52·5	45·8
Long-term debt	7·1	8·6	8·3	13·6	6·9
Bank credit	3·9	10·7	3·6	6·3	n.a.
Intracompany liabilities	11·0	11·0	n.a.	n.a.	15·9
Other liabilities	28·4	23·1	27·1	27·6	26·8
Total	100·0	100·0	100·0	100·0	100·0
Profitability (net profit after tax as a % of total assets)	8·5	5·6	6·1	4·2	4·5
Dividend payout annual average 1960–67 as a % of net profit after tax)	56		52		47

a. Aggregated accounts of certain overseas subsidiaries of twenty-seven British quoted companies in food, tobacco, beverages, and household products; chemicals; electrical engineering; non-electrical engineering; vehicles and automotive components. Data cover period 1955–64 and represent annual averages for the period. It should be noted that the definitions do not exactly conform to those used in this study. In particular, intracompany liabilities have been netted against intracompany assets. If these data for the 115 subsidiaries in the United Kingdom were similarly presented, their intracompany liabilities in 1967 would appear as 7·7 per cent instead of 11 per cent as shown above.

behaviour of all companies than in the overall effects of their behaviour which is revealed by aggregated data.

It was this problem that Tew had in mind in his study of the financial accounts of British quoted companies when he wrote about the need to 'preserve a high degree of disaggregation'.[7] His technique for meeting this requirement was based on the use of selected 'indicators' to describe certain characteristics and behaviour of the companies he was analysing. We have adopted a somewhat similar technique which we will describe below. For each of the 115 subsidiaries in our sample we prepared a series of financial ratios and certain other data. These included the following:

1. *Type of ownership*—wholly owned or quoted subsidiary.
2. *Nationality of parent company*—American or European.
3. *Industrial classification*—chemicals, machinery, etc.
4. *Profitability*—net profits after tax divided by total assets.
5. *Growth*—average annual increase in net operating assets (total assets less spontaneous sources of credit less liquid assets).
6. *Size*—total assets of the subsidiary as shown on its first and last balance sheets.
7. *Financial structure*—each of the following items shown as a ratio of total assets: ordinary shares, preference shares, net worth, long-term debt, bank loans, intracompany liabilities, other liabilities.
8. *Internal finance*—the percentage of new investment in fixed assets and net working capital needs that was financed from internal sources (retained earnings and depreciation). This was calculated for each year, and totalled for the period. Net working capital needs are defined as the net change in the following: current assets *less* spontaneous sources of finance (essentially trade credit and deferred taxes) *less* cash and marketable securities. While a minimum cash balance is required by the subsidiary to operate, we have excluded cash items from our calculations of working capital needs on the grounds that they act as a balancing mechanism, rising and falling with variations in the flow of funds from year to year.[8] Thus in some years cash balances are drawn on to meet the subsidiary's investment needs and represent a source of funds; in other years they increase as cash is generated (or raised from loans, etc.) and retained rather than being put to other use.
9. *Other sources and uses of funds*—increases or decreases in each of the following items: long-term debt, bank loans, equity capital, intracompany liabilities, and cash reserves. This was prepared for each year, and for the period.
10. *Dividend payments*—two measures: (1) percentage of current profits after tax that was distributed as ordinary dividends. This was prepared for each year and averaged for the period; (2) increases or decreases in the *amount* of dividend paid.

The full analysis of the above data as well as the methods and terminology used is shown at the end of this appendix. To reduce this mass of information to manageable proportions for use in our discussion, we handled it in two ways.

First, data relating to the entire period was recorded for each subsidiary on needle cards. For most characteristics (items 4, 5, 6, 7, 8, and 10), each series of values were divided into four equal groups, arranged in numerical order so that the highest value was at the top and the lowest at the bottom. Thus the first group included the smallest values, those below the lower quartile, the second group included values lying between the lower quartile and the median, and so on. To take an example, the average annual profitability (return on total assets) of the subsidiaries ranged from (a loss) −10·7 to 24·7 per cent with the median 6·6 per cent, the upper quartile 10·2 per cent and the lower quartile 3·5 per cent. This means that 25 per cent of the

Table AII.3 Sources and uses of funds (aggregated data)

Companies:	115 foreign subsidiaries in the United Kingdom 1960–67 Amount £ million	%	British quoted companies in manufacturing 1960–67 Amount £ million	%
Sources				
Cash flow from operations	1,079·2	68·2	12,019·0	69·4
Increases in:				
bank credit	156·0	9·9	1,038·0	6·0
long-term debt	101·8	6·4	1,967·0	11·4
intracompany liabilities	144·0	9·1	n.a.	n.a.
issued capital	78·8	5·1	2,193·0	12·7
Decreases in liquid assets	20·7	1·3	90·0	0·5
Total sources	1,580·5	100·0	17,307·0	100·0
Uses				
Fixed assets	822·6	52·0	10,910·0	63·0
Net working capital	402·4	25·6	2,869·0	16·6
Dividends	355·5	22·4	3,528·0	20·4
Total uses	1,580·5	100·0	17,307·0	100·0

Note. Cash flow from operations is the sum of depreciation allowances and earnings after taxes. Net working capital is current assets *less* spontaneous sources of finance (essentially accounts payable and accrued taxes), *less* cash and other liquid assets.

subsidiaries had a return of between −10·7 and 3·5 per cent, 25 per cent between 3·5 and 6·6 per cent, 25 per cent between 6·6 and 10·2 per cent, and the remaining 25 per cent over 10·2 per cent. By recording the data in this manner, the characteristics of all the subsidiaries are more readily observed, and the danger that the behaviour of the smaller might be concealed within

Table AII.4 Sources and uses of funds: foreign subsidiaries in the United Kingdom contrasted by ownership (aggregated data)

Type of ownership:	*Wholly-owned*	*American-owned*	*European-owned*
Number of subsidiaries:	103	90	25
Total uses of funds:			
monetary aggregate	£1,407·2m	£1,194·4m	£386·1m
as a % of total uses	89	69	31
Sources	%	%	%
Cash flow from operations	66·1	76·0	44·5
Increases in:			
bank credit	10·7	9·1	12·4
long-term debt	6·8	6·1	7·3
intracompany liabilities	10·0	3·9	25·3
issued capital	5·2	3·7	8·8
Decreases in liquid assets	1·2	1·2	1·7
Total sources	100·0	100·0	100·0
Uses			
Fixed assets	52·4	48·7	62·5
Net working capital	25·4	25·7	24·7
Dividends	22·2	25·6	12·8
Total uses	100·0	100·0	100·0

the mass of aggregated data is avoided. We can also cross-classify the subsidiaries' characteristics where this appears to be of interest. It is then possible to see whether a certain relationship exists between types of behaviour, such as, for example, whether companies using large credits are those undergoing rapid growth, and so on.

Secondly, data relating to the annual funds flows for each subsidiary were summarised so that the frequency of occurrence of each major source or use of finance could be calculated. In total, the sources and uses of funds were analysed for 914 subsidiary years. The year with its corresponding number of funds flows analysed is as follows:

1960—112	1962—114	1964—115	1966—115
1961—113	1963—115	1965—115	1967—115

The individual characteristics now available were those listed in items 8, 9, and 10 on page 311, namely the proportion of net operating assets that was financed from internal sources, increases or decreases in other sources and uses of funds, and increases or decreases in dividends. These could be observed for each year and for the period. To illustrate, let us take as an example how often the subsidiaries increased their bank borrowing.

Year	Subsidiaries increasing bank borrowing	Number of subsidiary years analysed	Relative frequency of bank borrowing %
1960	33	112	29
1961	41	113	36
1962	39	114	34
1963	42	115	37
1964	61	115	53
1965	63	115	55
1966	59	115	51
1967	50	115	44
Total period	388	914	42

From this summary, it is possible to extract a variety of information such as 'subsidiaries tended to borrow more frequently from the banks in the three years 1964–66 than on average', or 'on average, subsidiaries borrowed from the banks in more than two out of every five years observed', and so forth.

Finally, the data are probably best used to compare one type of behaviour with another; for example, the observation that the subsidiaries increased their bank borrowing on 42 per cent of the total occasions (subsidiary years) analysed takes on more meaning when we also note, say, that they increased their equity capital on only 6 per cent of the occasions analysed.

Tables AII.5 and AII.6 (pages 318–39)

Method and terminology

A. GENERAL

1. Subsidiaries are listed in order of the size of total assets in 1967. The symbol US-1, for example, refers to the largest United States-owned subsidiary of the sample in that year. EUR-6 refers to the sixth largest European-owned subsidiary of the sample in 1967.
2. The following symbols refer to the industries in which the different subsidiaries are included: Ph—pharmaceutical; F—food manufacturing; H/ap—home appliances; Ch—chemicals, including artificial fibres; Hs/p—household products including detergents; M—machinery; Off/e —office machines and computers; Ma/T—machine tools; El—electrical engineering, electronics, and precision instruments; Misc—all subsidiaries not included in one of the above industries.

3. Consolidated group accounts have been used in all instances where prepared by the subsidiary. In some cases, these included the accounts of overseas subsidiaries, i.e., a sub-subsidiary or third-tier company. However, these numbered less than 7 to 8 per cent of the total sample.

B. BALANCE SHEET DATA (table AII.5)

1. *Size*—total assets in millions of pounds sterling as shown on the balance sheets indicated.
2. *Issued capital*—ordinary and preference share capital as shown on the subsidiaries' balance sheets. Where the subsidiary had preference shares outstanding, the percentage is shown to the right of the percentage shown for ordinary shares, i.e. 16·2/6·1 means that ordinary shares were 16·2 per cent of total capital and liabilities, preference shares 6·1 per cent.
3. *Owners' equity*—the sum of issued capital, capital reserves, and revenue reserves.
4. *Long-term debt*—loans from United Kingdom financial institutions of over one year maturity, and loan stock and debentures issued in United Kingdom capital markets.
5. *Bank loans*—bank overdrafts and loans of short term nature from banking institutions resident in the United Kingdom. Loans from foreign branch banks resident in the United Kingdom, if any, were generally not identified separately in the accounts.
6. *Intracompany debt*—amounts owed to other members of the group including trade credit, loans—both short and long term,—dividends, and other accruals; companies in the sample did not always distinguish between liabilities arising from intracompany trading and loans from the parent or other members of the group. Frequently, trading liabilities are allowed to run over a period of time as a means of finance, and so by their very nature are difficult to define. Even where companies made such a distinction, the heading 'intracompany loan' often had many characteristics of a short-term liability, and was subject to considerable fluctuation. This also seemed to hold true, in almost every case, for intracompany loans which were labelled as 'long-term loans from the parent company' or given some analogous heading. For these reasons, it appeared impossible to subdivide the subsidiaries' liabilities to other members of the group in any meaningful way. For those companies which did make a distinction between categories of intracompany liabilities, those arising from trading represented about one-third of the total amount (based on the aggregated data for those companies).
7. *Other liabilities*—the sum of all other liabilities not included under one of the above headings.
8. *Net fixed assets*—all fixed assets *net* of accumulated depreciation *plus*

goodwill, investments in unconsolidated subsidiaries, and trade investments.

9. *Accumulated depreciation*—accumulated depreciation as shown on the balance sheets and expressed as a percentage of *gross* fixed assets.

10. *Return on total assets*—net profit after deduction of taxes, depreciation allowances, interest, and other charges, and preference dividends *divided* by total assets. The percentage shown represents the *mean* of the annual returns on total assets for the period.

11. *Dividend payout ratio*—ordinary dividends divided by net profits after deduction of taxes, depreciation allowances, interest and other charges, and preference dividends (unless held by the parent company). The percentage shown represents the total dividends and net profits for the period indicated.

C. SOURCES AND USES OF FUNDS DATA (table AII.6)

1. *Net fixed assets*—expenditure on net fixed assets as defined in B(8) above. The calculation of this item, in the absence of complete data, is based on certain assumptions and is therefore only an approximation. This calculation is made as follows:

   (*a*) Theoretically new investment should be equal to at least closing net fixed assets *plus* depreciation for the year *minus* opening net fixed assets. We have used this method, but since the accounts did not always indicate full details of assets sold or exchanged, there is a certain margin of error.

   (*b*) The figure derived from the above calculation is then adjusted, if required, to correct for any re-evaluation of assets that might have taken place, or for other reasons such as might arise from consolidation.

2. *Net working capital*—changes in current assets (including intracompany assets) *less* changes in spontaneous sources of credit (trade credit and deferred taxes essentially) *less* changes in liquid assets.

3. *Net cash flow*—retained earnings (after taxes) *plus* allowances for depreciation.

4. *Cash reserves*—changes in the amount of liquid assets held by the subsidiary. These defined to include cash, bank deposits, government securities easily converted into cash, and so forth.

5. *Bank loans*—changes in the amount of bank loans owed by the subsidiary.

6. *Long-term debt*—changes in the amount of long-term debt owed by the subsidiary.

7. *Intracompany debt*—changes in the liabilities owed to the parent company and other members of the group.

8. *Issued capital*—amounts of new capital subscribed by the shareholders of the subsidiary (i.e., the parent company). Preference shares have

been included, but represent a very minor portion of the total under this heading (subsidiary US-11 was the only one in the sample to have issued preference share capital). This does not include increases in the issued capital outstanding due to capitalisation of reserves or intra-company liabilities. A negative figure in the tables, if any, refers to the retirement of redeemable preference shares.

9. *Average growth*—the compound rate of growth between the beginning and ending balance sheet dates of (1) net fixed assets and net working capital; and (2) net profits after tax.

Table AII.5 Balance sheet and other selected financial data

Company/industry	Year	Size: total assets (£m)	Percent of total assets								1959–67 average Return on total assets (%)	Dividend payout ratio (%)
			Issued capital	Owners' equity	Long-term debt	Bank loans	Intra-company debt	Other liabilities	Net fixed assets	Acc. dep. (as % gross fixed assets)		
US-1 El	1959	35·7	33·6	42·0	9·5	25·7	1·6	21·2	21·2	59·5	4·5	50
	1967	98·9	14·7	30·1	11·9	24·0	3·2	30·8	27·2	49·0		
US-2 M	1959	46·9	2·9	21·4	25·1	—	24·1	29·4	44·7	19·2	2·5	55
	1967	77·7	3·8	34·8	29·2	3·2	6·7	26·1	28·8	52·0		
US-3 Off/e	1959	9·2	34·2	52·3	22·8	—	6·1	18·8	53·3	32·3	13·0	21
	1967	68·6	15·3	54·5	11·0	0·7	9·3	24·5	51·9	49·6		
US-4 Ch/Misc	1959	24·9	28·2	67·0	—	—	7·2	25·8	33·2	39·5	10·1	37
	1967	55·1	38·1	68·3	—	—	3·7	28·0	33·7	44·4		
US-5 F	1959	31·7	18·4/9·5	55·2	9·5	7·1	1·8	26·4	41·6	14·8	8·3	50
	1967	50·6a	41·5/4·9	60·8	7·4	1·0	1·3	29·5	41·8	29·1		
US-6 H/ap	1959	35·4	6·9/1·7	45·2	—	—	3·3	51·5	18·0	51·9	8·1	48
	1967	46·4b	10·6/1·3	70·4	—	0·2	2·1	27·3	23·6	60·8		
US-7 Misc	1959	18·6	31·6/6·5	57·3	30·3	—	1·1	11·3	41·8	49·3	5·6	27
	1967	40·2	14·6/3·0	55·7	10·4	13·1	0·3	20·5	43·8	47·8		
US-8 M	1959	19·3	42·8/2·1	81·0	—	1·0	1·7	16·3	34·0	42·8	9·3	48
	1967	34·9c	50·6	78·3	—	0·3	2·4	19·0	37·5	56·7		
US-9 Ch	1959	6·3	12·8	20·5	16·0	9·9	49·5	4·1	82·3	8·0	1·2	nil
	1967	31·8	7·5	67·5	—	14·2	10·5	7·8	66·5	20·0		
US-10 Ch	1959	28·9	18·7/10·4	45·2	22·8	0·3	5·6	26·1	59·0	29·6	3·9	52
	1967	30·2	17·9/9·9	55·9	18·6	—	4·6	20·9	45·2	53·5		
US-11 M	1959	14·0	17·8	34·0	—	21·4	34·8	9·8	50·8	19·7	4·8	6
	1967	28·9	19·9/13·0	73·1	—	3·2	1·7	22·0	28·2	53·2		

a. turnover 67·9m; b. turnover—51·0m, employees—88·6; c. turnover 30·0m, employees—10.046.

Company/ industry		Uses of funds		Net cash flow	Sources of funds					Other financial data		Average growth	
		Fixed assets	Net working capital		Cash reserves	Bank loans	Long-term debt	Intra-company debt	Issued capital	Profits	Dividends	Net assets (% pa)	Net profits (% pa)
US-1 EI	£'000	35,046	22,088	29,818	(800)	14,598	8,400	2,617	2,500	22,592	11,290	12	26
	% of total	61.4	38.6	52.2	(1.5)	25.6	14.7	4.6	4.4				
US-2 M	£'000	34,778	13,602	39,172	150	2,510	10,947	(6,044)	1,645	14,663	8,000	7	4
	% of total	71.9	28.1	81.0	0.3	5.2	22.6	(12.5)	3.4				
US-3 Off/e	£'000	75,945	13,257	73,172	304	449	5,470	5,814	3,991	35,128	7,253	29	36
	% of total	85.1	14.9	82.0	0.4	0.5	6.1	6.5	4.5				
US-4 Ch/Misc	£'000	22,784	9,408	33,158	(1,212)	(18)	—	261	—	32,519	12,110	12	11
	% of total	70.7	29.3	103.0	(3.7)	(0.1)	—	0.8	—				
US-5 F	£'000	15,678	3,625	21,594	(856)	(1,716)	741	71	(532)a	27,357	13,560	5	7
	% of total	81.2	18.8	111.8	(4.4)	(8.8)	3.8	0.4	(2.8)				
US-6 H/ap	£'000	15,417	14,891	26,599	3,822	109	—	(225)	—	25,642	12,202	24	-3
	% of total	50.9	49.1	87.8	12.6	0.4	—	(0.8)	—				
US-7 Misc	£'000	17,589	6,422	19,446	406	5,276	(1,050)	(68)	—	12,406	3,319	9	17
	% of total	73.4	26.6	80.7	1.7	21.9	(4.4)	(0.1)	—				
US-8 M	£'000	19,517	6,825	25,005	1,340	(97)	—	491	(400)a	20,041	9,527	10	4
	% of total	74.1	25.9	95.0	5.1	(0.5)	—	1.9	(1.5)				
US-9 Ch	£'000	21,450	7,365	6,874	14	3,882	(1,000)	5,995	13,051	1,645	nil	22	n.m.
	% of total	74.4	25.6	23.8	0.1	13.5	(3.5)	20.8	45.3				
US-10 Ch	£'000	12,797	5,135	20,620	(1,411)	(99)	(945)	(233)	—	9,866	5,142	1	nil
	% of total	71.4	28.6	115.0	(7.8)	(0.6)	(5.3)	(1.3)	—				
US-11 M	£'000	8,889	9,333	15,618	303	(2,065)	—	(4,383)	8,750	8,350	536	8	31
	% of total	48.8	51.2	85.8	1.7	(11.3)	—	(24.1)	47.9				

a. preference shares redeemed.

Table AII.5 Balance sheet and other selected financial data

Company/industry	Year	Size: total assets (£m)	Issued capital	Owners' equity	Long-term debt	Bank loans	Intra-company debt	Other liabilities	Net fixed assets	Acc. dep. (as % gross fixed assets)	1959–67 average Return on total assets (%)	Dividend payout ratio (%)
US-12 Off/e	1959	6.7	10.0	35.0	—	10.3	34.4	20.3	16.9	44.0	3.0	13
	1967	27.4	4.0	44.8	—	14.5	20.0	20.7	15.2	57.5		
US-13 M	1959	16.5	30.2	58.5	6.0	0.4	1.5	33.6	32.6	67.4	6.2	70
	1967	26.5	37.8	50.5	11.3	20.8	1.4	16.0	32.9	42.0		
US-14 off/e	1959	10.8	5.3	54.7	—	1.7	23.5	20.1	31.8	21.5	7.6	63
	1967	25.3	19.8	38.7	21.8	4.1	13.6	21.8	22.3	44.8		
US-15 off/e	1959	3.4	5.1	64.7	—	—	4.0	31.3	19.4	42.4	7.7	nil
	1967	28.2	0.6	38.6	7.1	21.4	15.8	17.1	30.3	42.0		
US-16 Hs/p	1959	17.9	19.8	45.8	11.2	—	0.4	42.6	31.5	37.1	11.3	96
	1967	25.3	14.0	35.8	14.7	8.7	1.3	39.5	32.5	43.8		
US-17 Misc	1959	12.7	1.1	35.8	—	14.2	29.9	21.0	34.2	49.2	5.5	29
	1967	22.2	0.6	41.8	20.2	20.3	—	17.7	35.4	52.0		
US-18 F	1959	7.8	32.2	39.0	19.3	14.8	4.9	22.0	61.3	31.2	6.7	36
	1967	21.9	30.8	54.2	25.1	4.8	0.5	15.4	59.2	31.6		
US-19 Misc	1959	12.7	19.7	59.3	—	—	0.6	40.1	38.8	46.3	5.1	72
	1967	21.4	11.7	44.4	—	23.7	10.5	21.4	33.2	59.8		
US-20 Off/e	1959	6.1	32.9	42.3	8.7	—	11.3	37.7	33.8	32.4	5.8	64
	1967	20.8	19.2	25.0	3.2	23.6	12.3	35.9	28.0	44.4		
US-21 Chem	1959	10.0	62.8	60.5	—	12.2	25.9	1.4	73.2	0.5	2.1	nil
	1967	20.5	30.4	42.3	—	33.6	13.3	10.8	40.3	51.2		
US-22 Ch	1962	7.2	34.8	44.6	—	—	44.6	11.1	40.0	n.a.	4.0	81
	1967	20.1	32.3	44.0	—	13.9	12.5	29.6	49.2	28.2		

Company/industry		Uses of funds		Net cash flow	Sources of funds					Profits	Dividends	Other financial data Average growth	
		Fixed assets	Net working capital		Cash reserves	Bank loans	Long-term debt	Intra-company debt	Issued capital			Net assets (% pa)	Net profits (% pa)
US-12 Off/e	£'000	6,900	11,152	8,572	18	3,297	—	3,234	2,933	4,537	602	20	8
	% of total	38·2	61·8	47·7	—	18·2	—	17·9	16·2				
US-13 M	£'000	9,043	10,484	9,406	2,549	5,451	2,000	122	—	12,438	8,765	13	-9
	% of total	46·4	53·6	48·2	13·0	27·9	10·2	0·7	—				
US-14 Off/e	£'000	6,107	9,132	7,880	109	844	5,500	905	—	10,634	6,655	11	3
	% of total	40·0	60·0	51·7	0·8	5·5	36·1	5·9	—				
US-15 Off/e	£'000	14,713	13,285	14,713	377	6,047	2,000	4,341	—	8,883	nil	36	20
	% of total	51·7	48·3	53·5	1·4	22·0	7·3	15·8	—				
US-16 Hs/p	£'000	7,394	3,066	5,675	613	2,211	1,721	244	—	20,136	19,270	9	-1
	% of total	70·7	29·3	54·3	5·9	21·2	16·5	2·2	—				
US-17 Misc	£'000	9,290	5,109	10,547	316	2,709	4,500	(3,674)	—	6,744	1,951	8	4
	% of total	64·4	35·6	73·4	2·2	18·8	31·2	(25·6)	—				
US-18 F	£'000	9,713	4,000	9,952	(254)	(100)	3,989	(274)	400	8,089	2,885	15	6
	% of total	70·8	29·2	72·5	(1·9)	(0·7)	29·2	(2·0)	2·9				
US-19 Misc	£'000	11,633	8,056	11,634	819	5,057	—	2,179	—	6,476	4,660	12	-9
	% of total	59·0	41·0	59·2	4·0	25·7	—	11·1	—				
US-20 Off/e	£'000	8,234	5,855	6,587	59	4,921	135	1,882	500	6,066	3,910	17	7
	% of total	58·4	41·6	46·8	0·2	35·0	1·0	13·4	3·6				
US-21 Ch	£'000	10,247	7,277	11,595	5	5,672	—	253	—	2,337	nil	8	33
	% of total	58·5	41·5	66·2	—	32·4	—	1·4	—				
US-22a Ch	£'000	6,879	978	4,082	(151)	2,803	—	1,122	—	3,551	2,868	17	1
	% of total	87·6	12·4	52·0	(2·0)	35·7	—	14·3	—				

a. 5 years, 1962–67.

Table AII.5 Balance sheet and other selected financial data

Company/ industry	Year	Size: total assets (£m)	Issued capital	Owners' equity	Long-term debt	Bank loans	Intra-company debt	Other liabilities	Net fixed assets	Acc. dep. (as % gross fixed assets)	1959–67 average Return on total assets (%)	Dividend payout ratio (%)
US-23 Ph	1959	9.3	32.4	53.0	—	—	9.6	37.4	52.6	20.7	6.7	58
	1967	18.8	36.2	68.0	4.0	3.6	4.2	20.2	53.0	42.6		
US-24 F	1959	3.5	2.1	68.2	—	—	—	31.8	30.6	37.7	10.2	58
	1967	17.3	0.4	32.5	49.0	—	—	18.5	47.7	19.8		
US-25 Ch	1959	1.2	51.1	45.9	—	—	13.7	40.4	39.6	19.7	4.6	nil
	1967	15.1	15.9	37.1	32.8	5.7	0.9	23.5	62.7	20.0		
US-26 Hs/p	1959	9.8	14.2	17.0	—	—	22.6	60.4	28.3	37.1	12.8	72
	1967	14.9	26.7	40.5	—	13.4	22.5	23.6	43.5	39.1		
US-27 Ph	1959	2.4	25.2	75.7	—	—	1.1	23.2	55.0	16.1	9.1	58
	1967	14.8	12.3	62.7	—	2.0	5.8	29.5	32.6	25.0		
US-28 H/ap	1959	9.2	21.8	81.0	—	—	1.5	17.5	51.3	—	0.2	∞[a]
	1967	13.9	14.4	48.6	—	24.4	18.3	8.7	46.1	—		
US-29 Misc	1959	6.4	15.6	72.6	—	—	—	27.4	26.9	48.5	10.4	98
	1967	13.1	7.6	37.1	12.0	21.6	0.1	29.2	33.4	61.8		
US-30 Ch	1959	4.7	30.5	56.9	11.5	—	4.1	27.5	35.0	31.8	13.8	44
	1967	13.0	41.4	64.2	3.5	—	4.9	27.4	45.8	32.2		
US-31 Hs/p	1959	4.7	27.7/9.4	58.2	—	—	4.3	37.5	21.6	44.5	10.6	46
	1967	12.5	23.9/2.5	57.3	6.8	5.0	3.3	27.6	33.6	35.6		
US-32 F	1959	7.2	19.4	33.4	20.8	—	19.5	26.3	39.5	14.5	6.4	68
	1967	12.1	11.5	35.1	25.0	4.9	6.3	28.7	46.4	34.7		
US-33 F	1959	5.0	0.02	50.9	—	—	4.3	44.8	37.4	45.7	23.4	90
	1967	11.3	0.009	36.4	2.4	19.5	5.1	36.6	47.7	44.8		

a. There was an overall loss for the 8-year period.

Company/industry		Uses of funds		Net cash flow	Sources of funds					Profits	Dividends	Other financial data — Average growth	
		Fixed assets	Net working capital		Cash reserves	Bank loans	Long-term debt	Intra-company debt	Issued capital			Net assets (% pa)	Net profits (% pa)
US-23 Ph	£'000	6,837	5,313	9,071	(50)	679	750	(100)	1,800	8,606	4,955	13	-4
	% of total	56·2	43·8	74·6	(0·4)	5·6	6·2	(0·8)	14·8				
US-24 F	£'000	10,491	1,624	6,648	(3,049)	—	8,500	19	—	8,020	4,658	28	6
	% of total	82·6	13·4	54·9	(25·3)	—	70·2	0·2	—				
US-25 Ch	£'000	10,754	1,908	4,984	50	865	4,972	480	1,311	3,039	nil	44	33
	% of total	84·9	15·1	39·4	0·3	6·8	39·3	3·8	10·4				
US-26 Hs/p	£'000	6,763	5,969	7,532	2,042	2,012	—	1,150	—	14,393	10,346	42	-11
	% of total	53·2	46·8	59·0	16·1	15·8	—	9·1	—				
US-27 Ph	£'000	3,561	4,235	6,024	(370)	301	—	583	1,258	7,912	4,550	22	18
	% of total	45·6	54·4	77·5	(4·8)	3·6	—	7·5	16·2				
US-28 H/ap	£'000	9,671	3,642	7,196	305	3,393	—	2,418	—	(147)	613	7	-7
	% of total	72·6	27·4	54·0	2·3	25·5	—	18·2	—				
US-29 Misc	£'000	5,444	3,306	2,923	1,421	2,827	1,567	13	—	7,277	7,115	15	1
	% of total	62·2	37·8	33·4	16·2	32·3	17·9	0·2	—				
US-30 Ch	£'000	7,287	1,335	8,652	(383)	—	(94)	447	—	10,096	4,407	18	7
	% of total	84·5	15·5	100·3	(4·4)	—	(1·1)	5·2	—				
US-31 Hs/p	£'000	4,705	1,063	5,704	(1,676)	627	853	205	47	7,205	3,281	18	13
	% of total	81·6	18·4	99·0	(29·0)	10·8	14·8	3·6	0·8				
US-32 F	£'000	4,963	768	4,113	145	596	1,525	(646)	—	5,238	3,529	11	-2
	% of total	86·6	13·4	71·8	2·5	10·4	26·6	(11·3)	—				
US-33 F	£'000	7,542	1,524	5,522	706	2,206	267	363	—	16,507	14,906	17	7
	% of total	83·2	16·8	61·0	7·8	24·3	2·9	4·0	—				

Table AII.5 Balance sheet and other selected financial data

| Company/industry | Year | Size: total assets (£m) | Percent of total assets | | | | | | | | 1959–67 average Return on total assets (%) | Dividend payout ratio (%) |
			Issued capital	Owners' equity	Long-term debt	Bank loans	Intra-company debt	Other liabilities	Net fixed assets	Acc. dep. (as % gross fixed assets)		
US-34 M	1959	4·4	5·6	73·3	2·6	—	1·2	22·9	30·7	—	8·4	89
	1967	10·9	2·3	34·3	—	32·3	9·9	23·5	9·9	—		
US-35 M	1959	3·7	27·3	23·3	—	54·1	6·3	16·3	61·0	28·6	7·4	12
	1967	10·8	9·4	48·3	—	21·0	5·4	25·3	47·1	46·4		
US-36 M	1959	5·2	38·6	69·0	—	—	0·1	30·9	12·6	47·4	12·1	67
	1967	10·0	20·1	61·6	—	2·9	9·3	26·2	15·8	45·8		
US-37 Ph	1959	2·2	2·2	50·4	—	—	0·2	49·4	16·8	40·0	9·6	34
	1967	9·9	13·2	48·8	6·1	11·2	8·8	25·1	49·3	—		
US-38 Ph	1959	0·3	12·0	(39·5)	10·5	—	121·3	18·2	34·6	4·0	18·8	67
	1967	9·7	10·3	21·5	—	—	15·8	52·6	22·4	19·7		
US-39 Ph	1959	3·3	7·2	39·4	—	—	0·3	60·3	30·2	16·3	24·2	75
	1967	9·5	9·5	52·1	—	—	2·8	45·1	21·5	37·3		
US-40 Ma/T	1959	2·1	6·7	62·4	—	—	8·8	28·8	23·4	39·3	12·7	55
	1967	9·2	1·5	41·5	6·0	11·2	10·2	31·1	26·7	33·4		
US-41 M	1959	3·7	19·6	62·3	—	—	6·9	30·8	27·9	37·3	5·8	76
	1967	9·1	15·8	42·2	32·8	1·5	1·6	21·9	27·9	37·7		
US-42 M	1959	1·9	5·4	(35·8)	—	17·9	105·4	12·5	40·3	26·1	1·2	nil
	1967	9·1	48·1	44·4	16·3	19·5	6·2	13·6	34·6	26·5		
US-43 Ch	1959	0·7	34·2	41·0	—	—	48·0	11·0	14·8	26·0	5·3	35
	1967	9·0	22·3	34·8	—	1·4	35·8	28·0	22·7	27·6		
US-44 H/ap	1959	7·1	8·4	28·6	—	21·7	39·4	10·3	25·7	34·9	2·9	35
	1967	8·8	20·4	53·6	1·5	9·2	23·7	12·0	39·0	37·8		

Company/industry	Uses of funds — Fixed assets	Uses of funds — Net working capital	Net cash flow	Sources of funds — Cash reserves	Sources of funds — Bank loans	Sources of funds — Long-term debt	Sources of funds — Intra-company debt	Sources of funds — Issued capital	Other financial data — Profits	Other financial data — Dividends	Average growth — Net assets (% pa)	Average growth — Net profits (% pa)
US-34 M — £'000	1,757	5,413	2,532	210	3,515	(118)	1,028	—	4,494	4,001	13	12
% of total	24.5	75.5	35.3	2.9	49.0	(1.5)	14.3	—				
US-35 M — £'000	6,555	2,206	8,106	44	266	(5)	354	—	4,987	600	13	26
% of total	74.8	25.2	92.6	0.4	3.0	—	4.0	—				
US-36 M — £'000	1,860	3,512	3,445	721	289	—	917	—	7,337	4,869	14	5
% of total	34.6	65.4	64.1	13.4	5.4	—	17.1	—				
US-37 Ph — £'000	6,070	2,725	4,097	945	1,109	600	2,043	—	3,834	1,302	19	0
% of total	69.0	31.0	46.5	10.7	12.6	6.8	23.4	—				
US-38 Ph — £'000	2,486	(1,363)	2,482	(3,535)	—	975	1,198	—	5,897	3,950	19	26
% of total	221.3	(121.3)	221.0	(314.3)	—	86.7	106.6	—				
US-39 Ph — £'000	2,287	2,426	4,399	53	5	—	257	—	13,030	9,770	39	12
% of total	48.6	51.4	93.0	1.5		—	5.5	—				
US-40 Ma/T — £'000	2,917	2,764	3,422	(64)	1,024	550	749	—	5,403	2,945	20	20
% of total	51.3	48.7	60.2	(1.1)	18.0	9.7	13.2	—				
US-41 M — £'000	2,443	2,813	2,097	134	135	3,000	(110)	—	3,337	2,523	15	-4
% of total	46.5	53.5	39.8	2.5	2.5	57.0	(1.8)	—				
US-42 M — £'000	3,628	3,850	1,640	2	1,445	1,488	2,905	—	423	nil	22	16
% of total	48.5	51.5	21.9	—	19.3	19.9	38.9	—				
US-43 Ch — £'000	2,395	3,842	1,430	42	122	—	3,862	781	1,537	536	37	23
% of total	38.3	61.7	23.0	0.7	2.0	—	62.0	12.3				
US-44 H/ap — £'000	2,856	(62)	3,937	175	(733)	136	(724)	—	2,702	939	3	-4
% of total	102.2	(2.2)	140.8	6.3	(26.2)	4.9	(25.8)	—				

Table AII.5 Balance sheet and other selected financial data

Company/ industry	Year	Size: total assets (£m)	Percent of total assets								1959–67 average Return on total assets (%)	Dividend payout ratio (%)
			Issued capital	Owners' equity	Long-term debt	Bank loans	Intra-company debt	Other liabilities	Net fixed assets	Acc. dep. (as % gross fixed assets)		
US-45 Ma/T	1959	4·3	9·4	71·4	—	—	3·9	24·7	29·2	43·4	10·8	45
	1967	8·8	4·6	69·1	7·0	—	2·0	27·9	36·5	38·9		
US-46 Off/e	1959	3·3	15·1	60·6	—	—	2·6	36·8	23·4	46·4	9·4	48
	1967	8·3	6·0	50·2	—	24·7	1·1	24·0	27·5	41·9		
US-47 Misc	1959	7·8	8·9/12·8	76·1	—	—	2·4	21·5	41·0	34·4	8·7	104
	1967	8·2	8·5/12·2	84·8	—	—	—	15·2	40·8	47·4		
US-48 El	1959	0·7	5·8	18·9	—	—	52·0	29·1	42·5	23·0	13·3	2
	1967	8·1	0·5	52·0	—	7·3	11·3	29·4	33·1	51·2		
US-49 H/ap	1959	2·6	19·6	63·1	—	—	23·6	36·9	21·4	—	9·3	73
	1967	7·8	6·4	34·6	0·2	10·5	—	31·1	28·4	36·0		
US-50 M	1959	0·3	11·5	68·0	—	—	6·3	25·7	38·6	23·8	2·3	nil
	1967	7·7	37·0	50·8	—	28·7	6·4	14·1	42·1	29·4		
US-51 Ma/T	1959	1·7	6·7	65·4	—	3·7	2·3	28·6	45·2	25·9	3·3	nil
	1967	7·3	1·5	32·9	—	31·8	18·7	16·6	39·2	27·8		
US-52 El	1960	5·0	20·1/10·0	31·7	—	38·0	—	30·3	30·1	35·5	-1·8	nil
	1967	7·1	364	33·3	—	31·2	7·0	28·5	17·9	47·7		
US-53 Ph	1959	1·2	0·8	47·1	—	2·7	13·3	36·9	41·3	—	9·8	15
	1967	7·4	13·5	57·0	—	1·2	4·6	37·2	35·2	33·0		
US-54 Ph	1959	6·9	2·9/7·2	36·4	—	—	10·3	53·3	11·7	24·4	24·7	96
	1967	7·0	2·9/7·1	45·6	—	—	3·2	51·2	18·6	50·7		
US-55 Ph	1959	4·1	36·9	72·4	—	—	1·1	26·5	24·3	34·0	6·5	59
	1967	6·8	29·3	65·1	6·6	1·5	—	26·8	38·8	28·8		

Company/industry		Uses of funds		Net cash flow	Sources of funds					Other financial data		Average growth	
		Fixed assets	Net working capital		Cash reserves	Bank loans	Long-term debt	Intra-company debt	Issued capital	Profits	Dividends	Net assets (% pa)	Net profits (% pa)
US-45 Ma/T	£'000	3,466	1,532	4,640	258	—	84	16	—	5,663	2,533	12	7
	% of total	69·2	30·8	93·0	5·2	—	1·7	0·1	—				
US-46 Off/e	£'000	2,932	2,966	3,658	191	2,040	—	9	—	4,310	2,081	16	2
	% of total	49·7	50·3	62·0	3·2	34·6	—	0·2	—				
US-47 Misc	£'000	943	1,467	1,782	807	—	—	(180)	—	5,831	6,040	4	–8
	% of total	39·2	60·8	74·0	33·4	—	—	(7·4)	—				
US-48 El	£'000	5,538	2,695	7,247	(163)	592	—	555	—	4,309	208	41	17
	% of total	67·3	32·7	88·0	(2·0)	7·2	—	6·8	—				
US-49 H/ap	£'000	2,743	2,230	2,040	252	814	12	1,837	—	3,779	2,769	19	8
	% of total	55·0	45·0	41·2	5·1	16·4	0·3	37·0	—				
US-50 M	£'000	4,918	3,199	2,722	14	2,218	—	1,324	1,840	920	nil	52	15
	% of total	60·6	39·4	33·5	0·2	27·3	—	16·3	22·7				
US-51 Ma/T	£'000	3,167	2,639	2,296	(81)	2,264	—	1,323	—	1,228	nil	22	0
	% of total	54·5	45·5	39·5	(1·3)	39·0	—	22·8	—				
US-52[a] El	£'000	225	2,131	235	194	332	—	996	600	(568)	nil	7	32[b]
	% of total	9·5	90·5	10·0	8·2	14·1	—	42·3	25·4				
US-53 Ph	£'000	3,618	889	5,170	(893)	53	—	179	—	4,313	643	23	33
	% of total	80·3	19·7	114·5	(19·7)	1·2	—	4·0	—				
US-54 Ph	£'000	1,635	2,299	1,812	2,142	—	—	(19)	—	16,708	16,040	17	–3
	% of total	41·5	58·5	46·1	54·5	—	—	(0·6)	—				
US-55 Ph	£'000	2,783	917	2,642	542	102	453	(18)	(21)	2,852	1,681	10	5
	% of total	75·2	24·8	71·5	14·6	2·7	12·3	(0·5)	(0·6)				

a. 7 years 1961–67. b. rate of decreasing losses.

Table AII.5 Balance sheet and other selected financial data

Company/industry	Year	Size: total assets (£m)	Percent of total assets								1959–67 average	
			Issued capital	Owners' equity	Long-term debt	Bank loans	Intra-company debt	Other liabilities	Net fixed assets	Acc. dep. (as % gross fixed assets)	Return on total assets (%)	Dividend payout ratio (%)
US-56 F	1959	3·7	1·2	47·0	—	—	—	53·0	23·8	28·1	14·5	77
	1967	6·6	9·1	47·4	—	—	5·1	45·6	29·5	45·7		
US-57 F	1959	3·8	6·6	44·3	—	28·6	—	27·1	6·9	52·0	2·4	41
	1967	6·5	7·7	35·5	—	43·5	0·6	20·6	8·9	46·3		
US-58 Hs/p	1959	5·3	18·9	53·8	—	—	1·7	44·5	34·1	36·7	13·1	98
	1967	6·4	15·7	47·0	—	3·3	0·3	49·4	47·3	44·4		
US-59 F	1959	4·3	11·5	65·9	3·3	6·9	1·8	29·0	45·5	17·0	6·0	81
	1967	6·4	7·9	45·5	25·0		0·7	21·9	52·5	30·0		
US-60 M	1959	1·9	5·4	69·4	—	—	—	30·6	10·4	56·6	4·0	nil
	1967	6·4	1·6	42·1	—	41·6	0·6	15·7	16·7	49·1		
US-61 Misc	1959	2·3	10·7	59·2	14·0	—	1·0	39·8	26·0	43·7	4·6	29
	1967	6·3	3·9	40·3	—	9·9	17·7	18·1	40·3	41·8		
US-62 F	1959	2·4	15·1	72·9	—	—	—	27·1	51·4	34·1	6·8	44
	1967	5·9	8·6	79·6	—	0·8	1·5	18·1	61·5	47·1		
US-63 Ma/t	1959	1·6	21·1	72·1	—	—	4·0	23·9	22·8	46·5	5·0	11
	1967	5·6	13·3	43·6	13·3	24·0	2·1	17·0	47·8	27·6		
US-64 Ph	1959	2·6	38·6	74·1	—	—	3·5	22·4	43·7	18·0	18·1	82
	1967	5·6	36·0	63·4	—	—	1·9	34·7	49·1	20·0		
US-65 Ph	1959	2·3	10·1	67·6	—	—	—	32·4	31·4	27·4	10·9	48
	1967	5·4	18·6	59·0	—	0·6	11·0	29·4	38·4	33·3		
US-66 Ch	1959	4·1	8·6	56·6	—	—	5·8	37·6	48·5	38·8	15·6	94
	1967	5·2	6·7	58·2	—	0·4	1·4	40·0	51·5	55·3		

Company/industry		Uses of funds		Sources of funds						Other financial data		Average growth	
		Fixed assets	Net working capital	Net cash flow	Cash reserves	Bank loans	Long-term debt	Intra-company debt	Issued capital	Profits	Dividends	Net assets (% pa)	Net profits (% pa)
US-56 F	£'000	2,813	962	3,150	170	125	—	331	—	6,136	4,745	11	8
	% of total	74.5	25.5	83.5	4.5	3.2	—	8.8	—				
US-57 F	£'000	755	2,094	1,065	4	1,740	—	38	—	1,057	430	8	-4
	% of total	26.5	73.5	37.4	0.2	61.1	—	1.3	—				
US-58 Hs/p	£'000	3,380	(841)	2,321	77	211	—	(71)	—	6,647	6,494	2	3
	% of total	133.2	(33.2)	91.5	3.0	8.3	—	(2.8)	—				
US-59 F	£'000	2,737	1,873	1,809	921	436	1,481	(37)	—	2,520	2,029	11	-4
	% of total	59.4	40.6	39.2	20.0	9.5	32.1	(0.8)	—				
US-60 M	£'000	1,879	3,779	2,502	440	2,678	—	38	—	1,501	nil	27	2
	% of total	33.3	66.7	44.2	7.8	47.2	—	0.8	—				
US-61 Misc	£'000	3,553	1,835	2,740	35	630	885	1,098	—	1,593	460	18	-9
	% of total	65.9	34.1	50.9	0.6	11.7	16.4	20.4	—				
US-62 F	£'000	4,515	775	3,575	183	46	—	89	1,401	2,500	1,100	12	3
	% of total	85.3	14.7	67.6	3.5	0.7	—	1.7	26.5				
US-63 Ma/T	£'000	3,350	1,408	2,310	294	1,352	750	52	—	1,427	150	22	n.m.[a]
	% of total	70.4	29.6	48.4	6.2	28.4	15.9	1.1	—				
US-64 Ph	£'000	2,725	(215)	2,692	(200)	—	—	16	—	6,232	5,125	9	7
	% of total	108.6	(8.6)	107.2	(7.8)	—	—	0.6	—				
US-65 Ph	£'000	1,973	645	2,342	(346)	34	—	592	—	3,298	1,582	14	9
	% of total	75.4	24.6	89.6	(13.5)	1.3	—	22.6	—				
US-66 Ch	£'000	2,564	514	2,565	655	23	—	(166)	—	5,306	5,008	7	8
	% of total	83.3	16.7	83.4	21.2	0.7	—	(5.3)	—				

a. loss—not meaningful.

Table AII.5 Balance sheet and other selected financial data

Company/industry	Year	Size: total assets (£m)	Percent of total assets								1959-67 average	
			Issued capital	Owners' equity	Long-term debt	Bank loans	Intra-company debt	Other liabilities	Net fixed assets	Acc. dep. (as % gross fixed assets)	Return on total assets (%)	Dividend payout ratio (%)
US-67 M	1959	3·1	19·5	32·6	21·1	1·6	2·2	42·5	30·8	22·8	-0·3	∞[a]
	1967	5·2	21·0	21·0	33·0	11·2	3·5	31·3	20·4	53·0		
US-68 F	1959	4·6	43·5	(2·5)	—	25·2	68·3	9·0	40·0	6·2	-10·7	nil.
	1967	4·9	61·7	53·0	5·1	30·3	5·6	6·0	56·1	35·3		
US-69 Ma/T	1959	2·6	28·7	72·4	—	—	2·6	25·0	38·3	36·0	7·3	60
	1967	4·7	24·2	72·4	—	13·2	1·6	12·8	43·8	46·5		
US-70 Misc	1959	4·0	27·5/10·1	71·7	—	—	9·2	19·1	20·9	46·4	7·0	38
	1967	4·6	23·7	82·8	—	—	2·0	15·2	50·3	7·3		
US-71 F	1959	0·8	0·6	40·5	—	10·2	2·3	47·0	37·7	23·6	8·2	19
	1967	4·3	23·5	45·5	—	17·1	4·3	33·1	49·2	28·8		
US-72 Hs/p	1959	2·6	0·1	60·3	—	—	2·1	37·6	30·0	20·7	18·4	99
	1967	4·1	24·2	46·0	—	—	0·8	53·2	47·1	30·2		
US-73 M	1959	1·2	46·7	65·1	—	9·9	5·5	19·5	12·0	58·5	2·6	nil
	1967	4·1	30·6	43·9	0·7	35·7	0·7	19·0	14·3	46·3		
US-74 Ph	1959	2·2	36·0	61·5	—	—	3·5	35·0	23·6	36·5	8·2	70
	1967	3·6	33·0	77·3	—	—	2·2	20·5	27·8	37·0		
US-75 Misc	1959	1·7	0·3	28·4	—	—	24·8	46·8	21·2	43·5	20·3	79
	1967	3·6	0·1	36·9	—	—	20·8	42·3	36·9	33·1		
US-76 F	1959	2·4	12·6	51·2	—	—	10·5	38·3	21·7	42·0	23·7	76
	1967	3·6	34·6	71·2	—	—	—	28·8	22·0	52·8		
US-77 F	1959	1·7	3·5	15·6	—	—	21·2	63·2	19·4	44·5	15·4	69
	1967	3·4	21·3	52·4	—	24·6	—	23·0	40·4	18·2		

a. due to loss for period.

Company/ industry		Uses of funds		Net cash flow	Sources of funds					Profits	Dividends	Other financial data Average growth	
		Fixed assets	Net working capital		Cash reserves	Bank loans	Long-term debt	Intra-company debt	Issued capital			Net assets (% pa)	Net profits (% pa)
US-67 M	£'000	1,232	1,529	658	4	539	1,076	118	366	(147)	303	9	-10
	% of total	44·7	55·3	23·8	0·3	19·5	38·9	4·3	13·2				
US-68 F	£'000	2,408	(487)	(2,915)	—	323	250	3,263	1,000	(4,420)	nil	1	7[a]
	% of total	125·4	(25·4)	(151·8)	—	16·8	13·0	170·0	52·0				
US-69 Ma/T	£'000	2,299	1,487	2,208	399	625	—	9	545	2,416	1,438	13	-7
	% of total	60·7	39·3	58·4	10·5	16·5	—	0·2	14·4				
US-70 Misc	£'000	2,802	918	2,652	1,735	—	—	(267)	(400)[b]	2,345	892	8	-7
	% of total	75·3	24·7	71·3	46·6	—	—	(7·2)	(10·7)				
US-71 F	£'000	2,693	520	2,425	(19)	644	—	162	—	1,856	350	26	-3
	% of total	83·8	16·2	75·5	(0·5)	20·0	—	5·0	—				
US-72 Hs/p	£'000	1,883	(406)	1,054	442	—	—	(22)	—	5,326	5,274	8	11
	% of total	127·5	(27·5)	71·5	29·9	—	—	(1·4)	—				
US-73 M	£'000	854	1,892	1,239	8	1,332	28	(39)	178	819	nil	16	11
	% of total	31·1	68·9	45·0	0·3	48·5	1·0	(1·3)	6·5				
US-74 Ph	£'000	225	1,365	1,171	412	—	—	4	—	2,228	1,550	17	-5
	% of total	14·0	86·0	73·7	25·9	—	—	0·4	—				
US-75 Misc	£'000	1,504	228	1,386	24	—	—	325	—	3,941	3,095	24	9
	% of total	86·8	13·2	80·0	1·4	—	—	18·6	—				
US-76 F	£'000	907	1,262	1,982	435	—	—	(250)	—	5,622	4,292	22	5
	% of total	41·7	58·3	91·4	20·1	—	—	(11·5)	—				
US-77 F	£'000	992	1,289	1,458	346	834	—	(358)	—	2,743	1,900	34	-2
	% of total	43·5	56·5	63·8	15·2	36·5	—	(15·5)	—				

a. rate of decreasing losses. b. preference shares retired.

Table AII.5 Balance sheet and other selected financial data

| Company/industry | Year | Size: total assets (£m) | Percent of total assets | | | | | | Net fixed assets | Acc. dep. (as % gross fixed assets) | 1959-67 average Return on total assets (%) | Dividend payout ratio (%) |
			Issued capital	Owners' equity	Long-term debt	Bank loans	Intra-company debt	Other liabilities				
US-78 Off/e	1959	0·7	21·4	39·5	23·1	—	1·8	35·6	32·6	38·2	-4·2	nil
	1967	3·2	29·1	13·5	19·6	29·8	16·5	20·6	30·8	51·2		
US-79 Hs/p	1959	1·4	36·5	61·7	—	—	—	38·3	20·3	35·4	10·6	54
	1967	2·8	36·2	66·1	—	—	1·4	32·5	39·8	37·8		
US-80 El	1962	0·1	44·3	8·9	—	—	86·0	5·1	31·7	0·0	9·3	nil
	1967	2·7	7·4	36·5	15·7	25·4	4·9	17·5	23·4	20·6		
US-81 M	1959	0·8	45·2	44·9	—	—	49·7	5·4	18·5	1·0	-2·0	nil
	1967	2·7	37·7	28·2	—	38·3	27·4	6·1	8·5	51·8		
US-82 Ch	1959	0·8	13·1	37·3	—	1·3	6·8	54·6	30·4	37·0	8·4	58
	1967	2·6	16·8	33·3	—	13·1	12·9	40·7	42·3	33·4		
US-83 H/ap	1959	2·5	48·7	48·5	5·4	—	11·1	35·0	29·6	41·0	1·1	nil
	1967	2·5	48·4	64·6	—	—	4·5	30·9	14·9	71·4		
US-84 El	1959	0·1	30·7	45·7	—	15·7	7·2	31·4	24·3	26·1	9·5	10
	1967	2·5	10·5	49·6	12·1	3·8	6·6	27·9	21·0	26·8		
US-85 El	1959	1·7	35·2/17·6	76·2	0·3	1·2	3·0	19·3	40·4	39·3	-1·0	8[a]
	1967	1·9	32·2/16·1	61·5	—	26·0	2·5	10·0	32·2	48·2		
US-86 Ch	1959	0·7	5·7	62·8	—	—	12·0	25·2	17·8	50·5	17·7	59
	1967	1·9	13·3	66·3	—	—	7·5	26·2	29·5	33·9		
US-87 El	1959	0·2	19·1	7·0	—	—	83·5	9·5	26·1	—	6·3	3
	1967	1·9	4·1	18·4	0·4	43·1	23·6	14·5	9·8	—		
US-88 Ph	1959	0·7	8·7	36·7	—	—	1·1	62·2	31·1	32·3	8·5	61
	1967	1·8	21·9	37·8	—	28·1	2·2	31·9	28·0	53·2		

[a] less payout ratio not meaningful

| | Uses of funds | | Net cash flow | Cash reserves | Sources of funds | | | | Other financial data | | Average growth | |
Company/industry	Fixed assets	Net working capital			Bank loans	Long-term debt	Intra-company debt	Issued capital	Profits	Dividends	Net assets (% pa)	Net profits (% pa)
US-78 Off/e £'000	1,782	1,435	359	58	982	480	981	357	(642)	nil	27	-17
% of total	55·3	44·7	11·2	1·8	30·6	14·9	30·5	11·0				
US-79 Hs/p £'000	1,761	147	1,922	(49)	—	—	35	—	2,122	1,141	21	7
% of total	92·3	7·7	101·8	(2·8)	—	—	1·8	—				
US-80[a] El £'000	850	1,546	1,056	6	683	422	114	115	995	nil	79	20
% of total	35·5	64·5	44·0	0·3	28·5	17·6	4·8	4·8				
US-81 M £'000	372	2,285	(60)	(26)	1,016	—	1,377	350	(328)	nil	17	n.m.[b]
% of total	13·8	86·2	(2·3)	(1·0)	38·3	—	51·8	13·2				
US-82 Ch £'000	1,534	352	1,000	28	332	—	285	240	1,155	671	22	6
% of total	81·3	18·7	53·0	1·6	17·6	—	15·1	12·7				
US-83 H/ap £'000	555	300	1,191	(38)	—	(133)	(163)	—	219	nil	1	n.m.[b]
% of total	64·9	35·1	139·4	(4·7)	—	(15·6)	(19·1)	—				
US-84 El £'000	735	1,185	1,190	1	73	300	154	204	1,059	106	45	38
% of total	38·3	61·7	62·0	—	3·8	15·6	8·0	10·6				
US-85 El £'000	346	482	348	25	464	(6)	(4)	—	(94)	38	3	3
% of total	41·8	58·2	42·2	3·0	56·0	(0·7)	(0·5)	—				
US-86 Ch £'000	612	486	968	73	—	—	57	—	1,765	1,038	19	15
% of total	55·7	44·3	88·2	6·7	—	—	5·1	—				
US-87 El £'000	308	1,412	585	(62)	833	8	325	30	441	15	40	43
% of total	17·7	82·3	34·0	(3·5)	48·4	0·5	18·9	1·7				
US-88 Ph £'000	829	681	969	18	494	—	30	—	979	600	22	-5
% of total	55·0	45·0	64·2	1·2	32·6	—	2·0	—				

a. 6 years, 1962-67. b. not meaningful—alternating losses and profits.

Table AII.5 Balance sheet and other selected financial data

Company/ industry	Year	Size: total assets (£m)	Percent of total assets								1959–67 average	
			Issued capital	Owners' equity	Long-term debt	Bank loans	Intra-company debt	Other liabilities	Net fixed assets	Acc. dep. (as % gross fixed assets)	Return on total assets (%)	Dividend payout ratio (%)
US-89 Misc	1959	0·4	1·3	19·0	—	—	48·0	33·0	1·0	67·0	12·0	22
	1967	0·8	0·6	52·6	—	—	20·6	26·8	17·5	34·2		
US-90 F	1959	0·4	4·7	62·4	—	—	—	37·6	12·0	51·0	8·5	143
	1967	0·6	3·6	25·2	—	35·9	6·3	32·6	15·2	49·0		
EUR-1 El	1959	54·0	8·9	44·8	13·4	3·0	15·5	23·3	38·5	—	0·6	46
	1967	150·3	20·0	37·4	5·9	8·6	30·4	17·7	52·4	—		
EUR-2 F	1959	26·5	37·7	52·4	—	—	19·7	27·9	40·2	11·2	3·0	146
	1967	68·3	29·3	30·0	—	20·2	37·2	12·6	51·2	18·8		
EUR-3 Misc	1959	13·5	7·4	50·9	18·6	—	11·8	18·7	30·2	—	5·4	45
	1967	50·0.	8·0	36·3	25·5	8·5	6·4	23·3	46·2	39·8		
EUR-4 Ph	1961	15·4	19·5	39·9	0·7	17·8	13·5	28·1	45·5	—	3·0	23
	1967	29·4	10·2	35·8	8·5	25·7	6·5	23·5	60·0	33·5		
EUR-5 Ph	1959	9·8	30·6	47·1	10·4	3·4	19·4	19·7	47·2	11·5	2·3	26
	1967	29·2	18·8	21·1	7·8	7·9	43·3	19·9	57·0	19·7		
EUR-6 Ch	1959	15·7	38·3/0·2	74·9	2·7	—	2·6	19·8	33·5	25·5	7·0	47
	1967	24·2	49·6/0·2	72·9	—	—	6·3	21·0	36·1	41·9		
EUR-7 M	1959	13·9	43·2	77·3	—	—	4·8	17·9	21·6	58·5	5·2	56
	1967	19·7	33·1	82·6	—	—	8·8	8·6	23·2	64·1		
EUR-8 Misc	1959	6·6	18·2	45·4	10·6	—	9·7	34·3	34·4	—	4·1	75
	1967	16·0	25·0	34·3	10·9	19·8	11·6	23·4	41·0	36·8		
EUR-9 Ch	1961	4·2	89·0	96·0	—	0·7	1·0	2·3	6·7	0·0	2·7	37
	1967	15·2	24·6	33·5	32·8	19·5	3·1	11·1	55·9	23·0		

Company/industry	Uses of funds		Sources of funds						Other financial data		Average growth	
	Fixed assets	Net working capital	Net cash flow	Cash reserves	Bank loans	Long-term debt	Intra-company debt	Issued capital	Profits	Dividends	Net assets (% pa)	Net profits (% pa)
US-89 Misc £'000	255	190	473	(13)	—	—	(12)	—	536	117	12	7
% of total	57·3	42·7	106·0	(3·0)	—	—	(3·0)	—				
US-90 F £'000	90	148	(64)	71	199	—	34	—	276	395	8	-8
% of total	37·8	62·2	(27·6)	29·8	83·5	—	14·3	—				
EUR-1 El £'000	84,400	20,600	34,355	648	11,387	1,651	44,463	12,500	4,774	2,160	16	n.m.[a]
% of total	80·4	19·6	32·7	0·9	10·7	1·6	42·2	11·9				
EUR-2 F £'000	29,385	18,641	2,917	1,141	13,786	—	20,182	10,000	10,428	15,260	16	-7
% of total	61·2	38·8	6·1	2·4	28·6	—	42·1	20·8				
EUR-3 Misc £'000	32,764	10,422	19,232	2,169	4,253	10,445	5,086	2,000	13,564	6,062	22	23
% of total	75·8	24·2	44·5	5·0	9·9	24·2	11·8	4·6				
EUR-4 Ph £'000	14,838	831	8,483	150	4,817	2,500	(282)	—	4,162	965	13	5
% of total	94·7	5·3	54·2	1·0	30·8	16·0	(2·0)	—				
EUR-5 Ph £'000	17,279	3,544	7,237	(463)	1,978	1,240	10,727	100	3,544	905	15	-7
% of total	83·4	16·6	34·7	(2·3)	9·5	6·0	51·6	0·5				
EUR-6 Ch £'000	8,128	4,768	10,346	1,847	—	(420)	1,123	—	11,533	5,437	9	0
% of total	63·0	37·0	80·3	14·3	—	(3·3)	8·7	—				
EUR-7 M £'000	6,036	5,709	8,275	716	—	—	1,068	1,685	7,878	4,430	7	-5
% of total	51·4	48·6	70·5	6·1	—	—	9·1	14·3				
EUR-8 Misc £'000	7,416	3,941	4,266	254	3,168	1,050	2,019	600	3,526	2,623	16	14
% of total	65·3	34·7	37·6	2·1	27·9	9·3	17·8	5·3				
EUR-9 Ch £'000[b]	10,775	4,878	3,561	(3)	2,968	5,000	377	3,750	1,627	618	68	n.m.[a]
% of total	68·8	31·2	22·8	—	19·0	32·0	2·2	24·0				

a. not meaningful—fluctuating losses and profits. b. 1961-67.

Table AII.5 Balance sheet and other selected financial data

Company/ industry	Year	Size: total assets (£m)	Issued capital	Owners' equity	Long-term debt	Bank loans	Intra-company debt	Other liabilities	Net fixed assets	Acc. dep. (as % gross fixed assets)	1959–67 average Return on total assets (%)	Dividend payout ratio (%)
							Percent of total assets					
EUR-10 H/ap	1959	7·7	38·9	54·5	—	—	8·6	36·9	24·6	37·4	3·1	47
	1967	13·5	51·7	70·6	—	2·1	4·3	23·0	18·0	57·4		
EUR-11 Ch	1959	6·3	27·8	71·8	1·7	5·2	5·2	16·1	47·6	52·4	3·2	27
	1967	12·9	13·5	53·5	20·2	17·6	3·0	5·7	64·7	—		
EUR-12 Ph	1959	3·5	5·7	16·1	—•	—	68·2	15·7	37·4	40·0	5·6	94
	1967	9·0	2·2	8·3	—	—	83·5	8·2	24·6	43·8		
EUR-13 El	1959	0·1	10·5	21·0	—	—	36·9	42·1	5·3	0·0	1·0	4
	1967	8·0	9·9	15·8	45·5	1·7	17·9	19·1	37·5	14·6		
EUR-14 Misc	1959	4·3	41·5	67·5	—	—	1·4	31·1	37·3	37·0	6·4	65
	1967	7·0	31·2	60·2	—	1·9	2·6	35·3	30·8	49·5		
EUR-15 Ph	1959	3·5	22·6	31·4	—	11·2	48·3	9·1	46·6	20·1	1·4	95
	1967	6·7	19·3	25·3	—	21·1	42·8	10·8	50·0	34·8		
EUR-16 Ph	1959	5·0	40·3	70·0	—	—	—	30·0	31·1	—	5·7	64
	1967	5·9	34·0	74·7	—	—	1·5	23·8	36·6	—		
EUR-17 Misc	1959	1·5	19·4/6·5	54·1	16·3	11·3	0·7	17·6	34·4	28·0	5·0	28
	1967	4·8	9·4/2·1	42·5	5·4	14·5	16·3	21·3	35·1	36·9		
EUR-18 M	1959	1·8	43·7	77·7	—	—	6·6	15·7	6·3	71·7	7·3	63
	1967	3·2	25·1	61·6	—	—	16·5	21·9	5·5	73·5		
EUR-19 Ch	1959	0·9	15·3	71·9	—	—	1·3	26·8	42·4	46·5	3·5	38
	1967	2·7	23·2	39·3	26·6	9·2	10·2	14·7	56·5	40·6		
EUR-20 M	1959	0·5	19·4	3·5	—	2·3	70·2	24·0	11·5	—	2·4	4
	1967	2·3	8·9	18·6	—	13·6	60·7	7·1	11·3	40·8		

Table AII.6 Sources and uses of funds and other selected financial data (eight years 1960-67)

Company/industry		Uses of funds		Sources of funds						Other financial data		Average growth	
		Fixed assets	Net working capital	Net cash flow	Cash reserves	Bank loans	Long-term debt	Intra-company debt	Issued capital	Profits	Dividends	Net assets (% pa)	Net profits (% pa)
EUR-10 H/ap	£'000	2,015	4,086	3,804	87	291	—	(81)	2,000	2,896	1,357	11	-2
	% of total	33.0	67.0	62.4	1.4	4.8	—	(1.4)	32.8				
EUR-11 Ch	£'000	9,128	731	6,048	(684)	1,941	2,500	54	—	2,745	745	10	-6
	% of total	92.6	7.4	61.2	(6.9)	19.7	25.4	0.6	—				
EUR-12 Ph	£'000	1,932	4,387	1,405	(193)	—	—	5,107	—	2,491	2,330	17	-6
	% of total	30.7	69.3	22.2	(3.2)	—	—	81.0	—				
EUR-13 El	£'000	3,365	3,280	711	(48)	136	3,626	1,617	603	284	10	107	n.m.[a]
	% of total	50.5	49.5	10.7	(1.0)	2.1	54.7	24.4	9.1				
EUR-14 Misc	£'000	1,673	252	2,238	(568)	130	—	125	—	2,859	1,840	5	4
	% of total	86.9	13.1	116.1	(29.4)	6.8	—	6.5	—				
EUR-15 Ph	£'000	2,949	1,024	1,454	(3)	1,023	—	1,169	330	671	635	8	-1
	% of total	74.2	25.8	36.4	—	25.8	—	29.4	8.4				
EUR-16 Ph	£'000	2,327	902	2,300	839	—	—	90	—	2,839	1,830	11	-3
	% of total	72.1	27.9	71.2	26.0	—	—	2.8	—				
EUR-17 Misc	£'000	1,770	1,277	1,551	(12)	514	3	769	220	1,135	323	14	12
	% of total	58.2	41.8	50.9	(0.1)	16.8		25.2	7.2				
EUR-18 M	£'000	421	1,276	900	393	—	—	404	—	1,439	901	10	14
	% of total	24.9	75.1	53.0	23.2	—	—	23.8	—				
EUR-19 Ch	£'000	1,739	648	1,047	127	245	709	259	—	438	167	20	-2
	% of total	72.8	27.2	43.9	5.3	10.3	29.7	10.8	—				
EUR-20	£'000	341	1,509	451	—	295	—	1,004	100	285	11	23	-12
	% of total	18.5	81.5	24.4	—	15.9	—	54.4	5.3				

a. not meaningful—fluctuating losses and profits.

Table AII.5 Balance sheet and other selected financial data

Company/industry	Year	Size: total assets (£m)	Percent of total assets							Acc. dep. (as % gross fixed assets)	1959–67 average	
			Issued capital	Owners' equity	Long-term debt	Bank loans	Intra-company debt	Other liabilities	Net fixed assets		Return on total assets (%)	Dividend payout ratio (%)
EUR-21 Ph	1959	0·6	46·8	57·1	—	11·2	8·3	23·4	14·0	49·7	3·0	12
	1967	2·2	27·5	40·8	—	19·7	19·2	20·3	12·7	46·0		
EUR-22 El	1959	1·3	39·6	80·9	—	—	4·4	14·7	26·4	63·5	-6·1	8[a]
	1967	2·0	25·2	(20·1)	—	30·6	83·5	6·0	42·2	55·0		
EUR-23 Ph	1959	0·6	2·5	35·9	—	—	38·0	26·1	20·4	—	10·7	29
	1967	1·7	28·6	57·3	—	—	11·1	31·6	15·8	52·5		
EUR-24 Ph	1959	0·8	83·9	75·4	—	1·2	15·5	7·9	62·4	23·4	2·6	nil
	1967	1·2	60·7	74·5	—	8·2	6·2	11·1	44·4	47·1		
EUR-25 F	1959	0·3	73·0	57·5	—	5·0	19·8	17·7	39·1	29·8	2·9	nil
	1967	0·8	30·8	39·7	—	—	30·5	29·8	27·3	54·0		

a. loss, payout ratio not meaningful.

Table AII.6 Sources and uses of funds and other selected financial data (eight years 1960–67)

Company/industry		Uses of funds		Sources of funds						Other financial data		Average growth	
		Fixed assets	Net working capital	Net cash flow	Cash reserves	Bank loans	Long-term debt	Intra-company debt	Issued capital	Profits	Dividends	Net assets (% pa)	Net profits (% pa)
EUR-21 Ph	£'000	462	1,031	570	(24)	357	—	591	—	289	34	17	16
	% of total	31·0	69·0	38·2	(1·6)	23·9	—	39·5	—				
EUR-22 El	£'000	1,062	464	(862)	181	606	—	1,600	—	(856)	573	10	n.m.[a]
	% of total	69·6	30·4	(56·7)	11·9	39·8	—	105·0	—				
EUR-23 Ph	£'000	504	513	1,063	(112)	—	—	(29)	95	1,005	290	14	14
	% of total	49·5	50·5	104·8	(11·0)	—	—	(3·1)	9·3				
EUR-24 Ph	£'000	445	271	664	(3)	84	—	(54)	25	194	nil	4	n.m.[a]
	% of total	62·1	37·9	92·7	(0·4)	11·7	—	(7·5)	3·5				
EUR-25 F	£'000	306	171	345	(30)	(17)	—	180	—	126	nil	8	n.m.[a]
	% of total	64·1	35·9	72·3	(6·5)	(3·6)	—	37·8	—				

a. not meaningful—fluctuating losses and profits.

Notes

PREFACE
1. *Le Monde*, Paris; 16 June 1965, p. 21. The quotations are translated from the French.

CHAPTER 1. THE MULTINATIONAL COMPANY
1. N. Machiavelli, *The Prince*; English edn, trans. W. K. Marriott, London 1908, ch. 2.
2. This is a recurring theme. See, for instance, *The Wealth of Nations*, Bk i, ch. 11, pt 1, and Bk iv, ch. 7.
3. See ch. 8, pp. 213–14.
4. This would not surprise those who follow Berle's argument that the firm is increasingly being led by what he calls non-state civil servants: 'We assume that our economic system is based on "private property". Yet most industrial property is no more private than a seat in a subway train, and indeed it is questionable whether much of it can be called "property" at all. We indignantly deny that we are collectivist, yet it is demonstrable that more than two-thirds of our enterprise is possible only because it is collectivist; what is really meant is that the state did not do the collectivising. . . .' See Berle 1960, p. 27.
5. This particular paradox has been well illustrated in a passage on postwar development in the European Iron and Steel Community in *The Multi-Millionaires* by Goronwy Rees, London, Chatto, 1961, p. 178. It can also be said that executives from business companies turn up much more regularly in places like Peking than politicians or missionaries.
6: See J. N. S. Oanh, 'Keynes today', *Harvard Business Review*, May–June 1960, p. 98.
7. For a discussion of the contribution of this study to the theory of organisational change see M. Z. Brooke, 'The multinational company: change factors in a complex organisation', published among the papers of the 1969 Rome Congress of the International Institute of Sociology.
8. See, for example, Robinson 1967, pp. 151 ff.
9. These are, of course, matters of vital concern to any local partners as well as to the tax and exchange control authorities of the host country. The point we wish to make is that they are conducted in private out of the public's eye.
10. Quoted from a speech at a private conference of executives of foreign companies by permission of the executive concerned.
11. W. J. Kenyon Jones, in *International Operations Conference Papers* 1966, paper 4.
12. Approximately 80 per cent of US direct investment overseas has been made by the three hundred largest US companies. A rather similar pattern emerges for UK investment overseas.
13. Aversion to risks is, of course, not confined to multinational operations, but is an attitude of management that plays a fundamental role in shaping company policies in all areas where there is uncertainty. Gordon wrote, for example, that managers '. . . may seek to some extent to play safe and to avoid some of the change and uncertainty which results from assiduous pursuit of every possible opportunity to increase profits further, . . . professional executives, emphasising care and caution and reacting only imperfectly to the lure of profits, may be slow to exploit new and unfamiliar lines of activity . . . [because] they do not receive the profits which may result from taking a chance, while their position in the firm may be jeopardised in the event of serious loss' (see R. A. Gordon 1961, pp. 324 and 327–9).

14. See Aharoni 1966, pp. 35–8.
15. See Veblen 1904.
16. See Gordon 1961, p. 306. The subsequent reference is to O. E. Williamson, 'A model of managerial behaviour', in Cyert and March 1963, ch. 9.
17. This account is based on the penetrating analysis of Amitai Etzioni, who uses the following typology:

'Kinds of Power	Kinds of Involvement		
	Alienative	Calculative	Moral
Coercive	1	2	3
Remunerative	4	5	6
Normative	7	8	9'

where 1, 5, 9 usually correspond.
See Etzioni 1961, p. 12. In ch. 1 of that book the author sets out a scheme for the study of power. Chapters 9 and 10 are especially illuminating in their implications for managers. The present study has sacrificed some of the precision of Etzioni's terms to avoid misunderstanding. Thus the words *normative* and *moral* are not used here. The word *voluntary* approximates to the meaning of these words. Thus if a person behaves in a certain way primarily because of the financial advantages or disadvantages to him, this is called *calculative*. He makes a calculation. If not, then the word *voluntary* is used. This is what he *wishes* to do and his action does not depend upon the financial advantages to himself.
18. An M.Sc. thesis on this subject by Christine Moffatt, University of Manchester, is in preparation (1970).
19. The points made in this paragraph are based on Cyert and March 1963, pp. 114–27.
20. This brief discussion on bureaucracy is included in the text to give a starting point for the understanding of the structures described. The most widely read English text on the subject is Weber 1948. Studies in the Weber tradition are listed in the Bibliography under the following: Blau 1955 and 1963, Merton 1952, Crozier 1964, Selznick 1949, Gouldner 1954. The word *Bureaucracy* is used here, as by Weber, in a neutral sense; it is meant to contrast with the rule of the personal autocrat.
21. We have used the words *job* and *position* here and elsewhere. The usual term in sociological writings is *office*, which is obviously more comprehensive. For a brief summary of Management by Objective, see Humble 1965 or 1968.
22. See below ch. 2. Product group projections are those units in the organisation handling the firm's interests in one particular product group. Geographical projections are concerned with the firm's interests in a particular locality, country or region of the world.
23. See Cyert and March 1963, p. 117.
24. See Metcalf and Urwick 1941, ch. 1.
25. This phrase is used by several writers on bureaucracy, especially Crozier 1964, ch. 7, on which the following is based.
26. A seminal discussion of this concept is to be found in Merton 1957, see especially pp. 368–84.
27. See Blau 1955.
28. On the significance of the 'innovating personality' see, for example, Touraine 1965.

PART I

CHAPTER 2. THE ORGANISATION
1. See Weber 1948, p. 216. See also chapter 1, note 20.
2. Other writers have referred to this conflict. See for instance, Lovell 1966, second page of summary entitled: 'Highlights for the Executive'.

3. This trend is being advocated by leading industrial consultants, who advocate autonomy and responsibility by product group.
4. Robinson 1964, p. 99. Later, on pp. 201–2, Robinson goes on to describe a system of book credits between divisions to overcome opposition to business abroad. A number of firms in our sample reported such a system.
5. One company described the initial processes of merger as follows:
   (1) Integration in one overseas area (an area where both merging companies had manufacturing operations).
   (2) The sales organisation of one company to handle the products of the other.
   (3) Some promotion from one company to the other. The effect on personnel was two-edged; it made wider opportunities for individuals but upset a well-planned management development programme in one of the companies.
   (4) Cross-fertilisation in ideas for sales promotion.
   (5) Some factories could use spare space by doing work for the other company. This was an example of a firm in which both partners to the mergers were already overseas; there were therefore special problems and the first moves to integration were taken at operating level. A firm which had been formed by a merger of three companies only one of which was already overseas took a different route. They had started integration at the top—a group capital budget, the beginnings of group services. Yet other companies notably integrate more rapidly.
6. See below, note 9.
7. This figure is quoted from Clee 1962.
8. This 'discovery' was made in many of the companies studied; it was never stated by members of the companies, but the following quotation is of interest: 'An important feature of the management of our overseas companies lies in the fact that the administrative structure closely follows that which operates in the parent company. This is not done in an attempt to set up in countries overseas a carbon copy of our headquarters organisation. But we have found that co-operation and exchange of "knowhow" are made easier—not only between the overseas companies and the British parent, but also between each overseas manager and his opposite number in other territories, if they are all accustomed to using the same methods, systems and management procedures' (John Oldham at a British Institute of Management Conference, Southport, April 1961).
9. The phrase is correctly applied to dealings between two companies in a group where pricing and other arrangements are made as if these were two separate companies. Some firms aver that they always transfer goods within the firm at 'arm's length'. Any other method causes trouble with the tax authorities, besides being bad for morale within the company; but few subsidiaries seem to accept that the arrangements are genuinely at 'arm's length'; and the obligation of negotiating with the tax authorities over transfer arrangements they would prefer not to make can be irritating. This point will be further discussed in chapters 4 and 6.
10. Lovell 1966, foreword p. 2.
11. See, for example, Vollmer and Mills 1966.
12. See Richardson and Walker 1948, an illuminating study of the subject.
13. Reported by J. Thackray, in 'ITT's one-man machine', *Management Today*, December 1966, p. 77. In another view of how this is intended to work, the Treasurer of ITT has this to say in a speech to the New York Society of Security Analysts: 'From our New York office we operate a rigid system of controls on inventories, receivables, debt levels, capital expenditures, G. and A. expense, profit forecasts, etc. through a highly sophisticated system of reporting. For example, no subsidiary can increase its level of debt over budget without justification to, and prior approval of, the Treasurer's office. It is also characteristic of our continuous attention that we make a worldwide check of the forecast of earnings at each division twice a month. If any of our subsidiaries forecasts a slippage in the approved budget levels in any of the areas mentioned above, immediate remedial steps are put into effect . . . by on-the-spot visits from appropriate regional staff.' (Quoted in Martyn 1967, p. 17.)

14. This problem is discussed more fully in ch. 4, pp. 113–15.
15. In one small British company which had been expanding rapidly overseas, the chief executive said that written policies would be impossible since 'they change every bloody night'. This was emphatically not a firm which could be said to be lacking in a sense of direction.
   Other examples from company manuals are given in ch. 4, pp. 92–5.
16. For a definition of *open* and *close*, see ch. 1, pp. 12–13. This will be taken up in detail in the next chapter.
17. See Lovell 1963, ch. 2.
18. N. V. Philips Gloeilampenfabrieken, *Report of the Board of Management*, Eindhoven 1964, p. 11. This report is quoted again in ch. 10, p. 248.
19. See Blau 1955 and Crozier 1964.
20. See Fenn 1957.

CHAPTER 3. RELATIONSHIPS BETWEEN HEAD OFFICE AND THE FOREIGN SUBSIDIARY— POWER SYSTEMS

1. For an explanation of the words used here, see ch. 1, pp. 11–12; for present purposes *voluntary* refers to non-economic motives.
2. For the theoretical discussion underlying this, see Etzioni 1961, chapters 1–3.
3. Whyte 1956.
4. This is further discussed in ch. 5, pp. 141–9.
5. See, for example, Etzioni 1961a, pp. 203–9, where the effect of the strong personality on the organisation is analysed.
6. Howard Coonley in the *Journal of Marketing*, 5, 1940, 106.
7. See R. A. Gordon 1961, ch. 5. For the reference in the following sentences, see Litterer 1965, ch. 19. The 'expected advantages' of decentralisation set out by Litterer bear some resemblance to the advantages actually claimed by one company, viz:

   (*a*) Creative thinking is stimulated by granting a large measure of initiative.
   (*b*) National company activities can be completely integrated in the national economy.
   (*c*) Full advantage is taken of international diversity of talent and natural abilities.
   (*d*) Quick action can be taken that is adapted to local needs.
   (*e*) The danger of central bureaucracy is limited.

   The truth of these claims has not been empirically tested.
8. This was suggested by some executives interviewed, but did not correspond with facts discovered in their own firms. The phrase *organisational distance* used later in this paragraph refers to the actual number of levels in the organisation.
9. See B. M. Gross 1964, pp. 385–7. Gross uses the phrase *vicious circle*, but we are using that phrase of a different situation, see e.g. ch. 1, p. 15.
10. See Donner 1967, pp. 35–6. See also above, p. 264.
11. This would appear to support the suggestion made later that modern management techniques are a principal centralising pressure. The small company cannot always afford these.
12. These are discussed again in ch. 9 in a general discussion of the reasons for the move abroad, see especially table 9.1, p. 227.
13. In the opinion of some observers, this is the ideal relationship. See, for instance, Layton 1966, p. 116.
14. This is the 'B type' organisation described above in ch. 2, see diagram 2.3.
15. See the *Financial Times*, London, 1 May 1964.
16. See 'Holding companies: tightening the reins', *The Stock Exchange Gazette*, London, 7 April 1967. The whole article illustrates this point very well, as does the *Annual Report* for 1966 of Norcros Ltd.

17. One Am rican company allowed its British subsidiary to drop one point from its survey, when the latter represented that it might produce ribald comments. The point was: 'I am proud to be working for — Corporation, strongly agree/agree/ disagree/strongly disagree.'
18. See Rocour 1963, especially pp. 54–6 and 197–9, where the position of American subsidiaries of European firms is discussed. It is pointed out that a situation described in our terms as very *open* can develop when a subsidiary is more advanced than head office.
19. See pp. 42–3.
20. See Cyert and March 1963, pp. 60–5.
21. Crozier 1964, ch. 7.
22. But Steiner (1963, p. 18) takes a different view: 'Because environmental influences vary widely among different countries of the world, the trend is for corporate headquarters of multinational companies to give local managers considerable delegated authority within broad policies and strategies determined at central headquarters.' It was frequently found in this study that statements beginning 'because' or 'as a result of' to suggest a commonsense consequence of a known condition were not supported by the investigation.
23. It will be noted that the present study contains no attempt to quantify the factors here being described. Although this account is based on considerable evidence, carefully crosschecked, and applying to all the companies studied, it has been found impossible to produce some reliable comparative measure of centralisation and independence. In saying this, the authors would like to pay tribute to the very significant pioneering work on organisation measurement undertaken at the University of Aston and the London Business School. Some of the publications describing this work are listed in the Bibliography below under Pugh. However, the following problems arise in connection with applying their techniques to multinational firms:

    (a) The contrast between the point where a decision is supposed to be taken, and that where it is actually made, already a problem in domestic companies, is a major difficulty in international firms.
    (b) The point of decision-making can vary from one subsidiary to another in the same firm.
    (c) The fact that a greater number of levels means a greater centralisation by level of the organisation.
    (d) The need to differentiate between centralisation of decision-making and independence of operation.

    We do not intend these points to be taken as a criticism of the work mentioned, and we know that the people concerned have their own answers to them. The problems remain, however, and cause difficulties in the way of producing a measure of centralisation in the international operations of the companies in our sample.
24. This distinction has already been used in connection with organisational arrangements in ch. 2, and will come up again in connection with appraisal problems in ch. 5.

CHAPTER 4. RELATIONSHIPS BETWEEN HEAD OFFICE AND THE FOREIGN SUBSIDIARY: CONTROL SYSTEMS
1. Gilbert 1957, p. 35.
2. See for example, Anthony *et al* 1965, Shillinglaw 1964, Taboulet 1965.
3. For a more detailed treatment see Anthony *et al* 1965, Steiner and Cannon 1966, pp. 8–16, Steiner 1963.
4. Again, there are a host of terms used to describe the process: planning, management planning, business planning, forward planning (as if one could plan an

other way but forward!), profit planning, budgeting, forecast, programming, and probably still others without venturing beyond the English language. For example, some companies referred to both budgets and forecasts. Budgets were for a one-year period, and seemed to be more for control, i.e. measurement of performance purposes. Forecasts covered various time periods and were more for planning purposes, i.e. to schedule or reschedule and coordinate other events. In other companies, choice of terms such as programming, or management planning appears often merely as an attempt to give budgeting a 'new look' such as when controls are being tightened up by head office.

5. J. Simon in *International Operations Conference Papers* 1966, paper 7.
6. Otto in Steiner and Cannon 1966, p. 108.
7. *Ibid.*
8. It is beyond the scope of this study to consider all the problems encountered in capital budgeting. For further discussion, see for example, Smith and Remmers 1966, B. R. Williams 1962.
9. For a detailed analysis and example of the appraisal of an overseas project, see Merritt and Sykes 1963, pp. 348–71. A discussion of the criteria used by companies in evaluation of foreign investments is presented in Polk, Meister and Veit 1966, pp. 62–76, and in Stonehill and Nathanson 1968, and in Aharoni 1966.
10 Even in the otherwise highly 'autonomous' foreign subsidiaries of European companies in the United States, this was the one decision area that was closely controlled by the parent company. Reported by Rocour 1963, pp. 165–7.
11. For further views on this point, see Merritt and Sykes 1963, pp. 364–71, and D. T. Smith 1966.
12. These are aggregate figures for all American and British overseas investments. We shall see that many subsidiaries remit virtually all their earnings; some reinvest virtually all earnings.
13. Stonehill and Nathanson 1968, table V, p. 49.
14. An approach suggested by J. S. Clapham in *International Operations Conference Papers*, 1966.
15. Pryor 1965.
16. About 35 per cent of the firms in Stonehill and Nathanson 1968 used this approach. See especially table VII, p. 50.
17. Polk, Meister and Veit 1966, p. 63. This view was generally confirmed by our interviews. A typical response might be, 'If the project looks good, we'll find the means to finance it.' *Looking good* in this sense usually meant an expected larger share of the market or a growth in sales volume.
18. And also internally in the subsidiary, though many of these deviations are recognised and corrected before ever appearing in a formal report.
19. This company's reporting of information was not especially unusual. One electronics company was required to forward to headquarters over 260 different reports. Another company which prided itself on granting the subsidiaries 'perhaps too much autonomy' required 74 different reports: 16 monthly, 17 quarterly, 11 semi-annually, 30 annually. Some of these were extremely detailed and long, one normally ran over 200 pages.
20. On this point see, for example, Shillinglaw 1964, pp. 153–5 and Drucker 1955, esp. pp. 113–17.
21. See Anthony 1965, p. 251.
22. For a discussion of some of the non-profit measures of performance, see Solomons 1965, pp. 277–86.
23. Net present worth has been defined as 'the difference between gross present worth and the amount of capital investments required to achieve the benefits being discussed'; (gross present worth being defined as 'equal to the capitalised value of the flow of future expected benefits, discounted [or capitalised] at a rate which reflects their certainty or uncertainty'), see Solomon 1963, p. 20.
24. Although the maintenance of a minimum level of earnings is crucial to the firm, there is considerable doubt whether the maximisation of earnings is the primary goal, at least in the larger companies. In summing up discussion on the goals

of the industrial system, Galbraith (1967, pp. 177–8) wrote: 'The first requirement is a secure earnings record. Any firm that fails this requirement is a dog. Its management is regarded with condescension, even pity. . . . Given a secure level of earnings the esteemed firms are those that are large—that have a record of achieved growth—or which are growing with particular speed. Increasingly, esteem is associated with the latter. And if a firm has a reputation for techno-logical innovation, it is additionally known as a smart outfit. Thereafter the dividend record will be mentioned.' On the same question, Marris (1964, p. 102) wrote: 'When a man takes decisions leading to successful expansion, he not only creates new openings but also recommends himself and his colleagues as particularly suitable candidates to fill them (and the colleagues, recognising this, will be glad to allow him a generous share of the utility-proceeds). He has demon-strated his powers as a manager and deserves his reward. So personal ability be-comes judged by achieved growth, and the encouragement of growth becomes a motive for not only collective but also individual advancement, thus reinforcing the basic connection. . . . This does not mean that a man's profit-earning ability will necessarily be ignored, for profits are required for growth and minimum profit is necessary for a minimum valuation ratio. But it does mean that a man is unlikely to be judged by his ability as a profit *maximiser*. By contrast he may well be judged by his ability to maximise, or at least promote, organisational growth.' See also, R. A. Gordon 1961, pp. 305–8 and Penrose 1959, pp. 26–30.

Despite the evidence of the importance of growth as an objective of companies, and as a measure of performance, it was impossible to elicit acknowledgement of this from the individuals we interviewed. 'Of course growth is important, but it is profit that really counts' was a typical response. Perhaps in conceptualising growth and profits distinctions between the two may, in practice, become blurred. In other words, they are equivalent in their minds. Profits are necessary to support the growth of the firm, and the firm would not invest if the expansion was not believed to be profitable.

25. These are internally derived, that is, self-imposed, yardsticks which are set down in the plan. An externally derived standard might also be used as a yardstick, but generally these would be taken into consideration during the planning process itself, and incorporated into the plan, or rejected as unattainable and left out of it.
26. See the discussion in the section on planning activities above, pp. 101–2.
27. For further discussion of this point, see Lewis 1965 and Solomons 1965, pp. 240–2.
28. Some subsidiaries, however, are set up as expense centres, and performance is measured in terms of how well they keep their costs down.
29. For a discussion of this general problem see, for example, Dean 1955, Hirschleifer 1957, M. J. Gordon 1964, Dearden 1960, Anthony *et al.* 1965, p. 165, Solomons 1965.
30. Shillinglaw 1964, p. 162.
31. Davidson 1964, p. 238.
32. Quoted from a speech at a private conference of executives of foreign subsidiaries by permission of the executive concerned.

CHAPTER 5. THE PERSONALITIES
1. But there is a major subject for study here. For a brief review of the subject of 'Personality and social structure' see an article of that title by A. Inkeles in Merton 1965, ii, 249–76. See also Lovell 1966. For a general study of management see Granick 1962. For the related subject of management education see Mosson 1965. Discusions of role theory can be found in Banton 1965, Merton 1957, N. C. Gross 1958, and Dahrendorf 1968, ch. 2. The last-named is an especially readable introduction.

2. See Robinson 1964, pp. 136–9.
3. Merton 1957, p. 369. The subsequent reference to mechanisms reducing the disorder in the role-set is to pp. 371–80. Dahrendorf uses the phrase 'position segment' instead of role-set.
4. See Barnard 1953, especially p. 75.
5. In one American company, the President comes to Europe in his private jet; he then settles in some centre and sends the plane to bring in the local executives to see him from various European cities. Another company ascribed its problems to the fact that the chief executive did not travel much and was not known overseas.
6. See, for example, the article by B. Levenson in Etzioni 1961, pp. 362–75.
7. The point made here is that the relationship discussed in chapter 3 has to do with the actual discretion left to the subsidiary. This, as explained below, is likely to be greater in a company which practises participative management, but this does not necessarily follow. There may be variations in practice anyway along the extended lines of a multinational company; but even if participation is practised all through, an organisation which has a large management team at each stage must limit the discretion at operating level. For a detailed exposition of the systems of organisation from what he calls the 'exploitive authoritative' to the 'participative' see the writings of Rensis Likert, especially Likert 1967, chapter 3.1.
8. For the discussion of the connection between personality and social structure, see Merton 1965, ii, 249–76.
9. This suggestion has been made by Barnard, 1953, ch. 12.
10. See above note 7.
11. See, 'A Consideration of Individual and Group Attitudes in an Expanding and Technically Changing Organisation', unpublished M.Sc. Thesis by W. W. Daniel, Faculty of Technology, University of Manchester, 1963.
12. See Gluckman 1959, pp. 51–3, and 1963, pp. 41–2 and 146–52. Gluckman calls the situation he describes the *intercalary* position.
13. Notably Blau 1955, where the whole purpose of one of the agencies described is shown as perverted by the appraisal methods used.
14. For a summary of this technique see Humble 1965 and 1968.
15. See Barnard 1953, ch. 12. The whole of this chapter throws light on questions raised by multinational companies.
16. One minor 'cultural difference' encountered here was over titles. For instance some British managers complained that their American masters did not appreciate the importance of the title 'director' in the United Kingdom. An interesting article on the problems of British managers in American firms was published in the *Financial Times*, London, 24 January 1967. This was entitled 'US subsidiaries— What future for British managers?' An account of the development of international management similar to that given here but couched in eccentric and unnecessary jargon was published by the same paper the following year; see 'A new way of looking at the international company', issue for 12 August 1968.
17. Quoted from a speech at a private conference of executives of foreign subsidiaries by permission of the executive concerned. Incidentally, the speaker later became a vice-president of his company.
18. The role of finance director abroad was one which caused some discussion. Those companies which kept this as an expatriate appointment did so on the grounds that a local national might feel a divided loyalty, as his main task was to find some means of getting money out of the country, and making other arrangements for the good of the company as a whole. However, companies which employed local nationals as finance directors could see no substance in this argument whatsoever.
19. Chester Barnard makes some points about the significance of an international grade of management, and the competitive advantages this brings to the company. See Barnard 1953, ch. 8 and 12.
20. The practices of British firms on salaries and conditions for expatriate managers have been surveyed by the British Institute of Management.

21. See above, p. 12.
22. See Fenn 1957, p. 132, where it is claimed that techniques at home change so rapidly that men who have been abroad for ten years are useless in the domestic operation. See also Hitchin, 1967.
23. Most multinational companies, no matter what the nationality of the parent company, used English as a common language for reports. This would be expected in an American or British group, but was also the case for Swedish, Dutch and German firms. The reason was clear enough in the case of the Swedish and Dutch and even German companies, because it would be unlikely that subsidiary management—unless they were expatriates from head office—would be fluent enough to correspond intelligibly in those languages. Therefore English was agreed upon as a compromise. However this enforced standardisation can make matters difficult for the subsidiary staff when bilingual or clerical staff are hard to find or are expensive. One subsidiary managing director complained to his superior at head office: 'Your requests and statistics have increased very considerably during the past few years. [The production manager] is the only Englishman in his department, and spends a disproportionate amount of his time on reports to London. Satisfactory bilingual secretaries are practically non-existent, and even if we did succeed in getting one who was suitable, it would be extremely costly.' In some subsidiaries, the task of corresponding in the group language was considered too burdensome (usually by French subsidiaries), and the parent company staff translated reports at head office. Obviously, these are *ad hoc* types of arrangements attempting to improve communications in the group. Too much should not be made of such matters, but they are, nevertheless, typical of the special, if only niggling, problems that complicate management in a multinational group.
24. The 'negotiated environment' is one in which competition between companies is to some extent limited by various methods such as agreements about prices. More and more of the industrial countries are introducing legislation designed to enforce greater competitiveness. The general difference in this from one country to another is one of the factors that increases the independence of the subsidiary. The transition from the negotiated to a more competitive environment is discussed in Haas 1967, ch. 12.
25. W. J. Kenyon-Jones, in *International Operations Conference Papers* 1966, paper 4.
26. In one national subsidiary the view was expressed that local executives would not stay if promotion to the home country was not made possible.

PART II

INTRODUCTION TO PART II

1. Once the subsidiary is established and operating, assuming also that it is profitable. Newly established subsidiaries, and those making losses are more dependent on funds from the parent company.
2. Also referred to as a trading or export company. This may or may not be a holding company, i.e. own the foreign subsidiaries. See above, pp. 205–8.
3. Net increases in equity capital and intracompany liabilities amounted to about £223 million. Dividends paid were about £356 million.
4. Based on data covering all US manufacturing companies in Europe and appearing in *Survey of Current Business*, US Department of Commerce (various issues).
5. This assumes that the subsidiary is profitable and that there are no restrictions on the repatriation of earnings and capital. But even this is not always a requirement. By means of the transfer price mechanism (see next chapter), a cash outflow can be achieved (or more precisely, the *effect* of an outflow can be obtained) without the necessity of making profits in the subsidiary and subsequently remitting them. Furthermore, looking at it from the point of view of the investor

country, this tendency has been reinforced by the massive growth and use of the Eurodollar capital markets by multinational companies during the latter half of the 1960s (see above, pp. 208–10).

CHAPTER 6. INTERNAL FINANCE

1. As an additional basis of comparison, we have included similar data, although over a shorter period of time, for US-owned companies in Europe. The smaller percentage of investment internally financed may be attributable to a more liberal dividend payout, faster growth, or lower profitability—especially associated with new investment.

2. One might ask how they were able to achieve such a high proportion of finance from internal sources. The rate of growth of fixed assets in these companies exceeded that of British quoted companies. Besides, they were remitting a slightly larger proportion of earnings as dividends which meant there were less remaining for reinvestment. Much of the answer is probably attributable to greater efficiency: the foreign subsidiaries earned a higher rate of return on their assets than domestic (British) companies.

3. Since the changes in the method of taxation of corporate income in the United Kingdom the ratio has increased.

4. There are a number of studies of dividend policy in companies. See, for example: Brittain 1966, pp. 139–44; Florence 1961, pp. 140–58; Lintner 1956, pp. 97–113; Solomon 1963; Walter 1956, pp. 29–41, and 1967.

5. Data appearing in the advertisement of Burroughs Machines Ltd., issue of debenture stock. *Financial Times*, London, 7 September 1966, p. 17.

6. Florence 1961, pp. 152–3.

7. One study of the practices of 180 American companies found that one of the main incentives to license was to get around foreign restrictions on currency remittances (Behrmann 1958, p. 244).

8. For example, both Kodak Ltd, and Procter & Gamble Ltd (the United Kingdom subsidiaries of the two American corporations of the same name) argued before the Monopolies Commission's 1966 inquiries that the royalties and fees paid to their parent companies represented only a portion of the full value of the contribution they received. Similar views were given by Reddaway 1967, p. 102. For further discussion, see also the Sainsbury Report 1967, para. 298 ff.

9. Based on US Department of Commerce data published periodically in *Survey of Current Business*, and UK Board of Trade data published in the *Board of Trade Journal*. A similar pattern overall was noted by Reddaway 1967. In his study, dividends amounted to about 48 per cent of net profits on average between 1955 and 1964 for the subsidiaries covered by the data; royalties and fees amounted to 10·6 per cent of earnings; interest 1·6 per cent. However, in some industries royalties and fees were much larger, e.g. electrical engineering, where they were about 35 per cent. We can only speculate whether this pattern would also be typical for subsidiaries of other national ownership, for comparable data is not published.

10. Dividend policy and other characteristics of jointly-owned subsidiaries will be considered in chapter 11. Generally speaking, where the subsidiary is itself quoted on a stock exchange, its dividend policy would be influenced by the factors discussed earlier, that is, a stable and consistent pattern of payments would be a primary consideration.

11. Zenoff 1967, p. 419.

12. Various tax guides have been published by some of the international groups of chartered accountants, for example, Price Waterhouse & Co. and Arthur Anderson & Co. These give a broad outline of the tax treatment of foreign income, information on tax reliefs, credits, and related matters, and are available for most

countries where international business is a significant activity. The reader is referred to these for more detailed description of the problem of taxation.

13. One might wonder if the possibility of such a reaction by companies occurred to the British policy-makers when the system of taxation was revised in 1965, for the effect would be to increase tax revenues in the United Kingdom at the expense of the overseas host countries. In any event such a policy would appear to be in conflict with the concept of 'tax neutrality'. In the absence of a uniform level of taxation among countries, perhaps the United States system which permits companies to pool all credits against all foreign income is a satisfactory alternative. Not only is this system more advantageous from the corporation's viewpoint than the present British system, but it also is probably more satisfactory from the point of view of the subsidiaries' host countries. If there were little or no advantage to substituting one form of payment for another, companies would have less incentive to shift profits away from the subsidiary, and the host country may realise more tax revenue as a result.

14. Some companies point out to their shareholders that some of the earnings are held overseas, and are not necessarily immediately available to the parent company. As an example, in its 1964 *Annual Report*, International Telephone and Telegraph had this to say: 'The undistributed earnings of foreign subsidiaries included in consolidated retained earnings should not be understood to represent US dollars immediately available, since the retained earnings of some foreign subsidiaries are subject to certain restrictions on the amount of dividends that may be paid and to taxes payable on declaration of dividends' (p. 30).

15. A general discussion of company practice can be found in Hepworth 1956; see also D. T. Smith 1966.

16. See pages 163–5 above for discussion related to the problem of taxation of foreign source income.

17. Witham 1965, p. 17.

18. Zenoff 1967, p. 423.

19. *Ibid.*, p. 423.

20. Zenoff reported a similar reaction among the firms included in his study; *ibid*, p. 423.

21. The above figures are aggregates. The median and quartile values for the 115 subsidiaries were in 1960: 1%, 7%, 15·3%; in 1967, 0·1%, 1%, 6%. By comparison, the British quoted companies in manufacturing held 8·4 per cent of their assets in cash and government securities in 1960, and 5·8 per cent in 1967. In 1966, a sample of American companies in the same industrial groups as our 115 subsidiaries held 7·8 per cent of their assets in cash and government securities. National Industrial Conference Board, *Economic Almanac 1967–1968*, New York, Macmillan 1967.

22. Asked what the point was for such an investment (from the parent company's side), it was explained that royalties and fees paid amounted to nearly 5 per cent of turnover. In another subsidiary, it was reported that 'virtually no dividends or royalties [had been sent back] since it began manufacture in Britain thirty years ago'. Here, the point was 'growth—the total worth of the company. US shareholders are interested in growth stocks as much as dividends'.(Winsbury 1967, p. 53).

23. According to one study, companies exhibiting such attitudes tended to be 'a primarily *domestic* concern with international interests' rather than a multinational concern, i.e. they were domestically-oriented, and also were often new to overseas operations (Polk *et al.* 1966, p. 62).

24. An analogy used to describe attitudes towards risk in some companies with regard to their South American subsidiaries (Robinson 1964, p. 188).

25. In some cases, what actually happened was that the subsidiary declared a dividend, but temporarily deferred payment, thereby creating an intracompany liability. The dividend was repatriated subsequent to the date on which the balance sheet was drawn up. At first glance, for the subsidiary to pay a dividend and then have finance provided by the parent company does not seem logical given

withholding taxes and the administrative inconvenience involved. However, as we have seen earlier, this could arise where the parent company wanted use of the foreign tax credits such a remittance would create.

26. The subsidiaries covered by the Reddaway Report paid out a similar percentage (47 per cent) over a different period (1955–1964) (Reddaway 1967, table G.6, p. 196). The change in the taxation of corporate profits in the United Kingdom tended to increase the dividend payout ratio of British companies after 1965. Were it not for this, the ratios would have been closer for British domestic and overseas companies.

27. This was offered by one observer as the reason why an American subsidiary which was quoted on the London stock exchange had stopped paying dividends: 'Despite soaring profits the parent has not paid a dividend since [1957] and the price of the shares had come up from the equivalent of around $2.75 to around $62. No doubt the Americans had visions of repeating this success here' (*The Sunday Times*, London, 20 March 1966).

28. This apparently happens because each case is judged on its own merits taking into consideration the company's exports, other types of foreign income, etc. We were told that the Bank of England avoids disclosing its guidelines regarding remittances, and periodically rotates its staff to prevent any personal relationships with companies' officials from being established; it allegedly enforces its rulings by requiring companies to purchase investment dollars (at a large premium) for the amount of dividends that it deemed should have been repatriated.

29. A similar differential exists between Switzerland and the United Kingdom. This is undoubtedly a major reason for the alleged practice of the Swiss pharmaceutical firms to inflate the transfer prices on materials shipped to their United Kingdom affiliates. See evidence reported in the Sainsbury Report 1967, p. 103, table 8; pp. 107–8, table 16; p. 84, para. 301.

30. This arises from Section 482 of the US Revenue Code which states: 'In any case of two or more organisations, trades or businesses, (whether or not incorporated, whether or not organised in the United States, and whether or not affiliated) owned or controlled directly or indirectly by the same interests, the Secretary or his delegate may distribute, apportion, or allocate gross income, deductions, credits or allowances between or among such organisations, trades or business, if he determines that such distributions, appointment, or allocation is necessary in order to prevent evasion of taxes or clearly to reflect the income of any such organisations, trades, or businesses.'

31. Under the Exchange Control Act, Part IV, Section 23, Subsection 1(b) which reads in part: 'The exportation of goods . . . is hereby prohibited except with the permission of the Treasury, unless the Commissioners of Customs and Excise are satisfied that the amount of the payment that has been made or is to be made is such as to represent a return for the goods which is in all the circumstances satisfactory in the national interest.'

32. This appears to be particularly true for US-owned subsidiaries in the United Kingdom. Dunning argued that 'there is little evidence that, in intragroup transactions, US firms either buy or sell at other than arm's-length prices. Neither the incentive nor the opportunity for international cost or profit shifting in favour of American subsidiaries in Britain is very great' (Dunning 1966, p. 9).

33. For a more complete discussion of the problems of transfer prices in multinational companies, see for example: Shulman 1966; Business International Research Report, *Solving International Pricing Problems*, Geneva, December 1965.

CHAPTER 7. EXTERNAL FINANCE

1. Local equity will not be discussed in this chapter, but will be considered in chapter 11, which deals with joint ventures.

2. The data covering 115 subsidiaries (and 914 subsidiary years of funds flow) has been built up in this way, that is, increases in trade credit, tax and other accruals have been netted against increases in non-liquid current assets.
3. Polk *et al.* 1966, p. 101.
4. For an interesting, though hypothetical, example of how this might work, see Clapham 1966, pp. 6.4–6.6.
5. Based on the Reddaway Report data which however pertained to non-current liabilities, i.e. long-term debt plus provisions for future taxation, etc. The figure given was 6·9 per cent of non-current liabilities to total capital and liabilities. Adapted from Reddaway 1967, pp. 195–6. Other sources give the ratio of non-current liabilities to total capital and liabilities in British foreign subsidiaries as: in Western Europe—8·6 per cent; in non-sterling area developed countries—16·5 per cent (adapted from 'Book values of overseas investments', *Board of Trade Journal*, London, 26 January 1968, table 5, p. xi).
6. Most are not listed on a stock exchange, and this can make it somewhat more difficult to market an issue of loan stock or debentures. We are referring to raising finance in a *national* capital market; other considerations apply to an *international* issue of Eurobonds.
7. Borrowing by foreign subsidiaries comes under the surveillance of the Bank of England which administers the exchange control regulations under the general policy guidelines of the British Treasury. The relevant passage from the regulations reads: 'Except with the permission of the Treasury, no person resident in the United Kingdom shall lend any money, Treasury bills or securities to any body corporate resident in the scheduled territories which is by any means controlled (whether directly or indirectly) by persons resident outside the scheduled territories' (*Exchange Control Act of 1947*, part V, section 30, subsection 3).
8. *Financial Times*, 7 September 1966, p. 17.
9. This is the general rule in Spain, for example. A company with 25 per cent or less foreign ownership is considered, for purposes of borrowing long- and medium-term funds, 100 per cent Spanish. Companies with over 25 per cent foreign ownership can borrow such funds up to 50 per cent of their capital. Beyond this limit, special authorisation might be obtained if foreign capital is also brought in. See Comisaría del Plan de Desarollo Económico y Social, *Foreign Investment in Spain*, Boletin Oficial del Estado, 1965, p. 17.
10. For a description of these institutions, see for example, Joint Economic Committee, *A Description and Analysis of Certain European Capital Markets, Paper No. 3*, Washington DC, US Government Printing Office, 1964; Organisation for Economic Co-operation and Development, *Capital Markets Study* (series), Paris, OECD Publications, 1967; Commission de la communauté économique européenne, *Le développement d'un marché européen des capitaux*, Bruxelles, Services des Publications des Communautés Européennes, 1966; Remmers 1964, 1966.
11. In the United Kingdom, the Board of Trade grants loans on a somewhat similar basis to firms investing in projects considered to be in the national interest.
12. This is a debated point. Some bankers claim that the nationality of the borrowers is irrelevant, but this is disputed by subsidiary officials. On balance, it could be probably decisive in marginal cases.
13. This may be a formal guarantee, or only a 'letter of intent' or some undertaking even more vague which, although it has no legal basis, amounts to a moral understanding between the bank and the parent company. This letter might be used where a guarantee could not (or would not) be provided because of legal restrictions or exchange controls on the parent, or where it wished not to show a contingent liability on its balance sheet.
14. Three of the very few public issues of debt that have been made during recent years by foreign subsidiaries in the United Kingdom are of special interest. These are the £6 million 3¾% convertible loan stock 1977/82 of Burroughs Machines Limited, the £6 million 4% sterling dollar convertible loan stock

1993/98 of The National Cash Register Company Limited (NCR-UK), both of which were issued in November 1968, and the £5 million 3¾% convertible unsecured loan stock 1978/94 of Cummins Engine Company Limited. The special feature of these loans is that they are convertible into the common stock of the American parent company. Ignoring the eventual dilution of the parent companies' equity upon conversion, the issues provided exceptionally low-cost finance to the subsidiaries—a non-convertible loan stock issued at the same time by NCR-UK carried an interest rate of 8½ per cent. In spite of the convertibles' low yield, and the fact that the investment dollar premium (39 per cent at the time of issue) will have to be paid at the time of conversion, the issues were well received by the market; the Burroughs Machines Limited issue was subscribed fourteen times over.

15. The usual form of short-term bank credit in some continental countries, e.g. the French *crédit escompte*.

16. Bank credit, and for that matter other short-term items such as trade credit and intracompany current accounts, often vary considerably during the year as stocks and debtors are increased or decreased with changes in the level of operations. For this reason, an analysis of this sort, based on company accounts which present a year-end position of a company, may present a somewhat inaccurate picture of the average amount of such items outstanding during the year. Some companies see fit to end their accounting year when current liabilities are at their lowest point, and therefore, to the extent that such practice is followed, bank credit may be understated.

17. The banks' discretion can, of course, be sometimes reduced or even eliminated by the central bank authorities. An example of this was in 1965 when the Bank of England withdrew the banks' authority to loan to foreign subsidiaries for working capital needs. It required new applications to be submitted by the banks on the behalf of their clients. These, numbering some 30,000 in all, were re-examined, and some subsidiaries were not permitted to have their credit facilities renewed—presumably on the grounds that their activities were of no special benefit to the country. The banks out of normal self-interest could be expected to put a strong case forward on the behalf of their valued clients; on the other hand, such interventions by the authorities could provide the banks with a handy excuse for discontinuing credit to some of their less valuable clients.

18. 'The removal of our main manufacturing operations to the depressed area of the Vosges, which was in accordance with the policy of the French authorities, produced greater difficulties than we had anticipated. Subsidies were made available to us on the basis of labour employed, and this induced the management to increase the numbers employed far too rapidly; moreover, in the areas concerned, the available labour had no experience of the methods of production appropriate to our industry, and it has proved more difficult than we had foreseen to train a labour force to the required standard. Furthermore, it proved almost equally difficult to recruit management with the necessary experience. Thus the factories have been operating inefficiently, costs have been far in excess of normal, and output has lagged behind targets' (*Chairman's Review*, Wilmot Breeden (Holdings) Limited, 31 December 1962).

19. Unfortunately, given the limitations of our data, it has not been possible to quantify all of the diverse and complex operations outlined above. Therefore, in the ensuing discussion we have chosen to assume that changes in the subsidiaries' capital and intracompany accounts, unless otherwise indicated, represent a transfer of funds. One should be aware that this is not always the case, and our data probably overstates the amount of parent company funds that was actually transferred.

20. There are sometimes exceptions where, for example, a foreign affiliate would be able to make the funds available for the investment, hence removing the need for them to be remitted by the parent company. From the subsidiary's viewpoint, however, these are still parent company funds.

21. This seemed to have been an important factor during the 1930s in the United

Kingdom where 'a number of promising but then financially struggling sub-sidiaries in this country were kept going solely by additional capital being supplied by their parent concern—a unique advantage which was not available to their competitors at that time' (Dunning 1958, p. 178).

22. However, under the US tax code at least, such remittances may be considered as a 'constructive dividend' to the parent company subject to tax on the grounds that it is in reality disguised equity. To avoid this, the fiscal authorities must be satisfied that the intracompany debt is a *bona-fide* loan carrying a rate of interest, a repayment schedule, etc.

23. See Behrman 1962, p. 106; Merritt and Sykes 1963; D. T. Smith 1952.

24. Merritt and Sykes 1963, p. 366.

25. Polk *et al.* 1966, p. 84.

26. Unless the repayment were held to be a 'constructive dividend'.

27. *Sunday Times*, London, 21 February 1965, p. 21.

28. There are other ways to hedge against devaluation and fluctuations in exchange rates—forward exchange contracts, swap arrangements, invoicing in a stable currency, etc.—which may sometimes be less expensive. For a discussion of these techniques and the general problems surrounding foreign exchange trans-actions, see for example, Crump 1963; Furlong 1966, pp. 244–52; L. W. Shaw 1965; N A.A. Research Report No. 36, *Management Accounting Problems in Foreign Operations*, New York, National Association of Accountants, 1960.

29. One of these, Crown Cork Company Limited, aroused considerable discussion by repurchasing their preference shares. See chapter 11.

30. Tew and Henderson 1959, pp. 73–4.

31. The service company is variously known as a trading company (one special example is the Western Hemisphere Trade Corporation used by US companies), export company, or domicile company (the Swiss 'letter-box' company whose operations must be conducted in a location elsewhere from its place of registration). For an extensive discussion of base companies, see National Industrial Conference Board, *Managing Foreign-Base Corporations*, New York, 1963.

32. For US-owned companies, the Revenue Act of 1962 eliminated most of the tax advantages of a base company. Profits arising out of intracompany transactions (Subpart F income) earned and retained by such companies are taxed as if remitted to the United States unless certain conditions are met.

33. This definition refers to Eurobond issues. A foreign bond issue, another type of an international issue, differs slightly in that it is underwritten by a national syndicate, is sold mainly in the country of the syndicate, and is denominated in the currency of that country. See Morgan Guaranty Trust Company, *World Financial Markets*, 27 December 1968, p. 3.

34. In order to qualify, a US company must have at least 80 per cent of its income from non-US sources.

35. For additional discussion and data on the international capital market, see: Banque de Bruxelles, *The Mechanics of Eurobond Issues*, Bruxelles, 1968; Morgan Guaranty Trust Company, *The Financing of Business with Euro dollars*; New York, November 1967; N. M. Rothschild and Sons, *The Eurobond Market*, London, February 1969.

PART III

CHAPTER 8. GROWTH AND PROFITABILITY OF DIRECT INVESTMENT ABROAD

1. The reader is referred to the statistical series published annually in *Survey of Current Business*, and in the *Board of Trade Journal*. Other studies of the growth and profitability of foreign investment include Cooper and Parker 1967; Dunning 1966; Dunning and Rowan 1968; Reddaway 1967, 1968.

2. *Survey of Current Business* (various issues 1960–67); *Board of Trade Journal*

(various issues 1961–69). The data shown in figs 8.1 and 8.2 for the book values of British overseas investment in 1966 and 1967 are *estimates* found by adding together the year-end values shown in the issue of 26 January 1968, table 2, p. viii, and the 1966 and 1967 net investment values shown in the issue of 9 May 1969, table C, p. 1312.

3. For data in support of this argument, see for example *Board of Trade Journal* 26 January 1968, table 15, p. xvii and table 31, p. xxii; Reddaway 1968, pp. 224–6.

4. Net operating asssets are defined as the sum of fixed and current assets *less* trade creditors, tax liabilities, sundry creditors, and liquid assets.

5. Growth was calculated by dividing the value shown on the beginning balance sheet into the corresponding value shown on the ending balance sheet. This gave an overall percentage increase in terms of the beginning assets; this figure was then converted into an annual rate to give us an average annual (compound) rate of growth. To illustrate, we may take an example of a subsidiary whose net operating assets were shown as £1 million on the 1959 balance sheet, and £3 million on the 1967 balance sheet. This gives us then,

(1) $\dfrac{3 \cdot 0}{1 \cdot 0}$ = 300 per cent total increase in net operating assets over the eight years; converting this to an annual compound rate r, we get,

(2) $(1+r)^8 = 300$

(3) $1 + r = \sqrt[8]{300}$; $r = 15$ per cent (approximately)

The subsidiaries whose rate of growth was extremely high were mostly newly established in 1959 and quite small.

6. Based on data appearing in *Business Ratios*, Spring 1968, table 5, p. 34.

7. Among the 115 subsidiaries, size and rate of growth were associated as follows:

	percentage of each group growing faster than median rate
29 smallest subsidiaries (less than £4·5 m of total assets in 1967)	62
29 medium-small subsidiaries (between £4·5 m and £8·6 m total assets in 1967)	38
29 medium-large subsidiaries (between £8·6 m and £19·3 m total assets in 1967)	55
28 largest subsidiaries (over £19·3 m of total assets in 1967)	36

8. Penrose 1959, pp. 212–13.

9. The Monopolies Commission (Colour Film) 1966, para. 204. It will be noted that our point is not exactly the same as Kodak's. We are merely saying that there should be some correlation between growth and profits; Kodak was arguing that for growth it is necessary to have profits, and was thus trying to defend its pricing policy which was considered by some to be excessively high as a result of its near-monopoly position in colour film.

10. Barna 1962, pp. 13, 30.

11. The coefficient of correlation was calculated to be 0·09 for our sample of 115 subsidiaries. A roughly similar lack of correlation (0·1) was reported in another study of a larger sample of foreign-owned subsidiaries in the United Kingdom. This is greatly different from a coefficient of between 0·6 and 0·7 found for independent British companies. See Cooper and Parker 1967, p. 10.

12. We have defined profitability as the net profits after tax, depreciation, and other charges divided by total assets measured at year-end (the sum of the fixed assets net of depreciation plus intangible assets plus current assets). The financial structure of many subsidiaries was highly geared, and overall the diversity was such that it was thought total assets would provide a more appropriate base to ensure comparable results. If we used the more popular measure, *return on capital employed* (total assets less current liabilities), some of our subsidiaries would have shown rather spectacular results. For example, one subsidiary

would have earned a return of over 68 per cent p.a. in 1967 using this method of computation whereas according to our measure its rate of return was 26·5 per cent. This rate of profit was considerably higher than that achieved by any quoted company, the highest of which in 1967 was the 48 per cent earned by the Nottingham Manufacturing Company (*The Times 500*, 1968, p.8).

13. *Average* profitability refers to the mean of the annual rates of profitability of each subsidiary for the eight-year period covered by the analysis.

14. This diversity is further brought out in a comparison with British quoted companies in three industries: food manufacturing, chemical and allied, radio and electronics. Net profit after tax divided by net assets (total assets less current liabilities) was approximately the following:

	Lower quartile	*Median*	*Upper quartile*
Food manufacturing:			
16 subsidiaries	6·2%	9·5%	18·2%
8 quoted companies	6·2	7·5	8·5
Chemical and allied:			
34 subsidiaries	4·1	9·9	24·6
28 quoted companies	5·9	9·2	10·7
Radio and electronic:			
18 subsidiaries	2·8	8·9	19·8
11 quoted companies	5·8	7·9	11·5

The rates of return shown for the quoted companies are only approximate based on data appearing in *Business Ratios*, Summer 1968, p. 33. The measure used for profit was profit after depreciation but *before* taxes and charges against income such as interest. The data related to 1967 at which time the total taxes on company income was of the order of 42·5 per cent. Therefore, the figures we have shown above were corrected to allow for deduction of taxes. Because of adjustments, investment allowances, etc. some companies of course would have paid less than 42·5 per cent in taxes, but the error is not significant enough to alter the results of our comparison.

15. See for example Dunning 1964, 1966, 1968, 1969a, 1969b; Cooper and Parker 1967.

16. Monopolies Commission (Colour Film), Appendix 7, pp. 134–6.

17. Monopolies Commission (Household Detergents) para. 154 (b).

18. Monopolies Commission (Colour Film) para. 67.

19. *Ibid.*, para. 200, 201 (our italics).

20. See for example, Dunning 1958. Dunning maintained that US-owned subsidiaries in the United Kingdom did so well because their research and development was subsidised to a large degree by the parent company. Reddaway argued similarly about the pricing of royalties and management fees to British overseas subsidiaries, maintaining that 'there was more under-pricing than over-pricing'. Reddaway 1967, p. 102. See also Dunning 1969b, p. 130 *et seq.*

21. Dunning 1958, p. 174, 305.

22. However, for most companies, this seems not likely to be a factor. One study reported that most US subsidiaries have been charged little or no interest on intracompany loans. Behrmann 1962, pp. 104–6. As further evidence in support of this, from 1962 to 1968, interest payments by United Kingdom subsidiaries to their overseas parent companies have, in the aggregate, only amounted to about 3–4 per cent of profits after tax.

23. For an argument in support of this thesis, see Dunning 1966, pp. 5–18.

24. Monopolies Commission (Colour Film), para. 190.

25. Monopolies Commission (Household Detergents), para. 133.

26. Between 1961 and 1965, the average profitability of the five Swiss-owned pharmaceuticals operating in the United Kingdom was less than half that of the American-owned, and also at least 30 per cent less than that of British, French, German, Dutch and Swedish-owned subsidiaries. Part of the explanation for

this, implied the authors of an official investigation into the pharmaceutical industry in the United Kingdom, was: 'Foreign firms reported a much higher cost of materials as a percentage of the total cost of manufacture than did British firms and we believe that the propriety of such costs should be investigated. . . . The highest percentage for manufacturing costs is shown by companies owned in Switzerland, but a large part of these costs represents materials at an advanced stage of manufacture, supplied by their parent companies at prices which as previously stated are not on an open-market basis.' Manufacturing cost of sales in the Swiss subsidiaries was on average 51·7 per cent between 1961 and 1965 compared to an average of 32·7 per cent in the American subsidiaries (*Sainsbury Report* 1967, pp. 84, 107, 115–18).

CHAPTER 9. STRATEGIC CONSIDERATIONS IN THE MOVE ABROAD

1. Once again it must be stressed that the 'move abroad' means the establishment of manufacture or the provision of services outside the home country. The phrase does *not* include exporting or the development of marketing subsidiaries in other countries. Indeed a considerable volume of existing foreign sales is assumed by the phrase 'defensive strategies' used in this chapter.
2. See Martyn 1964, a very readable introduction to the subject. The quotation is to be found on page 23. In ch. 3 of his book, Martyn also discusses the 'climate of opinion' among business men in support of developing abroad.
   For a detailed study of the economic issues involved in British investment overseas, see Reddaway 1967 and 1968. For some proposed strategies for United States firms see Clee and Lindsay 1961.
3. See ch. 10. Such a concentration has been noted in several parts of Europe. A clear and emphatic statement attaching little importance to government inducements, and saying that market considerations form the only sound basis for investment abroad is to be found in an article by Sven T. Aberg of Ericsson, in *Business Leadership in a Changing World*, ed. Baker 1962, pp. 386 ff.
   As noted above in ch. 7, companies are often forced rather than attracted into development areas.
4. Cf. *The Guardian*, London, 19 February 1969: '. . . Investment within EFTA by the three main capital exporting members, ourselves, the Swedes, and the Swiss, has tended to fall as the tariff barriers have come down. This is really no more than one would expect, but it does help to contradict a lot of loose thinking which sees the "multinational company" as just one aspect of freer world trade. It is the barriers to trade—the natural barriers of distance, or the artificial ones of politics—which make companies form foreign subsidiaries rather than supply direct.'
   More recently, however, the reverse process has been noted in the EEC.
5. Modern scheduling techniques have, as some companies suggested, reduced the advantage of long production runs.
6. They have, several, at least one as a joint venture.
7. Such a study is currently being undertaken (1970), at UMIST.
8. See *Report and Statement*, Mather and Platt Ltd, Manchester 1961.
9. Although one small company had moved into the manufacture of its own raw materials, this was because of the difficulty of getting adequate quality.
10. Harold Wincott in 'Labour's policies: strange meeting of minds', *Financial Times*, London, 23 June 1964. The whole article is valuable.
11. Discussing the investment prospects of a large engineering group, Robert Heller in *The Observer*, London, 7 November 1965, wrote that a sum spent on home investment if spent on the firm's 'substantial overseas interests would probably have boosted profits by £4 m; there's a thought'. A change of product line was also proposed, but the attractiveness of the overseas investment remains.

12. An executive of this company writes: 'On reflection one might now add to lack of capital the fear of increased personal and company tax liabilities.'
13. See above, pp. 70–1.
14. See R. A. Gordon 1961, p. 306, quoted above in ch. 1. See also Fayerweather 1962.
15. See above, p. 230, and in particular note 3.
16. See report in *Business Europe*, Geneva, 21 June 1967, pp. 195–7.
17. See *Fortune*, Chicago, 15 May 1969, pp. 244 and 250. The article names three other corporations which pulled out of Sicily in the same year.
18. This point is stressed in Clee 1962. The position of the licensing department is currently (1970) being investigated, at UMIST.
19. By Lord Chandos, late Chairman of AEI, in a conversation in connection with this study.

CHAPTER 10. COMPANIES AND COUNTRIES

1. See Reddaway 1967 and 1968. In Hufbauer and Adler 1968 and in Pizer and Cutler 1960 there is a discussion of the same subject from the American point of view. The latter shows, incidentally, how foreign investment is changing the patterns of trade.
2. A speech in connection with the development of a Shell Chemical plant in Cheshire, England. Local authorities had protested about the emission of sulphur dioxide into the atmosphere. The enquiry was reported in the *Stretford and Urmston Journal*, 13 March 1968.
3. For a forceful and witty statement of this trend by the chairman of a famous multinational company see: *Our Changing Customer the Consumer*, London, Unilever Ltd, 1968. Both the similarities and the differences among European countries are well expressed by Anthony Sampson in *The New Europeans*, 1968, ch. 11.
4. See Abegglen 1959. The quotations are from pages 7, 49, 50. See also: 'Personnel and labor management by foreign capitalised companies in Japan', *Management Japan*, vol. 2, nos 2 and 3, Tokyo 1968, pp. 12–14. This article shows interesting differences between locally owned and foreign owned firms in Japan on such matters as pay and promotion policies.
5. Granick (1962, p. 394) suggests, on the other hand, that the ability of some American firms to ignore European practices and customs should not be taken to mean that this can be done successfully as a general rule. An individual firm may be able to profit by an unorthodoxy which might not succeed all the time. In the same book (pp. 348–9), there is comment on the bringing of foreign capital to 'development areas' which is mentioned below in section 10.3.
6. See N. V. Philips Gloeilampenfabrieken *Annual Report for 1964*, American edition, p. 11. See also above, ch. 2, p. 61. For material relevant to the following paragraph see Ross and Hartman 1960.
7. Kahn 1960, p. 2.
8. See Hitchin 1967, p. 87, where a similar point is made.
9. Fayerweather 1957, p. 127.
10. See *The Observer*, London, 13 March 1966. The statement was made by the then Prime Minister, Dr Verwoerd. For a British criticism of the influence of ideology see: *Purpose and Progress 1965–1967*, London, United Kingdom–South Africa Trade Association 1967 (privately printed).
11. *The Sunday Times*, London, 27 August 1967. The same issue contains an article entitled 'The sanctions busters' which includes more in the same vein, such as: 'The major loopholes are the work of big international companies.'
12. See *American Economic Report*, May 1963, pp. 7–8, quoting the *Wall Street Journal*.

13. The building of a country's first factory was mentioned in the British American Tobacco Company's *Newsletter*, London, 4 November 1965, p. 12. The country was Sierra Leone.

14. See Fenn 1957, pp. 33–40, where integration in the local economy and company assistance for education and health projects are stressed.

15. Sir Jock Campbell (later Lord Campbell and President of Booker McConnell Ltd) in a lecture to a seminar at the London School of Economics in November 1959.

16. United States companies overseas become acceptable to governments, in spite of outcries about the domination of foreign capital, for the reasons mentioned in the text such as their ability to bring in funds and technical knowhow. It would appear, however, that the actual reason for their success in Europe has more to do with business methods than finance or technology. United States firms have more advantages in data processing, in analytical investigation systems and in management techniques generally, than they have in technology; and these advantages are made possible by the elaborate collection of information which European firms find so burdensome. Dr van der Haas has emphasised this (see Haas 1967, pp. 42–4 and elsewhere). The same point has also been made effectively by Dr Antonie T. Knoppers, President of Merck, Sharp and Dohme International, who quotes *Science* (issue of 22 April 1966) in support of his view that: 'Superior technology is the result of *superior management and management concepts*' (the emphasis is his). The article in *Science* refers to the success of IBM as an illustration of the thesis that 'the story of supposed technical mastery is really a story of the organisation of the firms'.

17. Servan-Schreiber 1967, p. 17 (trans. from the French).

18. Cerf 1967.

19. From another series of data for France, it was reported that at the end of 1962, slightly over 10 per cent of the value of total net assets in French industry belonged to foreign interests. Almost a third of this was from the United States, another third from the Common Market countries, about one-fifth was of Swiss origin, roughly one-tenth was British, and the rest was from miscellaneous sources. See *Recensement des investissements étrangers en France*, Paris, Ministère de l'Economie et des Finances, Mai 1967.

20. An estimate based on data appearing in *Industrial Profits and Assets* and *Survey of Current Business*, 1966. Another measure of the extent of foreign investment in the United Kingdom shows the total value of US assets to be about £2,900 m, and all foreign assets at about £4,200 m. This is about 10 per cent and 15 per cent respectively of the value of all British quoted companies in 1964 (see Cooper and Parker 1967, pp. 8–10; for the following sentence in the text see Dunning 1969b, p. 124).

21. An estimate based on data appearing in *National Income and Expenditure*, London: Central Statistical Office 1965; and *Survey of Current Business* 1966.

22. Quoted from Layton 1966, p. 19.

23. Robinson 1964, p. 45.

24. See 'Des Usines étrangères pourront s'installer en France' by Alain Weiller, *France-Soir*, Paris: 18 March 1966. This article announced that Arizona Motorola had been given permission to build a factory at Toulouse after a long delay. For figures of foreign ownership of French industry see table 10.1.

25. For instance: '650 ouvriers français ont failli devenir chômeurs parce que Johnson et Mao ne sont pas d'accord', *France-Soir*, Paris: 26 June 1965. Two days later the same paper reported the intervention of a French court. There was an article about the whole affair in the *Journal de Dimanche*, Paris, 11 July 1965, and the appeal was reported in the *Gazette du Palais*, Paris, 14–17 August 1965, pp. 2–3.

26. The Belgian Government has issued a series of booklets setting out the concessions and attractions available to foreign firms.

27. See the *Financial Times*, London, 6 November 1964, article entitled: 'Capital—a prohibited immigrant'.

28. See, for instance, *The Guardian*, London, 11 November 1968. The book mentioned in the next sentence is McMillan and Harris 1968.

29. See weekly *Hansard* no. 776, p. 491. For a discussion of the extent of foreign investment in Britain, see *The Observer*, London, 21 July 1968. In another study it was reported that US subsidiaries were exporting 25 per cent of their sales as opposed to a national average of 14 per cent. See Dunning 1969b.
30. For an example from General Motors, see above, ch. 4, p. 71.
31. See the *Financial Times*, London, 17 January 1962. For another reference to a similar controversy see: 'Parts made by US subsidiary on Cuba buses?', *The Guardian*, London, 11 November 1964.
32. See Samuel Brittain, 'Welcoming the dollar invaders', *The Observer*, London, 14 June 1964.
33. Issue for January 1962, p. 92, 'The American build-up in Scotland'.
34. For one nationalistic reaction, see 'Wir Kaufen die Ganze Deutsche Industrie', *Der Spiegel*, no. 41, 1965, pp. 49–64.
35. See Watkins 1968. This report contains suggestions on local participation in foreign businesses which are mentioned in the next chapter, pp. 273–4.
36. See Linfield 1960.
37. See pp. 42–3.

CHAPTER 11. OWNERSHIP POLICIES
1. For an extensive discussion of joint ventures in the less developed countries, see Friedmann and Kalmanoff 1961, and Robinson 1964, p. 146 ff.
2. See the footnotes to table 11.1 for some further remarks concerning these definitions.
3. Layton (1966, p. 118) reported that in 1964, almost one-half of new US direct investments in Europe were joint ventures. In another study covering the years 1960–66, it was reported that about 40 per cent of all new US direct investment took the form of joint ventures (Booz-Allen and Hamilton 1967).
4. See for example, *Who Owns Whom, U.K.*, 1968.
5. We are speaking of ownership policies regarding investment in European countries. In the less developed countries the pattern may be different. Nevertheless, in the US Department of Commerce census of 1957 (Pizer and Cutler 1960), only about 17 per cent of US direct investments in the less developed countries were joint ventures. Among other capital exporting countries, a similar pattern was reported for German direct investment abroad; on the other hand, joint ventures constituted the major part of Italian and Japanese direct investments (see Friedmann and Kalmanoff, 1961, p. 37). Other data suggest that British investment in the less developed countries includes a substantial proportion of joint ventures (see Reddaway 1967, especially the statistical data, and the *Board of Trade Journal*, 26 January 1968, p. xiv.
6. Twelve of these in manufacturing are analysed below. There are a number of subsidiaries with preference shares or debentures held by the general public in the United Kingdom; but, although it can be argued, we do not consider them to be joint ventures.
7. The original 10 per cent minority participation was acquired in 1966 in exchange for marketing and management knowhow from General Mills. Another 8 per cent of the equity was acquired for cash during 1966 and 1967. A £13 million bid for the remaining 82 per cent of the ordinary shares was tendered in November 1967. The company became a 100 per cent owned subsidiary eleven days after devaluation.
8. The so-called 'Buy-American' Act is an example of this kind of restriction. A foreign subsidiary in the United States, in sales to the government or one of its agencies, must if the foreign content of the goods in question exceeds 50 per cent of their total value, be able to prove that the sale is not a threat to the US national security, and offer a 6 to 12 per cent better price than the closest US bid. Other relatively minor obligations are also required. This comes under the Act

o

of 3 March 1933, ch. 212, title III, 47 stat. 1520 as amended; and Executive Order No. 10582, p. 2, 19 Fed. Reg. 8723 (1954).

9. Donner 1967, pp. 92–4. See also above, p. 71.
10. As far as could be determined from *The Stock Exchange Yearbook* for 1968, the sample included most companies in the manufacturing industries in which the *majority* of the ordinary shares were held by a non-resident owner. Since then, at least two additional companies fit into this category: the Rootes Motor Group, and Gallaher. The quoted subsidiaries included in our sample are: USA-6, USA-8, USA-10, USA-30, USA-31, USA-67, USA-70, Eur-7, Eur-9, Eur-14, Eur-17, Eur-19 (see Appendix II). There have been a number of changes to the ownership status of these firms recently. Company USA-10 offered the minority interest sterling-dollar convertible debentures in March 1969 in exchange for their ordinary shares. Eur-7 minority shareholders were bought out in February 1968 by the parent company, and the ordinary share quotation of Eur-17 was cancelled in 1965 with nearly 100 per cent of the ordinary shares in the hands of the parent company.
11. By comparison, the quoted companies in Professor Florence's study raised or held stable dividend payments 88 per cent of the time, but for the wholly-owned subsidiaries, it was only 70 per cent of the time (Florence 1961, p. 152, and table 6.3).
12. Rubner 1966, p. 117.
13. Lex, *Financial Times*, London, 1 November 1963. Actually the loans had been repaid by the parent company before the suspension of the dividend.
14. *Ibid.*, 12 November 1963.
15. *Ibid.*, 25 March 1964.
16. *Ibid.*, 25 April 1964.
17. *Financial Times*, 26 February 1965.
18. *Ibid.*, 17 March 1966.
19. Lex, *Financial Times*, London, 17 March 1966.
20. *Ibid.*, 27 February 1967.
21. *New York Herald Tribune—International Edition*, Paris, 8 March 1967.
22. This in fact was hinted by the chairman speaking after the annual meeting in June 1969 in which he was reported as stating, 'it was unlikely the company would pay another dividend before it was wholly taken over by its American parent' (*Financial Times*, London, 5 June 1969).
23. Quoted in Wilkins and Hill 1964, p. 423.
24. This was alleged to be the reason that the Xerox Corporation joined together with the Rank Organisation to produce and market its electrostatic copiers in markets outside of the United States. Growth of its US business was at such a rate that all available managerial resources were being absorbed at home; rather than lose out in the vast potential the overseas markets promised, Xerox opted for a partner.
25. On the point, see Aharoni 1966, pp. 155–9.
26. Friedmann and Kalmanoff 1961, pp. 65–80, esp. pp. 79–80.
27. Another company in our sample considered local shareholders to be a hedge against possible future controls over remittance of profits. They reasoned that the pressure from the local shareholders for dividends would help guarantee *their* dividend. Although this is an interesting argument, the transfer of dividends overseas could obviously still be blocked or limited in amount. For example, during World War II, the payment of dividends outside the UK was not allowed. In the case of Ford Ltd the local shareholders received their dividends during that period, but those paid to US Ford could not be transferred until well after the end of the war (Wilkins and Hill 1964, pp. 334, 377).
28. Reddaway 1967, p. 188.
29. See for example, Meyen, Friedmann and Weg 1966.
30. Duncan V. *International Operations Conference Papers* 1966.
31. Reported in *German International*, December 1965, p. 45. The article went on to quote a similar view held by a prominent and outspoken German industrialist,

Ernst Wolf Mommsen, general manager of the Phoenix Rheinrohr industrial complex. He considered that 'one way to improve public relations might be for the big American companies to put some stock of their European subsidiaries on the market in Europe, to create a stronger European interest in these companies'.

32. Watkins *et al.* 1968, pp. 216, 280, 294, 344, 412.
33. *Financial Times*, London, 17 March 1966. The general tone of the press had little changed at the time of the bid by General Mills for the Smiths Food Group at the end of 1967. Arguing that the terms of the takeover were none too generous in view of the expected future profits, *The Times* wrote: 'The alternative, a British minority in an American company, is well enough documented to make the acceptance forms flow in' (*The Times*, London, 29 November 1967).
34. From a letter by Sir William Letts to Henry Ford Sr, quoted in Wilkins and Hill 1964, p. 187.
35. Wilkins and Hill 1964, p. 195.
36. Somewhat ironically, a survey conducted after World War II by Ford in Germany showed that most Germans thought Ford-Werke (52 per cent owned by Ford USA) was an American company, whereas Opel (100 per cent owned by General Motors) was considered a German firm. This may have been partly due to the rather narrow distribution of local ownership. Of the original 40 per cent offering, 15 per cent was taken up by IG Farbenindustrie, and the remainder by Ford dealers and other selected individuals (Wilkins and Hill 1964, pp. 423 and 196).
37. The role of the press was noted in the US Chamber of Commerce survey cited earlier: '. . . The more sophisticated Europeans, the ones most prone to understand the salutary roles and real significance of US economic involvement, consistently turned out to be European bankers plus executives of larger corporations. However, national chambers of commerce and trade associations in Europe, and local press and elected politicians tended to be notably more xenophobic, inward looking. . . . An increasingly serious communications gap thus may well be growing between US and European business leaders on the one hand and, on the other hand, European mass communications media and politicians' (Cerf 1967, pp. 3–4).
38. Our underlying implication that companies should be advised to conceal or de-emphasise their foreign ownership is not always valid, for there are sometimes advantages to be gained from being foreign. In some countries, certain foreign-made products are considered to be of better quality than the domestic equivalent. The fact that a company is foreign-owned seldom appears to make much difference to the market, except when doing business with the public sector. Even here, the distinction that might be drawn is generally between locally produced and imported goods rather than the ownership. Usually the criteria used by government agencies are price, quality, delivery time, and other technical considerations. However, purchase by certain agencies—often the military—or of certain types of equipment may be limited to domestically owned companies. Often this is for security reasons, or to guarantee continuance of supplies. This has already been discussed in another context in ch. 10.
39. Donner 1967, p. 98.
40. To get round some of the tax and exchange control difficulties of owning foreign securities, Donner (1967, pp. 100–1) proposed that the local national subsidiaries would meet the dividend requirements of shareholders in a particular country rather than routing them via the parent company.
41. The convertible loan stock issues of the British affiliates of Burroughs Corporation, National Cash Register, and Cummins Engine Company can be viewed as steps in the same direction.
42. See also Watkins *et al.*, 1968, p. 282 ff.

CHAPTER 12. THE STRATEGY OF MULTINATIONAL ENTERPRISE

1. See Zwick 1964, pp. 35 ff.
2. Another of the safeguards that the parent company can take is by setting up a provision for losses arising from foreign operations. Losses would then be written off against this provision rather than appear as a charge against current income. As an example, the Burroughs Corporation, after writing off amounts totalling some 5 per cent of earnings in 1961 and over 15 per cent in 1962, set up a provision which was 'available to absorb any extraordinary losses which might arise from foreign operations including those associated with major currency devaluation'. This diverted approximately 5 per cent of the 1962–64 earnings, but would provide the company with the means to dampen the impact of future exchange losses on reported earnings. See Burroughs Corporation, *Annual Report* 1964, p. 20.
3. This hypothesis is currently (1970) being investigated at the University of Manchester Institute of Science and Technology, and some evidence is expected soon.
4. See Sampson 1968 ch. 2, where this is said about officials of organisations of the European Economic Community.
5. See above, pp. 71 and 264.
6. See Layton 1966.
7. For this reason we are sceptical of statements to the effect that world business will be dominated in the future by a limited number of very large companies. We are still more sceptical when we see that these statements are reinforced by suggestions that a company's ability to join the big league is somehow related to the internationalism of its organisation. More, much more, is involved. For an example of the view described, see David Jones, '300 Giant firms to rule world trade?', *The Times*, London, 29 April 1968. This article expounds the views of Howard Perlmutter of the Wharton School of Finance. It reads as if the author himself is sceptical of what is being suggested.
8. See 'Electronic firms in research link', *The Guardian*, London, 14 March 1969.

APPENDIX I. THE METHOD AND SCOPE OF THE FIELD RESEARCH

1. See Blau 1955, p. 4.
2. As Penrose has trenchantly demonstrated, see Penrose 1952.
3. See above, ch. 9, p. 229.
4. This is discussed above in chapters 2 and 3.
5. See Etzioni 1961.
6. See Gordon 1961 and Robinson 1964.
7. See Likert 1961 and Seashore in Likert and Hayes 1957.
8. See Barnard 1953, and Gouldner 1954.
9. See Cyert and March 1963.
10. This confirmed the view put forward in Barlow 1953.
11. On external systems see Haire 1959, pp. 158–62 and Homans 1950, p. 90. On centralisation and national differences see Butler and Dearden 1965; Clee 1961, 1962 and 1964; Crowther 1959; Fayerweather 1957 and Skinner 1964.
12. See Cyert and March 1963.
13. Following Barnard 1953, Blau 1955, Gouldner 1954 and others.
14. See Barnard 1953, Gordon 1961, Penrose 1959.
15. Crozier 1964, for example.
16. A question suggested by Richardson and Walker 1948.
17. The distinction between formal and informal is discussed above in ch. 2, pp. 61–3. The distinction gained importance in the interviews when it became obvious that company organisation was influenced by people familiar with the literature on this subject.
18. See Barlow 1953 and Martyn 1964; for a discussion on *role-set* see Merton 1957.
19. See, on this subject, especially Fayerweather 1962, R. A. Gordon 1961 and Martyn 1964.

APPENDIX II. THE FINANCIAL STATEMENTS
1. From various issues of *Survey of Current Business*, Office of Business Economics, US Department of Commerce, Washington, DC.
2. From various issues of *The Board of Trade Journal*, London.
3. Reddaway 1967 (Interim Report). It should be noted, however, that these statistics cover foreign subsidiaries both in Europe and in countries outside of Europe.
4. Additional data on American-owned companies appears in Mikesell 1962, pp. 77–111.
5. Data for the British quoted companies is based on the summarised accounts appearing in *Financial Statistics*, HMSO, London.
6. Reddaway 1967, p. 195.
7. Tew and Henderson 1959, p. 13.
8. This is based on the arguments used in Donaldson 1961, pp. 28–9.

Bibliography

The following list is of books and articles that have proved of some interest in the preparation of this present work. It is in no sense comprehensive. Some years ago two large bibliographies on international business were produced. These can be found below under Lindfors 1964 and Stewart 1964. Any books published since then are likely to be listed here, as are a number of significant articles; up-to-date information on the latter can be found in the Business Periodicals Index.

Newspapers and official publications, such as the *Board of Trade Journal*, are not listed here, but full details of references are given in the text and footnotes above.

ABEGGLEN, JAMES C. (1959). *The Japanese Factory*, Bombay, Asia Publishing House. (1st edn, New York 1958.)

AHARONI, Y. (1966). *The Foreign Investment Decision Process*, Harvard Business School.

AITKEN, T. (1962). *A Foreign Policy for American Business*, Harper.

ALBROW, M. C. (1964). 'The sociology of organisations', *British Journal of Sociology*, 15, 350–7.

ANTHONY, R. N. (1965). *Planning and Control Systems*, Harvard Business School.

ANTHONY, R. N., and others, eds. (1965). *Management Control Systems*, Homewood, Ill., Richard Irwin.

BAKER, R. L. (1962). *Business Leadership in a Changing World*, McGraw-Hill.

BANTON, MICHAEL (1965). *Roles*, Tavistock.

BARLOW, E. R. (1953). *Management of Foreign Manufacturing Subsidiaries*, Harvard University Press.

BARLOW, E. R., and WENDER, IRA T. (1955). *Foreign Investment and Taxation*, Prentice-Hall.

BARNA, T. (1962). *Investment and Growth Policies in British Industrial Firms*, Cambridge University Press.

BARNARD, CHESTER I. (1953). *The Functions of the Executive*, Harvard University Press.

BEAUVAIS, J. J. (1960). 'Internationalism: a new concept for U.S. business', *California Management Review* 2, no 2, 28–37.

BEHRMAN, J. N. (1958). 'Licensing abroad under patents, trade marks and know-how by U.S. companies', *Patent, Trade Mark and Copyright Journal of Research and Education*, June.

BEHRMAN, J. N. (1962). 'Foreign Associates and their Financing', in Mikesell 1962, *q.v.*

BERLE, A. A. (1954). *The Twentieth-Century Capitalist Revolution*, Harcourt Brace.

BERLE, A. A. (1960). *Power Without Property*, Sidgwick & Jackson. (1st edn, New York, 1959.)

BLAU, P. M. (1955). *The Dynamics of Bureaucracy*, University of Chicago Press.

BLAU, P. M., and SCOTT, W. P. (1963). *Formal Organisations*, Routledge.

BLAUGH, ROY (1960). *International Business Environment and Adaptation*, McGraw-Hill.

BONINI, C. P., and others, eds. (1964). *Seminar in Basic Research in Management Controls*, McGraw-Hill.

BOOZ-ALLEN and HAMILTON (1956). *The Making of Company Policy*, Chicago: published by the company.

BOOZ-ALLEN and HAMILTON (1965). *New Foreign Business Activity of U.S. Firms*, Chicago: published by the company.

BOOZ-ALLEN and HAMILTON (1967). *Six Years (1960–1966) of the New Foreign Business Activities of U.S. Firms*, New York: published by the company.

BRANNEN, T. R., and HODGSON, F. X. (1965). *Overseas Management*, McGraw-Hill.

BRASH, DONALD T. (1966). *American Investment in Australian Industry*, Australian National University Press.

BREWSTER, KINGMAN (1958). *Anti-Trust and American Business Abroad*, McGraw-Hill.

BRITTAIN, J. A. (1966). *Corporate Dividend Policy*, Washington, D.C., The Brookings Institution.

BROADWAY, F. (1966). 'World business—today's pacesetters', *The Statist*, London, Feb.

BROWN, W. B. D. (1960). *Explorations in Management*, Penguin Books (Pelican).

BRYSON, GEORGE D. (1964). *Profits from Abroad*, McGraw-Hill.

Business Ratios (1968), London, Dun and Bradstreet, Spring 1968.

BUTLER, W. J., and DEARDEN, JOHN (1965). 'Managing a worldwide business', *Harvard Business Review*, **43**, no. 3, 93.

Capital Markets Study (1967), Paris, OECD.

CARLSON, SUNE (1951). *Executive Behaviour*, Stockholm: Stromberg.

CERF, J. H. (1967). *European Investment Climate*, United States Chamber of Commerce.

CLAPHAM, M. J. S. (1966). 'Appraising, evaluating, and planning capital investment abroad', *International Operations Conference Papers*, British Institute of Management.

CLEE, G. H. (1965). 'Investing overseas', *Financial Times Supplement on the United States*, London, 12 April, 83.

CLEE, G. H. (1966). 'Guidelines for global enterprise', *Columbia Journal of World Business*, Winter.

CLEE, G. H., and DI SCIPIO, A. (1959). 'Creating a world enterprise', *Harvard Business Review*, 37, no. 6, 77–89.

CLEE, G. H., and LINDSAY, FRANKLIN A. (1961). 'New patterns for overseas management', *Harvard Business Review*, 39, no. 1, 65–73.

CLEE, G. H., and SACHTJEN, W. M. (1964). 'Organising a worldwide business', *Harvard Business Review*, 42, no. 6, 55–67.

CLEE, G. H., and others (1962). *International Enterprise—A New Dimension of American Business*, McKinsey.

COOPER, M. H., and PARKER, J. E. S. (1967). 'Profitability ratios and foreign-owned subsidiaries', *Business Ratios*, 1, no. 3, Dun and Bradstreet.

CROWTHER, F. D. (1959). 'Organising for overseas operations', *The Management Review* (New York), March, 9–13.

CROZIER, M. (1964). *The Bureaucratic Phenomenon*, trans. from the French by the author, Tavistock.

CRUMP, N. (1963). *The ABC of Foreign Exchange*, Macmillan.

CYERT, RICHARD M., and MARCH, JAMES G. (1963). *A Behavioural Theory of the Firm*, Prentice-Hall.

DAHL, R. A., and others (1959). *Social Science Research in Business*, Columbia University Press.

DAHRENDORF, RALPH (1959). *Class and Class Conflict in Industrial Society*, trans. by the author, Routledge.

DAHRENDORF, RALPH (1968). *Essays in the Theory of Society*, Routledge.

DALTON, MELVILLE (1959). *Men Who Manage*, Wiley.

DAVIDSON, S. (1964). 'The budgetary process and management control', in Bonini.

DEAN, J. (1955). 'Decentralisation and intra-company pricing', *Harvard Business Review*, 33, no. 4, 65.

DEAN, J. (1957). 'Profit performance measurement of division managers', *The Controller* (New York), Sept.

DEARDEN, J. (1960). 'Interdivisional pricing', *Harvard Business Review*, 38, no. 1, 117.

Description and Analysis of Certain European Capital Markets, A (Paper no. 3) (1964). US Government Printing Office.

Développement d'un Marché européen des Capitaux, Le (1966), Brussels: Service des Publications des Communautés Européennes.

DONALDSON, GORDON (1961). *Corporate Debt Capacity*, Harvard Business School.

DONNER, F. G. (1967). *The World-Wide Industrial Enterprise*, McGraw-Hill.

DRUCKER, PETER (1955). *The Practice of Management*, Heinemann.

DUNCAN, V. (1966). 'Developing and implementing company international objectives', *International Operations Conference Papers*, British Institute of Management.

DUNNING, JOHN H. (1958). *American Investment in British Manufacturing Industry*, Allen & Unwin.

o*

DUNNING, JOHN H. (1964), 'Does foreign investment pay?', *Moorgate and Wallstreet Journal* (New York), Autumn.

DUNNING, JOHN H. (1966). 'U.S. subsidiaries in Britain and their U.K. competitors', *Business Ratios*, Dun and Bradstreet, Autumn.

DUNNING, JOHN H. (1969a). 'American growth in Britain', *Management Today* (London), Feb.

DUNNING, JOHN H. (1969b). *The Role of American Investment in the British Economy*, London, PEP.

DUNNING, JOHN H., and ROWAN, D. C. (1968). 'Inter-firm efficiency comparisons: U.S. and U.K. manufacturing enterprises in Britain', *Quarterly Review*, Banca Nazionale del Lavoro (Rome), June.

EINZIG, P. (1965). *Foreign Dollar Loans in Europe*, Macmillan.

EMMET DOROTHY (1966). *Rules, Roles and Relations*, Macmillan.

ETZIONI, AMITAI (1961a). *A Comparative Analysis of Complex Organizations*, New York, Free Press of Glencoe.

ETZIONI, AMITAI (1961b). *Complex Organizations: A Sociological Reader*, Holt, Rinehart & Winston.

Eurobond Market, The (1969). N. M. Rothschild and Sons.

EWING, D. W. ed. (1958). *Long-Range Planning for Management*, Harper & Row.

EWING, JOHN S., and MEISSNER, FRANK (1964). *International Business Management, Readings and Cases*, Belmont, Calif., Wadsworth.

FARMER, RICHARD N. (1968). *International Management*, Belmont, Calif., Dickenson.

FARMER, RICHARD N., and RICHMAN, BARRY M. (1966). *International Business: An Operational Theory*, Homewood, Ill., Irwin.

FAYERWEATHER, J. (1957). 'Foreign operations—a guide for top management', *Harvard Business Review*, 35, no. 1, 127–35.

FAYERWEATHER, J. (1960). *Management of International Operations: Texts and Cases*, McGraw-Hill.

FAYERWEATHER, J. (1962). *Facts and Fallacies of International Business*, Holt, Rinehart & Winston.

FAYERWEATHER, J. (1965). *International Marketing*, Prentice-Hall.

FAYERWEATHER, J. (1966). 'Nineteenth-century ideology and twentieth-century reality', *Columbia Journal of World Business*, Winter.

FENN, D. H., ed. (1957). *Management Guide to Overseas Operations*, McGraw-Hill.

Financing Foreign Operations (1958), American Management Association.

Financing of Business with Euro-Dollars, The (1967), New York: Morgan Guaranty Trust.

FLORENCE, P. S. (1961), *Ownership, Control and Success of Large Companies*, Sweet & Maxwell.

Foreign Investment in Spain (1965), Madrid, Comisaria del Plan de Desarollo Economicó y Social.

'Foreign ownership in German enterprises' (1966), *Monthly Report*, Deutsches Bundesbank (Eng. edn), Nov.

FOURAKER, L. E., and STOPFORD, J. M. (1968), 'Organisational structure and multinational strategy', *Administrative Science Quarterly*, **13**, no. 1, New York, June.

FRIEDMANN, W. G., and KALMANOFF, G., eds. (1961). *Joint International Business Ventures*, Columbia University Press.

FRIEDMANN, W. G., and PUGH, R. C., eds. (1959). *Legal Aspects of Foreign Investment*, Little, Brown.

FURLONG, W. L. (1966). 'Minimising foreign exchange losses', *Accounting Review* (Chicago), **41**, no. 2, April.

GALBRAITH, J. K. (1967). *The New Industrial State*, Hamish Hamilton.

GELINIER, O. (1965). 'L'entreprise multinationale', *Les Documents de la Cegos*, Paris, Cegos.

GILBERT, T. J. (1957). 'Functions of the financial office in international operations', *Applying Financial Controls in Foreign Operations*, New York, International Management Association.

GLUCKMAN, M. (1959). *Custom and Conflict in Africa*, Blackwell.

GLUCKMAN, M. (1963). *Order and Rebellion in Tribal Africa*, Cohen & West.

GOETZ, BILLY E. (1949). *Management Planning and Control*, McGraw-Hill.

GORDON, M. J. (1964). 'The use of administered price systems to control large organizations', in Bonini.

GORDON, R. A. (1945; 1961). *Business Leadership in the Large Corporation*, Washington 1945; New edn, University of California Press 1961.

GOULDNER, A. (1954). *Patterns of Industrial Bureaucracy*, New York, Free Press of Glencoe.

GRANICK, D. (1962). *The European Executive*, Doubleday.

GROSS, B. M. (1964). *The Managing of Organisations*, New York, Free Press of Glencoe, 2 vols.

GROSS, N. C., and others (1958). *Explorations in Role Analysis*, Wiley.

HAAS, H. VAN DER (1967). *The Enterprise in Transition*, Tavistock.

HAIRE, M., ed. (1959). *Modern Organisation Theory*, Wiley.

HALL, E. T. (1959). *The Silent Language*, Doubleday.

HALL, E. T. (1960). 'The silent language in overseas business', *Harvard Business Review*, **38**, no. 3, 87–96.

HARBISON, F. H., and MYERS, C. A. (1959). *Management in the Industrial World: An International Analysis*, McGraw-Hill.

HEPWORTH, S. R. (1956). *Reporting Foreign Operations*, University of Michigan Press.

HIRSCHLEIFER, J. (1957). 'Economics of the decentralized firm', *The Journal of Business*, **30**.

HITCHIN, D. E. (1967). 'Pressures on the key executives overseas', *Business Horizons* (Bloomington, Indiana), Spring, 85–90.

HODGSON, R. W., and UYTERHOEVEN, H. E. R. (1962). 'Analysing Foreign Opportunities', *Harvard Business Review*, **40**, no. 2, 60–79.

HOMANS, G. C. (1950; 1962). *The Human Group*, New York 1950; new edn London: Routledge 1962.

HUFBAUER, G. C., and ADLER, F. M. (1968). *Overseas Manufacturing Investment and the Balance of Payments*, US Treasury Department.

HUMBLE, J. W. (1965). *Improving Management Performance*, British Institute of Management.

HUMBLE, J. W. (1968). *Improving Business Results*, McGraw-Hill.

International Bond Issues (1968), Chase Manhattan Bank, 26 Jan.

International Operations Conference Papers (1966). British Institute of Management.

KAHN, E. J. (1960). *The Big Drink*, Max Reinhardt (1st British edn).

KINDLEBERGER, C. P. (1966). 'European integration and the International Corporation', *Columbia Journal of World Business*, Winter.

KIRCHER, D. P. (1964). 'Now the transnational enterprise', *Harvard Business Review*, **42**, no. 2, 6–10, 172, 173, 176.

KRONSTEIN, HEINRICH (1952). 'The nationality of international enterprise', *Columbia Law Review*, **52**, Dec., 983–1002.

LANDAU, H., ed. (1962). *Doing Business Abroad*, New York, Practising Law Institute.

LAYTON, C. (1966). *Transatlantic Investment*, Boulogne-sur-Seine. The Atlantic Institute.

LEWIS, R. W. 'An industry view of budgeting', in Anthony and others, 1965, *q.v.*

Liaisons financières françaises, Les (1966). Paris, Société d'Editions Economiques et Financières.

LIKERT, RENSIS (1961). *New Patterns of Management*, McGraw-Hill.

LIKERT, RENSIS (1967). *The Human Organisation: Its Management and Value*, McGraw-Hill.

LIKERT, RENSIS, and HAYES, S. P., eds. (1957). *Some Applications of Behavioural Research*, Paris, Unesco.

LILIENTHAL, D. E. (1960). 'The multinational corporation', in Anshen, N., and Bach, G. L., eds., *Management and Corporation 1985*, McGraw-Hill.

LINDFORS, GRACE L., ed. (1964). *Multinational Business: A Bibliography*, Harvard University Press.

LINFIELD, S. L. (1960). 'Looking around: overseas operations', *Harvard Business Review*, **38**, no. 5, 41.

LINTNER, J. (1956). 'Distribution of income of corporations among dividends, retained earnings, and taxes', *American Economic Review*, **46**, no. 2.

LITTERER, J. A. (1965). *The Analysis of Organisations*, Wiley.

LOVELL, ENID BAIRD (1961). *Organising Foreign-Base Corporations*, New York, National Industrial Conference Board.

LOVELL, ENID BAIRD (1963). *Managing Foreign-Base Corporations*, New York, National Industrial Conference Board.

LOVELL, ENID BAIRD (1966). *The Changing Role of the International Executive*, New York, National Industrial Conference Board.

MACE, M. L. (1966). 'The President and international operations', *Harvard Business Review*, 44, no. 6, 72–84.

MCMILLAN, JAMES, and HARRIS, BERNARD (1968). *The American Take-over of Britain*, Frewin.

Management Accounting Problems in Foreign Operations (1960), New York, National Association of Accountants. (Research Report no. 36.)

Management Problems in a Parent-Subsidiary Company Relationship (1965), British Institute of Management.

MARRIS, R. (1964). *The Economic Theory of Managerial Capitalism*, Macmillan.

MARTYN, HOWE (1964). *International Business: Principles and Problems*, New York, Free Press of Glencoe.

MARTYN, HOWE (1967). 'Effects of multinational business affiliation on local management', *Michigan Business Review*, March.

Mechanics of the Euro-Bond Issue, The (1968), Banque de Bruxelles.

MERRITT, A. J., and SYKES, A. (1963). *The Finance and Analysis of Capital Projects*, Longmans.

MERTON, R. K. (1957). *Social Theory and Social Structure*, rev. edn, New York, Free Press of Glencoe.

MERTON, R. K., and others (1952). *Reader in Bureaucracy*, New York, Free Press of Glencoe.

MERTON, R. K., and others, eds. (1965). *Sociology Today*, New York, Harper. (New edn, 2 vols.)

METCALF, H. C., and URWICK, L., eds. (1941). *Dynamic Administration: The Collected Papers of Mary Parker Follett*, London, Management Publications Trust.

MEYEN, J., FRIEDMANN, W., and WEG, K. (1966). 'Joint ventures revisited', *Columbia Journal of World Business*, Spring.

MIKESELL, R. F., ed. (1962). *U.S. Private and Government Investment Abroad*, University of Oregon Press.

MIRACLE, G. E. (1966). *Management of International Advertising: The Role of Advertising Agencies*, University of Michigan Press.

Monopolies Commission, see under *Report*.

MOSSON, T. M. (1965). *Management Education in Five European Countries*, London Business Publications.

National Income and Expenditure (1965), HMSO.

NEWMAN, W. H., and LOGAN, J. P. (1965). *Business Policies and Central Management*, Cincinnati, South Western Publishing Co.

OTTO, D. D. (1966). 'Principles of planning as applied to Philips', in Steiner.

PANUCH, J. ANTHONY (1957). 'A businessman's philosophy for foreign affairs', *Harvard Business Review*, **35**, no. 2, 41–53.

PENROSE, E. T. (1952). 'Biological analogies in the theory of the firm', *American Economic Review*, Dec., 804–19.

PENROSE, E. T. (1959). *The Theory of the Growth of the Firm*, Blackwell.

PIZER, S., and CUTLER, F. (1960). *U.S. Business Investment in Foreign Countries*, US Department of Commerce.

PIZER, S., and WARNER, Z. V. (1962). *Foreign Investment in the U.S.*, US Government Printing Office.

POLK, J., MEISTER, I. W., and VIET, L. A. (1966). *U.S. Production Abroad and the Balance of Payments*, New York, National Industrial Conference Board.

PRINS, D. J. (1968). 'International business, a challenge to management and to education', *Management International*, Wiesbaden, **8**, no. 1, 123–7.

Pros and Cons of Joint Ventures Abroad (1963), New York, Business International Corporation, Management Monographs Series.

PRYOR, M. H. jnr. (1965). 'Planning in a world business', *Harvard Business Review*, **43**, no. 1, 130–9.

PUCKEY, WALTER (1963). *Organisation in Business Management*, Hutchinson.

PUGH, D. S. (1965). 'Modern Organisation Theory', *British Psychological Society Bulletin*, **18**, 59.

PUGH, D. S., and others (1963). 'A conceptual scheme for organisational analysis', *Administrative Science Quarterly*, New York, **8**, no. 3, 289–315.

PUGH, D. S., and others (1963). 'Dimensions of organisational structure', *Administrative Science Quarterly*, New York, **13**, no. 1, 65–105.

PUGH, D. S., and others (1964). *Writers on Organisations*, Hutchinson.

Rapport sur les Investissements étrangers dans l'Industrie française (1965), Paris, Ministère de l'Industrie, 17 August.

Recensement des Investissements étrangers en France (1967), Paris, Ministère de l'Economie et des Finances.

REDDAWAY, W. B. (1967). *Effects of U.K. Direct Investment Overseas: An Interim Report*, Cambridge University Press.

REDDAWAY, W. B. (1968). *Effects of U.K. Direct Investment Overseas: Final Report*, Cambridge University Press.

REMMERS, H. L. (1964, 1966). *The Capital Markets and Institutions in France, Germany, Italy and the United Kingdom*, Fontainebleau, INSEAD.

Report of the Committee of Enquiry into the Relationship of the Pharmaceutical Industry with the National Health Service 1965–1967 (Sainsbury Report, 1967), HMSO.

Report on the Supply of Household Detergents (1966), HMSO.

Report on the Supply and Processing of Colour Film (1966), HMSO.

RICHARDSON, F. L. W., and WALKER, C. R. (1948). *Human Relations in an Expanding Company*, Yale University Press.

ROBINSON, R. D. (1964). *International Business Policy*, Holt, Rinehart & Winston.

ROBINSON, R. D. (1966). 'Conflicting interests in international business investment', *Boston University Business Review*, 7, no. 1, Spring, 3–13.
ROBINSON, R. D. (1967). *International Management*, Holt, Rinehart & Winston.
ROBOCK, S. H., and SIMMONDS, K. (1966). 'What's new in international business?', *Business Horizons* (Indianapolis), Winter, 41–8.
ROCOUR, J.-L. (1963). 'Management of foreign subsidiaries in the U.S.', unpublished doctoral thesis, Cornell University.
ROETHLISBERGER, F. J., and DIXON, W. J. (1939). *Management and the Worker*, Harvard University Press.
ROSS, ARTHUR, and HARTMAN, PAUL J. (1960). *Changing Patterns of Industrial Conflict*, John Wiley.
RUBNER, A. (1966). *The Ensnared Shareholder*, Penguin Books (Pelican).
Sainsbury Report (1967), *Report of the Committee of Enquiry into the Relationships of the Pharmaceutical Industry with the National Health Service 1965–1967*, Chairman: Lord Sainsbury, Cmnd 3410, HMSO.
SAMPSON, A. (1965). *The Anatomy of Britain Today*, Hodder & Stoughton.
SAMPSON, A. (1968). *The New Europeans*, Hodder & Stoughton.
SELZNICK, PHILIP (1949). *T.V.A. and the Grass Roots*, University of California Press.
SERVAN-SCHREIBER, J.-J. (1967). *Le défi américain*, Paris: Editions Denoël.
SHAW, CRAWFORD, ed. (1962.) *Legal Problems in International Trade and Investment*, Dobs Ferry, N.Y., Oceana Publications.
SHAW, L. W. (1965). 'Coping with foreign exchange problems in international operations', *Financing International Operations*, American Management Association.
SHAW, ROBERT B. (1959). 'Joint ventures by American and foreign companies', *The Magazine of Wall Street*, 104, 15 Aug., 592–5.
SHELDON, OLIVER (1925). 'Policy and policy-Making', *Harvard Business Review*, 4, 1–6.
SHILLINGLAW, G. (1964). 'Divisional performance review: an extension of budgetary control', in Bonini.
SHUBIK, M. (1961). 'Approaches to the study of decision-making relevant to the firm', *Journal of Business*, April.
SHULMAN, J. S. (1966). 'Transfer pricing in multinational business', unpublished doctoral dissertation, Harvard Business School.
SKINNER, C. WICKHAM (1964). 'Management of international production', *Harvard Business Review*, 42, no. 5, 125.
SMITH, D. T. (1952). *Effects of Taxation—Corporate Financial Policy*, Harvard Business School.
SMITH, D. T. (1966). 'Financial variables in international business', *Harvard Business Review*, 44, no. 1, 93.
SMITH, J. E., and RAY, C. H. (1967). *Financial Aspects of Supervisory Management*, Nelson.

SMITH, P. L., and REMMERS, H. L. (1966). 'Investment decisions in French industry', *European Business Review* (Paris), Oct.

SOLOMON, EZRA (1963). *The Theory of Financial Management,* Columbia University Press, 8–9.

SOLOMONS, D. (1965). *Divisional Performance: Measurement and Control,* New York, Financial Executives Research Foundation.

STEINER, C. A., ed. (1963). *Managerial Long-Range Planning,* McGraw-Hill.

STEINER, C. A., and CANNON, W. M. (1966). *Multinational Corporate Planning,* New York, Macmillan Co.

STEWART, CHARLES F., and SIMMONS, GEORGE B. (1964). *A Bibliography of International Business,* Columbia University Press.

STONEHILL, A., and NATHANSON, L. (1968). 'Capital budgeting and the multinational corporation', *California Management Review,* Summer.

TABOULET, H. (1965). 'Les plans à long terme dans l'entreprise', *Direction et Gestion* (Paris), July–Aug., 5–18.

Taxation of Patent Royalties, Dividends, and Interest in Europe (1968), Amsterdam, International Bureau of Fiscal Documentation.

TEW, B., and HENDERSON, R. F. (1959). *Studies in Company Finance,* Cambridge University Press.

TOURAINE, A., and others (1965). *Workers' Attitudes to Technical Change,* Paris, OECD.

VEBLEN, T. B. (1904, 1958). *The Theory of Business Enterprise,* New York 1904; new edn, New American Library of World Literature 1958.

VERNON, R. (1967). 'Multinational enterprise and national sovereignty', *Harvard Business Review,* **45,** no. 2, 156.

VERNON, R. (1968). *Manager in the International Economy,* Prentice-Hall.

VOLLMER, H. M., and MILLS, D. L., eds. (1966). *Professionalisation,* Prentice Hall.

WALKER, E. W., and BAUGHN, W. H. (1961). *Financial Planning and Policy,* Harper & Row.

WALTER, J. E. (1956). 'Dividend policies and common stock prices', *Journal of Finance* (Chicago), March.

WALTER, J. E. (1967). *Dividend Policy and Enterprise Valuation,* Belmont, Calif., Wadsworth Publishing Co.

WATKINS, M. H., and others (1968). *Foreign Ownership and the Structure of Canadian Industry,* Ottawa, Queen's Printer.

WEBBER ROSS, A. (1969). *Culture and Management,* Homewood, Ill., Irwin.

WEBER, MAX (1948). *From Max Weber: Essays in Sociology,* H. H. Gerth and C. W. Mills, eds., Routledge.

WESTON, J. FRED, and BRIGHAM, EUGENE F. (1966). *Managerial Finance,* Holt, Rinehart & Winston, 3–15.

Who Owns Whom (1968), London, O. X. Roskill. (UK and continental editions.)

WHYTE, W. H. (1956). *The Organisation Man,* Simon & Schuster.

WILKINS, M., and HILL, F. E. (1964). *American Business Abroad*, Wayne State University Press.

WILLIAMS, B. R. (1962). *International Report on Factors in Investment Behaviour*, Paris, OECD.

WILLIAMS, C. R. (1967). 'Regional management overseas', *Harvard Business Review*, **45**, no. 1, 87.

WINDT, E. M. DE (1968). *The Role of the Multinational Company in the World Marketplace*, Cleveland, Ohio, Eaton, Yale & Towne.

WINSBURY, R. (1967). 'The shape of America's challenge', *Management Today* (London), Feb.

WITHAM, B. H. (1965). 'Some basic questions', in Falcon, W. D., ed., *Financing International Operations*, American Management Association.

YOSHIND, M. Y. (1966–67). 'International operations: what's the best strategy?', *Management Review* (New York), Nov.–Dec. 1966 and Jan. 1967.

ZENOFF, D. B. (1967). 'Remittance policies of U.S. subsidiaries in Europe', *The Banker* (London), May.

ZWICK, J. (1964). 'Aspects of the foreign capital rationing procedures of certain American manufacturing corporations', unpublished doctoral thesis, Harvard University.

ZWICK, J. (1966). 'Is top management really on top?', *Columbia Journal of World Business*, Winter.

Index